THE LAST YEARS OF

NAPOLEON

BOOKS BY RALPH KORNGOLD

ROBESPIERRE AND THE FOURTH ESTATE

SAINT-JUST

CITIZEN TOUSSAINT

TWO FRIENDS OF MAN
*The Story of William Lloyd Garrison and Wendell Phillips
and Their Relationship with Abraham Lincoln*

THADDEUS STEVENS
A Being Darkly Wise and Rudely Great

THE LAST YEARS OF NAPOLEON
His Captivity on St. Helena

The Last Years of

HIS CAPTIVITY ON ST. HELENA

BY RALPH KORNGOLD

Harcourt, Brace and Company
New York

Dedicated to the Memory of my Friend

RAYMOND THOMAS MOLONEY

FOREWORD

Interpretation of historical events is as important as are the events themselves. "Reason creates science; sentiment and creed shape history," the French sociologist and psychologist Le Bon has written. A study of the source material dealing with the St. Helena phase of Napoleon's career leads to the inevitable conclusion that, for one reason or another, an important aspect of the St. Helena tragedy has been neglected by historians.

The interpretation furnished by William Forsyth, R. C. Seaton, Douglas T. Pillans, and Norwood Young to the effect that Sir Hudson Lowe was "the real martyr of St. Helena" is more true than the authors imagined, but hardly in the sense in which they imagined it. His "martyrdom" was due to the fact that he was appointed to a post for which by character, temperament, and ability he was totally unfit. Haunted by fear and suspicion, crushed by a responsibility with which he was unable to cope, he became a mentally ill man, a "paranoid reaction type." French historians have been equally oblivious to the pathological nature of Sir Hudson Lowe's conduct; yet the record of his bizarre behavior, the testimony of Count Balmain, the Russian commissioner on the island, and of Lowe's personal friend and physician Dr. Baxter, leave no doubt concerning the matter.

I am indebted to Dr. John R. Adams, Professor of Neurology

and Psychiatry at Northwestern University, for the following opinion of Sir Hudson Lowe's disturbed state of mind:

"Sir Hudson suffered from a neurotic personality disturbance of the obsessive-compulsive variety. He sought to find in rules and procedures substitutes for the inner strength he lacked. Driven by uncertainty and doubt, his capacities for objectivity and for discerning judgment were increasingly eroded. His inner insecurity was projected outwardly in attitudes of suspicion and mistrust. His own indecisiveness was twisted into fears of what others might be up to.

"The stress for Lowe on St. Helena came close to being a composite of all that was most difficult for him. He was in charge. There was no higher authority on the island. But there was one who had been a much higher authority. He was in the dread position of having to control that authority and to cross its wishes. The manner in which he attempted to do this reveals the problem. As a second in command he could well have been a stodgy Colonel Blimp. As Governor he decompensated under the stress. The elaboration of suspicions and illogical fears became that kind of irrationality that is called paranoid. He was afraid and must have come very near to developing a severe psychosis—a total breakdown of personality function. Indeed, had his situation in physical actuality not been so protected and secure, had he been faced with a truly critical external situation, his collapse would likely have been complete."

TWO

Readers may be puzzled about why English liberals should have taken up the cudgels for Napoleon during the captivity. One reason was that there was about him an aura of the Revolution, which liberals throughout Europe had hailed as the dawning of a new era. Another, that he was the enemy of their enemies—men whom they considered responsible for the wretched state of a large portion of England's population by opposing necessary reforms. How deep the cleavage was between some of the liberal leaders and the Tory government may be judged from the fact that although England was an ally of Austria and at war with

France, Charles James Fox wrote to Lord Grey: "I confess that I go farther than you in my hatred of the English government: the triumph gained by France excited in me a joy I can scarcely conceal."

Still another reason was their realization that as far as his military exploits were concerned, Napoleon was a conqueror from necessity, a victim of circumstances. Most of the liberals agreed with the Tories that the government could not allow France to remain in possession of Belgium without jeopardizing England's safety. France was the most dynamic nation on the continent. Her armies had proved more than a match for the combined armed forces of her neighbors. As a maritime power she was second only to England. Her Parliament had declared its willingness to aid any people wishing to be free. To allow the French to retain control of Belgium, with its—from a maritime viewpoint—strategically located city of Antwerp, might have resulted in the loss of Ireland and have presented a constant threat to England.

Belgium, however, had been formally annexed by France in October, 1795, long before Napoleon's climb to power. When he became First Consul he had sworn never to give up Belgium and could not have gone back on his word without being overthrown. Having no army of her own that could measure itself with the French, England repeatedly subsidized Austria, Prussia, and Russia to make war upon France. The dynasts of Europe, who wished the Bourbons restored to the throne lest their own rule be endangered, were nothing loath. Shortly after becoming First Consul, Napoleon wrote to the King of England and to the Emperor of Austria asking that they come to terms with him and that the war cease. The English government replied that there could be no peace "without the restoration of that royal dynasty which has maintained for so many years the internal prosperity of France, and which has made it regarded with respect and consideration abroad."

Napoleon thereupon marched his army across the Alps and attacked England's ally Austria. He defeated the Austrians at Marengo, and two days after the battle, on June 16, 1800, wrote to the Emperor Francis: "With the cries of the wounded ringing in my ears and surrounded by 15,000 corpses, I beseech Your Majesty to listen to the voice of humanity and desist from a policy that has resulted in two brave and powerful nations injuring each other in a dispute about differences foreign to their own interests." But an additional subsidy of two million pound sterling offered Francis by Pitt had greater influence with the Austrian Emperor. It was not until the Austrians had been soundly trounced at Hohenlinden that Francis made a separate peace with Napoleon at Lunéville, in December of that year. Peace with England at Amiens, in March, 1802, was only an armistice, which England broke the following year by refusing to evacuate Malta, as specified by the peace treaty.

There followed a new coalition, with Russia as well as Austria as England's allies. Napoleon defeated the Austrians at Ulm and the combined Austrian and Russian armies at Austerlitz and made a separate peace with Austria at Presburg. He was marching his army back to France when word reached him that Prussia was arming and meant to join England and Russia in continuing the war. He wrote to the King of Prussia on October 12, 1806, telling him that he would find him a man "unwilling to spill blood in struggles with sovereigns with whom he had no industrial, commercial, or political quarrels," and warning him: "Sire, Your Majesty will be defeated. You will have imperiled the peace of your days, the lives of your subjects in vain." When this had no effect, he attacked, crushed the Prussians at Jena and at Auerstadt, and occupied Berlin. He defeated the Russians at Friedland, formed an alliance with Czar Alexander at Tilsit, and again offered peace to England, but to no avail.

The French fleet had been practically annihilated by Nelson at Trafalgar in October, 1805. Having no other weapon with which to combat England, Napoleon had issued a decree at Berlin in November, 1806, establishing the "Continental System," barring all English goods from the continent of Europe. He believed that a strict enforcement of the embargo would compel England to make a durable peace. He needed peace and wanted it, for himself as well as for France. The Emperor of

Austria, the King of Prussia, the Czar of Russia could lose battle after battle, their capitals could be occupied by enemy forces without endangering their thrones, for their roots went deep. But he was a parvenu among rulers, and if Paris was occupied he would lose all. Even his generals would turn against him. Many of them had been his colleagues, and there was more jealousy than loyalty in their hearts. He was to say after Waterloo: "If I had been my own grandson I still might have had a chance." It was his attempt to compel the nations of Europe to enforce the embargo that was his undoing. His aggression against Spain in 1808, against Russia in 1812, had no other purpose. The distinguished English historian John Richard Green has written: "It was to maintain the material unity of Europe against Britain that he was driven to aggression in North Germany and to demands upon Russia which threatened the league that had been formed at Tilsit. Above all it was hope of more effectively crushing the world power of Great Britain that drove him to his worst aggression against Spain."

Whether England could have afforded to make peace as long as France held Belgium is a moot question. Nevertheless, men like Lord Holland in Napoleon's time, Lord Rosebery at the beginning of this century, and numerous other Englishmen of note were conscious of the fact that England shared responsibility with Napoleon for the wars that had ravaged Europe, and less than any other nation had the moral right to wreak vengeance upon him.

RALPH KORNGOLD

CONTENTS

Part Five

ILLUSTRATIONS

I. The March to Paris

Napoleon had signed his abdication at Fontainebleau, had made his moving farewell address to the Old Guard, and was preparing to leave for the island of Elba.

In Paris his former secretary Bourrienne—who, having espoused the cause of the Bourbons, had been put in charge of the postal service—received a visit from a gentleman named de Maubreuil. The visitor exhibited credentials signed by two high military officials of the allied powers and produced an order bearing the signatures of two members of the King's cabinet. The order instructed Bourrienne to facilitate de Maubreuil's traveling plans in the matter of post-horses. "I did as instructed," he has written, "and a few days later learned to my astonishment that the purpose of the mission was to assassinate Napoleon."

The mission failed since the allied commissioners who accompanied the fallen Emperor on his journey were not in on the plot and did everything to protect him. An assassin was later sent to Elba but was arrested on his arrival, since Napoleon had been forewarned.

Nor were these the only manifestations of bad faith on the part of those who had made a treaty with Napoleon at the time of his abdication. The treaty provided that he was to receive an annual subsidy of two million francs "on the Great Book of France," that two and a half million francs were to be divided among various members of his family, and that his wife, Marie Louise, was to receive the Duchies of Parma, Piacenza, and Guastella, which his son was to inherit. These and other provisions of the treaty were ignored by the Bourbons and by the allied powers, co-signers of the document. Lord Rosebery has justly remarked: "Were it internationally correct that he [Napoleon] should be outlawed for the rupture of that treaty, all the other signatory sovereigns should have been outlawed too."

What prompted this amazing display of bad faith?

Lafayette has remarked in his memoirs that in failing to live up to the treaty the Bourbons intended to provoke Napoleon into some desperate move. Conscious of their unpopularity and feeling insecure, they considered Napoleon's relative freedom in close proximity to France a danger to them. They wanted him shut up in a fortress or deported to St. Helena. His removal to that island was discussed at the Congress of Vienna, but a pretext had been lacking. The Bourbons knew that without a subsidy he and those who had followed him into exile could not exist. They wished to provoke him into an attempt to leave Elba, confident that the British would intercept him.

That a man of Napoleon's dynamic personality would have remained on the island in straitened circumstances, knowing that his assassination or removal to St. Helena was being plotted, was hardly to be expected. His followers in France kept him informed about the growing disgust of the population with the regime imposed upon them. He knew about the mounting sentiment in his favor, about the dissatisfaction of the army, about officers and soldiers drinking the health of *le petit caporal*. There was moreover the possibility—which to him may well have appeared a probability—that confronted with a *fait accompli* the coalition might leave him in peace. Had there not been a time, in 1814 at Châtillon, when they had been willing to come to terms with him? All in all it must have appeared to him that he had everything to gain and nothing to lose by quitting Elba.

Would he have remained on the island had the French government met its treaty obligations? He told General Gourgaud that had he received the subsidy he would have made Elba a gathering place for the scholars of all Europe. He would have built a palace for their entertainment and have lived among them like a country gentleman. Considering that he was no longer young, that he had grown obese, and that his health was poor, this does not seem improbable. Nor does it appear improbable that if after his return the allies had left him in peace he might have devoted the remaining years of his life to making France great and prosperous in other ways than by extending her dominion over her neighbors. He is known primarily as a conqueror, but he was a statesman, administrator, and legislator of surpassing ability. Henry Clay, in a speech in the House of Representatives in 1844, referred to him as "The master spirit of the age. He appears to have comprehended, with the rapidity of intuition, the true interests of a state." There is considerable truth in the statement made by him to Las Cases: "The vulgar failed not to blame my ambition as the cause of all these wars. But they were not of my choosing; they were produced by the nature and force of events; they arose out of that conflict between the past and the future—that constant and permanent coalition of our enemies, which obliged us to subdue on pain of being subdued."

TWO

Napoleon left Elba on Sunday, February 25, 1815, when the British commissioner, Sir Neil Campbell, whose duty it was to observe and report his movements, was on a visit to Leghorn. The British sloop of war *Partridge*, which patrolled the waters around the island, was nowhere in sight when Bonaparte embarked his force of some nine hundred men on the brig *Inconstant* and on six smaller vessels. The *Partridge*, with the commissioner on board, later gave chase but caught up with the expedition only after it had disembarked.

The only incident during the voyage was the meeting of the *Inconstant* and a French frigate. The soldiers were ordered to go below or to lie down on the deck while the two ship-captains held a shouted conversation. The warship departed without suspecting anything.

On March 1, the expedition disembarked in the Gulf of St.

Juan, near the fishing village of Cannes. Camp was made in an olive grove. The soldiers hewed down some olive trees and soon campfires were blazing. Sentries posted on the road stopped a courier of the Prince of Monaco in a gold-bedizened uniform, and soon after the Prince himself, a former aide-de-camp of the Emperor. Both were questioned concerning the sentiments of the populace and of the army. The courier said that except in Provence, where royalism had always been rampant, the people were favorably inclined toward Napoleon, and the army almost wholly so. The Prince was more doubtful. "You have many partisans," he said, "but you do not lack enemies." The mayor of a village was even less encouraging. "We were just beginning to have a little peace," he grumbled; "now you come to spoil it again."

Peasants who were interrogated confirmed, however, the information Napoleon had received at Elba. During the Revolution land belonging to the Church and to the *émigrés* had been sequestered and sold. In the more than twenty years that had passed much of it had been resold several times, and it was now mostly in the hands of peasants whose holdings seldom exceeded five to six acres. According to a report presented in Parliament more than ten million people—one third of the population of the country—were directly involved. Yet efforts were being made to have the government repossess the land and return it to the original owners. Already such land could be neither mortgaged nor sold.

There were other grievances. There was talk of restoring the tithe. Thousands of disabled soldiers and families of the slain were not receiving their pensions. Soldiers discharged from the army often could not find employment, and nothing was being done for them. In Piedmont the use of torture had been resumed by the criminal courts, and Frenchmen were asking themselves how long it would be before the practice was renewed in France —how long it would be before people were again broken on the wheel and feudal rights were restored to the nobles. "The royalists of 1815 are no better than those of 1789," was a common observation.

Throughout his march to Paris many of those who came to

Napoleon's camp brought petitions. It was as if he had never ceased to be Emperor of France but had merely gone on a journey, leaving things in the hands of an unworthy steward about whom the people now came to complain. He always appointed someone to receive the petitions, and by the time he reached the capital there was a formidable stack of them. "I could march to Paris at the head of two million peasants," he was to say, then added: "But I don't want to be called King of the Jacquerie."

THREE

From Cannes he had sent a detachment of twenty-five soldiers to nearby Antibes in the hope that they would be able to persuade the garrison of about a thousand to join him. That hope was not fulfilled: they were placed under arrest. When news of this reached the camp at Cannes many officers demanded that he march upon Antibes. He would not hear of it. "Victory depends on speed," he said. "For me France is at Grenoble." At Grenoble there was a garrison of several thousand men, most of whom—he had been informed—were devoted to him. So, at about eleven o'clock in the evening, when the moon suffused the landscape with its phosphorescent glow, he broke camp and set off toward Grasse, whence toward the end of his reign he had ordered a road built over the mountains. He arrived there in the early morning of March 2, and learned to his disappointment that work on the road had been discontinued after his fall.

In five days he marched seventy-two miles over rough mountain terrain. On the 7th of March he met with the first armed resistance. General Marchand, commander of the Grenoble garrison, had ordered an aide-de-camp to go forth with a battalion of the Fifth Regiment of the Line and bring Napoleon to him dead or alive. The two marching columns confronted each other on the road between Mure and Vizille, some six miles from Grenoble. The fateful moment had come. Napoleon dismounted from the spirited mountain pony he had been riding and ordered a hundred of his Old Guard in their tall busbies to reverse arms and follow him. As Napoleon advanced the aide-de-camp gave the order to fire, but not a musket was raised.

Napoleon stopped and said: "Soldiers of the Fifth of the Line. I am your Emperor. You recognize me." Then advancing a few steps farther he held his gray military greatcoat open with both hands and said: "If there be those among you who have the heart to fire upon their Emperor, let them do so now." The soldiers looked at the familiar figure in the gray coat against the background of guardsmen and with one voice cried: *"Vive l'Empereur!"* Their commander, who was mounted, sought refuge in flight.

News of the Emperor's return had spread far and wide. He now marched on a road lined with cheering peasants. Girls strewed violets and mountain hyacinths in front of the marching column. A contemporary author hostile to Napoleon concedes that the people were "mad with joy." After reaching Paris Bonaparte was to say: "So well have they managed in the past ten months that I have but to make a sign—no, only to look the other way—and the nobles will be massacred in every province."

Among the old nobility, however, there were some, grown to maturity since the Revolution, who were his enthusiastic supporters. Labédoyère, the young colonel of the famous Seventh Regiment of the Line, stationed at Grenoble, was one of these. His men were equally devoted to *le petit caporal*. The white cockade of the Bourbons had replaced the tricolor cockade of the Republic and of the Empire on their shakos but not in their hearts, and the old insignia were being carefully preserved in a drum. It was this regiment General Marchand had the imprudence to choose for the task of stopping Napoleon's advance. The regiment was assembled on the *Grande Place* when Labédoyère, seated on his charger, received the order. He addressed his men, voice trembling with emotion: "Officers and soldiers of the Seventh, I have been ordered to lead you against the Emperor. I will not conduct you on the road to dishonor. I resign my command. I am no longer your colonel."

Cries of "No! No! Long live our colonel! *Vive l'Empereur!*" greeted the announcement.

Labédoyère held up his hand. "I thank you," he said. "But I am going to join the Emperor. Farewell, comrades."

An officer spoke up: "Colonel, you cannot forsake us. We are with you. Lead us to the Emperor."

This was greeted with frantic cheering. "Yes! Yes! We are with you! *Vive notre colonel! Vive l'Empereur!*"

A drummer ripped open his drum and produced tricolor cockades. They were quickly distributed, the white cockades flung into the dust. Someone fetched the old regimental eagle under which the regiment had so often marched to victory. Labédoyère swung his horse about. *"En avant!"* he cried. "Let those who love me follow me!" Commands rang out. The regiment marched toward the gate giving upon the road over which Napoleon was advancing.

It was dusk when the regiment joined Napoleon. The Emperor embraced Labédoyère, who told him that citizens as well as soldiers in the city were on his side. A small group of elderly gentlemen, scions of the old nobility, had tendered their services to General Marchand, but cries of *"Vive l'Empereur!"* resounded in every street.

When the marchers reached the city gate—now securely locked and bolted—darkness had fallen. Pitch-torches obtained in the faubourg were lighted. They illumined a weird and incongruous scene. Thousands of civilians from the faubourgs and from surrounding villages had joined the marchers. On the ramparts civilians, women as well as men, mingled with soldiers of the garrison and all were lustily shouting, *"Vive l'Empereur!"* But ten cannon loaded with shrapnel were trained on the crowd outside, and an aide-de-camp of Marchand was frantically urging the soldiers to fire them. Had a single one been discharged it might well have been the end of the drama, since Napoleon refused to seek a place of safety and was plainly visible by the light of the torches. He declined to give an order to force the gate. He wanted to reach Paris, he said, without firing a shot, without the use of force of any kind. He decided upon another audacious move. He had his drummers roll their drums to secure attention, then held up his hand and cried: "General Marchand is relieved of his command. Open the gate!" The extraordinary announcement was greeted with tremendous cheering, and a short time later the gate succumbed to blows of a beam used as a battering ram.

The multitude that swept out to greet him almost crushed him and his pony. When he had been extricated those in authority wished to conduct him to the prefecture, but he would not have it so. He knew, he said, that the Three Dolphins Inn was kept by a veteran of the Egyptian campaign. It was there he meant to stay. More than thirty thousand people cheered him on his way to the inn. He had hardly established himself in an upstairs room when a delegation of soldiers and civilians called upon him. They told him that General Marchand had fled, taking the keys of the city with him. Unable to present him with the keys, they had come to inform him that they had brought him the city gate through which he had passed. Upon their invitation he went to the window and saw the gate lying in the street, surrounded by a cheering multitude.

FOUR

Napoleon left Grenoble on March 8, with Lyon, second city of France, as his destination. He had thus far traveled either on foot or on horseback; in Grenoble he purchased a carriage. He had disembarked at the Gulf of St. Juan on March 1 with nine hundred men; on March 10, he entered Lyon with eight thousand men and thirty cannon. He encountered no resistance. Marshal Macdonald, commander of the troops in Lyon, had planned to resist, but had found it a hopeless undertaking. In his memoirs he has written that as soon as his men caught sight of Napoleon's advance guard "officers and soldiers mingled their cheers with the shouts of the populace; shakos were waved on bayonets in token of delight; the feeble barricades were thrown down; every one pressed forward to welcome the new arrivals. From that instant all was lost." He and his staff were forced to flee, as was the King's brother, the Comte d'Artois, who had come to Lyon in the hope of stiffening resistance.

In Lyon Napoleon issued several decrees. Purchasers of land that had belonged to the National Domain were confirmed in their possessions. *Emigrés* who had returned since the restoration were banished. The old nobility was abolished as well as all remaining feudal rights. He dissolved the Chambers and convoked an Extraordinary Assembly. In short, he conducted himself as the ruler of France.

He left Lyon for Paris on March 13, at the head of thirteen thousand men. Between him and the capital, at Lons-le-Saumier, was Marshal Ney with most of what remained of the King's forces. He had told Louis that he would bring Bonaparte to Paris "in a cage, like a wild beast." He now realized that his men would not fight against the Emperor and joined him with his entire army. "Labédoyère joined me from devotion to me; Ney from self-interest," Napoleon was to say at St. Helena.

Louis XVIII left Paris on March 19, at midnight, and was to set up court at Ghent. Napoleon entered Paris on the 20th in a carriage, accompanied by a cavalry escort. On March 13, the Congress of Vienna had declared him an outlaw, and the imminence of war had cast a pall over the city. Madame Junot informs us in her memoirs that "theaters were closed and the city had a mournful and sullen aspect." But a big crowd had assembled in front of the Tuileries while others had gathered at the palace to welcome him. There was wild cheering, and when he entered the palace people pressed upon him so impetuously that he cried out: "My friends, you stifle me!" His aides-de-camp had to carry him on their shoulders up the great stairway.

II. From Waterloo
to Malmaison

Upon embarking for France Napoleon made a serious miscalculation. It is generally conceded that his chances for remaining on the throne would have been far better had he waited for the dissolution of the Congress of Vienna, which took place about a month later. As it was, the Congress followed up its declaration of March 13, placing him outside the law, with one on March 25, vowing not to sheathe the sword until he had been driven from power. His confidant Lavalette, whom he had put in charge of the postal service, hoped that he would not force the issue but would abdicate in favor of his son. But Napoleon had no intention of abdicating. He busied himself with trying to convince the allies of his pacific intentions and with reorganization of the government, at the same time preparing to meet force with force.

He gave the country the *Acte Additionnel,* an addition to the constitution of the empire. There was to be a hereditary Chamber of Peers appointed by the Emperor, and a Chamber of Representatives elected by the people every five years. All taxes were to be voted by the lower Chamber and there could be no levy for the army without its consent. Ministers were to be responsible to that Chamber, judges were to be irrevocable, and trial was to be by jury. The rights of petition, of worship, of freedom of the press, and the inviolability of private property were recognized. He appointed a cabinet with Fouché as minister of police. The former Jacobin had held that office under him before, and after the second restoration was to hold it under Louis. It is as much a mystery why Louis appointed him as why Napoleon did. He betrayed both. The strangest part of the business is that Napoleon knew Fouché was betraying him, having obtained proof that he carried on a clandestine correspondence with Metternich.

His efforts to appease the allies having failed, he prepared to defend himself. By June 1, he had 200,000 effective troops under arms, less than a third of the number the allies planned to put in the field. He was to complain bitterly about the little co-operation he received from the Chambers. "They did nothing for me," he was to say. "They were mischievous before Waterloo and abandoned me after it." The fact was that the Chambers distrusted him. They feared that once he was victorious his good resolutions would go out of the window.

TWO

Reminiscing about the Hundred Days during his exile at St. Helena, Napoleon was to say that perhaps he made a mistake in attacking the allied armies—that had he assembled his army before Paris and waited, the allies might have reconsidered waging war upon him. Notwithstanding the unanimity of their proclamations, serious differences had arisen among them. But Napoleon was not a defensive general. With him the best way to defend was to attack. He decided to attack in Belgium, where Wellington was in command of an Anglo-Allied army of 106,000 men—Britons, Hanoverians, Belgians, and Hollanders—and Blücher commanded 120,000 Prussians. Napoleon had gathered 124,000 men for the Belgian campaign.

Murat recollected that in 1812, before the battle of Borodino, as Napoleon was "riding along observing the enemy line, he halted several times, dismounted, and with head resting upon a cannon, remained there for some time in an attitude of suffering." He was plagued by dysuria, stomach ulcers, headaches, and his legs often swelled. Nine years before, in Italy, he had said: "Health is indispensable in war, and nothing can replace

13

its loss." That his health, and as a consequence his military genius, failed him in the Belgian campaign admits of no doubt.

He knew that both Wellington and Blücher had made the serious mistake of scattering their forces in cantonments too far apart to make rapid concentration possible. He believed Blücher would be more prompt in gathering up his forces than Wellington and decided to deal with him first. He sent Ney with 45,000 men to deal with any concentration Wellington might make at Quatre-Bras—a strategic point on the road by which Anglo-Allied re-enforcements could be sent to Blücher—and, on June 16, attacked the Prussians at Ligny. Blücher had managed to concentrate 90,000 men, but they proved no match for the 80,000 French. The old field marshal himself was unhorsed in the rout and, but for the fact that darkness had fallen and the French cuirassiers galloping past him failed to recognize him, would have been taken prisoner.

If, after the victory at Ligny, Napoleon had marched, in the early morning of June 17, against Wellington's left at Quatre-Bras he would have been victorious—not only over Wellington, but subsequently again over Blücher. This has been admitted by no less an authority than General Sir James Shaw Kennedy, then a captain on Wellington's staff. He has written: "On the morning of the 17th of June . . . had Napoleon attacked the Anglo-Allied army with his whole force and succeeded in defeating it, there could be little question of his being able to defeat afterwards the Prussian army." That on the morning of the 17th Napoleon could have made short work of Wellington can hardly be doubted, considering the fact that the latter had managed to concentrate only some 50,000 men at Quatre-Bras, while Napoleon's and Ney's combined forces would have been more than double that number.

But on the morning of June 17, Napoleon, who had grown corpulent and tired easily, got up late—too late to execute the maneuver that would have spelled Wellington's doom—and then proceeded to seal his own fate by greatly weakening the army that had routed the Prussians. He sent Grouchy with 33,000 men in pursuit of Blücher—now so far away that the French marshal could not possibly have caught up with him, even if he had had any certainty where the Prussians were headed, which he had not. The Napoleon of Rivoli and Wagram would not have made such a tactical blunder.[1] When finally he marched to attack Wellington's left flank it was too late. He arrived at Quatre-Bras at noon; Wellington had withdrawn two hours earlier. Had he arrived in time he might well have remained on the French throne. "What would have become of the coalition and of the whole story of the Congress [of Vienna] if the battle [of Waterloo] had been lost?" Gneisenau, the Prussian chief-of-staff, has written. There would have been no battle of Waterloo if Napoleon had got up early and had not weakened his army by sending Grouchy on a wild goose chase.

Thus the outcome of the famous battle of Waterloo, on June 18, was decided the previous day. The fighting had hardly begun when Prussian re-enforcements began to arrive. Even when 30,000 Prussians under Bülow, who had not participated in the battle of Ligny, were attacking Napoleon's right flank, Wellington, whose army now nearly equaled Napoleon's in size, remained on the defensive. In vain Napoleon waited for Grouchy to join him. The French marshal was far away at Wavre where Thielemann with 15,000 men kept him occupied, while Blücher with 50,000 was marching to Waterloo. He arrived when darkness was falling and stove in Napoleon's right, while at the same time Wellington ordered a general assault by his Anglo-Allied army. The French, greatly outnumbered, panicked, and all was over.

Napoleon was to remark repeatedly at St. Helena that Blücher, not Wellington, should be credited with the victory at Waterloo.

THREE

"The play is over!" was the remark of one of Napoleon's generals when the rumor reached him that the Emperor had perished

---

[1] Colonel Charles C. Chesney, late professor of military art and history at the Royal Staff College, was to concede that Wellington "owed something that day to Fortune"—a considerable understatement.

during the last phase of the battle. He was indeed prevented from throwing himself into the thick of the fray by Marshal Soult, who seized his horse's bridle, exclaiming that he would not be killed but taken prisoner. Seeing the army dissolving and men fleeing everywhere he left the battlefield and, accompanied by Soult, Bertrand, Gourgaud, Labédoyère, Drouot, Flahaut, and a few others, took the road to Jemappes. He was so fatigued that had Gourgaud not supported him he would have fallen from his horse. All night they rode over the rain-soaked roads, and at five in the morning reached Charleroi. Here Napoleon attempted to rally some of the shattered units. The attempt failed and they rode on toward Philippeville.

From Philippeville Napoleon traveled to Paris in a carriage belonging to the commander of the garrison. He arrived at the Elysée Palace on June 21, at eight in the morning. Caulaincourt, his minister of foreign affairs, met him on the palace steps. The Emperor convoked a ministerial council and went to take a bath. Lavalette, who soon after came to see him, has written that Napoleon received him with a hysterical laugh and the exclamation, "Oh, my God! My God!" But he soon collected himself and asked what went on in the House of Representatives. When told that the majority of the deputies were determined he should resign, he remarked: "I have accustomed them to such great victories that they don't know how to bear up under one day's misfortune."

He breakfasted with his brothers, Joseph and Lucien, and then went to the council chamber to confer with his ministers. He explained the seriousness of the situation and said that a temporary dictatorship was imperative to save the country from foreign domination. The ministers remained silent. When asked to express themselves, only Carnot, the old revolutionary, was in favor of the plan. Fouché opposed it. Waterloo was no disappointment to him. The previous month he had said to Pasquier: "As soon as he is gone to the army we shall be masters of the situation. He will win one or two battles, but will lose the third. Then it will be our turn." He now scribbled a note to one of his henchmen in the House of Representatives and gave it to a page, with instructions that it be delivered instantly.

Napoleon outlined the measures he meant to take and did it so convincingly that some of the ministers were won over. While the matter was being discussed a message from the House of Representatives was handed to him. It informed him that the Chamber had declared itself in permanent session; that any attempt to dissolve it would be regarded as treason against the state; that he who attempted it would be considered a traitor and would be tried for high treason.

That evening the liberal leader Benjamin Constant came to see him, and they went walking together in the palace garden. The crowd assembled before the palace had no sooner recognized the Emperor than a mighty cheer went up. *"Vive l'Empereur!* Down with the Bourbons! Death to the traitors!" Napoleon smiled and waved his hand to the crowd. "Do you hear?" he said to Constant. "Those are not the men whom I have loaded with riches and honors. These people owe me nothing. I found them poor and I left them poor. But theirs is the voice of France calling to me. If I were to permit it, in an hour the rebellious Chamber would cease to exist. But I did not come from Elba to inundate Paris with blood."

The generals who had accompanied him from the battlefield had taken counsel together and had agreed that on his arrival in Paris, stained with the grime of battle, he should go to the Chambers, give an account of what had occurred, and appeal to the patriotism of the deputies to help organize resistance. Having done this he should immediately leave Paris, place himself at the head of Grouchy's corps and such other forces as could be gathered, and prepare to defend the capital. Why did he not follow their advice? At St. Helena he was to say to Gourgaud: "Yes, I should have gone to the Chambers, but I was dog-tired, and I could not anticipate that they would turn against me so quickly. I arrived at eight o'clock, and at noon they were in insurrection." Then, passing his hand wearily over his face, he was to add: "After all, I am only a man. I might indeed have put myself

17

at the head of the army, which was in favor of my son, and whatever would have happened, it would have been better than St. Helena."

FOUR

The demand for Napoleon's abdication was mainly due to the belief on the part of the deputies that it would save Paris from foreign occupation. Had not the coalition emphasized that they were not making war upon France but upon Bonaparte? He felt certain that they would no more keep their word with France than they had kept it with him, but yielded to the pressure. On June 22, 1815, he signed the second abdication. The Chambers appointed a committee of five, with Fouché as chairman, to exercise provisionally the powers of government. Napoleon remained at the Elysée Palace, urging that his son, in whose favor he had abdicated, be proclaimed Emperor, burning many of his papers, offering advice about the defense of Paris.

His stepdaughter Hortense, who had hastened to the Elysée Palace as soon as she had heard of his arrival, urged him to reach a decision. She was a slender young woman of thirty-two with a profusion of blond hair and appealing violet-blue eyes. Madame Junot has said of her that she was "gay, gentle, and amiable, and combined Creole languor with the vivacity of France." She now pleaded with him to write to the Emperor Alexander, who at one time had professed great friendship for him and who had a reputation for generosity. If not that, then he should communicate with his father-in-law, the Emperor Francis, and ask asylum in his domain. If he meant to seek refuge in America, then he should hasten to one of the Atlantic ports before the British got wind of his plan. He replied: "Never will I write to my father-in-law. I have too much to complain about his having kept my wife and child from me. As for Alexander, he is like other men. I would prefer to address myself to a people, to England." Finally, however, he reached a decision: he would go to America. On June 23, the day after his abdication, he sent a message to Decrès, minister of marine, asking that two frigates in the harbor of Rochefort—the *Saale* and the *Méduse*—be placed at his disposal. Decrès promised to take up the matter promptly with the provisional government.

Fouché and his colleagues found his presence at the Elysée Palace embarrassing. Crowds continued to gather in the Avenue de Marigny demonstrating in his favor. It was suggested to him that he move to Malmaison, the beautiful country house nine miles from Paris that had belonged to Josephine. She had died while he was at Elba, leaving the property to Hortense. Napoleon consented to leave, and Hortense departed immediately to prepare the mansion for his reception. On June 25, at about noon, the Emperor left for Malmaison. To avoid a popular demonstration his six-horse carriage, with the imperial arms, drew up in front of the palace, while he and Marshal Bertrand slipped out at the garden gate giving upon the Champs Elysée, where a carriage and pair were waiting. General Gourgaud and Count Las Cases followed in the coach of state.

FIVE

Besides Hortense only a couple of chamberlains and a few pages were at Malmaison to welcome the fallen monarch. One of the first callers was the banker Laffite, whom the Emperor had entrusted with four million, two hundred and thirty thousand francs, by far the greater part of his private fortune. Napoleon wished to know what could be done to keep the money from being confiscated if the Bourbons returned to power. We do not know what assurance Laffite was able to give him, but we know what means the banker employed to prevent seizure. When the King's minister of finance demanded that he declare under oath if he had any deposits belonging to Bonaparte, Laffite obtained an audience with the King. He told him about the finance minister's demand, at the same time informing him that on his arrival at the Tuileries, Napoleon, having obtained information that Louis had seven million francs on deposit with him, had summoned him and had told him: "That money belongs to the King personally. Private affairs are entirely distinct from political matters." As a result of the interview Napoleon's fortune was not seized.

That evening General Beker came at the head of three hundred men of the Old Guard and forty dragoons. He had received an order from Davout, minister of war, to watch over Napoleon's safety and "to prevent ill-disposed persons from provoking disorders in his name." The Emperor received him in the library. When Beker showed him Davout's letter, he said severely: "I cannot regard this order as a measure of surveillance. Such a measure would be entirely unnecessary. I have no intention of disavowing any engagement I have entered into." The general excused himself. He was an old soldier, he said, and had accepted the assignment solely in the hope of being useful to the Emperor. Gourgaud has written that Beker "did everything possible so his mission would not be disagreeable to the Emperor."

During the next few days there were many callers. Napoleon's mother, Letizia, came with her half-brother Cardinal Fesch, Joseph came, but neither Lucien nor Jerome called. Labédoyère, Lavalette, Maret, Talma, Planat, Savary, Lallemand, many others called. His former mistress Countess Walewska came with little Alexander, the son she had borne him. Léon, his son by the actress Eleonore Denuelle, who bore a striking resemblance to him, came in charge of his tutor, Baron de Mauvière. Corvisart, Napoleon's favorite doctor, called. After his departure the Emperor handed a phial to his valet Marchand with instructions to put it where it would be always at his disposal. It contained a poison that would kill instantly. Some came out of devotion to the great man; most, because they expected him to aid them in the difficult situation they found themselves in as a result of his fall. Many wished to accompany him to America. When finally he left for Rochefort there were sixty-four persons—men, women, and children—in his party.

SIX

On the 26th of June Napoleon sent Beker to Paris to inquire what decision had been reached regarding the two frigates. The general was given a written order to the effect that they were at Napoleon's disposal, but were not to sail until a safe-conduct, application for which had been made to the British, had been received. When the Emperor had read the order he said he would remain at Malmaison until the restriction had been removed. This was not to the liking of Fouché and his colleagues. The populace in Paris kept demonstrating in favor of the Emperor, and Malmaison was too near for comfort.

On the morning of June 28, Napoleon sent General Flahaut to Paris to demand categorically that the restriction concerning the departure of the frigates be lifted. Davout shouted angrily: "Tell your Bonaparte that he must leave. If he does not, I'll have him arrested. I'll arrest him myself!" The young general replied just as heatedly that it ill became a man who less than two weeks earlier had been almost on his knees before the Emperor to use such language. Tearing off his epaulets he flung them at the feet of Davout saying: "I would disgrace my uniform if I were to continue to serve under you." [2]

In the meantime Wellington and Blücher were marching upon Paris. The two armies had again become separated, Blücher marching far ahead. He had learned the whereabouts of Napoleon and had sent a regiment of hussars and two battalions of infantry, under the command of his brother-in-law, with instructions to capture him. In a letter to his wife he expresses his intention of having him shot. Wellington, on the other hand, made it known that if Napoleon was to be executed it was not he who would carry out the order.

The provisional government was in a quandary. It did not dare to incur the displeasure of the allies by helping Napoleon escape, but neither did it care to arouse the wrath of the populace by having him fall into the hands of Blücher. Beker received orders to burn the bridge at Châtou. Cannon fire could now be distinctly heard at Malmaison, but, except for selling a packet of bonds, Napoleon made no preparations for departure.

Fouché and his colleagues were extricated from their awkward situation by a letter from de Bonnefoux, maritime prefect at Rochefort. He wrote that the straits were now so closely blockaded by the British that escape would be impossible. This meant

[2] It is interesting to note that General Flahaut was the natural son of Talleyrand.

that on his arrival at Rochefort Napoleon would be confronted with the choice of voluntarily surrendering to the British or waiting to be arrested by the Bourbons. That a safe-conduct would be granted by the British appeared highly improbable. The letter arrived late in the evening of June 28. Decrès was instructed personally to inform Napoleon as speedily as possible that the restriction to which he had objected had been removed. He arrived at Malmaison at four in the morning. The Emperor, who received him in his dressing-gown, informed him that he would depart that day.

After the interview with the minister of marine Napoleon had dressed and had gone into the library. There, on the table, a map was spread in which colored pins were stuck. He had been furnished with precise information about the movements of the allied armies by several of his visitors. He now looked at the gap separating Blücher's army from Wellington's and realized the opportunity this presented.

Toward nine o'clock Lavalette and Maret, his former minister of the interior, called. Napoleon received them in the library, where Joseph and Flahaut had joined him. Lavalette gave the latest news: Marshal Grouchy and General Vandamme had arrived in Paris with a considerable force. While his companions were conversing, Napoleon sat brooding. Suddenly the cry of "*Vive l'Empereur!*" was heard outside. A regiment returning from the Vendée was passing on the highroad to Saint-Germain, and the soldiers were cheering their idol. Napoleon rose to his feet. The lethargy that had enveloped him since his abdication had dropped from him like a cloak. "France," he cried, "must not submit to a handful of Prussians! I can still crush the enemy and give the government the opportunity to negotiate with the allies."

He summoned Beker and told him to ride to Paris immediately, see the members of the provisional government, and tell them that he stood ready to take command of the army, "not as Emperor, but as a general whose name and reputation can still have a great influence upon the country's destiny." When he had repulsed the enemy he would relinquish the command and sail for the United States. The order was given in a tone of command that brooked no argument. Beker saluted and hastened to carry it out.

Napoleon felt confident that his offer would be accepted. He dressed carefully in the uniform of a colonel of the *Chasseurs de la Garde,* riding boots and sword. He seemed to have grown ten years younger as he impatiently awaited Beker's return, ready to mount his horse and be off to confront the enemy.

In the meantime Beker had arrived at the Tuileries, where the provisional government was in session. He was admitted to the council chamber and delivered his message. Fouché burst out: "Is he making fun of us? Don't we know how he would keep his word if we were to accept his offer? Why do you come here with proposals such as this when it is your duty to see to it that he leaves immediately? Go and tell him that it is our fixed resolution to change nothing in the dispositions already taken." Beker demanded a written reply. It was given him in the form of a letter to the Duke de Bassano (Maret) asking him to use his influence to get Napoleon to depart, as he stood in imminent danger of capture by the Prussians.

When Napoleon was shown the letter he said: "These people have no conception of the spirit of France. They will live to regret this. Give the order to start for Rochefort. When everything is ready come and tell me."

He went to his room, took off his uniform, and dressed in mufti—a brown frock coat, blue trousers, a round felt hat. The phial with the reddish liquid Corvisart had given him was in a little pocket Marchand had attached to his suspenders. He embraced his mother and Hortense, bade farewell to Cardinal Fesch and to such of his officers as had chosen to remain in France. He tried to persuade Labédoyère to accompany him, but the young colonel did not take his advice. Hortense insisted that he take her diamond necklace, which she had sewed into a girdle to be worn under the clothing. After some hesitation he took it, later entrusting it to Las Cases. By five o'clock all was ready. As before at the Elysée Palace, he left by a back door giving upon the garden. With him were Bertrand, Beker, and Savary. They mounted into a yellow coach drawn by four horses in charge of two postilions. Napoleon's valet Ali mounted upon the box in front, and they set off at a gallop toward Rambouillet. His suite departed a short time later, some taking a different route, so there might be no shortage of post-horses.

Notwithstanding Napoleon's insistence on the annulment of the provision that the *Saale* and the *Méduse* must not sail without a safe-conduct from the British, he must have expected that the document would be forthcoming. How else explain why he allowed so many—including women and children—to attach themselves to his party? Decrès, who was devoted to him, apparently did not believe the British would grant a safe-conduct. He had written to the captains of the *Saale* and the *Méduse* that the Emperor and his suite should embark on the *Saale*, the swifter of the two vessels, while the other should, if necessary, sacrifice itself to cover their escape. The order was later countermanded.

III. From Malmaison to the "Bellerophon"

The yellow coach sped on over the dusty road. The heat was stifling. Nobody spoke. Now and then Beker produced an ivory snuff-box and held it out open to Napoleon, who would take a pinch of snuff. It was his habit not to sniff it in, merely to smell it, then drop it. Having noticed that Marie Louise's profile was carved on the lid, he, on one occasion, took the box from Beker's hand, examined the effigy, then handed it back without a word. He knew about his wife's liaison with the Austrian Count Neipperg.

Darkness had fallen when they reached Rambouillet. Beker had intended to travel through the night, but the Emperor wanted to spend the night at the castle. Was he trying to gain time? Did he still hope something might happen that would make it unnecessary for him to continue his flight? He delayed his departure until eleven o'clock in the forenoon. Then, however, he and his companions traveled almost uninterruptedly for thirty-six hours. They drove through Châteaudun, Vendôme, Tours, and Poitiers, stopping only for meals and to change horses. On July 1, at ten in the evening, they arrived at Niort and stopped at an inn. The Emperor's presence soon became known, and in the morning the prefect of the department hurried over to invite him to stay at the prefecture. After his arrival there a crowd gathered and acclaimed him, but he did not show himself. He received a visit from his brother Joseph who was on his way to Bordeaux, where he expected to embark for the United States. The officers of two regiments of hussars stationed in the town sent a delegation to beg him to place himself at the head of their men and join the army of the Loire. He refused. It would mean civil war, he said. He had asked de Bonnefoux, maritime prefect of Rochefort, to meet him at Niort. The prefect sent his excuses, claiming to be indisposed, and the information that it would be impossible to slip through the blockade. After reading the message Napoleon had Beker write to the provisional government asking permission to communicate with the British squadron, and renewed his offer to place himself at the head of the army "as a general who has no other thought than to be of service to his country." He left Niort on July 3, at four in the morning. Even at that early hour a crowd had assembled and there were cries of "*Vive l'Empereur!*" and "Don't forsake us!" An honor guard of hussars, swords drawn, escorted him to the next relay station.

TWO

Napoleon arrived at Rochefort on July 3, at eight in the morning. He was received with enthusiasm by the populace. When he had visited the town in 1808, an apartment of state had been prepared for him at the prefecture. This was now placed at his disposal by de Bonnefoux. A great crowd gathered before the building and acclaimed him. He went out upon the balcony several times in response to cheers.

That same day a council of naval and military officers was held to decide on the possibility of sailing without being stopped by the British. It reached the unanimous decision that it could not be done. Yet, had the order of Decrès that the *Méduse*, the slower of the two frigates, should if necessary sacrifice itself not been countermanded, there can be no doubt that he could have escaped on the *Saale*. There were at that time only two British warships blockading Rochefort—the cruiser *Bellerophon* and the brig *Myrmidon*. The former, a vessel carrying seventy-four guns, was old and slow, while the *Saale* was one of the newest and fastest ships in the French navy.

During the next few days various possibilities were discussed. Since British attention appeared to be focused upon Rochefort, why not escape in a merchant vessel from nearby La Rochelle or Bordeaux? The French captain of a Danish brig with a cargo of gin offered to take Napoleon and four of his officers on board, hide them in empty barrels if the British boarded his vessel, and take them to the United States. Napoleon did not appear interested in any of the proposals. He still hoped that the British would grant him a safe-conduct to America, and, if not, that he and his suite would be granted asylum in England. He had faith in British magnanimity and hospitality.

On the evening of the 7th, Beker received a reply to the letter he had written at Niort. Napoleon's offer to lead the army was again rejected. He was to go immediately on board the *Saale* and there await the result of negotiations concerning him. He was forbidden to communicate with the British. If he refused to obey, force was to be used. Beker informed the Emperor of the contents of the letter, calling attention to the fact that once the Bourbons had taken over, the situation would be desperate. Napoleon decided to obey. In the afternoon of July 8, he went to the little port of Fouras and was carried to a barge on the back of a sailor while a crowd on shore cheered and waved good-by. His suite followed. Captain Philibert of the *Saale* was a Royalist, but received Napoleon with all honors due him except the firing of cannon, which might have alerted the British.

The following morning the Emperor decided to visit the island of Aix, which he had been examining through a spyglass. During his reign he had had powerful defense works constructed there. He was rowed to the island in company with Gourgaud and Las Cases. Beker, whom the move made uneasy, followed in another boat. It was Sunday, and almost the entire population was at the landing stage to receive the Emperor. He visited the defense works, had the officers introduced to him, and reviewed a regiment of marines. Everywhere a crowd followed and ac-

27

claimed him. He might have imagined himself at the height of his power.

When he returned to the *Saale* he found de Bonnefoux awaiting him with new orders from Paris. The maritime prefect was instructed to insist that Napoleon and his suite leave at once on the frigates placed at their disposal. If he preferred going on board the British cruiser, means for doing so were to be furnished him upon his written request. "Under no circumstances is the commander of the vessel on which Napoleon might find himself to disembark him anywhere on French soil on pain of being tried for high treason." The provisional government apparently wished to give him the opportunity to surrender voluntarily to the British, but did not care to run the risk of having him join the army of the Loire.

THREE

After a conference with Beker and Bertrand, Napoleon decided to send emissaries to the commander of the *Bellerophon*. He dictated a letter, which Bertrand signed, asking if a safe-conduct had been received, and in case it had not, if the commander would oppose the Emperor's departure for America. Las Cases and Savary were chosen for the mission. The former had lived in England ten years as an *émigré* and knew English fairly well, but was instructed not to betray that knowledge, as this might enable him to gain some useful information. They departed in the early morning under a flag of truce.

Arrived at the *Bellerophon* the emissaries delivered the letter to Captain Maitland, who asked if they spoke English. Savary replied that they did not. Having read the letter, Maitland, who spoke French fluently, said that the latest information he had received was that Napoleon had been defeated at Waterloo. Having no orders concerning him he would have to forward the letter to his commanding officer, Admiral Hotham, who was at Quiberon Bay. This was far from being the truth. Hotham had written him that Napoleon had abdicated, that a safe-conduct had been applied for on his behalf and had been refused, that in all probability he was on his way to Rochefort, and that if he tried to escape Maitland should intercept him. More than that. Royalists on shore had kept Maitland informed of every move Napoleon was making since his arrival at Rochefort. It appears that the captain of the *Bellerophon* was by no means sure of his ability to keep Napoleon from escaping if the French frigates showed fight and wished to gain time so the reinforcements he had asked for could reach him.

Maitland invited the two envoys to breakfast. While they were at table the *Falmouth* arrived with dispatches from the admiral. Hotham wrote that if Maitland succeeded in intercepting Napoleon, he should transfer him and his retinue to the *Bellerophon* and proceed with all possible speed to the nearest British port. On arrival at the port he should not permit any communication with the shore. Needless to say Maitland said nothing of this to the emissaries, but gave them the following written reply: "I cannot say what the intentions of my government may be, but, the two countries being at present in a state of war, it is impossible for me to permit any ship of war to put to sea from the port of Rochefort. As to the proposal made by the Duc de Rovigo [Savary] and Count Las Cases, of allowing the Emperor to proceed in a merchant vessel, it is out of my power, without the sanction of my commanding officer, Sir Henry Hotham—who is at present at Quiberon Bay, and to whom I have forwarded your dispatch—to allow any vessel, under whatever flag she may be, to pass with a personage of such consequence."

There was some further conversation during which Maitland said: "Why not ask an asylum in England?" It is mainly upon this remark that Napoleon was to base his claim that he had been decoyed by the British.

FOUR

Napoleon sent Lallemand to Royan, at the mouth of the Gironde, to interview Baudin, captain of the *Bayadère*, who had offered to take him to the United States. He was still willing, but the order of the provisional government forbidding anyone to land the fallen monarch on French soil made it impossible for Napoleon to reach Royan. On the 11th newspapers that ar-

rived on board the *Saale* announced the entry of the King into
Paris. Consternation reigned among the refugees.

The following day Napoleon left the *Saale* and installed himself in the house of the military commander of the island of Aix,
who was away from home. The move was a violation of the order of the provisional government that he should not be landed
anywhere on French soil, but Philibert chose to interpret this as
meaning the French mainland. The reception he received from
the people and the military on the island was as enthusiastic as
on his previous visit. Young marine officers offered to take him
and his suite out to sea at night in swift coasting vessels. They
would board the first merchant ship they encountered, and its
captain was to be induced or compelled to set sail for the United
States. It was a hairbrained scheme, but with the Bourbons in
Paris the situation was truly desperate.

On the 13th Joseph came. He had chartered a ship at Bordeaux to take him to the United States. The Emperor would
have gone with him had he been able to reach the mainland.
Joseph, who bore a striking resemblance to his brother, suggested that they change clothing and that Napoleon should im-
personate him. The Emperor refused. In the meantime Maitland
had received reinforcements, making it appear even more haz-
ardous to try to run the blockade.

Gourgaud has written that on the 13th Napoleon favored taking advantage of the offer of the French captain of the Danish
brig, and asked his opinion. The young general advised against
it, saying that if the vessel was searched and Napoleon's hiding
place discovered he might be subjected to ill usage. "He assured
me," he writes, "that in that case he would still remain master
of his destiny, that he would kill himself. 'No,' I replied, 'Your
Majesty cannot do that. A gambler kills himself, a great man
braves misfortune.'" He advised Napoleon to surrender to the
British.

While they were talking a little bird flew in through the open
window, "It's a sign of good luck!" Gourgaud exclaimed. He
caught the bird and held it in his hand. Napoleon remarked:

"There's enough misery in the world—let it go." As Gourgaud obeyed, the Emperor said: "Let's watch for an omen." The bird fluttered for a moment, then flew to the right. "Sire, he is flying towards the British cruiser!" the young man cried. Yet, at nightfall, some of Napoleon's effects were put aboard the Danish brig. At midnight the order was countermanded: he had decided to send Las Cases and Lallemand to the *Bellerophon* to negotiate surrender.

FIVE

The two emissaries departed for the *Bellerophon* at four in the morning on July 14. They were received by Maitland, who thought it prudent to have Captain Sartorious of the *Slaney* present at the interview. Las Cases said that Napoleon could, if he wished, join the army of the Loire but, desiring to avoid further bloodshed, had resolved to go to America. He was prepared to sail on a French or a British cruiser or on a merchant vessel. Maitland replied: "I have no authority to agree to any arrangement of that sort, nor do I believe my government would consent to it; but I think I may venture to receive him onto this ship, and convey him to England; if, however, he adopts that plan, I cannot enter into any promise as to the reception he may meet with." Las Cases has written: "He further declared it as his private opinion that there was not the least doubt of Napoleon's meeting with all possible respect and good treatment." Lallemand, who had been proscribed by the Bourbons, asked if persons implicated in the dissension in France who went voluntarily to England had any reason to fear that they would be turned over to the French authorities. Maitland assured him "that they had not: repelling the doubt as an insult."

The emissaries were back at the island before noon. A council was held. With the exception of Lallemand and Montholon, all favored surrender to the British. Lallemand believed there was still a possibility of joining the army of the Loire. Such a move, he thought, might decide the allies to offer the Emperor reasonable terms. Montholon favored escape in the Danish brig. Napoleon, however, had already made up his mind. Before the council had assembled he had composed the following letter to the Prince Regent:

ROYAL HIGHNESS,

A victim of the factions that divide my country, and of the enmity of the greatest Powers of Europe, I have terminated my political career, and I come, like Themistocles, to seat myself at the hearth of the British people. I place myself under the protection of their laws, which I claim of your Royal Highness as of the most powerful, the most constant, and the most generous of my enemies.

Napoleon

As the council broke up the Emperor motioned to Gourgaud to remain. He showed him the letter, the contents of which moved the young general to tears, and gave him the following instructions: He and Las Cases were to go to the *Bellerophon* that afternoon. Las Cases would carry a letter from Bertrand to Maitland informing him that the Emperor and his suite would arrive on board early the following morning. The letter to the Prince Regent would be entrusted to Gourgaud unsealed, so he could show it to Maitland. He should request to be sent to London immediately so he might deliver it personally to the Prince Regent. He was to ask the Prince that passports to the United States be granted to the Emperor and his suite, and if this was found inexpedient that they be granted asylum in England. Napoleon should like to settle down in a country house ten or twelve miles from London, sufficiently large to shelter him and members of his suite. He would live incognito as Colonel Muiron or Baron Duroc and would not object to the presence of an English commissioner.

Gourgaud and Las Cases arrived on the *Bellerophon* at about seven o'clock that evening. Las Cases gave Maitland Bertrand's letter, after which Gourgaud handed the captain the letter to the Prince Regent. Maitland and several of his officers read Napoleon's message to the Prince and expressed their admiration of its wording. Gourgaud was taken to the *Slaney*, which immediately set sail for England, while Las Cases remained on the *Bellerophon*.

That evening there arrived at Rochefort a representative of the King with new instructions. Napoleon was not to be allowed to communicate with the British and was not to leave the *Saale*, where the commander of the British squadron would claim him as a prisoner of war. De Bonnefoux immediately set to work to have the well-laid plans of the Bourbons miscarry. He was helped by Philibert, who although a Royalist did not feel Napoleon should be deprived of whatever advantage was to be derived from voluntary surrender. The maritime prefect sent a letter to Philibert telling him what was afoot and asking him to warn the Emperor. Philibert promptly forwarded the letter to Beker, who was with Napoleon on the island, together with a note of his own urging him to tell Napoleon "not to lose a moment in embarking." To make it appear that he was trying to execute the King's order, de Bonnefoux went on board the *Saale*, where he knew Napoleon was not, remained there all night, and in the morning informed the King's representative that Napoleon had already surrendered to the British.

IV. From the "Bellerophon" to the "Northumberland"

Napoleon had risen at midnight. His valet Marchand helped him dress. Since leaving Malmaison he had worn mufti, now he donned the uniform of colonel of the *Chasseurs de la Garde*— green, with red facings and hooked-back skirts, white waistcoat, white breeches, and high riding boots. His breast was adorned with the star of the Legion of Honor, the small cross and the iron crown. At his side was a sword, and on his head the famous cocked hat with three-colored cockade.

Accompanied by members of his suite he went to the landing stage, where the *Épervier*—the brig that was to carry them to the *Bellerophon*—was waiting. General Beker had asked whether he should accompany him, but Napoleon had replied: "That would make it appear as if you were delivering me up to the British. I do not want this ever to be imputed to France. My surrender is voluntary."

Few people were about. Those who were saluted respectfully. Some were visibly moved. It was three in the morning on July 15 when the *Épervier* hove anchor and sailed toward the British squadron. There was little wind, and at daybreak the brig was still about a mile from the *Bellerophon*. Captain Maitland, standing on the quarter-deck with his officers and Las Cases and watching the vessel through a telescope, saw that it was making scant headway and ordered a barge to go to meet it. When the barge was on its return trip, he kept his telescope trained upon it and felt relieved when he distinguished Napoleon among the occupants. Admiral Hotham's flagship the *Superb* was visible at a distance sailing into the straits and he had feared the Emperor might decide to surrender to him.

When the barge reached the cruiser, Bertrand climbed aboard and announced the Emperor's arrival. Maitland made no reply. A moment later Napoleon appeared. Las Cases went to meet him and escorted him to the quarter-deck. The Emperor raised his hat and said: "Commander, I have come to place myself under the protection of your Prince and of the laws of your country."

No special honors were shown Napoleon. Having received no instructions in the matter, Maitland took advantage of the regulation that before eight in the morning and after sunset ceremony could be dispensed with. He ushered the Emperor into the captain's cabin, which he placed at his disposal, and introduced his officers to him. At nine o'clock an ample breakfast was served, but as it was in the English style Napoleon ate little. Maitland gave orders that henceforth the Emperor's chef was to prepare the food for the French. Later he and Napoleon strolled together on the deck chatting, and he was amazed at the nautical knowledge the Emperor displayed.

TWO

In the meantime the *Superb* had dropped anchor close to the *Bellerophon*. Maitland went to report to the admiral, and in the afternoon Hotham came on board and treated Napoleon with the utmost deference. The Emperor invited him to dinner, which was prepared by his chef and served by his servants on the imperial plate he had brought with him from the Tuileries. Maitland has written: "Bonaparte, viewing himself as a royal personage, which he continued to do while on board the *Bellerophon*, and which, under the circumstances, I considered it would have been both ungracious and uncalled for in me to have disputed, led the way into the dining room. He seated himself in the center at one side of the table, requesting Sir Henry Hotham to sit at his right hand, and Madame Bertrand on his left." The admiral invited the Emperor and his suite to have breakfast with him on board the flagship the following morning.

Napoleon's reception on board the *Superb* left nothing to be desired. With the exception of the firing of the cannon every honor was shown him. The yards were manned and an honor guard presented arms. The Emperor's hope rose. He was heard to remark: "I must learn to conform to English ways. I shall probably spend the rest of my life in England." Hotham expressed the hope that his guest would remain on the *Superb* for the voyage to England, but not wishing to offend Maitland Napoleon declined. When he returned to the *Bellerophon* he was pleased to see that following the example of the admiral, Maitland had manned the yards and that the captain's guard stood at attention.

Shortly after Napoleon's return, the *Bellerophon*—accompanied by the *Myrmidon,* on which the less important members of the Emperor's suite had been accommodated—sailed for England. Napoleon had exchanged his colonel's uniform for the green frock coat, white vest, and white breeches in which he is usually pictured. The high military boots had given place to white silk stockings and gold-buckled shoes. He was beginning to feel very much at home. Las Cases has written: "The captain, officers, and crew soon adopted the etiquette of his suite, showing him exactly the same attention and respect. The captain addressed him either as *Sire* or *Your Majesty*. When he appeared on deck, every one took off his hat, and remained uncovered while he was present—this was not the case at first. There was no entering his cabin, except by passing the attendants. No person but those who were invited appeared at his table. Napoleon was, in fact, an Emperor on board the *Bellerophon*." He rose late and went to bed early. He often appeared on deck, and with Las Cases as interpreter conversed with members of the crew.

THREE

The ship dropped anchor in the harbor of Torbay on July 24, at about eight in the morning. Shortly after its arrival doubt began to creep in among the French about British intentions. The *Slaney,* on which Gourgaud had been dispatched with Napoleon's letter to the Prince Regent, was in the harbor, and a short time later the young general presented himself. He had not been allowed to land and brought the letter with him, which he had refused to surrender. It was later forwarded to London. Maitland had received orders not to allow anybody to land or to come on board without an order from Lord Keith, admiral of the channel fleet, who was at Plymouth. Newspapers that arrived on board carried the ominous news that Napoleon's ultimate destination would be the Tower of London, a fortress in Scotland, or St. Helena. The only bright spot on the darkening horizon was the following paragraph in Keith's letter to Maitland, which the captain communicated to the Emperor: "You may say to Napoleon, that I am under the greatest personal obligation to him for his attention to my nephew, who was taken and brought before him at Belle Alliance, and who must have died, if he had not ordered a surgeon to dress him immediately, and sent him to a hut."

But if the attitude of the British government was one of cold aloofness and severity, the British public was differently inclined. The admiralty was swamped with requests from people of note wishing to visit the *Bellerophon* in the hope of seeing Bonaparte. The owner of an estate in the neighborhood of Torbay sent him a basket of fruit. Boatloads of the curious swarmed around the vessel and Maitland had to put out guard-boats to keep them at a distance.

In the meantime the government was negotiating with its allies about the prisoner's fate. On July 20, Lord Liverpool, the prime minister, had written to Castlereagh, secretary of foreign affairs: "We are all decidedly of the opinion that it would not answer to confine him in this country. Very nice legal questions might arise upon the subject, which would be particularly embarrassing. But, independent of these considerations, you know enough of the feelings of people in this country not to doubt he would become an object of curiosity immediately, and possibly of compassion, in the course of a few months; and the circumstances of being here, or indeed, anywhere in Europe, would contribute to keep up a certain degree of ferment in France." He favored St. Helena as a place of detention because: "The situation is particularly healthy. There is only one place in the circuit of the island where ships can anchor, and we have the power of excluding neutral vessels altogether, if we should think it necessary. At such a distance and in such a place, all intrigue would be impossible; and being withdrawn so far from the European world, he would very soon be forgotten." Although no agreement had yet been reached with the allies, Lord Bathurst, secretary of state for the colonies, proceeded to make arrangement with the East India Company, to whom the island belonged, to turn it over temporarily to the Crown.

FOUR

Maitland received instructions to take his ship to Plymouth, where it arrived in the afternoon of the 26th. Here the afflux of spectators bordered on the fantastic. People came from all over England and Scotland. Post-horses were at a premium. Rowboats rented for as high as sixty pounds and were packed so closely that no water was visible between them. When Napoleon would show himself men removed their hats and women waved handkerchiefs. Many wore a red carnation, symbol of the Bonapartists. Lord Keith had two frigates, the *Liffy* and the *Eurotas,* anchor on either side of the *Bellerophon,* so close that their sides almost touched. Shots were fired over the heads of the crowd. But all this did not discourage the curious. "On July 30," wrote Maitland, "the number of boats was greater than I had yet seen. I am sure I do not exaggerate by saying that there were over a thousand, with an average of eight persons in each." Guard-boats from the warships began charging the multitude. A boat was upset and a man was drowned.

Immediately after the ship's arrival at Plymouth Napoleon had asked to see Lord Keith. The admiral wished to postpone the interview until he had something definite to communicate, but on the 28th made a short courtesy call. Newspapers arriving on board now stated as a positive fact that Napoleon would be exiled to St. Helena and that Sir Henry Bunbury, under-secretary of state, was leaving for Plymouth to communicate the government's decision to him. On the 31st of July, Lord Keith and the under-secretary arrived and were closeted with the Emperor. Bunbury read to the prisoner a French translation of a letter addressed to Lord Keith by Lord Melville, first lord of the admiralty. It contained the following stipulations:

Napoleon (referred to in the letter as "General Bonaparte") was to reside at St. Helena.

He could choose from his suite three officers (but not Lallemand and Savary, proscribed by the Bourbons) and twelve servants, who together with his surgeon would be permitted to accompany him.

Rear-Admiral Sir George Cockburn would convey General Bonaparte and his suite to St. Helena and would receive detailed instructions concerning the matter.

As the admiral would be ready to sail in a few days, General Bonaparte was requested to make the choice of the persons whom he wished to accompany him as speedily as possible.

Napoleon made an indignant protest. Lord Keith suggested that he put it in writing, promising to forward it to London. When he and Bunbury had departed, the Emperor wrote:

"I am England's guest, having come to this country on board the English vessel the *Bellerophon* after communicating to its captain the letter I wrote to the Prince Regent, and having received the assurance that he had orders to receive me on board and convey me and my suite to England if I expressed the desire to go there. Admiral Hotham has since given me the same assurance. From the moment that I voluntarily set foot on the *Bellerophon* I was under the protection of your country's laws. It is my desire to live in the interior of England under the protection and surveillance of those laws. . . . I have no intention of engaging in correspondence with any one in France or to mix in politics in any manner. . . . I put my trust in the honor of the Prince Regent and in the laws of your country."

FIVE

News of the government's decision created consternation among Napoleon's suite. Lallemand and Savary now felt convinced that they would be turned over to the Bourbons, which would have meant court-martial and the firing squad. They wrote to Lord Bathurst and bitterly complained to Maitland. The captain, feeling that the assurance he had given Lallemand was responsible for that officer's and Savary's presence on board, bestirred himself on their behalf. (They were deported to Malta and released in April of the following year.) Madame Bertrand tried to persuade Captain Maitland to use his influence so the choice of those who were to accompany Napoleon to St. Helena would be made by the British government, and begged him to try to arrange matters so her husband would not be chosen. When he told her that there was nothing he could do, she stormed unannounced into the Emperor's cabin and demanded that he promise her not to choose Bertrand. Failing to obtain that assurance she was with difficulty prevented from jumping overboard. Las Cases, who had been the most optimistic regarding the reception that awaited Napoleon in England, was particularly downcast.

England's allies had readily consented to Lord Liverpool's proposal to banish Napoleon to St. Helena. On August 2, treaties were signed between Great Britain on the one hand and Austria, Prussia, and Russia on the other specifying that Napoleon was to be prisoner of the allies, but that responsibility for his safe-keeping was to devolve entirely upon Great Britain. Each allied sovereign was, however, to appoint a commissioner who was to reside at the place of exile, but whose duty would be restricted to assuring himself of Bonaparte's presence. The King of France would likewise be invited to send such an official.

In the meantime Napoleon's admirers in England—of whom there were many in the Whig party—had not been idle. The *Morning Chronicle* received more than a hundred letters belaboring the government for its treatment of the former Emperor. A gentleman who signed his communication "Practicing Barrister" wrote: "The policy of imprisoning for life a forlorn and abdicated monarch by way of security . . . is the policy of cowards!" The venerable Capel Lofft, juris-consult, classical scholar, abolitionist and reformer, whom Boswell called "this little David of the popular spirit" wrote that the deportation would be a violation of the Magna Charta, the Habeas Corpus Act, and the Bill of Rights—"in fact, of our whole Criminal Law, which permits not transportation unless in cases for which the Statute Law has expressly provided." Lady Clavering, a friend of Las Cases, hired a lawyer to try to obtain a writ of habeas corpus. A barrister named Anthony McKenrot took advantage of a court action he had initiated some nine years before and which was still pending to obtain a *subpoena duces tecum,* calling upon those who had custody of Napoleon to produce him in court as a witness. All this, together with the mounting popular sympathy for "Boney," alarmed the government, and the admiralty gave orders that the *Bellerophon* should leave Plymouth Roads and cruise in the channel until the arrival of the *Northumberland,* a more seaworthy vessel that was to take the captive to St. Helena. The doughty McKenrot, thwarted in his attempt to serve the subpoena on Captain Maitland, tried to serve it on Lord Keith, who fled through the back door of his house, was pursued by McKenrot to the *Tonnant,* escaped from there just as his pursuer was climbing aboard, fled back to Plymouth, and finally wound up on the *Prometheus,* breathless, but still unserved.

SIX

Napoleon had told Gourgaud that he would not go to St. Helena; that to do so would mean to terminate his career in an ignoble fashion; that his blood would stain the *Bellerophon.* On the morning of August 4, he did not breakfast with his suite but remained in bed. He had Marchand read to him Plutarch's life of Cato the Younger, who committed suicide rather than surrender to Cæsar. Later in the day he appeared on deck and talked with Las Cases. "My friend," he said, "I have sometimes an idea of quitting you, and this would not be very difficult. It is only

41

necessary to create a little excitement, and I shall soon have escaped. All will be over, and you can then quietly rejoin your families. It would be all the more easy as I am not opposed to it in principle." Las Cases tried to dissuade him, as Gourgaud had done on the island of Aix. "But what can we do in that desolate place?" the Emperor asked. "Sire," replied the chamberlain, "we will live on the past; there is enough there to satisfy us. You will re-peruse yourself, Sire!" "Be it so!" rejoined Napoleón. "We will write our memoirs. Yes, we must be employed. Occupation is the scythe of time. After all, a man ought to fulfill his destiny."

SEVEN

Admiral Keith had returned to the *Tonnant,* which joined the *Bellerophon* and the *Eurotas,* to which most of those who had come with Napoleon had been transferred, in the channel. The three ships cruised about aimlessly until August 6, when they dropped anchor at Start-Point, near Torbay. That same day the *Northumberland* arrived, flying the flag of Rear-Admiral Sir George Cockburn and followed by transports and other vessels carrying reinforcements and supplies for the garrison at St. Helena. Admiral Keith came on board the *Bellerophon* accompanied by Rear-Admiral Cockburn, whom he introduced to Napoleon. Soon after, the Emperor was informed of the regulations to which he and his companions in exile were to be subjected. They were, in part:

His belongings and those of persons accompanying him were to be searched.

All money, negotiable bills, diamonds, and other valuables, except the "General's" silverplate, must be delivered up and would remain in the custody of the British government, so as to prevent their use for purposes of escape. Arms of any description must likewise be surrendered.

If any attempt at escape were made by the "General" he would thereby "expose himself to close imprisonment," as would any one aiding him in the attempt. (Later, by Act of Parliament, any person aiding him to escape was to incur the death penalty.)

All letters addressed to him or to any member of his suite, and all letters written by them, had to pass through the hands of the admiral, and later through those of the newly appointed governor, Sir Hudson Lowe.

"The Governor and the Admiral have received positive orders to forward to His Majesty's government any request or representation he [Bonaparte] may think proper to make. Nothing is left to their discretion on this point; but the paper on which such representations shall be written is to remain open, in order that they may subjoin such observations as they may think expedient."

Napoleon sent Las Cases aboard the *Tonnant* to protest to Admiral Keith against these regulations, especially against the searching of their belongings. He considered this humiliating and said he would prefer having them thrown overboard. Keith received the emissary with punctilious courtesy but said it was not in his power to change the regulations. Would he go so far, asked Las Cases, as to demand that the Emperor surrender his sword? Keith replied that an exception would be made in the case of "General" Bonaparte. A secretary present called the admiral's attention to the fact that the regulations made no such exception. He received the curt reply: "Mind your own business, sir, and leave us to ours." In the end all the officers were allowed to keep their swords. Their firearms were returned to them at St. Helena.

Fourteen officers had followed the Emperor from Malmaison, of whom he could choose three to accompany him into exile. He chose Marshal Bertrand, Count de Montholon, and Colonel Planat de la Faye. The last-named had been transferred to the *Eurotas*, hence was unable to plead his cause, while Gourgand pleaded his own so passionately that Napoleon allowed himself to be persuaded and substituted him for Planat, a decision he would live to regret. Lord Keith, having noticed that Napoleon found Las Cases particularly useful, decided that he, too, could go as the "General's" secretary. He moreover raised no objection to Bertrand taking his wife and three children with him, Montholon his wife and child, and Las Cases his son, a boy of fifteen. A doctor and fourteen servants were added to the party.

The belongings of those who were to be transported to St. Helena were searched by a custom-house officer and his assistants, under the personal supervision of Admiral Cockburn. Neither Napoleon nor any of his officers deigned to be present, but the Emperor's loyal servitor Marchand kept a watchful eye. The search was perfunctory. Montholon informs us that a box containing four thousand napoleons was all that fell into the hands of the British, and that the exiles were able to conceal on their persons four hundred thousand francs in gold, between three and four hundred thousand francs in diamonds, and the letter of credit from the banker Laffite.

On August 7, between one and two o'clock in the afternoon, Napoleon bade farewell in his cabin to those of his suite who were to remain behind. Most of them on entering the cabin could not withhold their tears. Savary threw himself at the Emperor's feet and kissed his hand. Napoleon raised him up and embraced him. Las Cases remarked to Lord Keith, present at the scene: "You see, my Lord, that the only persons who shed tears are those who are to remain."

When the Emperor left the cabin the drum rolled and the guard presented arms. He went up to Captain Maitland, thanked him for the courtesy shown him, and asked him to convey his thanks to his officers and crew. Then, turning to the officers, he said: "Gentlemen, I have requested the Captain to express my gratitude to you for your attentions to me and to those who have followed my fortunes." Before going down the ship's side he bowed. He was followed into the barge by Madame Bertrand, Madame Montholon, the officers who were to share his exile, and finally by Lord Keith. As the barge left the cruiser he remained standing for a while, then saluted and seated himself beside the admiral.

V. On the "Northumberland"

William Warden, surgeon on the *Northumberland,* thus describes Napoleon's arrival aboard the vessel:

"Our quarter-deck was covered with officers, and there were also some individuals of rank who had come round from motives of curiosity.

"The marines occupied the front of the poop, and the officers kept the quarter-deck. A universal silence prevailed when the barge reached the side, and there was a grave but anxious aspect in all the spectators, which, in the opinion of others as well as in my own, was no small addition to the solemnity of the ceremonial. Count Bertrand ascended first and, having bowed, retired a few steps to give place to him whom he still considered as his master, and in whose presence he appeared to feel all his most respectful homage was still due. The whole ship's company seemed at this moment to be in breathless expectation. Lord Keith was the last who quitted the barge, and I cannot give you a more complete idea of the rapt attention of all on board to the figure of Napoleon, than that his Lordship, high as he is in naval character, Admiral also of the Channel Fleet, to which we belonged, and arrayed in the full uniform of his rank, emblazoned with the decorations of his order, did not seem to be noticed, nor scarcely even to be seen, among the group which was subject to him.

"With a slow step Bonaparte mounted the gangway, and, on feeling himself firm on the quarter-deck, he raised his hat, when the guard presented arms and the drum rolled. The officers of the *Northumberland,* who were uncovered, stood considerably in advance. Those he approached, and saluted with an air of the most affable politeness. . . ."

Napoleon was pleased with this reception, but was soon to be disillusioned. The ceremonial was not in his honor but in honor of Lord Keith. The admiralty had been much displeased by the honors shown him by Admiral Hotham and on the *Bellerophon,* and had given strict orders to Rear-Admiral Cockburn that this was not to happen again. He was to be treated as a general and was to be addressed as General Bonaparte—or, as Lord Bathurst preferred to spell it, Buonaparte. Thus, throughout the journey, the officers of the *Northumberland* remained covered in his presence, but neither they nor the admiral could refrain from showing him some of the consideration due to his rank and fame.

Admiral Cockburn conducted him to the after-cabin, where he presented to him Captain Ross of the *Northumberland* and his principal officers, Colonel George Bingham of the 53rd regiment—soon to be promoted to brigadier-general and placed in command of the garrison at St. Helena—and two members of Parliament, Lord Lowther and Mr. Lyttelton. The latter, who spoke French fluently, had a long conversation with Napoleon. Before the ship hove anchor those of Napoleon's followers who were remaining behind were permitted to pay him another visit. Among them was Captain Piontkowski, a Polish officer who had been with him at Elba and now begged permission to accompany him to St. Helena. When Napoleon told him that he was helpless in the matter, he turned to Lord Keith and, with tears coursing down his cheeks, offered to go as a domestic if he could not do so as an officer.

The decision that Napoleon should bear the title of general was to result in endless complications. Throughout his exile he was to refuse to receive any communication addressed to "General Bonaparte." He was willing to assume an incognito and be known as Colonel Murion or as Baron Duroc,[1] but the British decision to reduce him to the rank of general he considered an insult to the people of France who had twice conferred imperial rank upon him by a plebiscite. "The throne of France was granted before to Hugues Capet by a few bishops and nobles," he said to O'Meara at St. Helena. "The Imperial throne was given to me by the desire of the people, whose wishes were three times verified in a solemn manner. The Pope crossed the Alps to crown and anoint me." At another time he said: "I did not usurp the crown, I picked it up out of the gutter; the people placed it on my head; let their acts be respected."

TWO

What manner of men and women were they who were to accompany Napoleon to his grim island prison in the Atlantic?

Count Henri Gratien Bertrand deserves first mention. Of him an English officer, Dr. Walter Henry, assistant-surgeon of the 66th regiment stationed at St. Helena, has written: "I believe Marshal Bertrand was the most honest and honorable man of the Longwood establishment, perhaps of the whole court of Napoleon." Bertrand, who had been with Napoleon on the island of Elba, was forty-two when he decided to accompany him to St. Helena. He was of medium height, sparely built and balding. He had taken part in the campaigns in Italy, Egypt, Germany, and Russia, usually in charge of engineers. He became brigadier general at the age of twenty-seven, then, successively, aide-de-camp of the Emperor, divisional general, commander in chief of engineers with the army in Germany. In 1808 he became count of the empire and three years later governor-general of Illyria. While capable and resourceful as an engineer he was reputed to have been but an indifferent general. He came by the title of marshal through his appointment, in the fall of 1813, to grand marshal of the palace, an office not requiring military

---

[1] Murion was killed at Arcola while covering Napoleon with his body. Duroc, Bertrand's predecessor as grand marshal of the palace, came nearer being regarded by Napoleon as an intimate friend than any other man. He was killed during the campaign of 1813.

talent. Of the genuineness of his devotion to Napoleon there can be no doubt, yet it should be noted that he, too, had been proscribed by the Bourbons, a circumstance Lord Keith had chosen to overlook. In May, 1816, he was condemned to death in absentia. Had he not gone to St. Helena he would have had to live abroad until the political atmosphere had cleared in France. He apparently realized this, for he had taken the precaution to transfer his not inconsiderable fortune to England.

Napoleon's opinion of Bertrand varied with the mood he was in. At one time he said: "The name of Bertrand is linked with mine; as long as I live, he will live." At another time he referred to him as "the best military engineer in Europe," but on several occasions he called him a "nincompoop" and once declared that he had come to St. Helena not on account of any devotion to him, but because otherwise he would have shared the fate of Labédoyère and Ney, executed by the Bourbons.

Countess Françoise Elizabeth Bertrand, whose maiden name was Fanny Dillon, was the daughter of General Arthur Dillon—scion of an English lord of Irish extraction who had adopted French nationality—and of a Creole lady related to the Empress Josephine. Her father had been executed during the Revolution and she had spent a part of her childhood with relatives in England, hence spoke English fluently. At the time of her departure for St. Helena she was thirty and the mother of three children. She was tall and graceful, with golden-blond hair that contrasted piquantly with her dark eyes. She could, when she chose, be exceedingly charming, but disliking Madame de Montholon, feuded with her from the beginning.

Napoleon had been very generous to the Bertrands at the time of their wedding. He had presented them with an estate and with over half a million francs in money and valuables. When Bertrand had been governor-general of Illyria, and later at the Tuileries, they had lived in grand style. Fanny had been dissatisfied at Elba, and the idea of living on a rock in the Atlantic filled her with horror. Not only had she tried to get Maitland to intervene with the British government to prevent her husband from going, but she had written to Lord Bathurst, asking for his aid in the matter. Finally she had extracted a promise from Bertrand that they would remain on the island only a year. But for his condemnation by the court-martial he might have kept that promise.

The Bertrands' three children were Napoleon, seven; Hortense, five; and Henri, three. A boy they named Arthur, after his grandfather, was born to them at St. Helena in January, 1817. Napoleon was fond of children and was never happier than when playing with the Bertrand brood. They amused him and he teased them, pinching their ears and noses, which he was in the habit of doing even with adults when in a good humor.

THREE

Charles Tristan, Marquis de Montholon and Comte de Lee, was the son of a colonel of dragoons, chief huntsman of the Duc de Provence who was to become Louis XVIII, King of France. His father died when he was five. Two years later his mother married de Sémonville, an astute and influential politician and councillor of the Parliament. When Montholon was nine, his stepfather was appointed ambassador to Turkey and journeyed to Constantinople by way of Corsica, taking the boy with him. At Ajaccio they became acquainted with the Bonapartes. Montholon has claimed that he lived for a time with the Bonaparte family, that Napoleon's brother Lucien taught him Latin, and Napoleon himself, home on leave from the French army, gave him lessons in mathematics. This, as many another statement made by him, is of doubtful veracity.

Montholon was thirty-two when he accompanied Napoleon to St. Helena. He was of medium height, handsome, and well-proportioned. His manners were courtly and he had a ready flow of speech. It has been said of him that he was more of a diplomat than a general and more of a courtier than a diplomat. He was, however, proud of his military career, which, after Napoleon's first abdication, he summarized as follows in a letter to Louis XVIII: "Thirteen campaigns, ten great battles in which I have taken part, three times wounded, several horses shot under me." It has, however, been established that his military career was devoid of all distinction. If at twenty-six he was commissioned colonel it was due to the influence of de Sémonville; and if he was created chamberlain and minister plenipotentiary to the Grand Duke of Würzburg, it was due to that same influence and to the favor of the Empress Josephine, who had a weakness for well-proportioned, handsome young men. However, he soon fell into disgrace by marrying a divorcee and was deprived of both offices.

When in 1814 France was invaded by the allied armies, Montholon was put in charge of a force of four to five thousand men in the department of the Loire. He acquitted himself poorly and finished by turning over the command, without authorization, to a subordinate, while he went to join the Emperor at Fontainebleau. After Napoleon's abdication he offered his services in the most obsequious fashion to the Bourbon King and was commissioned brigadier general. He again fell into disgrace when it was discovered that while in command in the department of the Loire he had seized the treasury of a town, supposedly to pay his soldiers, but had given no accounting of any sort. Family influence saved him from being court-martialed, but he emerged from the affair without employment and with a damaged reputation.

When Napoleon returned from Elba, Montholon decided to gamble on his success. He hastened to meet him at Fontainebleau and offered him his services. The Emperor reappointed him brigadier general, but made no use of him in his campaign in Belgium. After Waterloo Montholon's situation was desperate. He had dissipated his wife's as well as his own fortune and was heavily in debt. He had nothing to expect from the Bourbons except a court-martial. What more natural than that he should have offered to accompany Napoleon to St. Helena? If after a few years the political atmosphere cleared in France, he could return, a lion among the Bonapartists, and Napoleon would surely have made some financial provision for him.

In 1846-1847, a quarter of a century after Napoleon's death, Montholon published a book entitled *Récits de la Captivité de l'Empereur Napoléon à Sainte-Hélène*. He took few notes during the captivity and had to rely almost entirely upon his memory. Worse than that—he invents, falsifies, and romanticizes, proves himself worthy of the epithet "the Liar" given him by the servants of Napoleon's establishment at St. Helena. Much of what he has written can be believed only if corroborated by others.

In insinuating himself into Napoleon's favor Montholon was ably seconded by his wife, whose maiden name was Albine Hélène de Vassal and whom Bertrand characterized as "a scheming woman, who knows where her best interests lie." She was three years older than her husband, a coquettish if somewhat faded beauty. She had been married to a Swiss financier, Daniel Roger, by whom, in 1803, she had had a son, Edouard. Roger divorced her in 1812 and that same year she married Montholon. Unlike Madame Bertrand, who made little attempt to please Napoleon, she did everything to gain his favor, even to the extent of becoming his mistress. She sang and played the piano for him and, according to Gourgaud, flattered him outrageously.

The Montholons had a son, Charles Tristan, born in 1812, whom they took with them to St. Helena.

FOUR

Gaspard Gourgaud, born in 1783, was the son of a violinist in the King's private orchestra at Versailles. His mother was nurse to the Duc de Berry, son of the Comte D'Artois, younger brother of Louis XVIII. He was educated for the army, and in 1802 became second lieutenant in an artillery regiment. He was brave and capable but somewhat of a braggart. He distinguished himself in campaigns in Austria, Prussia, Poland, Spain, and Russia. In 1811, he was chosen by Napoleon to be one of his orderly officers. In Russia, before pontoon bridges were laid across the Berezina, he swam the river under fire to explore the opposite bank. In Moscow he was among the first to enter the Kremlin and discovered the mine with which the Russians had hoped to blow up the Emperor and his staff. He was rewarded by being created baron of the empire. In 1813, Napoleon created for him the post of first orderly officer, which gave him the opportunity to be much in the Emperor's company. He conceived an affection for Napoleon that bordered on the pathological. In 1814, during the battle of Brienne, he claimed to have saved the Emperor's life a second time by shooting a cossack who was about to transfix the monarch with his lance. He had an account of the affair engraved upon his sword, but Napoleon has stated that he had no recollection of it. After his first abdication at Fontainebleau the Emperor wrote a letter to him thanking him for his services and expressing the hope that he would serve the new sovereign as faithfully as he had served him. Gourgaud remained in the army, but found it difficult to keep his tongue from wagging. The Duc de Berry saved him from the consequences of his impetuosity.

When Napoleon returned from Elba, Gourgaud was torn between his love for the Emperor and his duty toward the King. He feigned illness and did not participate in any of the futile attempts to stop Napoleon's march to Paris. He did not, however, offer him his services until after the King had fled. The Emperor, feeling he should have done so sooner, refused to accept them. Gourgaud wept and pleaded, was finally forgiven, and was with the Emperor at Waterloo. He was promoted to brigadier general after Napoleon's return to Paris. It has been claimed that the promotion was made when the Emperor had already abdicated, but that the document was predated.

Gourgaud was a bachelor, but had a mother and sister in Paris to whom he was greatly attached. He was of medium height, with a swarthy complexion, accentuated by closely clipped black sideburns. He had a projecting mouth and a receding chin which, according to one observer, "calls to mind the muzzle of a snarling dog ever ready to bark and bite." He was indeed difficult to get along with—vain, jealous, blunt-spoken, moody, given to contradicting, easily offended. The fact that unlike his companions he had neither wife nor child with him at St. Helena aggravated the situation for him. Lord Rosebery has written: "He was a brilliant young officer, devoted to his master with an unreasonable, petulant jealousy, which made his devotion intolerable; and above all, he was perpetually bored—bored with the island, bored with confinement, bored with isolation, bored with celibacy, bored with court life in a shanty, involving all the burdens without the splendor of a palace, bored with inaction, and bored with himself for being bored."

Gourgaud kept a journal at St. Helena, not intended for publication, but which was published in 1899. It is a revealing document. Together with Bertrand's journal it is by far the most important material we have concerning the captivity.

FIVE

Emanuel Auguste Dieudonné Marius Joseph, Marquis de Las Cases, born in 1766, was a scion of the old nobility. The family, of Spanish origin, had owned extensive properties at Languedoc which were confiscated during the Revolution. In his youth he had been a naval officer and had participated in war against the British. In 1790 he emigrated and together with other *émigrés* took part in an unsuccessful invasion of France. He then migrated to England where he made a meager living by teaching French. His situation vastly improved when, in 1799, he published, under the pseudonym of Le Sage, a work entitled *Atlas historique et généalogique*. The book had a phenomenal success, and besides making him a small fortune gave him a reputation as a scholar. He remained in England ten years, returning to France when Napoleon lifted the ban on *émigrés*. Having conceived a great admiration for the new ruler he sought and obtained government employment, being entrusted with several missions of more or less importance. He was moreover appointed councillor of state and chamberlain, but was never called to active service at the palace.

After the first abdication Las Cases served the Bourbons as councillor of state and had the rank of captain in the navy conferred upon him, but he was among those who greeted Napoleon at the Tuileries on his arrival from Elba. After Waterloo he told the Emperor that he stood ready to follow him wherever he went. Napoleon, who hardly knew him, said: "Do you realize where that may lead you?" Las Cases replied: "I have made no calculation concerning the matter, but it is my ardent wish that my offer should be accepted."

At this period of his career Las Cases was nearly fifty—a little man, about five feet, one inch in height, sparely built, vain, ambitious, and given to impassioned rhetoric. He did not follow Napoleon to St. Helena (where Las Cases remained only thirteen months), solely from devotion to the great man. He wished to link his name with the Emperor's to gain immortality, and he wished to write a book. He had already tasted the fruit of successful publication, but how could that compare with the success to be derived from a book about Napoleon's captivity by a companion in exile? His *Mémoiral de Sainte-Hélène* appeared in 1823, simultaneously in French and in English, was translated into almost every European language, and is said to have netted him two million francs. It is not without historical value, but it is too rhetorical and has been rendered suspect by the fact that it contains four letters which have been proved to be forgeries. Three of these, however, had appeared in print before, and Las Cases may well have believed all of them to be genuine.

Las Cases was more useful to Napoleon than any other member of his suite. His knowledge of English was invaluable, and he proved a devoted secretary. Already in 1814, when bidding farewell to the Imperial Guard, Napoleon had said: "I want to write about the great things we have accomplished together." Dictating his memoirs to a historian stimulated him. The Emperor liked to talk, and Las Cases was a starry-eyed, uncritical listener. He never ventured to contradict, as Gourgaud was in the habit of doing. When Napoleon felt like listening, Las Cases, having been an *émigré* and having lived in England, could tell him many things that were novel to him. It is therefore hardly surprising that he should have become Napoleon's favorite companion. For this he was disliked by all the others, particularly by Gourgaud. They called him "the Jesuit."

Las Cases had with him his eldest son, Emanuel, a boy of fifteen, with an intelligence far above his years.

SIX

Napoleon's suite was further composed of a surgeon, Barry Edward O'Meara, and fourteen servants: Marchand, first *valet-de-chambre;* Cipriani, *maître-d'hôtel;* Pierron, butler; Saint-Denis (usually called Ali), Noverraz, and Santini, *valets-de-chambre;* Lepage, cook; Rousseau, steward; two Archambault brothers, grooms; Gentilini, footman; Heymann and wife, servants of the Bertrands; Josephine Brule, maid of the Montholons.

O'Meara, who was to play an important role in the drama of St. Helena, had been engaged under the following circumstances:

Napoleon's physician, Corvisart, had recommended to him a young doctor named Louis Pierre Maingault who agreed to accompany the fallen monarch to the United States. But when it developed that Napoleon's destination was to be St. Helena, he was no longer willing. He had been seasick during the voyage, and when Planat and Gourgaud were indisposed, the ship's surgeon, O'Meara, was called. He thus came in contact with Napoleon, who, having discovered that he spoke Italian fluently, had had several conversations with him and was favorably impressed. When the difficulty with Maingault arose, Napoleon instructed Savary to ask the surgeon if he would be willing to accompany him to St. Helena as his personal physician. O'Meara declared himself willing provided Captain Maitland and Lord Keith raised no objection. Maitland gave his consent and recommended him highly to Napoleon, while Keith agreed to O'Meara's terms, which were that he was to remain a British naval surgeon at full pay and should have the right to resign his new post whenever he chose.

O'Meara was an Irish Protestant, born in 1786. Napoleon was to take a liking to him and to talk to him freely. What the Emperor did not know was that the surgeon communicated everything of interest that he said or that went on among the French to his friend John Finlaison, an employee of the admiralty, who passed on his letters to Lord Melville, first lord of the admiralty.

55

O'Meara was not paid for spying on the French and there is no evidence that he had been solicited to do so, but he knew that Lord Melville read his letters and expected that this would advance his career.

O'Meara, like Las Cases, appears to have made up his mind from the beginning to write a book about the captivity. He made voluminous notes, copies of which he sent to an agent in London, a certain William Holmes. In 1822, he published his famous *Napoleon in Exile* or *A voice from St. Helena,* which wrecked the career of Sir Hudson Lowe.

SEVEN

On August 9, the *Northumberland,* at the head of a small squadron consisting of a frigate, two transports, and several brigs, set sail for St. Helena. "He [Napoleon] appeared in a good humor," Admiral Cockburn has written, "chatted in a very good-natured mood with everybody, and retired to his bedroom apparently as much at his ease as if he had belonged to the ship all his life." On the 9th, as the ship was leaving the channel, clouds that had shrouded the French coast lifted. "France! France!" cried several of the French excitedly. Napoleon who had been pacing the deck, stopped, looked in the direction of the French coast, and remained motionless until it disappeared from view. French and English officers remained at a respectful distance.

During the voyage the Emperor breakfasted in his cabin. At about eleven he sent for one of his officers to learn the news of the day. He began taking lessons in English from Las Cases, but soon tired of it and spent most of the morning and part of the afternoon reading. Toward three he dressed and went to the aftercabin to play chess with Gourgaud or Montholon. Contrary to what might be expected he was an indifferent chess player and often lost. Dinner was served in the messroom at five o'clock. After dinner he walked on deck, usually in the company of Bertrand and Las Cases. In the evening *vingt-et-un* or whist was played. Admiral Cockburn, his secretary Glover, Captain Ross, Colonel Bingham, and the ladies participated.

At the dinner table Napoleon occupied the place of honor,

with the admiral on his right and Madame Bertrand on his left. Behind his chair stood two of his valets who served him, while the admiral pointed out choice morsels to them. Others at table were the French officers, Madame de Montholon, Captain Ross, Colonel Bingham, Glover, and sometimes O'Meara, Warden, the ship's chaplain or whatever other officers the admiral chose to invite. Glover noted that Napoleon made little use of his fork, but ate with his fingers. At table French was spoken, Las Cases serving as interpreter for those who did not speak the language.

The Emperor had been too busy a man to acquire habits of conviviality. He had seldom spent more than half an hour at dinner. The British officers were accustomed to spending a leisurely one hour and a half, after which they remained at table at least another hour drinking wine and conversing. The Emperor endured this for three days, but on the fourth rose as soon as he had swallowed his coffee, motioned to Bertrand and Las Cases to follow him, and went on deck. All present rose and remained standing until he had left the room; then, however, the admiral caustically remarked: "I believe the General has never read Lord Chesterfield." Madame Bertrand flushed with annoyance and said: "Don't forget, admiral, that your guest is a man who has governed a large portion of the world, and that kings once contended for the honor of being admitted to his table." Cockburn meekly replied: "Very true," and thenceforth not only shortened the time spent at dinner, but ordered coffee served to Napoleon and his suite before the English had finished eating. He soon succumbed to Napoleon's charm and was never happier than when the Emperor would link his arm through his and they would walk up and down the deck together. Napoleon asked many questions about India and the islands of the Atlantic. He told Cockburn of his Egyptian and Russian campaigns, about his rise to power, about his plans for the invasion of England, about the attempts on his life during his reign, about the organization of the French navy.

The admiral was somewhat worried about Napoleon's increasing popularity with officers and men. "The difficulty of repressing the inclination to pay him marked attention is evident,"

Glover has written. The young midshipmen especially could not do enough to show their admiration for him. There was a cannon on the quarter-deck against which Napoleon often leaned while looking out meditatively over the sea. It became known among the crew as the "Emperor's gun" and was polished with especial care. Napoleon liked to converse with the sailors and managed to do so with the aid of Las Cases. Once he talked with a petty officer who appeared to him uncommonly intelligent, so much so that he invited him to dinner the following day. Flattered but embarrassed the man said: "The admiral and the captain will not be willing that I should sit at their table." "Very well," said Napoleon, "if they do not, so much the worse for them. You shall dine with me in my cabin." When Cockburn heard of this he instructed the man to appear for dinner, saying that rules of etiquette were suspended for anyone General Bonaparte wished to have as his guest. After this incident Napoleon's popularity with the crew reached its zenith.

EIGHT

On August 23, the squadron arrived at Funchal, on the island of Madeira. The sirocco was blowing and the sea was rough. Cockburn and his secretary were the only ones to go ashore. Supplies were taken on with difficulty, and the ships departed after a two days' stay.

Tired of idleness Napoleon decided to begin work on his memoirs. Beginning September 9, he sent for Las Cases every morning and, walking up and down his cabin in his dressing gown, dictated to him his experiences during the siege of Toulon and the story of his campaign in Italy. "The Emperor dictates very rapidly, almost as fast as he speaks in ordinary conversation. I was therefore obliged to invent a kind of hieroglyphic writing; and I in my turn dictated to my son," Las Cases has written. As the work progressed the Emperor became more and more interested and took considerable pains. When Las Cases would read to him what he had dictated the previous day he would often dictate the same thing over again, amplifying and correcting. If not entirely satisfied with the second version, he would dictate a third, a fourth, sometimes even a tenth.

Knowing that Las Cases was writing memoirs of his own concerning him, he often twitted him with it, calling him "illustrious memorialist" or the "Sully of St. Helena." Seriously he told him: "These memoirs will be as celebrated as any that have preceded them. You will survive as long as any previous memoirwriter. It will be impossible to dwell upon the great events of our time, or to write about me without referring to you." This was music to the ears of the vain little man.

On September 23, the ship crossed the equator. Neptune and Amphitrite, fantastically arrayed and assisted by half a hundred tritons, naked to the waist and bedaubed with screaming colors, sat in judgment of those crossing the line for the first time. The victims had their faces lathered with a concoction the principal ingredient of which was pitch, were shaved with an enormous razor, and drenched with seawater. The Emperor did not appear on deck. With his usual generosity he instructed Bertrand to present Neptune and his aids with one hundred napoleons. Cockburn who felt that the prisoner's popularity with the crew had already reached dangerous proportions insisted that this should be reduced to five napoleons. Bertrand considered such an offering unworthy of the Emperor, and the men got nothing.

Ships sailing to St. Helena usually steered toward the coast of Brazil. Cockburn, however, had decided to experiment and had steered toward the African coast. The experiment was not a success and prolonged the voyage by some twenty days. The southeast trade wind he had hoped to encounter did not make itself felt until the ship had almost reached the mouth of the Congo. There had been little harmony among Napoleon's suite from the beginning. The tediousness and discomfort of the long voyage aggravated the situation. Bingham has written: "His attendants are divided into parties and do nothing but abuse each other behind their backs." Cockburn wrote that Napoleon showed more patience and equanimity of temper than any member of his suite, but even he lost his temper when he heard that Gourgaud had contradicted something he had told the admiral, and administered a sharp rebuke to the young general. Gourgaud and Montholon had an altercation at the dinner table, to the embarrassment of all present. Madame Bertrand and Madame Montholon gossiped about each other. Las Cases and Gourgaud had a serious quarrel when the former asked the latter why he had come since he was so dissatisfied. He received the answer: "Sir, if I have come with the Emperor it is because I have been with him for four years, and have followed him wherever he went, except to Elba. I have saved his life, and one loves those to whom one has rendered such service. But you, sir, hardly know the Emperor and he hardly knows you. Whence therefore all this devotion?"

On October 14, when dinner was being served, the lookout cried: "Land!" After a journey of seventy-one days St. Helena came into view. It was as yet but a shadow on the horizon, barely visible to the naked eye. Not until the following morning did Napoleon behold the island which the British army surgeon Walter Henry described as "the ugliest and most dismal rock conceivable, of rugged and splintered surface, rising like an enormous black wart from the face of the deep." And like an oasis in this perpendicular desert of basalt, from which many a cannon frowned, was a whitewashed little town at the extremity of a V-shaped bay. It was Jamestown, the only town on the island, where Napoleon was to spend the remainder of his life.

2

VI. St. Helena

St. Helena was discovered in 1502 by the Portuguese navigator Juan de Nova Castella. The discovery having been made on May 21, the anniversary of Helena, mother of the Emperor Constantine, he named it St. Helena. The island is ten miles long, seven miles wide, has a circumference of twenty-eight miles and an area of forty-seven square miles. It is located 700 miles from the island of Ascension, 1,750 from Capetown, 1,800 from South America, and 4,400 from England. In 1651, the English East India Company took possession of it. In 1672, the Dutch moved in but were driven out the following year. When St. Helena was chosen as a place of exile for Napoleon, an agreement was made that a governor was to be nominated by the Crown and appointed by the Company directors, who were to remain responsible for its civil government. As expenses would vastly increase, the Company was to pay the average it had spent during the preceding three years, while the British government undertook to pay the difference. In 1836, the island became a Crown colony.

When Napoleon and his suite landed at St. Helena its population, including the garrison of over one thousand, was about four thousand. Only 776 of the civilians were white; the rest were Negroes, Chinese, and Lascars. Three fourths of the more than 1,800 Negroes were slaves. Native whites were referred to as

Yamstocks, yams being the principal article of diet of the majority. During Napoleon's captivity the garrison and the white population greatly increased.

Gloomy and forbidding as was the appearance of the island when viewed from the sea, it was considerably less so in the interior. There were ridges of mountains alternating with deep ravines, and tall peaks, the tallest of which, Diana's Peak, rose to a height of 2,700 feet. Some of the peaks were devoid of vegetation and were slate- or ochre-colored; others were covered with trees. While parts of the island were dreary and desolate, betraying its volcanic origin, other parts had beauty and even grandeur. "The view from Sandy Bay Ridge and from Diana's Peak is sublime," O'Meara has written. There were pleasant valleys some of which sheltered country houses with well-kept grounds, shade and fruit trees, and a profusion of flowers. The most imposing was Plantation House, the governor's residence. It was a two-story white-stuccoed building, containing forty rooms and fronting a wide stretch of lawn, surrounded by low hills planted with a great variety of trees and shrubs. It lacked architectural beauty but was comfortably furnished and fully protected from the southeast trade wind which was to cause such discomfort to Napoleon. Four other country houses deserve mention—Colonel Smith's Rosemary Hall, Mr. Doveton's Mount Pleasant, Mr. Balcombe's The Briars, and Miss Mason's Orange Grove. The mimosa of New South Wales, the pine of the North, and the bamboo of India flourished in their gardens, as did vines, figs, apples, oranges, and lemons.

TWO

Jamestown boasted only two streets: the Marino, a short street parallel with the wharf—from which it was separated by a rampart and a moat spanned by a drawbridge—and the main street which extended about a mile inland between two steep hills, Rupert Hill and Ladder Hill. On the Marino, fronting a terrace, stood the Castle, the governor's town residence. There were about one hundred and sixty houses and a church with a square tower. The houses, built of stone, whitewashed, and roofed with shingles or with boards covered with earth, were for the most part shops and boardinghouses. Here and there a huge rock jutted out over the roof of a house, and it sometimes happened that one became detached and came crashing down upon the dwelling.

The cost of living on the island was extraordinarily high, about four times what it was in England. Major General Alexander Beatson, governor of St. Helena from 1803 to 1813, wrote on December 26, 1815, to Prince Esterhazy: "If any of the houses here were for rent it could scarcely be had for less than two or three hundred pounds sterling a year, of course entirely unprovided with furniture. . . . Living is much dearer than in the most expensive hotels in London. A master, man or woman, pays thirty shillings a day for board and lodging; a servant of either sex, and even down to the smallest child, fifteen shillings a day." Coal and nearly all manufactured articles were imported from England. Wood was scarce and one needed permission from the governor and the council to fell a tree. Most of the meat came from cattle imported from the Cape colony and was high-priced. As the animals suffered in transit, the quality was poor. Poultry, too, was expensive. Chickens sold at from six to ten shillings; ducks, ten shillings; geese, fifteen; turkeys, from one pound five to two pound sterling. There were rabbits, partridges, and pheasants on the island. One could hunt the first two; the last were reserved for the governor's table. Potatoes sold at ten to twelve shillings a bushel, eggs at three to four shillings a dozen. Governor Beatson warned, moreover, that "it appears probable, not to say certain, that the increase of the garrison, the presence of naval forces, and the crowd of newcomers, as a result of the new importance which has just been given to the island, will cause prices of all articles to rise to a point where they have never been before."

THREE

There has been considerable controversy regarding the climate of St. Helena and its effect upon Europeans. Lowe's apologist Norwood Young has claimed that "the climate of St. Helena has been praised in terms which would seem exaggerated if they were not unanimous." [1] Upon investigation the unanimity is found to be confined to those whom Young has chosen to quote.

The salubrity of the island left much to be desired. The official record shows the average annual death rate in regiments stationed at St. Helena during the captivity to have been 40 per thousand, as compared with 17 per thousand in regiments stationed in England. The high death rate has been ascribed to the climate by some of Napoleon's partisans, and the accusation has been made that the English government had chosen St. Helena as the place of detention with the express purpose of shortening his life. That the climate was not principally to blame is evident from the fact that in modern times the death rate on the island has been considerably lower than in England, though the fact that few Europeans now live at St. Helena should be taken into account. What appears to have been principally responsible was that, in Napoleon's time, the drinking water, allowed to run through open ditches, was polluted by grazing cattle.[2] O'Meara has written: "The most prevalent complaints are dysentery, inflammation of the bowels, liver affections, and fevers—all of them generally violent in form." All, or nearly all, appear to have been parts of the same disease. Whether that disease was hepatitis or amoebic dysentery, it was so prevalent on the island as to appear endemic, and had a decided effect on the health and longevity of the population.

John R. Glover, Secretary to Admiral Cockburn, believed with others of his time that the prevalence of poor health was due to the climate. He has written that the climate was "by no means so healthy as it is generally described to be, the children being sickly, and the adults suffering from the liver, of which complaint many of our men died. . . . During our eight months'

[1] Norwood Young, *Napoleon in Exile at St. Helena* (*1815-1821*), The John C. Winston Company, Philadelphia, 1935.

[2] It is now generally believed by the medical profession that hepatitis, or inflammation of the liver, is caused by a specific virus which invades that organ. A few years ago a contaminated utility water supply in North Carolina was held responsible for an outbreak of the disease in that state.

residence we experienced very little variation and had continued rains."

Thomas Henry Brooke, Secretary of the Council of St. Helena and acting governor after the departure of Sir Hudson Lowe, wrote in his *History of St. Helena*, published in 1808, that there were "few instances among the islanders of longevity."

Count Balmain, the Russian commissioner, reported in November, 1819, to his government that one third of the soldiers of the 20th regiment were hospitalized. Indeed, Sir Hudson himself was to write to Lord Bathurst on June 19, 1817: "In the autumnal season of the year fevers and dysenteries prevail here in a very great degree."

VII. The Briars

On October 15, at about noon, the *Northumberland* dropped anchor at Jamestown Roads. Several vessels belonging to the squadron were already there. Admiral Cockburn and Colonel Bingham went ashore to call on the governor, returning a couple of hours later accompanied by him. The governor, Colonel Mark Wilks (soon to be replaced by Lieutenant General Sir Hudson Lowe), was a white-haired distinguished-looking man of fifty-five. He had served with success in India, had written several learned papers for the Asiatic Society of which he was a vice-president, and had published a book entitled *Historical Sketches of South India*. Napoleon took an immediate liking to him and asked him many questions about the island, its climate, its history, and its population, to which Wilks replied with great amiability.

Early the following morning Cockburn, Bingham, and Wilks set out on horseback in search of a suitable dwelling for Napoleon and his suite. The East India Company had specified in its agreement with the government that Plantation House must remain the governor's residence. Colonel Smith's Rosemary Hall was considered, but was found to be too small and too difficult to guard. Governor Wilks suggested Longwood House, residence of Lieutenant Governor John Skelton. His office was to be abolished when the new governor took over, and in the meantime the

68

Skeltons could be accommodated elsewhere. The house was situated on a large plateau, bordered on all sides by deep ravines, with only a narrow tongue of land giving access to it. It was found on inspection that it would have to be enlarged and stood badly in need of repairs, so arrangements were made with a man named Porteous for Napoleon and his suite to be housed temporarily at an inn he owned at Jamestown.

Cockburn told Napoleon of the arrangements that had been made and expatiated on the advantages of Longwood House, which he is said to have compared with the palace at St. Cloud. It was agreed that the Emperor and his suite were to disembark the following evening after sunset, so as to escape the curiosity of the populace, and that on the morning of the 18th Napoleon and Bertrand were to visit Longwood in the company of the admiral.

On October 17, at seven o'clock in the evening, the Emperor, accompanied by Cockburn and Bertrand, was rowed to the landing stage. Members of his suite followed in a barge. Before leaving, Napoleon thanked Captain Ross for the courtesy shown him during the voyage and asked him to convey his thanks to officers and crew. Somehow news of the proposed debarkation had spread through the island, and hundreds of the curious, carrying lanterns, were massed on the quay. Soldiers with fixed bayonets had to clear the way for the French.

TWO

When morning came Cockburn, Bertrand, and Napoleon's valets Marchand and Ali, who were to accompany the party, were ready at the appointed time for the ride to Longwood. The Emperor, however, was late in putting in an appearance and Cockburn expressed his displeasure. When told of this Napoleon remarked: "The admiral is an ill-bred person." He who had had kings patiently awaiting his convenience found it difficult to accustom himself to the changed circumstances.

They rode down the main street, the cynosure of all eyes, then turned into a mountain road bordered on one side by an ochre-colored rock wall with flowering aloes bursting from fissures, on the other side by a stone parapet. It was nearly five miles to Longwood and the road climbed steadily. Napoleon beheld a landscape that must have reminded him of Corsica. There were bare crags and lofty peaks, green mountain slopes on which cattle and sheep were grazing, here and there a cottage in the midst of olive trees or dwarf oaks. They reached Alarm House from which the east coast was visible and vessels approaching the island were signaled to Jamestown by the firing of a gun. The road now skirted a yawning abyss, known as the Devil's Punch Bowl. Near Hutt's Gate, about a mile and a quarter from Longwood, there was a charming little valley where there was a spring, myrtle and briar grew, and weeping willows hung their drooping foliage. Napoleon was to call it Geranium Valley, having been impressed on a later visit by a giant geranium that grew against the wall of a cottage.

They crossed the tongue of land giving access to the plateau, passed between two stone pillars near each of which stood a whitewashed guardhouse, and rode up the avenue toward the house.

Colonel and Mrs. Skelton received the visitors hospitably. Napoleon strolled about the grounds with the colonel and surveyed the plain to which he would virtually be confined for the remainder of his life. It consisted of some fifteen hundred acres, for the most part uncultivated, nearly eighteen hundred feet above sea level. It was sparsely covered with coarse grass, with here and there a forlorn-looking gumwood tree. Close to the house the gumwoods formed a wood which extended eastward for about two miles. The trees all inclined in the same direction as a result of constant buffeting by the southeast trade wind. There was little shade, for the leaves of the gumwood tree are small, narrow, and confined to the extremities of twigs and branches. A part of the plain, about half a mile north of the house, was known as Deadwood and was soon to be transformed into a soldiers' camp. O'Meara has said of the plateau: "The soil is tenacious, argillacious clay, which in wet weather collects and adheres to the shoes of the pedestrian forming so ponderous a mass as materially to impede his progress. For a month or six weeks during the year there is fine weather; for two or three a powerful vertical sun prevails; and for seven or eight, the weather is wet and most disagreeable." Napoleon was to complain that "the wind constantly beat on his face, or the sun scorched his brain. . . . It is at the same time, the driest and most humid climate in the world." That his complaints were not unjustified is evident from the testimony of John Charles Mellins, civil engineer in the British colonies, who spent a great part of his life at St. Helena and wrote in 1873: "Longwood is a bleak, cold, exposed situation, and the complaints of Napoleon's staff against it as such were not without some reason."

On Napoleon's first visit to Longwood the weather was fine, so he was not too unfavorably impressed. The visitors had lunch with the Skeltons, and as Mrs. Skelton spoke French fluently time passed pleasantly. When the Emperor was established at Longwood he invited the Skeltons to dinner on several occasions. At her farewell visit Mrs. Skelton offered to convey messages from the exiles to friends and relatives. Hudson Lowe learned of this and not only complained to her husband but to Lord Bathurst. She wrote to Napoleon's mother about her son and received a grateful acknowledgment from Cardinal Fesch.

THREE

On his way to Longwood, about a mile from town, Napoleon had noticed in the valley below a pleasant country house built in the Indian style and situated with its grounds in an amphitheatre of towering rocks. A grass-grown avenue of banyan trees led toward the house. The grounds were shaded by huge lacos, evergreens, pomegranates, and clusters of myrtle. The cactus hedge was bright with large white roses and wild geraniums. A waterfall, leaping from a height of some two hundred feet volatilized into silver spray before reaching the bottom. The Emperor had inquired the name of the proprietor and had been told that The Briars, as the estate was named, belonged to William Balcombe, a minor East India Company official and member of a firm of purveyors to ships touching at St. Helena. On the way back to Jamestown, as he again looked down on the estate below, he asked Cockburn if it might not be possible to obtain lodging there while the house at Longwood was got ready. The admiral opined that perhaps it might be arranged, so they descended into the valley. Betsy Balcombe, a girl of thirteen, the younger of the proprietor's two daughters, gave in later life the following description of her first meeting with Napoleon:

"The party arrived at the gate, and there being no carriage road, they all dismounted, excepting the Emperor. He retained his seat and rode up the avenue, his horse's feet cutting up the turf on our pretty lawn. Sir George Cockburn walked on one side of his horse, and General Bertrand on the other. How vividly I recollect my feelings of dread, mingled with admiration, as I now first looked upon him whom I had learned to fear so much. His appearance on horseback was noble and imposing. The animal he rode was a superb one; his color jet black; and as he proudly stepped up the avenue, arching his neck and champing his bit, I thought he looked worthy to be the bearer of him who was once the ruler of nearly the whole European world.

"Napoleon's position on horseback, by adding height to his figure, supplied all that was wanting to make me think him the most majestic person I had ever seen. His dress was green and covered with orders, and his saddle and housings were of crimson velvet richly embroidered with gold. He alighted at our house, and we all moved to the entrance to receive him. Sir George Cockburn introduced us to him.

"While he was talking to Mamma, I had an opportunity of scrutinizing his features, which I did with the keenest interest; and certainly I have never seen any one with so remarkable and striking a physiognomy. The portraits of him give a good general idea of his features; but his smile, and the expression of his eye, could not be transmitted to canvas, and these constituted Napoleon's chief charm. His hair was dark brown, and as fine and silky as a child's, rather too much so indeed for a man, as its very softness caused it to look thin. His teeth were even, but rather dark, and I afterwards found that this arose from his constant habit of eating liquorice, of which he always kept a supply in his waistcoat pocket."

FOUR

Napoleon did not return to Jamestown. On an eminence some fifty yards from Balcombe's house stood a pavilion consisting of a room twenty-two by sixteen feet, a small anteroom, and two garrets. The Emperor thought this would suit him very well, and the Balcombes felt honored to have him as a lodger. They even offered to vacate their cottage so he could live in that, but he would not hear of it. So Bertrand was told to send over Las Cases (soon to be joined by his son), while Marchand and Ali were sent to fetch the Emperor's camp-bed and other necessities. With the assistance of the Balcombes the pavilion was soon made habitable. Las Cases and his son were to sleep in the garrets, Marchand and Ali on mattresses in the anteroom. After a couple of days Colonel Bingham had soldiers put up a marquee to serve as a dining room. Later a second marquee was added in which Gourgaud often slept. The faithful Marchand carved an imperial crown in the turf between the pavilion and the marquee. Meals were at first brought by slaves from Jamestown, but as they arrived cold, Napoleon's cook and his assistants used to come over from town to prepare the food.

It cannot be said that the Emperor was comfortably housed— he lacked bathing facilities—but he who had so often slept on a camp-bed in far worse surroundings would not have minded had not the fact that he was a prisoner constantly intruded itself upon him. An orderly officer was stationed at Balcombe's house, and two sergeants in the avenue followed every move made by him. The latter were finally withdrawn after a protest from Balcombe. Horses were put at Napoleon's disposal, but as he was not allowed to go out riding without being followed by the orderly officer, he made no use of them except for an occasional canter about the lawn. Only twice during his stay at The Briars is he known to have left the boundaries of the estate: once when he paid an impromptu visit to the neighboring estate of Major Hodson, another time when he went walking with Las Cases and his son on the road to Jamestown. Hodson was a tall man—over six feet and powerfully built. Napoleon henceforth always referred to him as the "Hercules."

During the walk on the road to Jamestown they met Mrs. Balcombe and a Mrs. Stuart who had stopped over at St. Helena on her way from Bombay to England. Mrs. Balcombe introduced her friend, who was young and pretty. Both ladies spoke a little French, and there ensued a conversation during which Napoleon did most of the talking. While they were conversing several heavily laden slaves tried to pass. Mrs. Balcombe rebuked them, ordering them to wait. The Emperor, however, said: "Respect the burden, Madam," and stepped aside, motioning them to pass. Mrs. Stuart later expressed her surprise at such consideration on the part of a man whom she had learned to regard as a monster in human form.

FIVE

Behind the pavilion was a garden—a long, steep, narrow strip of land where there were myrtle groves, vines, lemon trees, orange trees, mangoes, and guavas, and flowers bloomed in colorful profusion. There were well-kept paths, a trellised grape walk, a vine-covered arbor with a rustic table and bench, and a pond with gold and silver fish. On its western side the waterfall leaped down a towering rock wall.

Napoleon would rise early, drink a cup of coffee Marchand had prepared for him, and go for a stroll in the garden. He made friends with "Uncle" Toby, the gardener, a Malay slave whom Balcombe hired from his owner and who lived in a hut at the far end of the garden. He had been kidnaped by British sailors, smuggled ashore at St. Helena, and sold into slavery. The Emperor seldom left the garden without slipping a piece of money into old Toby's hand. He even tried to buy him and have him returned to his native land, but official red tape and the opposition of Sir Hudson Lowe—who undoubtedly feared such a procedure might make the prisoner too popular with the many slaves on the island—frustrated the plan. When the Emperor left The Briars he had Bertrand give twenty napoleons to Toby, who ever after spoke of him as "that good man Boney."

He breakfasted at ten. After breakfast he dictated to Las Cases —in the arbor when the weather was propitious, otherwise in the pavilion. Often he dictated without interruption until five in the afternoon. At six dinner was served in the marquee. One or more members of his suite invariably came over from Jamestown to keep him company at dinner, and Las Cases and his son were always present. Cipriani, the *maître d'hôtel*, ceremoniously announced: "His Majesty's dinner is served."

The evenings were the most trying. Las Cases did not play chess or any game of cards. The visitors from town had to depart early, for anyone found on the road after nine in the evening was arrested and had to spend the night in the guardhouse. Until late in November, when Gourgaud came to stay permanently at The Briars, there was only conversation to fall back upon. When the weather was fine the Emperor and the chamberlain would go walking in the garden, and there, with the sound of the waterfall for accompaniment, Napoleon would talk. Las Cases has said of these monologues: "He speaks of his past history as if it had occurred three centuries ago. In his recitals and his observations he speaks the language of past ages. He is like a spirit discoursing in the Elysian fields; his conversations are true Dialogues of the Dead. He speaks of himself as of a third person, noticing the Emperor's actions, pointing out the faults with which history may reproach him, and analyzing the reasons and the motives which might be alleged in his justification." Toward eleven he usually retired, but sometimes, when the moon shone brightly, would get up, put on his dressing gown, go down into the garden and muse. At other times he would light a candle and read.

SIX

Sometimes he spent the evening at the Balcombes'. There were four children in the family—Jane, fifteen; Betsy, thirteen; and two little boys, one seven, the other five. The girls had studied French when the family lived in England, and having had a French maid with whom they had practiced conversation spoke French with considerable ease. When Napoleon called there would usually be a game of whist, in which the girls participated. Sugarplums served as counters. At other times they spent the evening talking. The girls soon lost their awe of the great man and asked innumerable questions, which he answered with great good humor. Betsy, a mischievous little minx, blond, blue-eyed, and very pretty, once asked him if it was true that when he was in Egypt he had become a Mohammedan. He replied laughingly: "I always adopt the religion of the country I am in."

Betsy became his favorite. He teased her about Las Cases' boy, who, he said, would make a good husband for her. When she appeared more serious than was her wont, he would say in his faulty English: "Has *le petit* Las Cases been inconstant? If he have—bring him to me." Once he held her hands and told the boy to kiss her. He did, and got his ears boxed as soon as her hands were free. That same day the Emperor, Las Cases, his son, Jane and Betsy, in the order named, were going down the steep, narrow path that led from the pavilion to the house, where they planned to play whist. This seemed to Betsy a heaven-sent opportunity to get even with Napoleon. She allowed the others to proceed, herself remaining a little behind. Then, with a rush, her hands outstretched, she ran against Jane, who fell against young Las Cases, who collided with his father, who bumped into the Emperor and almost upset him. Las Cases, after suitable apologies to Napoleon, went after the culprit, of whose identity there could be no doubt, for Betsy was laughing and jumping in glee at the success of her prank. He seized her by the shoulders, shook her, and forced her down upon a rock, hurting her. She began to cry and called to Napoleon: "Oh, Sir, he has hurt me!" The Emperor, amused rather than offended, called back: "Never mind, *ne pleures pas*—I will hold him so you can punish him." And hold him he did, while Betsy boxed the chamberlain's ears. When he released him, Las Cases ran away, with Betsy after him. Napoleon shook with laughter and encouraged her as she chased the little man about the lawn.

Another time, when Napoleon sat in the arbor reading some of the dictation young Las Cases had copied, Betsy snatched the papers from the table and ran away crying: "Now I'll find out all your secrets!" Still another time, when he was sitting on a bench near the pond, she led Admiral Cockburn's huge New-foundland dog, Tom Pipes, to the pond and had him disport himself in it. When he was thoroughly wet she led him to the bench where, as she had expected, he shook himself, bespatter-ing the Emperor from head to foot, while she ran away laughing. On neither occasion did the great man lose his temper, but when an opportunity presented itself to pay her back in her own coin he took advantage of it. The admiral was giving a ball to which the Balcombes were invited. Betsy's father thought her too young to go to a ball, but Napoleon interceded for her. A few days before the occasion she showed him the pretty dress she was going to wear, then laid it down on the sofa. He snatched it and ran away with it. She ran after him, but he reached the pavilion first and locked himself in. Entreaties in English and in French proved unavailing. He said he meant to keep the dress, that she was a naughty girl and might as well make up her mind she was not going to the ball. She thought he meant it, went home, and threw herself on her bed crying. The next day and the next he was just as inexorable. She was heartbroken. But a few hours before the ball he himself brought the dress to her and said: "Here, Miss Betsee, I have brought you your dress. I hope you are a good girl now, and that you will like the ball; and mind that you dance with Gourgaud."

If he thought this would cure her of playing pranks on him, he was mistaken. When some time later he showed her a beauti-ful parade sword, she drew it from its scabbard and brandished it about, telling him he had better say his prayers, for she was going to kill him. He had to back up against the wall to keep from getting hurt. When she finally desisted he pinched her ear and her nose.

He possessed a variety of beautiful seals and sometimes amused himself by making sealing wax impressions of them. One day while he was thus engaged she came into the pavilion, watched him for a little while, then mischievously nudged his elbow. The hot wax dripped on one of his fingers, raising a blis-ter. This she had not foreseen and humbly apologized. He for-gave her.

When they were conversing he often tried to speak English. Some of these attempts were sufficiently comical. One day he told her teasingly that English ladies, like English men, were heavy drinkers; then he asked: "You laike veree mosh dreenk, Meess, sometime brandee, geen?"

That Betsy's anecdotes about Napoleon—which she related in her *Recollections,* published in 1844, when she was Mrs. Abell—were not invented is evident from the fact that they became the talk of the island. The French commissioner, the Marquis de Montchenu, who came to St. Helena in June, 1816, related them in a letter to a Paris newspaper. The letter was promptly translated into English and German. He said that she was the wildest little girl he had ever seen—*une folle.* When Napoleon heard about the letter he sent a message to Betsy telling her how to get even with the marquis. The nobleman wore an old-fashioned wig, with a cue at the back tied with a ribbon. He told her to wind a rag around a stick, dip it in acid, sneak up behind him, and burn off the cue. If she sent her trophy to him he would reward her with the most beautiful fan to be found in Solomon's shop at Jamestown. Betsy was more than willing to carry out the imperial order, but her mother forbade it.

Napoleon was kind to all the Balcombe children. He had his pastry cook make dainties for them, played blindman's buff with them, had one of his servants make toy balloons for the boys and a little toy wagon to which four mice were hitched. When they complained that they could not get the mice to pull it he told them to pinch the tails of the leaders, which had the desired effect. On several occasions he gave valuable presents to the girls and to their mother, who, he said, reminded him of Josephine. Betsy has written: "I never met with anyone who bore childish liberties so well as Napoleon. He seemed to enter into every sort of mirth or fun with the glee of a child, and though I have often tried his patience severely, I never knew him to lose his temper or fall back upon his rank or age, to shield himself from the consequences of his own familiarity, or of his indulgence to me."

When Napoleon and his suite moved to Longwood the girls often came to visit him, their father having been appointed by Cockburn purveyor to the Longwood establishment. The Emperor tried to teach Betsy to play billiards, but the little "hoiden" (as Las Cases called her) was more interested in having the ball strike his fingers.

Balcombe was to serve as intermediary to the French in forwarding clandestine correspondence and in cashing bills of exchange drawn on a London bank or on Prince Eugene—Napoleon's stepson, who had married a Bavarian princess and with whom the Emperor had 800,000 francs.

SEVEN

The two months Napoleon spent at The Briars were the least unhappy of his exile at St. Helena. He might even have been reasonably contented had it not been for the constant tale of woe members of his suite poured into his ears. They complained about the discomforts they had to endure and the surveillance to which they were subjected. Realizing that lack of occupation was partly responsible for their discontent, he began giving dictation to Gourgaud, Montholon, and Bertrand, as well as to Las Cases. The complaints, however, did not cease and began to affect him. Once when they were all assembled at The Briars, he indulged in a harangue against those responsible for his exile and urged his retinue to give as much publicity as possible to their unhappy lot. "Make your complaints, gentlemen. Let indignant Europe hear them. Complaints from me would be beneath my dignity and character. I must command or be silent."

But he did not remain silent. The very next day, a ship captain who expressed his willingness to carry a message from him to England visited him. Napoleon dictated a lengthy protest in which, speaking of himself in the third person, he declaimed: "The first principles of Christian morality, and that great duty imposed upon man to pursue his fate, whatever it may be, may withhold him from terminating with his own hand a wretched existence. The Emperor glories in being superior to such a feeling. But if the British Ministry should persist in the course of injustice and violence toward him, he would consider it a favor if they would put him to death."

He dictated a letter of protest which Bertrand was to sign and send to Admiral Cockburn. On second thought Bertrand decided not to send it, but the complaints continued. When Napoleon learned that the letter had not been sent, he said to Bertrand: "If you did not deliver the letter because you considered it couched in offensive terms, you performed a duty of friendship. But surely this did not require a delay of more than twenty-four hours. A fortnight has elapsed without your mentioning it to me." Bertrand's reply was unsatisfactory and the Emperor, growing angry, called him a "nincompoop." The grand marshal, raising his voice, said the Emperor had not heeded his advice. Napoleon said reproachfully: "You would not have spoken to me in that tone of voice at the Tuileries"; then he added: "Before long the *Weymouth* will arrive bringing permission for any one who wishes to leave me to do so." Gourgaud spoke up and said: "All of us have come to share Your Majesty's lot, and the harder that lot becomes the more we want to share it. We will only leave when Your Majesty orders us to do so."

Bertrand finally wrote a letter to the admiral complaining about the scanty accommodations provided for the Emperor and about the irksome surveillance to which he and other officers of his suite were subjected. "Why," he asked, "can the authorities not increase the guard on the coast and allow us to ramble over the island without restraint?" Cockburn replied that he had "no cognizance of any Emperor being actually upon this island," and that it was "incompatible with my instructions to permit of your passing beyond the established line of sentries without your being accompanied by an English officer or noncommissioned officer."

As a result of all this, relations between Napoleon and the admiral became strained. On a couple of occasions when Cockburn came to see him he sent word that he was indisposed, at the same time leaving the pavilion for a walk in the garden "to indicate," says Gourgaud, "that he was quite well but did not care to receive the Englishman." In the presence of Sir George Bingham he once referred to the admiral as a "veritable shark," and to members of his suite he sometimes called him an "assassin." When Cockburn invited him to dinner at the Castle he declined.

On November 20, the admiral's ball took place. Napoleon ignored the invitation addressed to "General Bonaparte," but had no objection to his suite attending the function. It was generally believed, however, that he would attend, and invitations were eagerly sought. The French officers looked smart in their gold-braided uniforms and attracted general attention. It is indicative of the tolerance shown by Admiral Cockburn that although diamonds and other precious stones were supposed to have been surrendered when Napoleon and his suite were transferred to the *Northumberland*, Madame de Montholon wore with impunity a parure of diamonds and emeralds estimated to be worth £1,000. Sir George Bingham, who danced with Madame Bertrand, has written that her dress must have cost at least £500. Both ladies appeared to enjoy themselves, and Las Cases basked in the attention paid him as Napoleon's favorite companion, but Gourgaud was in an ill humor. He had hoped to dance with the governor's daughter Laura, a striking beauty who had set his heart palpitating, but the admiral had taken it upon himself to select his partners for him. The list included Betsy and the lovely Miss Knipe—a farmer's daughter whose beauty had sufficiently impressed the French to earn her the sobriquet of *Bouton de Rose*—but not the ravishing Laura. At the supper following the dancing the governor sat on the admiral's left and the governor's lady on his right. When Napoleon was told about this he waxed indignant. Madame Bertrand, he said, should have sat on Cockburn's right, she being the wife of a grand marshal, a far more distinguished personage than the wife of a petty governor. It was decided that rather than endure such slights the French would in the future not attend official functions.

EIGHT

All this took place while the house at Longwood was being repaired and enlarged. Not only all available skilled labor on the island, but many sailors were employed to speed the work. Until March, 1816, from fifty to two hundred were daily sent up to Longwood to work on the house and grounds. At the beginning of December, 1815, the work was far enough advanced to make the place habitable. The admiral called and informed Napoleon that the house was ready for occupancy. Marchand and several other servants were sent to arrange the furniture, and Napoleon announced that he would move on December 10.

On the morning of his last day at The Briars he invited Balcombe to have breakfast with him. Mrs. Balcombe was ill in bed, but before leaving he went up to her room to bid her good-by. He sat down on the bed, took her hand in his, and thanked her for her hospitality. Then he produced a gold snuff box and asked her to present it to her husband with his compliments. He told good-by to the girls, giving each a little bonbonnière. Betsy's eyes filled with tears, and he said: "You must not cry, Mademoiselle Betsee; you must come and see me next week and very often." She ran away weeping.

At about two in the afternoon Admiral Cockburn arrived on horseback accompanied by several British officers. Napoleon's suite had assembled at The Briars. His officers were mounted, the women and children were in carriages drawn by oxen. The Emperor, dressed in his green frock coat, with the star of the Legion of Honor upon his breast, white trousers, top boots, and his little cocked hat, mounted a sprightly little horse purchased for him at the Cape. A British officer headed the procession toward the mountain road. From the lawn of The Briars Jane and Betsy watched its progress until it had disappeared from view.

At the entrance to Longwood the guard presented arms and a drum rolled. Napoleon's horse shied and had to be given the spurs to advance up the avenue. When they reached the house Cockburn jumped from his horse and went up to Napoleon to help him dismount. He seemed anxious to please. As he showed him through the house he watched his face for signs of approval. The Emperor was not displeased. The disadvantages of the house and of its location were not immediately perceptible, and after months aboard a man-of-war and the makeshift accommodations at The Briars, Longwood appeared a decided improvement.

Adjoining the Emperor's bedroom was a smaller room in which the carpenter of the *Northumberland* had constructed a bath. It was a crude contraption—a long wooden box lined with tin—that would soon be replaced by a bathtub from London. But Napoleon, who had a veritable mania for bathing and had lacked facilities for doing so since leaving Malmaison, was delighted with it. The carpenter was rewarded with a gold snuff box, made especially valuable by the presence upon the cover of Napoleon's initial, surmounted by the imperial crown. No sooner had the admiral departed than the Emperor ordered Marchand to prepare a hot bath. He stewed in it for over an hour while talking to Las Cases, whom he told that he was welcome to use the bath. The chamberlain demurred, considering it too great a privilege and perhaps reflecting that it might excite increased envy among his colleagues. Napoleon dismissed his objections saying: "My dear Las Cases, fellow-prisoners must aid one another." When finally he left the bath he did not dress but put on his dressing gown. He had dinner in his room and went to bed early.

VIII. Longwood

Longwood House with the additions made by Cockburn was a collection of buildings grouped around a court and branching off behind. Most of the work on the additions was done after Napoleon moved in. In the meantime Gourgaud, O'Meara, and Captain Poppleton—the orderly officer—were housed in tents, while the Montholons and the Las Caseses occupied temporary quarters. When the work was completed, there were thirty-six rooms on the ground floor and a number of attics.

The building in front and one at the back were of stone and had been erected in 1753—not to serve as a habitation but as a cowhouse and barn. In 1787, Lieutenant Governor Robson had transformed the cowhouse into a four-room dwelling. At right angles with it, so that the two constructions formed a recumbent T, he had added a fifth room. At the back were a courtyard, five smaller rooms (remodeled slave shacks), a kitchen, and a barn. Cockburn had considerably lengthened the projection in front by adding another room and a trellised veranda accessible by four stone steps. The barn was being transformed into an apartment for the Montholons.

The house faced north, equivalent to southern exposure in the northern hemisphere. There was no cellar and no air space under the floors of most of the rooms. In the moist maritime climate of St. Helena this made the house damp and unhealthy.

Captain Masselin of the French engineers, who in 1859 was sent by his government to St. Helena and remained there two years, reported about the house: "Silk stuffs and gloves, even when placed in closed boxes, become quickly covered with ineffaceable reddish spots; leather articles are, in the space of a few days, thickly coated with mildew."

The antechamber built by Cockburn was of wood and was elevated well above the ground. It was the largest and cheeriest room in the house. Three sash windows in the west wall gave upon the avenue and upon a mountain range where perched the fortress of High Knoll. Two such windows in the opposite wall, on either side of a fireplace, commanded a view of The Barn—a mountain the shape of an enormous sarcophagus—and of the sea. In one of the Venetian blinds, usually kept lowered and closed to insure privacy, Napoleon had an opening carved to enable him to survey the environs through a spyglass without being observed. The room was at first used as a dining room but, when in July, 1816, a billiard table was installed, it became known as the billiard-room. It was here, his maps spread on the billiard-table, that Napoleon did most of his dictating while walking back and forth.

From the antechamber a door led to the drawing room. In this room Napoleon was to receive his visitors, and he and his suite were to while away the evenings with reading, conversation, card games, and chess. Next came the dining room, almost as large as the antechamber, but lighted only by a window-door opening onto the garden. East of the dining room was a fairly large chamber in which the Montholons were temporarily housed, but which was to serve as a library. Saint-Denis was appointed custodian of the library, where at the time of Napoleon's death 3,370 volumes had accumulated.

A door opposite the one leading into the library gave access to Napoleon's private quarters, consisting of two rooms giving upon the garden, a bathroom, and a small chamber in which slept the valet on night duty. One of the rooms served as a study, the other as a bedroom, but one of Napoleon's two folding camp-beds with green silk curtains had been placed in each. In the bedroom, where the Emperor spent most of his time, there was a couch, usually cluttered with books that overflowed upon the carpeted floor, and a fireplace surmounted by a mirror, on either side of which were miniatures of Marie Louise, Josephine, and the King of Rome. Cockburn had purchased the furniture second hand and, except for a washstand with a silver ewer and basin—which Napoleon had brought with him from the Tuileries and which stood in a corner of the bedroom, it was somewhat shabby. In May of the following year, however, furniture for the drawing room, which Bertrand informs us had belonged to a "great English lord," arrived from England.

TWO

When work on the additions to the house was fully completed, the Montholons came to occupy five rooms and a bath. Las Cases and his son were assigned three small rooms, one of which was occupied by their mulatto servant. Gourgaud, O'Meara, and Captain Poppleton had two rooms each. There was a servants' hall opposite the kitchen, but with one or two exceptions the servants slept in the attics, unbearably hot in summer and far from rainproof.

As on the island of Elba, so now at St. Helena, Madame Bertrand had made up her mind to preserve her independence by maintaining an establishment of her own. Bertrand knew that Napoleon would be displeased, but was too uxorious to oppose her. The admiral consenting, they moved into a two-story seven-room house at Hutt's Gate. It was far from comfortable, and the gallant admiral ordered ground broken immediately for a new dwelling for the family. Madame Bertrand, who was more English than French, was a favorite with him and with most of the officers of the garrison. The new house, completed in October, 1816, was located about 120 yards from Longwood House. The Bertrands kept their own table, but the marshal and his wife were expected to have dinner regularly with the Emperor. As one of Madame Bertrand's outstanding characteristics was lack of punctuality, the arrangement did not work out well.

The additions to Longwood House were wretchedly constructed. Roofs were of wood, covered with brown paper smeared with a mixture of tar and pitch that cracked in the sun and let the rain through. Among the Lowe papers in the British Museum there are more than a score of complaints from Captain Poppleton with variations on the theme: "The rain comes into my room at many places."

The house was infested with rats, as was the entire island. In 1875, John Charles Mellis wrote in his volume on St. Helena: "Rats abound everywhere, from the water-edge to the mountain-top, building their nests in holes or in high trees, just as rooks and crows do in England." Longwood seemed to have had a particular attraction for them. Partitions between the rooms at Longwood House being double, with an air space in between, the rats could be heard scampering about inside the walls at all hours. They made numerous outlets, which the servants patched with pieces of tin. They gamboled in the attics and romped under the floors of Napoleon's private chambers, where the ground sloped away from the house. Once when the Emperor picked up his hat, which he had placed bottom side up upon the sideboard before sitting down to dinner, a huge rat jumped out and scampered away between his feet. They gnawed holes in the blankets and ate the bark off the trees in the garden. An attempt to raise poultry had to be abandoned, as the pests invaded the coop, killed the hens, and feasted upon the eggs. When Madame Montholon gave birth to a daughter, she lived in constant fear that notwithstanding all precautions, they might harm the infant. Several dogs and cats were acquired, and sometimes a rat hunt was organized. The servants would arm themselves with sticks and, taking the dogs with them, would go to some part of the house that was particularly infested. The patches of tin would be removed from the rat holes and the hunt was on. However, when unable to get away, the rats put up such a desperate resistance that the dogs grew discouraged. To poison the vermin was impractical as they might die inside the partitions and make the house uninhabitable. Indeed, on several occasions a partition had to be opened to extract a putrid carcass.

News that Napoleon was plagued by rats spread through England and France. Cartoonists had a heyday. They scented the comic possibilities of the business and proceeded to exploit them. They pictured the fallen monarch as reading his *Acte Additionnel* to an assembly of rats; as fleeing from them in terror; as drilling them as soldiers; as leading an army of cats against them, seated upon a goat; as being served at table by liveried rats; as plotting with them in a cave a fresh invasion of France; as caught in a rat-trap, with rats outside mocking him; as having taken refuge on the roof of his house with an ocean of rats surrounding him.

THREE

The squadron was the British government's first line of defense against any attempt to free the prisoner. Major General Beatson, former governor of St. Helena, wrote in a memorandum in July, 1815, that there were only four accessible landing places on the island—Jamestown, Rupert's Bay, and Lemon Valley on the north and Sandy Bay on the south. All were defended by powerful shore batteries and considered impregnable. Ample precautions had been taken against a landing, clandestine or otherwise, anywhere on the island. The uninhabited island of Ascension, seven hundred miles from St. Helena, which might have served would-be rescuers as a base of operations, was occupied by British sailors. Three frigates and two armed vessels were kept in constant readiness at Jamestown Roads, while six brigs circumnavigated the island night and day.

St. Helena was defended by 2,784 officers and men, 500 battery pieces, 24 campaign pieces, and a number of mortars. All roads were guarded. Anyone found upon a road after nine in the evening without a pass was arrested. Soldiers were encamped at all strategic points. At Deadwood, in full view of Longwood House, there were five hundred men. On all the principal heights were look-out stations that semaphored to headquarters anything in the least suspicious on sea or land. Ships could be sighted at a distance of sixty miles and were immediately reported.

Napoleon's freedom of movement was strictly circumscribed. The house, the garden, and what was known as the park—a growth of pines and gumwood trees with a carriage road and footpaths—an area about four miles in circumference, was encompassed by a low stone wall. Along the wall sentries were posted within sight of each other. At fall of darkness, when the cannon at Alarm House boomed, they were drawn in around the house. No one was allowed to enter or leave until the cannon boomed again at sunrise. Napoleon and his suite were not, however, restricted to the confines of the enclosure. They could walk, ride, or drive at will over virtually the whole of Longwood-Deadwood plain, the circumference of which was about twelve miles, down the full length of Fisher's Valley southeast of Longwood and thence to Hutt's Gate, Geranium Valley, and Alarm House. If they wished to go farther afield they had to be accompanied by the orderly officer. It was the duty of the orderly officer to assure himself of Napoleon's presence "at least twice in the twenty-four hours."

Semaphore signals were arranged for informing the admiral of the prisoner's movements. The code signals were: "All is well with respect to General Bonaparte and family"; "General Bonaparte is unwell"; "General Bonaparte is out, properly attended, beyond the cordon of sentries"; "General Bonaparte is out, but within the cordon of sentries"; "General Bonaparte has been out longer than usual, and is supposed to have passed the sentries, not properly attended"; "General Bonaparte is missing"; "General Bonaparte has returned home"; "General Bonaparte is in want of . . ." If the signal read "General Bonaparte is missing," a blue flag was to be hoisted at the command post, whereupon every signal post was to do the same. Army contingents in every part of the island thereupon were to undertake an intensive search of territory previously assigned to them. If the signal read that he had passed beyond the cordon of sentries not properly attended, the blue flag was not to be hoisted, but troops throughout the island were to be alerted.

Napoleon had to complain repeatedly about being stopped by sentries where he had a right to go. At one time, in Fisher's Valley, a sentry pointed his musket at him when he and Las Cases, exasperated by the unwarranted interference, refused to stop and gave their horses the spurs. In every such case Sir George Bingham personally apologized to Napoleon, and the soldier who had threatened to shoot would have been court-martialed had the Emperor not asked that the matter be dropped. Throughout the captivity, members of his suite were to complain of being stopped by sentries and forced to turn back in violation of the regulations. The least that can be said is that in this, as in many other respects, things were badly managed.

Cockburn had issued an order forbidding any one to pass Hutt's Gate or the gate leading to Longwood House without a written order signed by him, by the governor, or by the commander of the garrison, Sir George Bingham. Napoleon was indignant about this and the admiral relented. On December 31, 1815, he wrote to Bingham: "An invitation from Comte de Bertrand to any person to come to Longwood may be considered in future as a sufficient pass."

IX. Napoleon's Household

Shortly after his arrival at Longwood Napoleon proceeded to organize his household. Displeased with Bertrand for setting up an establishment of his own, he entrusted the management to Montholon. Las Cases, given a supernumerary office under him, decided to confine himself to secretarial duties. Gourgaud was put in charge of the stables, in which there were twelve horses. Two of these, Frengant and Vizir, Napoleon had brought with him from France; the others Cockburn had imported from the Cape.

The appointment of Montholon to the management of the establishment came as a shock to Bertrand. It was all the more humiliating as Napoleon did not trouble to inform him but allowed the news to reach him through the servants. When on December 13, the Bertrands failed to show up for dinner, Napoleon realized that he had been too brusque. The following day he sent Gourgaud over to explain that Montholon had been appointed because the grand marshal, living at a distance, could not exercise proper supervision, but that he continued to hold first place in the imperial household. Bertrand listened in silence, but when dinner time came he and his wife remained at home.

The Montholons took advantage of the situation to fish in troubled waters. Later in the month Madame Bertrand complained to Gourgaud that Montholon had lied when he told the

Emperor that they were using his servants to wait upon them and that she had bought a tea service decorated with the King's arms. In the meantime, however, she and her husband were again dining at Longwood, but not for long. On December 29, when dinner was announced, the grand marshal was present, but his wife had not yet put in an appearance. Gourgaud was sent to fetch her. When she entered the parlor Napoleon said severely: "I am not in the habit of waiting for anybody." The following day he remarked to Gourgaud: "They behave as they did at Elba. They think only of themselves. They have forgotten what they owe me. They use my house as if it were an inn. Let them come to dinner regularly or not at all."

Bertrand on his part complained bitterly to Gourgaud about the treatment he and his wife were receiving from the Emperor. "I have known for a long time that he is an egoist," he said. Gourgaud explained that Napoleon was displeased because Madame Bertrand had gone to Jamestown to dine with the admiral and had stayed overnight "at the house of Porteous and Hamilton." [1]

The name of Captain Hamilton recurs repeatedly in Gourgaud's journal in connection with Madame Bertrand. He was captain of the *Savannah*, one of the ships that had escorted the *Northumberland* to St. Helena. Tall, blond, and handsome, he was a favorite with the ladies. Napoleon believed that Madame Bertrand had become enamored of him, indeed, that she was his mistress. The *Savannah*, with Colonel Wilks and his family on board, left St. Helena on April 23, 1816, for England, but by that time the gossip concerning its handsome captain and Madame Bertrand had taken firm root. In September, 1817, we find Napoleon remarking to Gourgaud: "I believe Hamilton has cuckolded poor Bertrand." The following month he told him that gossip had it that the son born to Madame Bertrand in January of that year was the offspring of Hamilton. In February, 1818, we find Madame Bertrand beseeching Gourgaud to defend her against the calumny bandied about concerning her and Hamilton.

[1] Gourgaud writes, *"chez Porteous et Hamilton."* The inn belonged to Porteous. Captain Hamilton appears to have had lodgings there.

TWO

The feud between the Emperor and the Bertrands subsided for a while after the new year, but flared up again at the beginning of April, when Madame Bertrand failed to show up for dinner twice in succession—the first time because she had again accepted an invitation to dine with the admiral, the second because she felt fatigued after her trip to Jamestown. Napoleon's pride was hurt. Was it then no longer considered a privilege to dine and spend the evening with him? "I know," he said to Las Cases, "that one is often inclined to be unreasonable and susceptible, so, when I am mistrustful of myself, I ask: 'Should I have been treated that way had I been still at the Tuileries?' That is my infallible test." To Gourgaud he said that it was perfectly ridiculous the way Madame Bertrand was gadding about and sleeping away from home. She was flighty, like all Creoles. He instructed the young general to call on her and inform her that if she cared for his good opinion she must change her ways. Unless she meant to do so she had henceforth better dine at home. He was not running a *table d'hôte*.

Gourgaud, who was on good terms with the Bertrands, delivered the message reluctantly. Madame Bertrand burst into tears. Her husband came to her defense. He said he had not deserved such treatment from the Emperor. He could see no wrong in a young matron seeking a little diversion. Had she not occasionally accepted an invitation to dine in town, he himself would have urged her to do so. Since it was his intention to remain at St. Helena as long as possible, he did not want her to despair and to droop with ennui. Knowing the Emperor as he did, he felt certain that when he got over his huff he would appraise the situation differently. It was evident that he had fallen under the influence of intriguers—meaning the Montholons. Henceforth, he said, his wife and he would dine at home.

When Gourgaud returned to Longwood he found the Emperor walking meditatively in the garden. He told him what Bertrand had said and tried to act as a peacemaker. "The Emperor grew angry," he has written. "He said that he might be

wrong, but that his entourage had always found their greatest
satisfaction in being with him. He had tried to live like a private
person, but had found that he could not. Lack of consideration
was infinitely more painful to him now than it had been in Paris."

It was a pathetic confession. He obviously hated to face the
fact that now that his power had departed people no longer
found the same satisfaction in his presence—that it was not
Napoleon himself but the effulgence of his glory and high office
that had been the principal attraction.

A week after this incident Gourgaud called Napoleon's attention to the fact that the following day was Sunday and that the
Bertrands would undoubtedly appreciate an invitation to dinner. "Then go ahead and ask them," Napoleon replied. Gourgaud
sent a note to Madame Bertrand, inviting her and her husband,
in the name of the Emperor, to come to Longwood on Sunday at
four o'clock and to remain for dinner. She replied that they
would come at six. Bertrand was there at the appointed time, but
she did not put in an appearance until half an hour later. When
Napoleon entered the drawing room she curtsied with an injured
mien. Nevertheless it was agreed that they were to dine at Longwood regularly on Sunday.

THREE

On December 30—twenty days after Napoleon had moved to
Longwood—his household was augmented by the arrival of
Captain Piontkowski. We have already met him on the deck of
the *Northumberland* where with tears in his eyes he had begged
to be allowed to accompany Napoleon to St. Helena, if only as a
servant. Lord Keith had taken pity on him and, having consulted
the proper authorities, had allowed him to depart on the *Cor-
morant* to join his idol. He had arrived at Jamestown the previous day, and the admiral, thinking Napoleon would be pleased
to see him, had personally conducted him as far as Hutt's Gate.

Charles Frederic Jules Piontkowski was born in Poland in
1786. The historian Masson has painted an unflattering portrait
of him, based on insufficient research. G. L. de St. M. Watson has
written a book about him setting the record straight. Others who

A View of St. Helena

Sir Hudson Lowe
Governor of St. Helena

Marquis de Las Cases

*Napoleon Dictating
to General Gourgaud
at St. Helena*

Marshal Bertrand

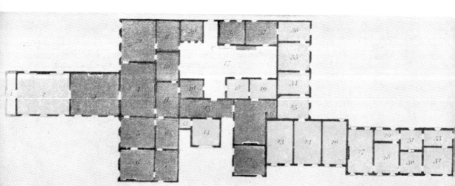

A View and Plan of Longwood House, the Residence of Napoleon

have written about the captivity barely mention him. True that his role was a very minor one, but the reactions of the principal actors to his appearance on the scene are not devoid of interest.

Piontkowski had been a first lieutenant in the Polish Lancers with the French army, most of whom had enlisted in the hope that Napoleon would some day free their country from foreign domination. He had taken part in the campaign in Saxony and was wounded and taken prisoner before Dresden. After the Emperor's abdication at Fontainebleau, there being no opening for him as a lieutenant in Napoleon's Elban army, he had enrolled as a private. During the Hundred Days he regained his rank of lieutenant in the Lancers and fought at Waterloo. After the second abdication Bertrand gave him written permission to follow the Emperor to Malmaison, and on the journey to Rochefort entrusted his wife and children to his care. His right to the rank of captain has been challenged, but the fact that Bertrand never questioned it makes it appear probable that he got him promoted, somewhat irregularly, after the abdication, as Napoleon had done with Gourgaud.

It has been claimed that Piontkowski was an adventurer who capitalized on his stay at St. Helena by living all the rest of his life on the bounty bestowed upon him by admirers of Napoleon for his devotion to the great man. Yet that devotion appears to have been genuine. When he says, "I never had any other motive than my admiration, any other ambition than to serve him as best I could," we are inclined to believe him. He declined a proposal that he write his memoirs, saying: "I am only a pigmy, and so much has been written about Napoleon." In his letters to Sir Robert Wilson, who befriended him during his stay in England, he speaks about his role at St. Helena with becoming modesty and blames himself for the unfriendly reception he received from members of Napoleon's suite.

On Piontkowski's arrival at Longwood, Montholon, Gourgaud, and Las Cases gave him the cold shoulder. This was mostly due to snobbism: they did not like to have a subaltern for a companion. They expressed the opinion that he might be a spy. "I cannot blame them if the devotion they bore Napoleon rendered rather suspicious in their eyes the permission I, and I alone, had obtained to rejoin the Emperor," he was to comment in a letter to Wilson. He likewise admits that, dazzled by his good fortune, he had perhaps been insufficiently respectful toward his superiors in rank. Napoleon at first refused to receive him, but Bertrand interceded for him. After a severe interrogatory the Emperor relented and instructed him to be at his table for dinner.

His appearance at dinner provoked black looks from his table companions. They considered it a breach of etiquette, an assault upon their cherished prerogatives. Napoleon was a stickler for etiquette himself, but only in the case of those of high rank or elevated social position. He could be quite informal with soldiers, subalterns, and men and women of the people. It was one of the secrets of his popularity. It had not been at all uncommon with him to sit down at a bivouac fire with soldiers, converse, joke and laugh with them, taste their soup, and eat their bread. "My soldiers were much at their ease and made very free with me, often addressing me familiarly with the pronoun thou," he told Las Cases. No cabinet officer or grand marshal would have ventured to do that. Some of this may have been histrionics, but to succeed as it did there must have been a considerable admixture of the genuine and spontaneous. It is the strict etiquette he exacted from those of high rank that appears forced and artificial.

Piontkowski had the good sense to realize that to continue to appear at the Emperor's table was not likely to improve his relationship with the generals. He told Montholon that henceforth he would eat alone. He did so for a time, but was soon invited by O'Meara and the orderly officer to share their table with them. Napoleon occasionally invited him to lunch in the marquee Cockburn had had put up in the garden. He at first slept in a tent, but later was assigned a wretched little attic room by Montholon. When he accidentally injured himself while hunting and the Emperor expressed the intention to visit him, Montholon had him hurriedly change rooms with his wife's maid, who had a room on the ground floor. The Pole was appointed equerry, which meant that he would have to assist Gourgaud in supervision over the stables. Considering Gourgaud's irascibility, it was not a pleasant assignment.

FOUR

Speaking about the discord among members of Napoleon's suite Las Cases wrote: "Though attachment to the person of the Emperor had united us around him, yet chance and not sympathy had brought us together. Our connection was purely fortuitous, and not the result of any natural affinity. Thus, at Longwood, we were encircled round a center, but without any cohesion with each other. How could it be otherwise? We were almost strangers to one another, and, unfortunately, our different conditions, ages, and characters, were calculated to make us continue so."

Had they been better suited to one another dissension would have come anyway. With the exception of Las Cases, who kept himself and his son busy with the memoirs which were to make him rich and famous, members of Napoleon's suite had little to occupy them. They were bored with one another and with themselves. Napoleon's insistence that they should spend all their evenings with him did not greatly affect the situation, since under Hudson Lowe's regime they could not have spent them elsewhere, unless they remained in their wretched little rooms. The etiquette he imposed upon them may appear absurd, but one is inclined to believe that without it the situation would have deteriorated even more rapidly.

The Emperor was not a unifying element at Longwood but rather the opposite. It was around him that the jealousies, ambitions, and hopes of his followers raged. While he was anxious to maintain a semblance of majesty, they were striving for first place in his imitation court—for the satisfaction of being preferred by him—for the realization of their hopes of receiving a rich reward from his ample resources. The Montholons were scheming to displace the Bertrands. They and Gourgaud hated Las Cases because of the favor he found with the Emperor. Gourgaud hated Montholon, who, although his equal in rank was forging ahead of him. He hated Madame Montholon whom he believed to be the weaver of schemes for her husband's pre-ferment. About Las Cases Gourgaud wrote in his journal that if he again tried to go before him into the dining room he would kick him. About Montholon he said: "I have had a discussion with my colleague regarding the places we should oc-cupy at table. I have told him that I would yield to him in noth-ing. Sooner I'll fight him." It was not long, however, before Gourgaud and Montholon realized that they had a mutual rival in Las Cases and had better join forces against him. Las Cases was again giving the Emperor English lessons and was more in his company than any of them.

Time and again Napoleon tried to allay the discord. When on the first of the new year his followers came in a body to offer him their good wishes, he asked them to keep in mind that con-sideration for one another was the sole means of making life bearable in their isolation. In April, 1816, he said: "You should try to live as members of one family. You have followed me with the idea of lightening my burden of sorrow. Should this then not be your principal consideration? If sympathy for me is not a suf-ficient incentive, then let reason be your guide. We must learn to curb ill temper. That little misunderstandings should arise among you is natural enough, but they should be followed by mutual explanations, not by ill humor. The first will produce re-sults; the second will only aggravate matters."

Later in the month he spoke more forcibly: "You followed me with the view of cheering me in my captivity. Be brothers then —otherwise you but annoy me. You talk of fighting, and that before my face! You forget that the attention of foreigners is fixed upon you." In July of that year he said: "Some day, when you are restored to the world, you will consider yourselves as brothers, because of me. My memory will oblige you to do so. Then do so now."

FIVE

Let us take a look at the lower household.

If Bertrand deserves first mention among the officers, Louis Marchand deserves it among the servants. Indeed, as far as devotion is concerned, he rates ahead of Bertrand. He was twenty-three when he went with Napoleon to St. Helena. His mother, a cradle-rocker to the King of Rome, had followed Marie Louise to Vienna in 1814. Marchand had received a fair education, was intelligent, well-mannered, trustworthy, discreet, and possessed some talent as a landscapist, which he exercised at St. Helena. He had entered into service at the Tuileries in 1811, but did not come into close contact with the Emperor until three years later. When, in 1814, Napoleon abdicated at Fontainebleau and his two valets, Constant and Roustan, abandoned him, Bertrand appointed Marchand first *valet de chambre*. He followed the Emperor to Elba, and at St. Helena the relationship between master and servant took on a tinge of intimacy and affection. He was an excellent reader, and when the Emperor could not sleep would read to him until late into the night. There were times when Napoleon unburdened his heart to him. In 1819, when half of those who had come with him from France had left him, he said sadly to Marchand: "If this keeps up only you and I will remain here. You will read to me, you will close my eyes, and return to France to live on the legacy I shall leave you." Napoleon did, indeed, leave him a generous legacy. More than that—he named him, together with Bertrand and Montholon, his testamentary executor. Marchand married the daughter of General Brayer and in 1869, seven years before his death, was created a count by Napoleon III.

Next in importance was Cipriani Franceschi, the major-domo, a Corsican of uncertain age and mysterious antecedents. He was an avowed Republican and unbeliever, a hater of emperors and kings, but somehow managed to make an exception of Napoleon. A relationship of long standing, the exact nature of which is unknown, existed between him and the Bonaparte family. His son was in the service of Cardinal Fesch, his daughter in that of Napoleon's mother. In 1808, he had served as an undercover agent at Capri, where Hudson Lowe then commanded a force of Corsican rebels in the service of the British. He had followed Napoleon to Elba, but had spent most of his time at Vienna, whence he forwarded the information that the Congress of

Vienna was discussing the advisability of transferring Napoleon to St. Helena. He thus may have been partly responsible for the Emperor's decision to leave Elba. On St. Helena he was employed mainly in gathering information that might be of value to Napoleon, with whom he had frequent conferences. "He would give us all for Cipriani," Gourgaud once jealously remarked.

The remaining servants were of far less importance. Giovanni Natale Santini, born in Corsica in 1790, had served in the campaigns in Austria and Germany and as orderly at headquarters during the invasion of Russia. He had followed Napoleon to Elba, where he served as usher and keeper of the portfolio. He possessed some knowledge of tailoring, of barbering, and of shoe repairing, and at St. Helena looked after the Emperor's wardrobe and trimmed his hair. He was fanatically loyal to Napoleon and conceived a hatred for Hudson Lowe that might have ended tragically had the Emperor not intervened.

Louis Etienne Saint-Denis, Napoleon's second valet, was born in 1788. He had at one time served the Emperor in the costume of a Mameluke and became known as Ali. Besides serving as a valet and groom he had charge of the library, and as he wrote a fair hand was often in demand as amanuensis.

Jean Abram Noverraz, born in Switzerland in 1790, had been in service at the Tuileries since 1809. When after the first abdication the Emperor traveled to Fréjus, where he was to embark for Elba, Noverraz sat on the box behind. At Orgon, a royalist stronghold, an angry mob surrounded the carriage. Noverraz, tall and broad-shouldered, jumped to the ground and with a sword in one hand and a pistol in the other prepared to charge, but was restrained by Bertrand. The mob, however, had recoiled before him and the carriage was able to proceed. At St. Helena he served as a valet and usher. When he stood at the door leading from the antechamber to the drawing room, no one whom the Emperor did not care to receive could have entered except over his dead body. Napoleon called him "my Swiss bear."

The two Archambault brothers, Achille Thomas and Joseph Olivier, had served as hostlers at the Tuileries and had followed Napoleon to Elba. At St. Helena they again looked after the horses. Both were skillful coachmen and postilions, which was fortunate, for when Napoleon went out driving it was with a span of six and at breakneck speed. At Longwood this meant running the risk of smashing into a tree, and on the road skirting the Punch Bowl the even greater risk of plunging into the abyss.

Pierron, chief steward and confectioner, had been kitchen assistant at the Tuileries. In 1818, when Lepage, the cook, returned to France, Pierron took charge of the kitchen. Lepage had been employed by Napoleon's brother Joseph and was the only French servant who had not been with the Emperor on Elba. Rousseau, candleman in Paris, was in charge of the silverware, a prodigious quantity of which Napoleon brought with him from the Tuileries. Gentilini, a native of Elba, served as a footman. The remaining French servants were Bernard Heymann and his wife and son, servants of the Bertrands; and Josephine Brule, Madame Montholon's maid. There were besides eleven English sailors (later replaced by an equal number of soldiers) and seven men and one woman of the island. Poppleton and his assistant Lieutenant Jackson had three orderlies. With O'Meara, the English officers and their orderlies, Napoleon's household, at the beginning of the captivity at Longwood, consisted of sixteen principals (men, women, and children) and thirty-eight servants. From time to time Chinese were hired to assist with the work.

SIX

The establishment was overstaffed. Few of the servants had enough to do. Montholon was far from being a good manager. A man who had run through his own and his wife's fortune could hardly have been expected to have an eye on economy. Napoleon should have known this. But he who had had three hundred million in his coffers at the Tuileries and had ruled half of Europe did not think of economy in such a matter as running a household. The servants had little respect for Montholon. Among themselves they referred to him as "the Liar." There was overindulgence in wine and constant bickering.

The servants Napoleon had brought with him from France divided into an upper and a lower echelon. Marchand, Cipriani, Pierron, and Saint-Denis were upper servants and did not eat at the same table with the others. The English sailors and people of the island had a table of their own. The French servants were as jealous of their prerogatives as were the officers. When Montholon hired a personal servant, a Persian who spoke French, and assigned him a seat at the table of the lower echelon, it required Napoleon's personal intervention to prevent a mutiny.

Thieving went on continually. It became especially bad when the *Northumberland* left for England and soldiers took the place of the sailors. The Tommies carried off bottles of wine and anything else they could lay their hands on. One was caught with twenty pounds of Longwood candles in his possession. When the room of another was searched, ninety-two pound sterling were found, the provenance of which he could not explain. The outside larder was robbed repeatedly, which could not have happened without the connivance of the sentries.

Napoleon was far from satisfied with Montholon's management, and his mendacity exasperated him. But having alienated Bertrand by making the appointment, he did not care to alienate Montholon by revoking it. Sometimes, however, he lost patience with him. One day he discovered that the sentries—who although drawn closer around the house at nine o'clock in the evening had yet remained at a reasonable distance—were now posted before the doors and windows. When he asked Montholon what he knew about the matter, the latter replied that he did not know the reason, but that the admiral had given the order. Napoleon promptly protested to Cockburn, who said that it had been done at the request of Montholon, who had complained about prowlers. He had told the admiral that either the servants were bringing in wenches during the night or fanatics were trying to break in to assassinate Napoleon. The Emperor flew into a rage. He told Montholon: "You must have sunk pretty low to act as our jailer! If this goes on, pretty soon there will be sentries in my bedroom. Who put the idea into your head that my life is in danger—that sailors or the people of the island want to get rid of me by assassinating me? It's rank nonsense! Even if it were true one of my officers could sleep near my bedroom. I don't need English sentries to protect me. You say they are bringing in wenches? If it gets to be a nuisance you can stop it without the aid of the British. What do you think this is, a convent? Get out!" As Montholon was leaving, Napoleon said to Gourgaud: "A veritable scullery maid that Montholon."

A few days later, when Montholon was going to town, he told him: "Don't bring me back any lies as news. Bertrand is going to town tomorrow and I'll find out the truth."

Cockburn gave orders that the sentries should be posted as they had been before Montholon's complaint.

On December 30, 1815, when out riding with Las Cases and Gourgaud, Napoleon had told them that it was his intention to give his officers a quarterly allowance. "It is a trifle, to be sure," he had said, "but everything must be proportioned to the circumstances, and to me this is truly the widow's mite." Later, when they were alone, Las Cases told him that since he had 80,000 francs of his own he did not need an allowance. Bertrand, too, declined to accept it. The fact that Montholon received a considerably larger allowance than Gourgaud was to contribute to the dissension.

X. Life at Longwood

Napoleon usually awoke at dawn. The valet on duty would respond to the bell and would come from the little chamber adjoining the bathroom where he had spent the night. The Emperor would get up, retaining around his head the red madras handkerchief he wore at night, and would don a pair of white trousers with heel-straps, a white quilted dressing gown, and red morocco slippers. Thus attired he would seat himself on the sofa before a little round table and sip the cup of black coffee the servant had brought.

At his toilet he was assisted by three valets—Marchand, Saint-Denis, and Noverraz. He began by shaving. One valet would hold the mirror, another the shaving implements. When he had gone over one side of his face, he would ask, "Is it done?" before beginning on the other. Having finished, he would examine his face carefully. If any part had been neglected he would give the valet a tap on the cheek and say, "Ah, you rascal! why did you say it was done?" Stripped to the waist he would wash at the silver basin from the Tuileries. He would scrub his arms, shoulders, and chest vigorously with a hard brush, and would then hand it to Noverraz to brush his back. "Come, brush hard, as if you were scrubbing a donkey," he was in the habit of saying. This finished, Noverraz would rub his chest and back with *eau de Cologne*. "He used almost to drown himself in *eau de Cologne*," Las Cases has written.

Marchand assisted him in dressing. At Longwood he did not wear a military uniform, but he never discarded the familiar cocked hat with tricolor cockade. He donned breeches and a waistcoat of white cashmere and a green hunting coat with velvet collar and cuffs and silver buttons embossed with animal heads. On his breast he wore the silver plaque of the Legion of Honor. At the beginning of his captivity at Longwood he went out riding at seven in the morning when the weather permitted. At such times he pulled on riding boots, otherwise he wore shoes with gold buckles and white silk stockings.

His usual riding companions were Las Cases and Gourgaud; Bertrand and Montholon accompanied him only occasionally. Saint-Denis or Noverraz followed on horseback at a little distance. Twelve miles is not much of a riding circuit, especially if it is the same twelve miles that constitute one's principal outing. "It is like being confined in a riding school," he told Las Cases. He could have gone riding in other parts of the island accompanied by the orderly officer, but disliked doing so. "The officer might say I ride too fast, or too slow, or it was time to go home, which is what I will not submit to," he was to say to Sir Pulteney Malcolm, who was to succeed Admiral Cockburn as commander of the squadron. To make the ride last longer they usually walked their horses. One day when riding past a field where a farmer was plowing, Napoleon dismounted, took the handles of the plow from the farmer's hands with a friendly nod, and plowed a remarkably straight furrow.

TWO

There was one other ride Napoleon could make unaccompanied by the orderly officer. It was through Fisher's Valley toward Miss Mason's cottage, thence to Hutt's Gate and Alarm House. What was called Fisher's Valley was a deep ravine through which flowed a shallow but limpid stream. There were some marshy places where a horse could easily become mired if one ventured off the narrow road, but the masses of foliage, the interplay of light and shadow, the turquoise sky overhead, and the awesome silence combined to give the place the solemnity of a

105

cathedral. On his first visit Napoleon reined in his horse and listened as if waiting for some great mystery to reveal itself. Then, as if waking from a dream, he said: "The Valley of Silence!"

There were a few cottages in the valley inhabited by tenant farmers. Napoleon visited the cottage of a man named Legy, who had a wife and six children. The farmer addressed him as "Sir Emperor" or "Sir General." In reply to Napoleon's usual interrogatory he said that he had a hundred acres, mostly in vegetables, and that things had greatly improved since "Sir Emperor" had come to the island. Before that he had had to wait for the coming of a fleet from India or China to dispose of his produce and much of it often spoilt. Now he had a ready market at Longwood. With the aid of Las Cases, Napoleon also spoke to the woman, complimenting her on her brood and asking about the children's ages and schooling. He had Las Cases distribute coins among the children, while he playfully pinched their ears and noses and pulled their hair. By this time the family felt quite at ease. The farmer produced a bottle of Cape wine, and he and the visitors drank together. Dr. Warden, who knew the family, tells us that the children often inquired of him: "When will Boney come to see us again?"

There was one cottage where Napoleon was to be a frequent visitor. On one of their rides in the valley they had come upon a girl of sixteen or seventeen, who, although shabbily dressed, possessed a grace and beauty that appealed even to Napoleon's sophisticated taste. They stopped to talk to her and learned that her name was Mary Ann Robinson and that her father was a tenant farmer who lived in a cottage farther up the valley. Napoleon called her the "Nymph," and the Valley of Silence became the Valley of the Nymph.

The following morning he went again for a ride in the valley, undoubtedly in the hope of catching another glimpse of the "Nymph." With him were Bertrand, Las Cases, and Gourgaud. It was not long before they saw her. She had apparently been expecting them, for she was dressed in her Sunday best, not nearly as becoming to her as the faded frock of the preceding day. What particularly displeased Napoleon was that her interest seemed to be centered on Gourgaud, by far the youngest of the party. She did not disguise her interest, but asked Bertrand: "Is this General Gourgaud?" The young general felt flattered, and Napoleon, feigning indifference, remarked: "She pays more attention to you than to me. She probably knows that you are a bachelor. Ah, those young ladies! All they care about is to catch a husband."

As they rode away Napoleon was morose and told Las Cases that on second look the "Nymph" had proved disappointing. The chamberlain, courtier fashion, agreed with him. He wrote in his diary: "Our pretty blossom of the field now appeared to us nothing more than an ordinary garden flower."

Several days later the Emperor, Las Cases, and Gourgaud again came upon the girl. Had she discussed the meetings with her father and had the practical Yamstock instructed her how to proceed so as to draw the greatest possible benefit from the affair? Anyway, this time she had no eyes for Gourgaud, but asked Las Cases to tell the Emperor that she went walking alone in the valley every morning.

It was an unmistakable invitation to a flirtation or more, and Napoleon was not the man to neglect such an opportunity. Having had a wide experience in such matters, he felt reasonably certain that she had been advised by her father. He called at the cottage and became acquainted with her father and brother. What happened after that? We have only fragmentary evidence. O'Meara, in an interview with Lowe, was to say that Bonaparte visited the cottage "twelve or fourteen times, twice in one day." Robinson, questioned by the new governor, said that Bonaparte had done him a favor by "saving a cow" and that he had "given tips" to his son. He made the significant admission that Piontkowski had brought him a message from Bonaparte "saying when his daughter was married [to Lieutenant Impett of the 53rd] he would make her a present of five hundred pounds." A subaltern reported that Robinson had toasted Napoleon in his presence and when plied with wine had endeavored to get him interested in helping the prisoner escape. Robinson denied the charge and was not prosecuted, there being no corroborative evidence. But there is sufficient evidence to justify the suspicion, if not the assumption, that Napoleon's relationship with the "Nymph" was not an innocent one and that her father and her brother were involved in the affair.

Mary Ann did not marry an impecunious young lieutenant. The attention Napoleon had been paying her—before he apparently decided to get her safely married—made her fortune. The news of his infatuation had spread throughout the island and thence to England and France. Soon all Europe knew about the "Nymph." There were suitors galore. In the fall of 1817, she married Captain Edwards of the *Dora,* a merchant vessel the captain operated for his own account. In a memorandum to Bathurst, Lowe has given these further details, which he claims to have obtained from Robinson: "After she had been married to Captain Edwards they spent about two hours with Bonaparte and all his attendants; he seemed dejected at her leaving the island, filled a glass of wine, and insisted on carrying it himself to her. On their leaving the house he stood in a studious manner until they had walked on some way, then followed them; on overtaking them he embraced Captain Edwards, saying he could not help it, he put him so much in mind of his own brother Joseph."

THREE

After a ride Napoleon always took a bath. For him bathing had ever been a voluptuous enjoyment. Now that there was so little to occupy his time, he abandoned himself to it as another might have taken to drink. It became not unusual with him to spend three to four hours in the bath, either with a book or lulled in a *dolce far niente.* He often bathed as many as three times a day. He liked his bath very hot, and Marchand was kept busy carrying boiling water from the kitchen to maintain the temperature. The excessive bathing sapped his strength, but he would not admit this. Hot baths, fasting, and drinking large quantities of barley water he believed to be infallible remedies for most bodily afflictions.

After—and sometimes during—the bath he received Dr.

O'Meara. He had as little faith in doctors as he had in the cura-
tive value of their pills and potions. When a doctor was introduced to him it was his standing joke to ask: "In the course of
your practice how many people have you killed?" or "How many
did you bleed today?" But he respected surgeons. "With respect
to surgery, he professed a far different opinion, and acknowledged the great utility of that science," O'Meara has written. He
moreover believed in vaccination, and once asked Dr. Warden:
"Have not the people of England given me some credit for my
having adopted, encouraged, and, indeed, decreed the rigid ob-
servance of Dr. Jenner's system?"

He looked forward to O'Meara's daily visit, not because he felt
in need of his ministrations, but because the doctor was an inexhaustible fount of salty gossip. Able to go freely about the
island and welcomed at the officers' mess at Deadwood, he knew
all the scandal, civil and military, and told it with gusto. St.
Helena's crop of scandal was perennial. Whether, as claimed by
some, it was due to the climate or, as appears more probable, to
the presence of many unmarried officers and soldiers, the wench-
ing was terrific, and there were few married women on the island
who were not suspected of adultery. Napoleon had liked to listen to gossip even at the height of his power. It amused him
and he believed one could garner much useful information from
it if one used common sense in sifting it. The doctor's Italian being more fluent than his French, it was in that language they
usually conversed. The Emperor liked to talk as well as to listen, and expatiated to O'Meara about his career and about the
difficulties he was having with Cockburn and later with Lowe.
After each visit O'Meara noted down carefully what he had said.
Like Las Cases, he meant to publish a book.

After the doctor's visit it was time for lunch. If the weather
was inclement Napoleon ate at the little round table in his bedroom, in dressing gown and slippers. If it was pleasant outside,
he lunched in the marquee. He usually invited one or two of his
officers to lunch with him. In the beginning the officers had
lunched together, but relations among them had become so
strained that this had to be given up. Bertrand and Montholon

lunched with their families, Las Cases with his son; but Gourgaud, unless the Emperor or the Bertrands invited him, ate alone in his dreary little room. It increased his feeling of loneliness and made him more irascible. *"Ennui! Ennui! Ennui!"* he exclaims over and over in his journal, or *"Ennui! Tristesse!"*

Napoleon's lunch consisted of soup, which had to be served steaming hot, two meat courses, and a side dish of vegetables. He was a modest drinker: half a bottle of claret sufficed him either at lunch or dinner and he nearly always diluted it with water.

After lunch he might spend several hours dictating, sometimes in his study, more often in the billiard-room, where it was easier for him to pace back and forth. He kept his spyglass always handy and from time to time would stop and peer through the hole in one of the Venetian blinds. For Bertrand—who considered serving as amanuensis beneath his rank and ill-concealed his displeasure—was reserved the story of the campaign in Egypt and Syria; for Las Cases, the first Italian campaign; for Gourgaud, Waterloo. Montholon was given dictation on varied topics; Marchand and Saint-Denis, on Cæsar's wars. "I cannot recollect," Las Cases has written, "ever having seen him occupied with two different topics at the same time. The story of Cæsar simultaneously dictating dispatches in various languages to several secretaries made him laugh." When ill health, difficulties with the governor and in his own household became more and more troublesome, he lost most of his interest in the work and dictated only occasionally. Toward the middle of 1819, he ceased doing so altogether.

FOUR

During the early part of Napoleon's residence at Longwood there were many callers, a fair proportion of whom were dinner guests. Among the visitors were Governor Wilks, Admiral Cockburn, Lieutenant Governor and Mrs. Skelton, Colonel Bingham, Major and Mrs. Hodson, Major Fehrzen, the Balcombes, Captain Ross and Dr. Warden of the *Northumberland.* Ship captains, distinguished travelers, and members of the St. Helena council vied with one another for the privilege of being introduced to the great man. Colonel Bingham presented to him the officers of the 53rd; Cockburn's successor Admiral Malcolm, the officers of his squadron.

While Admiral Cockburn was in command a pass issued by Marshal Bertrand sufficed. Later no one was admitted to the Longwood enclosure without a pass from the governor, seldom granted without a severe interrogatory. To obtain an audience with the Emperor it was still necessary to apply to Bertrand. Napoleon increasingly received only those in whom he took a special interest: he did not care to exhibit himself to the curious. If an audience had been granted and the visitor was a person of note, there was considerable ceremony. Montholon and Gourgaud, sometimes also Bertrand, in resplendent gold-braided uniforms, would receive him in the billiard-room. Santini or Noverraz, in green tail-coat with gold-embroidered collar and cuffs, white vest, black silk breeches, white silk stockings, and buckled shoes, would open the door of the drawing room and announce the visitor. The Emperor would be standing, his hat under his arm, with Las Cases close by to serve as interpreter. Persons of less consequence were sometimes received informally in the garden.

After August, 1816, Napoleon received but seldom and there was only one invitation to dinner. Between October 31, 1817, and his death three and a half years later, he received only twice.

Cockburn had ordered a calash sent from the Cape, and toward four o'clock Napoleon liked to go out driving.[1] With the Archambaults as postilions and never less than four horses, the carriage would go flying down the avenue through the wood. Bertrand, Las Cases, and one of the ladies would be seated in the calash with the Emperor; Montholon and Gourgaud followed on horseback. Sometimes they would race down the road from Hutt's Gate to Alarm House, which, though skirting the dizzy abyss called the Punch Bowl, was unprovided

---

[1] Octave Aubry has written: "It was an old carriage of Wilks, which, for want of anything better, the governor had sent to Longwood." Gourgaud informs us that on December 21, 1815, a calash arrived from the Cape.

with a parapet. Betsy Balcombe, who on her visits to Longwood sometimes participated in this breath-taking experience, has written: "These were drives which seemed to inspire Bonaparte with a mischievous pleasure. He added to my fright by repeatedly assuring me that the horses were running away, and that we should be all dashed to pieces."

Indeed, the drives sometimes seemed to put Napoleon in a hilarious mood. Dr. Warden of the *Northumberland* thus describes a drive to which he was invited: "I declare, if it had been a party in a jaunting-car to a country fair in Ireland there would not have been more mirth, ease, and affability. The carriage drove off at a pretty round pace, and the pleasantry of Napoleon seemed to keep pace with it. He began to talk English, and having thrown his arm half-round Madame Bertrand's neck he exclaimed, addressing himself to me, 'This is my mistress,' while the lady was endeavoring to extricate herself, and the count, her husband, was bursting with laughter. He then asked if he had made a mistake, and being informed of the English interpretation of the word, he cried out, 'Oh, no, no! I say my friend, my love. No, not my love; my friend, my friend.' In short, to use a well-known English phrase, he was the life of the party."

Sometimes he and his suite went walking instead of driving. Napoleon would wear his green hunting coat and little cocked hat. His officers, in dress uniform, carried their plumed hats in their hands, as required by etiquette. The ladies wore the short-waisted, puffed-sleeved, long-flowing dresses of the period. The Emperor would lead the procession with Madame Bertrand. It was not a pleasurable walk. The gumwood trees were hardly objects of beauty and gave little shade. Travelers have compared them with ragged umbrellas turned inside out. The promenaders must have felt exceedingly uncomfortable in their court dress, with the sun beating down upon them and upon the dusty road. Yet Madame Montholon informs us that the walks sometimes lasted for hours. One can hardly blame her for trying to slip away. She seldom succeeded. Napoleon kept a watchful eye on his followers and, when one of them tried to save himself down a side path, would say reproachfully: "Look at . . . running away."

FIVE

Winter at St. Helena commenced officially on June 21, summer on December 22. In winter, rain and fog were frequent at Longwood and Napoleon spent most of his time in his rooms. A fire would be laid in the fireplace, and Saint-Denis would bring stacks of books from the library and place them on the little round table. Napoleon would sit on the sofa in his dressing gown and read. He read very fast. One of his contemporaries has said that he read "with his thumb." Madame Montholon has written that she had known him to go through a twenty-two volume history in three days. He had a way of taking in a page almost at a glance, and he remembered all he found of interest. Sometimes he made observations on the margins, and there are a few books he annotated from cover to cover. When he finished a book he was in the habit of throwing it on the floor, so that after a few hours books would be scattered over the carpet like autumn leaves after a gale.

History, memoirs, military and social science, geography, and travel narratives were his favorite reading. Novels he read but seldom, but he liked plays, especially tragedies. In his youth he had been fond of lyric poetry, Italian as well as French, and still knew many poems by heart; but he lost his taste for poetry as he grew older. At St. Helena the only poet he sometimes perused was Ossian, whom he read in an Italian translation. Mrs. Abell (Betsy Balcombe) has written: "I have heard him speak slightingly of poets, and call them *rêveurs,* and still I believe the most visionary of them all was the only one he ever perused. His own vast and undefined schemes of ambition seemed to have found something congenial in the dreamy sublimities of Ossian."

In his boyhood he had been fond of Rousseau; later Voltaire became his favorite. Roederer quotes him as saying in 1803, when he was First Consul: "Until I was sixteen I would have fought for Rousseau against the friends of Voltaire. Now it is the other way around." He especially liked *Zaïre,* which Voltaire himself considered his best play. He seemed to have preferred Corneille to Racine, and one evening said: "Gentlemen, had he lived in my time I would have made him a prince."

His library was fairly well stocked and became increasingly so as fresh shipments arrived from England. He lacked, however, reference works and documents he needed for the writing of his memoirs. This was a constant source of irritation to him. He had brought with him some six hundred volumes from the libraries at the Trianon and Malmaison, and when the *Northumberland* stopped at Madeira had had Bertrand send a long list of books to the British government with the request that they be sent to him. Some thirteen cases of books arrived in June, 1816, and he was so delighted that he helped to unpack them. But he was indignant when the British government sent him a bill for £1,396, which he claimed was about double what they must have cost and which he refused to pay. Most of the books he received after that were sent him by Lady Holland, wife of the Whig leader. Between June, 1817, and March, 1821, she sent six shipments, the last arriving after his death.

He was not allowed to subscribe to any newspaper or magazine, English or French, but while Cockburn was in command he sent him what newspapers he received, often before he had read them himself. Nor did it matter to him whether it was *The Times,* that supported the government, or the *Morning Chronicle,* that opposed it. The papers were usually three months old, but Napoleon read them avidly. They were his principal—and, when he ceased to receive visitors, his only—contact with a world in which he had played a stellar part, but which now was forever lost to him. Las Cases had not succeeded in getting him to speak more than a few English sentences intelligibly, but he was able to read English newspapers with the aid of a dictionary. After the arrival of Lowe it was a great privation to him to receive, as he said in a letter of protest, "only occasionally a few copies of *The Times.*" This was an exaggeration, for Lowe did sometimes send him other papers, including files of the *Journal des Débats.* That, however, after Lowe's arrival, the reading matter was censored there can be no doubt.[2]

SIX

One day, at the beginning of February, 1816, the Emperor and Las Cases were walking in the garden when newspapers arrived from Jamestown. Napoleon ordered that they be brought to him and he and the chamberlain sat down in the marquee where Las Cases proceeded to translate the contents to him. There was a dispatch from Vienna which told how Murat, Napoleon's brother-in-law, wishing to imitate his return from Elba, had landed in Calabria with a handful of soldiers in the hope of regaining his kingdom. He had been seized and shot. Las Cases translated the dispatch. There was a silence, then the Emperor said: "The Calabrians were more humane than those who sent me here." The chamberlain waited, but Napoleon said nothing more and he went on with the reading.

In March the news arrived that Ney and Labédoyère had died before a firing squad. He had said once that he would give all the gold in his coffers for another general like Ney—"bravest of the brave!" Labédoyère, a scion of the old nobility, had died out of devotion to him. Both had been with him at Waterloo. Commenting on their execution he remarked that the King could not have pardoned Labédoyère without laying himself open to the charge of discriminating in favor of the old aristocracy, but that clemency to Ney would have been of advantage to him. If he was moved by the death of the two men he did not show it. But he often spoke about them and about Murat, who had betrayed him in 1814.

SEVEN

At five in the evening Napoleon's followers assembled in the candlelit drawing room—the gentlemen in uniform, the ladies in low-necked evening gowns. None ventured to sit down until

[2] Lowe's apologists have denied this. He himself admits it in a letter to Lady Holland, March 5, 1821, and to Lord Bathurst, March 18, 1821.

the Emperor entered and bade the ladies be seated. The men remained standing, unless cards were played.

At St. Helena piquet and reversi were Napoleon's favorite games. Madame Junot has written that when as a young lieutenant he played cards at her mother's house he often cheated—not for the sake of the winnings, but because, among friends, he thought it a great joke. When the game was over he would return what he had won and tell his partners they were boobies not to have noticed that they were being fooled. If caught cheating he was not at all embarrassed but laughed heartily. He does not appear to have indulged this peculiar sense of humor at St. Helena. He proposed that all winnings be put in a common fund to buy the freedom of a slave. The proposal was accepted, but must have run afoul of the governor, for there is no record of any slave having been freed by the French.

At chess, when his opponent touched a piece, he insisted that it must be played, but himself did not obey the rule. His was not the temperament for chess. In a game resembling the maneuvering of armies he was impatient with rules made by another and became reckless. As he hated to lose, Bertrand and Montholon often permitted him to win when they could have beaten him. Gourgaud was not sufficient of a courtier to indulge him and often won. It was hard on his officers when he chose to play chess. No matter how long the game lasted, etiquette required that the onlookers remain standing.

At eight Cipriani would open the door to the dining room and announce: "His Majesty's dinner is served." Napoleon would rise, offer his arm to Madame Montholon, and proceed toward the dining room. The Bertrands, who after the quarrel about their irregular attendance dined at Longwood only on Sundays or on special occasions, would excuse themselves and depart. The others would follow in the Emperor's wake—first Montholon, then Gourgaud, finally Las Cases and his son. There had been considerable quarreling about precedence before this arrangement was finally agreed upon, and ill will concerning it never ceased.

The dining room was lit with wax candles in silver candelabra.

The table service was of silver. Liveried servants stood all about. Saint-Denis and Noverraz, erect behind the Emperor's chair, waited only on him. He would seat himself with his back toward the fireplace, with Madame Montholon on his right, Las Cases on his left. Opposite them sat Gourgaud, Montholon, and young Las Cases. Dinner consisted of soup, a *relevé,* two *entrées,* a roast, and two sweets. Dessert was served on exquisite Sèvres china, a gift from the city of Paris. Sir George Bingham thus described a dinner at Longwood:

"It was a most superb dinner which lasted only forty minutes, at the end of which we all retired into the drawing room to play cards. The dessert service was Sèvres china, with gold knives, forks, and spoons. The coffee cups were the most beautiful I ever saw; on each cup was an Egyptian view, and on the saucer a portrait of some Bey or other distinguished character. . . . The dinner was stupid enough; the people who lived with him scarcely spoke above a whisper; and he was so much engaged in eating that he hardly said a word to anyone. He had so filled the room with wax candles that it was as hot as an oven. He said to me after I had entered the drawingroom, 'You are not accustomed to such short dinners.'"

Yet forty minutes was about double the time Napoleon usually spent at dinner. It had been a saying in Paris that if you were invited to dine at the Tuileries, you had better dine at home first, since unless you bolted your food you would get up from the table hungry.

EIGHT

After dinner Napoleon and his suite returned to the drawing room. The gentlemen as well as the ladies were now permitted to seat themselves, and coffee was served. The Emperor might ask Madame Montholon to oblige with a song and she would sing a French ballad, accompanying herself on the piano. Her voice was thin, but not unpleasing. Sometimes they would play cards; at other times he would read to them a play of Corneille, Racine, Voltaire, Molière, Beaumarchais, Sophocles, or a novel —*Don Quichotte, Faublas, Manon Lescaut, Paul et Virginie.*

During the reading he often stopped to criticize or to analyze, asking the others to join in.

He read well. Cockburn's secretary Glover, who heard him read on the *Northumberland,* has said: "He reads distinctly, much slower than he speaks, and with good emphasis." Madame Montholon opined that he read with feeling but had no sense of rhythm, often lengthening or shortening a line and spoiling the meter. Proper names he frequently mispronounced. Once, when they asked him to read from the Bible, he said: "This is very edifying. It would never be believed in Europe." "He read to us from the book of Joshua," Las Cases has written, "observing at almost every town or village that he named: 'I encamped here; I carried that place by assault; I gave battle here.'" In winter the room was usually overheated, since Napoleon was susceptible to cold. This and the reading sometimes made one or another of the listeners drowsy. He was quick to notice when one began to nod and would say severely: "Gourgaud, wake up!" or "Madame Montholon, you are sleeping!" and for punishment would pass the book to the offender for further reading. After a few minutes he himself would begin to nod and on a couple of occasions fell fast asleep. No one dared leave the room until he had awakened.

Occasionally the evening would be spent in conversation. Napoleon's remarks to the ladies on such occasions, as recorded by Gourgaud, were not always in good taste and at times rude and inconsiderate. So, for example, he once remarked that "a woman likes nothing better than a good-looking young man," then, turning to Madame Montholon: "Isn't that right, Madame Montholon? You should know something about that. I have heard it said that you have had a good many adventures." The poor woman blushed, but he went on: "By the way, is it true that you have had three husbands—been divorced twice? I know you have been married to Monsieur Roger, and of course to Montholon, but who was the third?" She replied, on the verge of tears: "I can't imagine who invented the story that I have had a third husband." Once when Madame Bertrand had been somewhat neglectful of her toilette he told her that she looked like a washerwoman, and at another time remarked that she had no teeth. When, however, he was in the mood he could be quite complimentary, even excessively so. Thus one evening he said to Madame Montholon: "How beautiful you are!" and once, when Madame Bertrand looked her best, he embarrassed her with his attentions. Gourgaud writes: "The Emperor kissed Madame Bertrand and caressed her. He insisted that she be his partner at chess, although she knew nothing about the game. She sat down to play with him. Madame Montholon was almost bursting with jealousy."

In conversation with his officers he sometimes displayed a lack of reticence that justified the charge of vulgarity made against him. It should be considered that he was primarily a soldier, and it is understandable that in the company of army men his conversation should sometimes have smacked of the barrack room and the army camp. But he exceeded the bounds when in October, 1817, he sent for Gourgaud and in the presence of Marchand proceeded to entertain him with details of his first night with Marie Louise, assuring him that he had married a virgin—"The chambermaids saw the blood on the bedsheets in the morning." Then, turning to Marchand, who, he knew, had acquired a mulatto mistress named Esther: "Not like your Esther, who lost her maidenhead long before you knew her."

There were, however, evenings his followers must have remembered to the end of their days. Those were the times when he told them about his campaigns, about the sixty battles he had fought—about Marengo which gave him dominion over Italy, Ulm where a whole army was annihilated, Jena which delivered the Prussian monarchy into his hands, Friedland which opened the gate to the Russian empire, Wagram which decided the outcome of a war. He told them about the capitals he had entered victoriously, about Emperors and Kings who came to sue for peace, about his generals and his cabinet ministers, about his miraculous escapes from assassination. He told them about his aspirations—the founding of a great Empire of the East, a united Europe with Paris for its capital, his plan of joining the Mediterranean and the Red Sea by means of a canal. They listened entranced. It was like listening to Alexander or Cæsar tell about his exploits. The walls of the room seemed to dissolve. Space was filled with heroic images. Once, when he finished speaking, he sat for a while staring into space, then said: "After all, what a romance my life has been!" He glanced at the clock. It was long past midnight. "We have made a conquest of time," he said and retired to his rooms.

NINE

Relations between Napoleon and Admiral Cockburn had not improved after the move to Longwood. It did not take the Emperor long to discover that his first impression of Longwood had been far too favorable. Even Arthur Young, who views the location through rose-colored glasses, has written: "Rain falls at Hutt's Gate on two days out of three, and at Longwood nearly as often, probably four days in the week. In the winter there is misty sea fog and much cloudy weather. Even in summer there can never be any certainty of a rainless day." [3] When one considers that the argillacious soil made walking after a rain well-nigh impossible and riding far from pleasant, that in summer the plateau swarmed with mosquitoes, that there was virtually no shade, and that from the beginning poorly instructed sentries interfered with the movements of Napoleon and his followers in places where they had a right to go, one can well understand his growing dissatisfaction. Moreover, while at the beginning O'Meara had sufficed as an escort outside the limits, on the 18th of December the order was revoked and Poppleton's presence was made mandatory.

Two days after he had moved to Longwood, Napoleon advised his officers to complain about the admiral to the British government. Two days later when Cockburn came to pay his respects, accompanied by Colonel Skelton, Napoleon had a valet inform him that he was indisposed, at the same time instructing the servant to express to the colonel, but not to the admiral, his regret at being unable to receive him. On December 20, he told Montholon that the admiral was an "assassin" and

[3] *Op. cit.*

ordered him to write a vigorous protest. On December 24, he
again advised his followers to lodge a complaint with the government and forbade Gourgaud to accept an invitation to dinner
the admiral had sent him.

This prolonged outburst of ill temper made no sense. Cockburn was a reasonable man and an hour's conversation with him
would have remedied what grievances Napoleon had, as far as
it was in the admiral's power to remedy them. The Emperor
himself was later to admit this; when comparing Admiral Cockburn with Sir Hudson Lowe he said to Sir Pulteney Malcolm:
"On many accounts I had cause to complain of Sir George
Cockburn, but we never conversed together without coming to
a satisfactory understanding; but it is impossible to converse
with Sir Hudson. It was possible to live under the regulations established by Sir George, but now we are tortured to death by
pinpricks."

On December 21, Montholon wrote the letter of protest the
Emperor had ordered him to write. It was couched in offensive
terms and demanded that the limits beyond which the French
could not go without an escort be considerably extended—that
Napoleon be allowed to receive whom he pleased—that O'Meara
be authorized, as before, to serve as escort outside the limits—
that a different habitation in a more pleasant and more salubri-
ous part of the island be provided for the Emperor and his following.

Cockburn, in his reply, rebuked Montholon for the tenor of
his epistle and conceded nothing, which, considering the tone of
the letter, might have been expected. However, when more than
a week had passed, he decided to call on Napoleon and talk
things over. On December 30, he called and after some prelimi-
naries was admitted.

Lord Keith in reply to the question of what objection there
could be to Napoleon being allowed to have a personal interview with the Prince Regent had said: "That would never do! In
half an hour they would be the best of friends." During his interview with Admiral Cockburn Napoleon did not get all his demands satisfied, but he got a great deal. The limits were to be

somewhat extended. O'Meara was not to be authorized to serve as escort outside the limits, but Poppleton, when serving as escort to Napoleon, was to be dressed in mufti and to remain at some thirty or forty paces behind him. Bertrand was to be given the right to issue a pass to anyone Napoleon cared to receive. Montholon having complained that since the Emperor's firearms had been taken from him he was deprived of the pleasures of the hunt, they were returned.

TEN

On January 3, Governor Wilks gave a party at Plantation House to which some thirty people, including Napoleon and his suite, were invited. The Emperor considered it his duty to ignore the invitation, as it was addressed to "General Bonaparte," but he urged his suite to attend. He decided to make an excursion that day to Sandy Bay, considered the most beautiful spot on the island. When on the morning of the 3rd of January he went to the stables, he was surprised to find there not the orderly officer but the admiral waiting for him. Cockburn explained that having learned over the semaphore of Napoleon's intention he had come to accompany him. It was a courteous gesture. After the ride, which the Emperor greatly enjoyed, he invited the admiral for dinner on January 5, when Major and Mrs. Hodson, and Major Fehrzen were likewise to be his guests.

The dinner and the subsequent gathering in the drawing room, where coffee was served, were a great success. The previous day Napoleon had told Gourgaud that during the ride he had "conquered" the admiral. And, indeed, as they sat together on the sofa chatting they seemed to be on the best of terms. They discussed the relative strength of various fortified towns, and Cockburn asked the Emperor if it was true that he had at one time contemplated an attack on Gibraltar. Napoleon laughed and said: "Oh, no! Except as an object of national pride the place is of no value to you, and its possession earns you the enmity of the Spaniards. Why should I have wanted to disturb such an admirable arrangement?" The admiral told Napoleon that the 66th regiment was coming soon to re-enforce the 53rd, and Napoleon laughed again and asked if he did not think he had enough soldiers to keep him from escaping. Did he not think an additional seventy-four would be more useful? Time passed quickly and when the guests had departed Napoleon was in the best of humor. He pinched Gourgaud's ear and told him that he could do what he liked with the admiral.

The following day the Emperor, accompanied by Bertrand and Gourgaud, went for a ride outside the limits, in the direction of Sandy Bay. Captain Poppleton, in mufti, followed at a distance, looking more like a groom than like an army officer. They visited several cottages and finally crossed a ditch at the bottom of the valley. Here Napoleon called to Bertrand: "Tell Poppleton not to follow so close." Bertrand relayed the message, and the obliging captain reined in his horse, while the Emperor and Gourgaud rounded a hill. They had no sooner done so than Napoleon cried: "Gourgaud, at a gallop!" and gave his horse the spurs. They galloped down a side road by which Cockburn had taken the Emperor to Sandy Bay and did not stop until they reached a villa named Rock Rose Hill. Here, with the permission of its owner, a widow, they walked about the garden. "We rounded a hillock," Gourgaud has written, "and discovered two valleys giving out upon the sea. The Emperor told me not to tell anyone where he had been and had me give a napoleon to the gardener and to a slave." They were back at Longwood at seven in the evening.

In the meantime Poppleton had galloped up one road and down another looking for the fugitives. He finally semaphored, "General Bonaparte is missing," and went in search of the admiral. He found him at The Briars, where a party was in progress. Bingham and several officers were there and the news created some excitement. Cockburn remained calm. "It's nothing," he said. "There is no danger. But it is a lesson."

Three days later Napoleon decided to go on another ride outside the limits. Gourgaud was to accompany him. Horses were saddled. The Emperor had his foot in the stirrup when Gourgaud came running and told him that Poppleton had said he could no longer follow at a distance but must remain close to

Napoleon. The Emperor, furious, took his foot out of the stirrup and ordered the horses unsaddled. He said the admiral had broken faith with him—had gone back on his word. He retired to his rooms and did not appear for dinner.

ELEVEN

Did Napoleon's escapade have any significance? Was it in any way connected with a plan of escape, as claimed by some? There is every reason to believe that it was not, that it was like his cheating at cards—a prank. There was a good deal of the prankster about him. Some years later, when a young Corsican priest was sent by Cardinal Fesch to keep him company, he had him dress up in a green coat and a planters' hat he often wore in the garden and gallop away, to the consternation of the orderly officer.

Napoleon was aware from the beginning that escape from the island was impossible. Referring to Sir Hudson Lowe's pathological fear that he might escape he was to say: "If I had really any intention of effecting my escape, instead of quarreling with the governor I would caress and flatter him, endeavor to be on the best of terms with him, and try to make him believe I was contented, and thereby lull him to sleep."

This does not mean that he had given up hope of leaving St. Helena. He cherished that hope to the end, *and it was a powerful deterrent against any attempt at escape.* He hoped that the Tories would be overthrown and Lord Holland or some other Whig leader favorable to him would become prime minister. He hoped that the Prince Regent—that "fat Adonis of fifty," as Leigh Hunt called him—might die and Princess Charlotte, an ardent admirer of his, might ascend the throne. He hoped that when the armed forces of the coalition were withdrawn from France, there would be a popular uprising and the Bourbons would have to flee. Lord Holland or Princess Charlotte might permit him to live in England or if not that, on an island in the Mediterranean. If Louis was forced to flee, either he or his son might be called to the throne. Had not, in 1814, at Châtillon, the coalition been willing to leave him on the throne of France if he would agree to their terms? He had no intention of jeopardizing these possibilities by foolhardy attempts at escape. Indeed, even without these hopes it is doubtful if he would have tried to escape had an opportunity offered. Gourgaud, after quarreling with him, told Baron Stürmer, the Austrian commissioner at St. Helena: "However miserable he may be here he secretly enjoys the importance attached to his detention, the interest taken in it by all the Powers of Europe, the care with which his smallest remarks are reported, and so on. He has many times said to us, 'I can no longer live as a private person; I prefer being a prisoner here to living in the United States.'" Montholon has given similar testimony. He quotes Napoleon as saying: "I should not be six months in America without being assassinated by an agent of the Comte d'Artois. . . . I see in America nothing but assassination or oblivion. I prefer St. Helena."

It was oblivion he feared most. A Prometheus on a rock in the Atlantic, guarded by infantry, artillery, and a squadron, he was still a world-figure. It was a finale not unworthy of such a career as his. His sense of the dramatic, of the fitness of things, told him that to live as a fugitive in America was not for him.

Napoleon's escapade terminated, however, the friendly relationship so recently re-established between him and Admiral Cockburn. He decided to complain about him to the Prince Regent. On March 13, 1816, Bertrand wrote to the admiral asking if he would forward a sealed letter from the Emperor to the Prince. Cockburn prefaced his reply with the puerile remark he had made once before in a letter to Bertrand that he had "no knowledge of the person designated by you 'the Emperor,' there being no person on this island I consider entitled to such dignity." He then called attention to an enclosed copy of his instructions, requiring such communications to be left open, so the governor and admiral "may be enabled to accompany it with such observations as they may think expedient." He received an acrimonious protest from the marshal, one sentence of which read: "Nothing, certainly, that is unjust, or contrary to the rights of man and the custom of civilized nations, can surprise the Emperor on the part of those who have violated in his person the rights of hospitality—rights held sacred even among barbarians."

On April 14, 1816, the new governor, Sir Hudson Lowe, arrived at St. Helena.

3

XI. Sir Hudson Lowe

Sir Hudson Lowe was born in Galway, Ireland, July 28, 1769. His father was an English army surgeon attached to the 50th regiment. At an early age he was taken by his parents to the island of St. Vincent in the West Indies, to which the 50th had been transferred and where his mother and sister died. Eventually the regiment returned to Salisbury, where he attended grammar school. When the 50th was sent to Gibraltar his father took him along. In 1787, at the age of eighteen, he was appointed ensign in the regiment. He had a talent for languages and studied French, Italian, and Spanish. He was a lieutenant of twenty-three when he took a leave of absence, traveled in Italy, and studied for several months at Pisa, improving his knowledge of Italian, which he learned to speak fluently.

In 1794, we find him with the regiment at Ajaccio, Corsica. Two years later, as a result of Napoleon's victories in Italy, the British evacuated Corsica, and the regiment was sent to Elba. The previous year Lowe had been promoted to captain and appointed deputy judge advocate. From Elba the peripatetic regiment was sent to Portugal, where it remained two years, giving Lowe the opportunity to learn Portuguese. It was then transferred to the island of Minorca where many Corsicans who had been in the service of the British had taken refuge. The English commandant of the island had organized some two hundred of the refugees into a corps known as the Corsican Rangers, and owing to his knowledge of Italian, Lowe was appointed commander of the corps.

The following year the Corsican Rangers were sent to Gibraltar to join an expedition to Egypt. Lowe was given the "temporary" rank of major. He does not appear to have particularly distinguished himself, but did well enough to obtain confirmation of his "temporary" rank. From Egypt the Corsican Rangers were sent to Malta, and in 1802, when the treaty of Amiens terminated the second coalition war, the corps was disbanded and Lowe was put on half pay.

With the renewal of the war he was appointed to the 7th Fusilliers, and in July, 1803, was sent on a secret mission to Portugal to ascertain if the frontiers of that country could be successfully defended against the French. He was next entrusted with the task of raising a force to be known as Royal Corsican Rangers. He managed to enlist about seven hundred men, the majority of whom were Corsicans, and was appointed commander of the corps with the rank of lieutenant colonel. The corps took part in an unsuccessful attack on Naples and retired to Sicily.

TWO

In 1806, the British captured the island of Capri. Lowe had nothing to do with the capture, but was appointed governor of the island, his first independent command. It was part of his duty to obtain all the information he could concerning happenings on the mainland, for which he employed a couple of spies. One of these was Cipriani Franceschi, Napoleon's future major domo at St. Helena. Cipriani did not come into personal contact with Lowe while in his service and was known to him by another name, hence Lowe never discovered that one of Napoleon's domestics at St. Helena was his former agent. Cipriani has revealed that he and his colleague Suzzarelli had actually been in the service of France, and that it was their assignment to lead Lowe by the nose by furnishing him false reports while gathering information about the situation at Capri.

In October, 1808, the French decided to make an attempt to

recapture the island, which had been strongly fortified by the British. Its garrison consisted of five companies of Royal Corsican Rangers, a Maltese regiment, and a detachment of artillery —1,400 men in all. Lowe has claimed that the French general Lamarque had 3,000 men, which, considering the strength of the British position, could hardly have been called excessive. French historians insist, however, that Lamarque's force did not exceed 1,600 men, and that Lowe had at least as many since he had called into service the local militia he had equipped and trained.

Lamarque's assault on the Marina Grande, defended by the Royal Corsican Rangers, was repulsed. He then made a landing at Anacapri, defended by the Maltese, and won a sweeping victory. Most of the Maltese surrendered. Lowe, with about eight hundred men, held out for thirteen days behind the fortifications of the town of Capri before accepting the terms of surrender offered him: he was to embark with the remainder of his force on the British squadron that had arrived with re-enforcements, leaving all war material and supplies in the hands of the French. According to the French version, the British squadron had already disembarked four hundred men and debarkation of eight hundred more was awaiting favorable weather when Lowe decided to quit. Nevertheless, Norwood Young has written: "There was no suggestion at the time that Lowe's conduct had been other than highly creditable to himself and the British army. . . . The attack upon him . . . was retrospective; it was an emanation from the foul gases of O'Meara and Las Cases." [1]

If the term "British army" applies also to the Maltese, then it can hardly be said that its performance was "highly creditable." Nor is it true that "at the time" there was no criticism of Lowe. Lowe's foremost champion, William Forsyth, has admitted that the Capri fiasco well-nigh terminated his military career. He has written: "Sometime after Colonel Lowe arrived in Sicily he felt annoyed that his official report of the fall of Capri was not published in the 'London Gazette,' and, thinking that his professional reputation was at stake, he applied for leave to go to England to vindicate himself from any imputation that might

[1] *Op. cit.*

be attached to his character, for the loss of the place. Indeed, at the time, owing to this circumstance and the unpleasant deportment of [Lieutenant General] Sir John Stuart toward him, he seriously contemplated retiring from the army."

Equally questionable is the statement that "the attack upon him . . . was an emanation from the foul gases of O'Meara and Las Cases." It appears highly improbable that the English general and historian Sir William Francis Patrick Napier allowed himself to be influenced by O'Meara and Las Cases when he pronounced the following judgment on Lowe's defense of Capri in his *History of the Peninsular War:* "Sir Hudson Lowe first became known in history by losing in a few days a post that, without any pretensions to celebrity, might have been defended for as many years." It appears probable that after the Capri affair Lowe was saved from disgrace by his knowledge of languages. A military man who spoke French, Italian, Spanish, and Portuguese was invaluable in the Mediterranean at that period.

THREE

In 1809, Hudson Lowe and his Royal Corsican Rangers took part in an expedition against Ionian islands occupied by Albanians in the service of France. After their capture Lowe was appointed—on the recommendation of General Oswald, commander of the expedition—governor of two of the islands. Considering his performance at Capri the general must have felt confident that the islands were safe from attack.

In 1812, Lowe was promoted to full colonel. When one considers that he did not reach that rank until he was over forty-two and had behind him twenty-four years of service, during eighteen of which England had been almost constantly at war, it is obvious that military authorities could not have regarded his war record as particularly brilliant.

Shortly after receiving his promotion he went to England on leave and remained unemployed for over a year, which in time of war would hardly have been the case had he been an officer of recognized merit. In January, 1813, he was summoned by Lord Bathurst. The secretary of state for war wished him to inspect the Russo-German Legion, formed by order of Czar Alexander of soldiers from the Rhineland who had deserted or been taken prisoner during Napoleon's invasion of Russia. The British government was financing the Legion and wished to assure itself of its fitness for service. Bernadotte, Napoleon's former marshal —who having been adopted by the Swedish King had become Crown Prince of Sweden—was expected to command the Legion, and Lowe's first assignment was to accompany General Hope to Stockholm for a conference with the prince.

At Stockholm Lowe was presented to the King, the Queen, the Crown Prince, and met the celebrated Madame de Staël. He then journeyed to Kalish, in Poland, where Czar Alexander had his military headquarters, and reported to Lord Cathcart, the British ambassador, who got him an audience with the Czar. When he finally went on his tour of inspection he had the opportunity to witness the battle of Bautzen, during which, with the aid of a field telescope, he got his first glimpse of Napoleon.

Lowe remained with the allied army throughout the armistice, then was sent to the mouth of the Elbe to inspect other German levies in the pay of the British. Thereafter he joined Field Marshal Blücher at his headquarters, first as unofficial observer, then as British liaison officer. He was with the field marshal throughout the campaign in Germany and in France, until Napoleon's first abdication. He has been credited by his apologists with a large part of the responsibility for Napoleon's fall in 1814. The claim is not altogether without validity, but unfortunately for his military reputation this was due not to the wisdom but to the stupidity of his advice. Peace negotiations between Napoleon and the allies were then in progress at Châtillon. Napoleon had been prevailed upon to agree to give up Belgium, the left bank of the Rhine, and Piedmont. Preliminary articles of peace had been drawn up and signed. Caulaincourt, who represented Napoleon, sent the document to him for his approval. But the Emperor had changed his mind and decided to hold out for better terms. For this Lowe was partly responsible. He had urged Blücher to march upon Paris without waiting for a junction with the Austrian and Russian armies. The old field marshal, reckless by nature, had taken his advice and crossed the Marne. The English historian John Gibson Lockhart has written: "The blunder was great, yet in the end its consequences were disastrous, not to those who committed, but to him whose eagle eye detected it, and who could not resist the temptation which it presented to make one warlike effort more." Blücher was defeated and suffered such great loss of men and equipment that Napoleon decided to fight on. The decision cost him his throne.

Nevertheless Lowe's post as liaison officer with the Prussian army paid off handsomely. He had sung the praises of Blücher and his chief of staff Gneisenau so consistently in his reports that when Napoleon abdicated at Fontainebleau, they made it possible for him to reach London with news of the abdication ahead of any other messenger. The Prince Regent, to whom he delivered the message, was so pleased that he knighted him and had him promoted to major general.

FOUR

In the summer of 1814, Lowe was appointed quartermaster general to the British troops in the Low Countries under the command of the Prince of Orange. He still held that post when Napoleon returned from Elba. When in April, 1815, the Duke of Wellington came to take charge of the Anglo-Allied army, it was not long before Lowe got on his nerves. His punctiliousness, his hesitancy, his frequent changes of mind, his inability to reach a decision without first checking the remotest risk were more than he could stand. Once, on horseback and accompanied by several members of his staff, he asked Lowe: "Where does this road lead to, Sir Hudson?" Lowe produced a map from his pocket, unfolded it, and proceeded to scan it carefully. The duke waited, got tired of waiting, muttered between his teeth, but loud enough for one of his officers to hear, "Damned fool!" and galloped away. Soon afterward he asked that Lowe be transferred.

Lowe was transferred to Genoa, where he arrived the day before the battle of Waterloo. On July 2, Lord Exmouth's squadron appeared before the city, and Lowe embarked for Marseilles with his troops. Napoleon had abdicated, and the garrisons at

Marseilles and Toulon for the second time recognized Louis XVIII as King of France. One cannot help wondering what sort of showing Lowe would have made had the garrisons resisted. He probably would have spent weeks in preparation, changed his mind several times, and have deluged the war office with lengthy reports. It is doubtful if there ever was a military commander who combined such a minimum of achievement with such voluminous paper work. His letters, orders, and reports have been preserved in no less than 240 bulky volumes.

Such had been the military career of Sir Hudson Lowe when on August 1, 1815, he received notice that he had been appointed to take charge of Napoleon at St. Helena. John Gibson Lockhart, in his *Life of Napoleon*, has said with a touch of irony that Lowe's "antecedents were not splendid."

FIVE

The letter notifying Lowe of his appointment summoned him to London. He departed immediately, making a stopover in Paris, where many notables were assembled—the Duke of Wellington, Lord Castlereagh, Field Marshal Blücher, Prince Metternich, Count Pozzo di Borgo, and others. He had received instructions to wait upon Wellington and Castlereagh. It has been claimed that he had received the appointment to compensate him for the snub inflicted upon him by Wellington in Belgium in demanding that he be transferred. Proof of this is lacking. It is certain, however, that had the duke been consulted Lowe would not have been appointed. Lord Stanhope, in his *Notes of Conversations with the Duke of Wellington*, has written: "The duke said that he thought the government had been mistaken in removing the old East India Company governor, Colonel Wilks. He was a very intelligent, well-read man, and knew everything that had been passing in Europe, and Napoleon had become really attached to him." As for Lowe, the duke had a very poor opinion of him. He told Stanhope on one occasion: "Sir Hudson Lowe was a very bad choice. He was a man wanting in education and judgment"; and on another: "I knew him very well. He was a stupid man. He was not an ill-natured

135

man. But he knew nothing at all of the world, and like all men who know nothing of the world, he was suspicious and jealous."

Lowe's interview with Lord Castlereagh gives us a clue to his bizarre behavior at St. Helena. The secretary of foreign affairs asked him if he thought it possible for Bonaparte to escape from the island. Lowe has written: "I told him at once that I saw no chance of it [other] than that which might result from exciting a mutiny or disaffection amongst the troops, recollecting two instances of formidable mutinies having occurred at St. Helena, in which several lives were lost, and in both of which the governor had very narrowly escaped with his life." Considering the composition of the garrison destined for the island, he believed the danger of mutiny "proportionally diminished, although attempts to tamper with the officers and men I thought it very likely might be made."

It can therefore not be too strongly emphasized that Lowe's fear of Napoleon's escape was essentially a fear that he might incite a mutiny.

Soon after his arrival in London, Lowe received confirmation of his appointment from the East India Company at an annual salary of £12,000. Numerous perquisites of the office more than doubled his salary. The governor's residence, Plantation House, with its grounds and appurtenances was cared for by sixty slaves maintained by the Company. The high cost of living on the island would affect him but little, as the property had its own fruit and vegetable gardens and pasturage for horses and cattle. The government granted him the "local" rank of lieutenant general, which, while far from equivalent to the "army" rank, would heighten his prestige. On September 12, Lord Bathurst gave him his instructions, which read, in part: "You will observe that the desire of His Majesty's government is to allow every indulgence to General Bonaparte which may be compatible with the entire security of his person: that he should not by any means escape, or hold communication with any person whatever (excepting through your agency), must be your unremitted care; and these points being made sure, every resource and amusement which may serve to reconcile Bonaparte to his confinement may be permitted." The instructions contained the following provision, which left considerable leeway for leniency as well as severity in the hands of the governor: "Many things, however, must be determined by local circumstances."

Arrangements for the departure of Lowe and his staff were not completed until the end of January, 1816, and in the meantime he did some courting. On December 31, he married the charming Susan Johnson, widow of Colonel William Johnson and sister of Colonel Sir William Howe de Lancey who had taken Lowe's place as quartermaster general with Wellington's army and had been killed by a cannon ball during the battle of Waterloo. Mrs. Johnson had two daughters, Charlotte and Susanna, both in their early teens. On January 23, another honor was conferred upon Lowe—he was appointed knight commander of the bath. Finally, on January 29, accompanied by his family and a staff of six, the governor sailed for St. Helena in the frigate *Phaëton*.

SIX

In May, 1820, when Lowe had been governor of St. Helena for four years, Montholon offered to send some beans, grown in the vegetable garden at Longwood, to the French commissioner, the Marquis de Montchenu—the old royalist who still wore his hair in a cue in fond memory of the *ancien régime*. Montholon asked the commissioner whether he preferred white beans (*haricots blancs*) or green beans (*haricots verts*). The marquis replied that he might send some of both. As Lowe insisted that all communications between Longwood and anyone on the island must pass through his hands, he learned about the offer and its acceptance. His suspicion was immediately aroused. He wrote to Lord Bathurst: "Whether the '*haricots blancs*' and '*haricots verts*' bear any reference to the '*drapeau blanc*' of the Bourbons, and the '*habit vert*' of General Bonaparte himself, and the livery of his servants at Longwood, I am unable to say: but the Marquis de Montchenu, it appears to me, would have acted with more propriety if he had declined receiving either, or limited himself to a demand for the white alone."

Lord Bathurst's reaction to this remarkable state paper is not known, but one feels reasonably sure that had the Duke of Wellington been in his place he would again have muttered, "Damned fool!"

The affair of the beans—which Lowe considered so important that he wrote about it a second time to the war office—was only one of many which have made one of Lowe's critics suspect that his fear that Napoleon might escape affected his sanity. Here are three more of a similar nature:

Count Balmain, the Russian commissioner on the island, wrote a letter to Lowe in which he said: "I am as independent upon this rock as you are." "Upon this rock"—where had Lowe heard that before? He remembered! Three years earlier Count Montholon had used the phrase in a letter of protest (undoubtedly dictated by Bonaparte) which had become public and had made quite a stir. Balmain must be quoting from the letter! Proof positive that he is in sympathy with Bonaparte! Lowe immediately communicated his astute deduction to Bathurst and told Montchenu that his fellow-commissioner was a Bonapartist!

Montchenu, however, became just as suspect. Not only had he accepted a gift of beans from a member of the prisoner's suite the color of Napoleon's hunting jacket and of his servants' livery, but speaking one day to the governor about the prisoner, he referred to him, not as "General Bonaparte," but as "Napoleon"! Lowe, greatly disturbed, unbosomed himself to Bathurst in this fashion: "I am not without some doubts of a certain degree of combination between him [Bonaparte], or his followers, and the Marquis de Montchenu, whose language in the last two conversations he had with me appeared most extraordinary. . . . I never heard him pronounce the name 'Napoleon' with such emphasis; he formerly used to call him only 'Bonaparte.'"

Napoleon's valet Marchand had made a sketch of Longwood House and grounds. In front of the house he had sketched in the figures of Napoleon, Bertrand, Montholon, and O'Meara. He had presented the sketch to Madame Bertrand, who had had it framed and hung in her living room. Captain Lutyens, orderly officer at Longwood from February 10, 1820, to April 26, 1821, paid a visit to the Bertrands and looked at the sketch. He had never known O'Meara, who had quarreled with Lowe and had left the island eight months before the arrival of the regiment to which the captain belonged. So Madame Bertrand remarked to him: "The figure in the foreground is O'Meara." An innocent remark, you will say, and a natural one under the circumstances. Not when there was a Lowe around to fathom its hidden meaning. He questioned everyone who came in contact with the inhabitants of Longwood. No sooner had Lutyens mentioned the name of O'Meara than the sinister meaning of the sketch became clear to him. He wrote to Bathurst: "The picture is meant to serve as a kind of *touchstone* to judge the disposition of occasional visitors."

The absurdity of this is all the more apparent when one considers that Lowe was keeping a record of visitors at Longwood, hence knew that since April 2, 1819—ten months before Lutyens became orderly officer—there had not been a single visitor. There was to be none after that date until Napoleon's death.

SEVEN

It was the opinion of Dr. Alexander Baxter, deputy inspector of hospitals at St. Helena and Lowe's personal physician, that Lowe was suffering from what in modern times is known as an "anxiety neurosis." On July 18, 1816, three months after Lowe's arrival on the island, he made the significant statement to Marshal Bertrand that he considered Sir Hudson "unsuited" for the post he occupied, as he was too "agitated"; that although knowing how difficult it would be for Napoleon to escape, he yet "trembled"; that his "fear" was such as to drive him to the adoption of all sorts of measures to prevent the dreaded escape, but that all this failed to "tranquilize" him. He added that Lady Lowe had asked him to express her regret at her inability to visit Madame Bertrand; that she wanted the French to know that she was in no way responsible for the measures the governor was taking, and regretted them very much, considering them too severe.[2]

Dr. Baxter's opinion fully accords with that of Count Balmain, the Russian commissioner on the island, of whom Lowe's champion Norwood Young has written: "Balmain was a man of ability, tact, and good sense. He had also a quality which was very precious and singularly rare at St. Helena, a sense of humor."[3] On May 1, 1817, the commissioner reported to his government: "The responsibility with which he [Lowe] has been entrusted makes him tremble. He becomes alarmed at the slightest incident, puzzles his brain for hours about nothing, and does with an immense expenditure of energy what another would accomplish in a minute. If asked a question about Bonaparte his forehead wrinkles with suspicion. He believes one is trying to entrap him and gives an evasive reply. He never expresses himself clearly and logically, so that listening to him one becomes confused. He is quick to anger, and if one attempts to reason with him or contradicts him in any way, he loses his head and no longer knows what he is saying. To do business with him and to feel relaxed and at one's ease is an impossibility."

On October 1, 1817, he wrote: "He is killing his people by inches. His is a weak, stubborn mentality which becomes frightened at almost nothing."[4]

Lowe had the infantile habit of putting his forefinger in a corner of his mouth and sucking it when he felt perplexed, which may or may not have had psychological significance.

[2] Bertrand's journal, like Gourgaud's, was not written for publication. He was so fearful lest anybody might read it that he wrote it in cipher. It was not brought to light until the autumn of 1946, through the efforts of Paul Fleuriot de Langle, who spent years deciphering it. Two volumes have thus far been published by Flammarion, Paris, 1951, under the title *Calhiers de Sainte-Hélène*. The part dealing with Napoleon's last illness and death (January-May, 1821) was published in an English translation by Doubleday & Company, Inc. Copyright, 1952.

[3] *Op. cit.*

[4] *Le Prisonnier de Sainte-Hélène.* D'Après les rapports officiels du Commissaire du Gouvernement Russe. Revue Bleue du 8 mai au 12 juin, 1897. Abridged English translation: *Napoleon in Captivity: The Reports of Count Balmain,* 1927.

EIGHT

Sir Hudson was acutely conscious of his lack of ability to inspire a feeling of personal loyalty in those he commanded. His very appearance and manner were against him. Count Balmain speaks of his "cold suspicious nature and repulsive exterior." Thomas Henry Brooke, secretary of the council of St. Helena, in an attempt to get Bertrand to take a more favorable view of the governor, told him that while Lowe's appearance was "repulsive," he "improved on acquaintance." One of Lowe's most ardent defenders, the assistant army surgeon Walter Henry, concedes that "his countenance is unpleasing." His foremost champion, William Forsyth, has written: "We admit that his manner was not attractive." The fact is that most people far from being attracted felt repelled by him.

Napoleon on the other hand had that indescribable something called personality, the fascination of which even his enemies found difficult to resist. The *Morning Chronicle*, in its issue of July 25, 1815, had reported: "All 'hostility' vanished the moment the Emperor set foot on the English ship, and one and all fell under the charm of his manner. A note of wonder runs through the countless depositions to that effect." The Marquis de Montchenu reported to his government that the crew of the *Northumberland*—still at St. Helena at the time of his arrival—sympathized with Bonaparte, and that one of the ship's officers had said to his secretary: "He is a fine man, an excellent man, and does not deserve the fate that has befallen him." The marquis was to tell Lowe that if he were governor he would not permit any traveler to visit Bonaparte. "All who go to Longwood," he said, "return wildly enthusiastic about him. They carry that feeling with them to Europe, which is hardly to our advantage." It was to be reported to Lowe that a workingman at Jamestown, after reading one of his proclamations concerning the prisoner, had remarked: "Damn me if I would mind giving five pounds to assist in getting him off!"

What weapon had a man like Lowe against a man like Napoleon? None except to keep him as isolated as possible. That, if given the freedom of the island, Napoleon *could* have incited a rebellion is possible; that he *would* have done so is highly improbable. To enable him to escape, a mutiny would have had to involve the squadron as well as the garrison. This would have been too much of a feat to accomplish, even for him. Moreover, he had put his faith in a change of government in England and did not want oblivion in America. Had Lowe been a man sure of himself he would not have feared a mutiny. Wellington, or someone like him, would not have feared it. Lord Stanhope has reported that the duke said to him: "If I had been Lord Bathurst, I would have adopted a different plan for his confinement. There are only very few landing-places along the coast of St. Helena.[5] These I would have strictly guarded, and insisted upon his showing himself to an English officer every night and morning, and then for the rest of the time I would have let him do [whatever] or go wherever he pleased. This would have avoided most matters of dispute, and then he might have received and sent as many letters as he chose." [6]

[5] Wellington had visited St. Helena in 1805 and had inspected its defenses.

[6] When Hon. Creevey, former whip of the Whig party in Parliament, asked Wellington in 1818 what he thought of Sir Hudson Lowe, and of the means employed by the government to insure the safekeeping of Napoleon at St. Helena, the duke replied: "As for the means of keeping him there, there never was anything so damned absurd. I know the island of St. Helena well. . . . As for Lowe, he is a damned fool."

XII. The Emperor and the New Governor

When Napoleon heard about the expected arrival of the new governor he was not displeased. The breach between him and Admiral Cockburn had not healed. Moreover, since an article in the *Morning Chronicle* had severely criticised the government for its lack of generosity toward him, might it not be that the new governor had instructions to give him greater freedom? He had heard that Sir Hudson had been received by the Czar, by the King of Sweden, and by the Prince Regent; hence he would undoubtedly know how to conduct himself in the presence of a man like Napoleon. He would not sit down without being invited to do so, as the admiral had done, or indulge in other familiarities. When on the morning of April 14, Sir George Bingham came to inform him that the *Phaëton* had been sighted and would probably be in port that day, he said: "I am glad of it; I am tired of the admiral, and there are many things I should like to talk over with Sir Hudson Lowe; he is a soldier and has served; he was with Blücher; besides, he commanded a Corsican regiment, and must know many of my friends and acquaintances."

Had he been able to read a letter Sir Hudson wrote concerning him on January 13, 1816, to Sir Henry Bunbury, under-secretary of state, he would have thought differently. In the letter we read: "A law declaring it felony in any person whatever even to hold communication with him or with the persons of his adherents, except with the authority of the government, would appear to me as a necessary check. In respect to such a person as Napoleon Bonaparte, even the weakness, the ignorance, or the compassion of the persons around him require the strongest checks which prohibitory laws can order."

The *Phaëton* dropped anchor at Jamestown in the evening of April 14, but the governor, his family, and his suite did not disembark until the following morning. Soon after, a message was sent by aerial telegraph to the orderly officer at Longwood inquiring at what hour the following day it would be convenient for General Bonaparte to receive the governor, who would be accompanied by the admiral and by two members of his staff. Captain Poppleton, instead of replying that he would have to consult Marshal Bertrand, took it upon himself to semaphore that he believed nine o'clock in the forenoon, when Bonaparte returned from his usual morning ride, or four o'clock in the afternoon would be suitable. He received the reply that the governor and his party would arrive at Longwood at nine the following morning.

Now, since his arrival at Longwood, Napoleon had never received visitors in the morning. When informed by Bertrand at what hour the visit was to take place, he was furious. When the grand marshal later informed him that he had learned from Captain Poppleton that the admiral would accompany the governor for the purpose of introducing him, he exclaimed: "I wasn't told that! If the admiral comes I will receive nobody!" He later told Dr. O'Meara: "He [the admiral] wished to embroil me with the governor, and for that purpose persuaded him to come up here at nine o'clock in the morning, though he well knew that I never received any persons, nor ever would, at that hour."

The visitors arrived in the morning of April 16, in a driving rain. Napoleon had not gone out riding. He was in his study, in his dressing gown, peering through the opening in the Venetian blind. Montholon, Las Cases, and Gourgaud received the visitors in the billiard-room, and Montholon informed the governor that His Majesty was indisposed and could not receive him. Las Cases has written that the admiral was "quite triumphant" and Gourgaud, too, remarks that he "seemed quite pleased." This lends verisimilitude to Napoleon's supposition that the admiral had suggested the early morning hour in the expectation that the governor would not be received. He had not been too successful in handling Napoleon and might have wished to demonstrate to his successor how difficult a personage he had had to deal with. The governor felt annoyed, but restrained himself, and the visitors departed. They stopped at Hutt's Gate to see Bertrand. The grand marshal assured the governor that the Emperor never received visitors in the morning and that Captain Poppleton should have known this. Sir Hudson apologized. An appointment was made for four o'clock the following day.

TWO

Sir Hudson Lowe arrived at Longwood at the appointed time, accompanied by Admiral Cockburn and by two members of his staff—Lieutenant Colonel Sir Thomas Reade and Major Gideon Gorrequer.

Reade, deputy adjutant general, was a stocky man of thirty whose moon-shaped face was wreathed in a perpetual smile many considered hypocritical. Letters written by him prove that he favored even greater severity toward the exiles than was to be practiced by his chief. Count Balmain was to consider him neither "pleasant" nor "cultured." The Emperor took an intense dislike to him. "Napoleon scorns to see him or to talk to him, and the English fear him," Balmain was to write.

Gorrequer, aide-de-camp and acting military secretary to the governor, was a slightly built man of thirty-five with a keen ferret's face, redeemed by the humorous twinkle of his brown eyes. His manners were faultless and he spoke French fluently. Outwardly he gave his full support to the governor, but the Austrian commissioner Baron Stürmer and others received the impression that he did so from a sense of duty and was not in sympathy with Lowe's policies. It is significant that in later life he could never be prevailed upon to discuss the St. Helena episode. In his dealings with the exiles he exhibited far more finesse than his chief, and he was generally liked by them.

The visitors were received in the billiard-room by the grand marshal and the Emperor's three other officers in dress uniforms. At the door leading to the drawing room, where the reception was to take place, stood Noverraz, Napoleon's "Swiss bear," in green gold-braided livery. Bertrand excused himself and went to the drawing room to await the Emperor. Napoleon was in no hurry. It was fully half an hour before he arrived and told Bertrand to have the governor admitted.

It had been agreed between Sir Hudson and the admiral that the latter was to enter first to introduce him. But Lowe, apparently flustered by the prospect of meeting the great man, hastened to the door and went in as soon as Marshal Bertrand pronounced his name. When Admiral Cockburn tried to follow, Noverraz held forth a restraining arm and closed the door. The admiral retired in dudgeon to a window, before which he remained standing, "nursing his wrath to keep it warm."

Sir Hudson Lowe found Napoleon standing at ease behind a Pembroke table, his hat under his arm; in the background stood Marshal Bertrand, his plumed hat in his hand. The Emperor wore his green hunting jacket on which shone the plaque of the Legion of Honor, white breeches, white silk stockings, and buckled shoes. Forsyth has written that "almost from the first moment of seeing Hudson Lowe, Napoleon conceived a dislike for him, and this soon ripened into aversion." That Lowe's appearance was against him has already been noted. He was of medium height, spare, and angular. His head was egg-shaped, with a high forehead, a long upper lip, and long pointed chin. His reddish-blond hair was stiff and unruly; his nose, long and pointed; his mouth, a taut line. His eyes, heavy-lidded and surmounted by beetling eyebrows, were small, restless, glancing furtively about—"hyena's eyes" Napoleon was to call them. His face was freckled and disfigured by eczemic red patches. Sir Hudson waited for Napoleon to address him, but as the Emperor merely regarded him with a mingling of curiosity and indifference, he broke the silence with the words: "I am come, Sir, to present my respects to you."

Napoleon waited for a moment before replying, then said: "You speak French, Sir, I perceive; but you also speak Italian. You once commanded a regiment of Corsicans." The governor replied that the language made no difference to him. "We will speak, then, in Italian," the Emperor said.

The interview lasted about half an hour. Napoleon asked if Sir Hudson had been in Egypt with his Corsican regiment and, when the governor replied in the affirmative, spoke about the operations of the British with a knowledge of detail that amazed the visitor. He said of Egypt that "it was the most important geographical point in the world, and had always been considered so. He had reconnoitered the line of the canal across the Isthmus of Suez; he had calculated the expense of it at ten or twelve millions of livres—half a million sterling." In the course of the conversation he made the oft-quoted remark: "In war victory is always with him who makes the fewest mistakes." He asked Sir Hudson how long he had been in the service and, having received the reply, "Twenty-eight years," remarked: "Then I am an older soldier than you." This gave the governor the opportunity to make the flattering remark: "History will reckon the years of your service as so many centuries." Napoleon acknowledged the compliment with a smile, but made no reply. Sir Hudson then asked permission to present the two members of his staff he had brought with him, and, the Emperor consenting, they were admitted. Napoleon put a few questions to them in his characteristic fashion, then bowed and withdrew.

Las Cases claims that after the interview Napoleon said to him concerning the governor: "He is hideous. He has a most villainous face. But we must not decide too hastily. His disposition may perhaps make amends for the unfavorable impression his face produces." O'Meara, to whom he spoke about Sir Hudson the following day, quotes him as saying: "The new governor is a man of very few words, but he appears to be a polite man.

However, it is only from a man's conduct for some time that you can judge of him."

Napoleon was unaware of Admiral Cockburn's misadventure. When told about it he laughed and acted, says Las Cases, "like a schoolboy who had successfully played a trick on his teacher." Rubbing his hands gleefully he exclaimed: "Ah, my good Noverraz, you have done a clever thing for once in your life! He had heard me say that I would not see the admiral again, and thought it his duty to shut the door in his face." Becoming more serious, he remarked: "After all it was entirely the governor's fault. He should have requested that the admiral be admitted, especially as he had said that he could be presented only by him. Why did he not request the admiral's admission when he presented his officers? He alone is to blame." The following day, however, he had Count Montholon call on the admiral to express his regret for what had occurred. Cockburn refused to be reconciled. When in June of that year Admiral Sir Pulteney Malcolm came to replace him as commander of the squadron, he did not accompany his successor to Longwood to introduce him. He left St. Helena without taking leave of Napoleon. They never saw each other again.

In fairness to Cockburn it should be said that he had modified some of Lord Bathurst's instructions to Napoleon's advantage. Admiral Keith had done the same when he allowed Las Cases to accompany Napoleon to St. Helena and permitted the fallen monarch and his officers to keep their swords. The most unreasonable instruction given to Cockburn read as follows: "The General must be *always* attended by an officer appointed by the admiral or governor, as the case may be. If the General be permitted to move beyond the boundaries where the sentries are placed, *the officer should be attended by one orderly at least.*" This would have meant close confinement, as Napoleon would have refused to leave the house.

THREE

When Sir Hudson Lowe's first attempt to see Napoleon had miscarried and he had gone to see Bertrand to make a new appointment, he had given the grand marshal a disturbing piece of news. All who had accompanied the Emperor to St. Helena had from the beginning been subject to the same regulations as he. The governor now informed the grand marshal that servants as well as officers must sign a declaration promising to abide by the regulations, and binding themselves *to remain on the island for the duration of Napoleon's captivity!* Failure to agree to either meant to be deported to the Cape, where in due time facilities would be provided for departure to Europe. Having communicated this startling news to Bertrand, the governor handed him a copy of the supplementary instructions he had received from Lord Bathurst, in which, however, there was no mention whatever of the second stipulation. When the grand marshal called the governor's attention to this, he replied that that part had been communicated to him verbally by Lord Bathurst.

The demand that members of Napoleon's suite bind themselves to remain with him for the duration of the captivity had no relation to the safekeeping of the exile. It was made for the purpose of economy. Lord Bathurst expected that a substantial number of Napoleon's following would refuse to sign. This would result in their deportation, reducing the expense for the upkeep of Napoleon's establishment, which he considered excessive. He evidently realized that the employment of so shoddy a tactic for the attainment of so paltry an end would be severely criticised by the Opposition, and hence preferred not to make it a part of the official instructions.

The demand created consternation at Longwood and at the Bertrands'. Madame Bertrand wept, seeing no possibility of educating her children properly on the island and shuddering at the thought of spending what remained of her youth at St. Helena. Bertrand, in a letter to the governor, said that he had told Admiral Keith and Sir Henry Bunbury that family reasons would oblige him to return to Europe after a year, and that Lord Keith had told him repeatedly there would be no objection to this, while Sir Henry had given Madame Bertrand the same assurance. Gourgaud exclaimed: "They want to rob us of all hope of ever seeing our families again!" There was a good deal of running back and forth between Longwood and Plantation House, and Longwood and the Castle, where Admiral Cockburn resided. The admiral, who appears to have suspected the purpose of the maneuver and did not like it, expressed the opinion to Montholon that it would not be enforced—that after a year or eighteen months at most no one would be compelled to remain on the island. Sir Hudson, however, remained adamant: whoever did not sign would be deported. He notified Marshal Bertrand that the *Phaëton* was sailing for the Cape on April 29, and would be ready to take him and his family aboard.

In the end no one signed the formula prepared by Bathurst. Each of the officers sent Lowe a declaration of his own composition, declaiming against the unjust treatment the Emperor and he were receiving, but promising to obey the regulations. As for the promise to remain on the island for the duration of the captivity, Bertrand wrote: "I declare it to be my wish to remain at St. Helena." The others were equally equivocal. The servants signed a short declaration prepared by Napoleon promising to abide by the regulations and consenting to "remain here."

Sir Hudson Lowe had decided not to insist on a strict adherence to Lord Bathurst's formula. He was, however, disappointed that none of the French servants had declined to sign. He wrote to Lord Bathurst: "The declaration from the servants was quite unlooked for: I shall have a further communication with them." He asked to question the servants. Montholon, after consultation with Napoleon, told him that the Emperor was powerless to stop him, but that he resented a demand which implied that the servants might have been coerced. All the French servants declared that they had signed of their own free will.

Thus the questionable maneuver to reduce the expense of Napoleon's establishment—which at its height did not exceed 8 per cent of the total expense of keeping him on the island— miscarried. Sir Hudson, apparently fearing that Lord Bathurst might be displeased with the result, now proposed to him a more effective way of achieving the same end. He wrote: "With the present feelings of the persons attached to General Bonaparte, I conceive the whole of them, with the exception perhaps of Las Cases, had better be removed; and the insolent manner with which they manifest their opinions on all occasions might afford a sufficient pretext."

FOUR

Next to being denied the freedom of the island, Napoleon's principal grievance was the denial of freedom of correspondence. As long as Cockburn was in charge, and for a short time thereafter, the Emperor and his household were free to communicate with anyone on the island. Later Lowe was to forbid all unauthorized communication, written or verbal, between the French and the island's inhabitants. As for communication with the rest of the world, all letters written by the French had to be delivered to the governor unsealed, while anything sent to them from abroad had to be addressed to Lord Bathurst's office for examination.

Since Napoleon considered himself a prisoner *de facto*, but not *de jure*, he refused to recognize the right of the British to interfere with his correspondence and felt justified in doing everything in his power to circumvent the regulation. O'Meara, Balcombe, travelers, merchants in Jamestown, sailors, ship captains were ready to aid him. Few who did so received any remuneration. There was satisfaction in doing something for the great Napoleon. "What has struck me from the beginning of my arrival," Count Balmain was to report to Count Nesselrode, "is the enormous ascendancy which this man, surrounded by guards, by rocks, by precipices, still exercises over men's minds. Even those who guard him solicit a look, an interview, a word."

What was the nature of the clandestine correspondence? No letter written at St. Helena by Napoleon or any member of his suite has come to light dealing with plans of escape or of subversion in France or elsewhere. They dealt principally with his grievances. Some dealt with funds on deposit in England and France, the whereabouts of which the exiles wished to keep secret for fear they might be impounded or confiscated. A few might have dealt with personal matters of an intimate nature. Members of the Emperor's suite sent nearly all their letters through official channels. Napoleon, however, refused to do so since this would have meant recognition of the governor's right to examine his correspondence.

It should be said that Napoleon was hardly in a position to express indignation about his correspondence being examined. When he had been in power he had done the same with the correspondence of all diplomatic and suspected persons. Letters written by, or addressed to, such persons went to a special bureau where they were opened in a manner that left no trace. "If they [the employees of the bureau] met with a seal for which they had no facsimile, they could get one made in twenty-four hours," he told O'Meara. Nevertheless, when in May, 1816, he received a letter from his mother that had been opened in London, he angrily tore it to bits after having read it. A few days later Bertrand wrote to the governor: "I am ordered not to receive any more open letters for him. Should any arrive you are at liberty to burn them." Lowe refused to take this seriously and continued to deliver them.

Few persons about to depart for England who came in contact with the French escaped being solicited to take letters with them. On April 19, 1816, four days before he was to sail for England with his family, former governor Wilks received a visit from Marshal Bertrand who asked him if he would take charge of a communication from the Emperor to the Prince Regent. That Wilks considered some of Lord Bathurst's instructions so unreasonable as to justify their amendment by the official in charge at St. Helena is evident from the fact that it was he who had advised Admiral Cockburn to give Napoleon the freedom of Longwood plateau. But he would not lend himself to do anything secretly. He told the grand marshal he would receive the communication only if it was handed to him by Sir Hudson. Bertrand did not insist. Wilks was to depart on the *Savannah*, of which Captain Hamilton was the commander. On April 21, Madame Bertrand had dinner with Admiral Cockburn. She remained at Jamestown overnight, and the following day was accompanied to Hutt's Gate by Captain Hamilton, who remained at her house for dinner. On that day an entry in Bertrand's journal reads: *"Paquet remis."*

On April 20, Wilks, his wife, and their daughter Laura called at Longwood House for a farewell visit. Napoleon had heard Gourgaud rave about Laura but had never met her. Madame Bertrand now presented her to him, and he was enchanted with her beauty. Judging by an existing portrait of her, Petrarch's Laura could hardly have outshone her. The Emperor told her gallantly that she surpassed any description given him of her. On April 23, at two in the afternoon, the roar of cannon saluted the departure of the *Savannah* with former governor Wilks and his family on board. Gourgaud heard it and with a sigh wrote in his diary: *"Adieu, Laure!"*

Two days later the governor came to Longwood, inspected the rooms occupied by Las Cases and his son and those of the Montholons, and finding them in a deplorable state promised to order immediate repairs. He had, he said, brought from 1,500 to 2,000 French volumes with him from England, which, as soon as they had been arranged, would be at the service of General Bonaparte and his suite. That same evening he sent over material concerning the grand army and official documents relating to the Egyptian campaign, which, he thought, might be of interest to Napoleon. Throughout the remainder of the captivity such courtesies alternated with restrictive measures that increasingly isolated the exiles from the life of the island.

FIVE

Lord Bathurst's original instructions required the orderly officer to assure himself twice daily—in the morning and in the evening —of Napoleon's presence at Longwood. Admiral Cockburn had paid but little attention to this—so little that the French were unaware of the existence of such a rule. It sufficed him to know that Dr. O'Meara saw Bonaparte nearly every day and would communicate with him or with the orderly officer if anything was amiss. Sir Hudson Lowe, however, had what Count Balmain called a "tyrannical precision in fulfilling his duty."

153

When Captain Poppleton informed him that Napoleon, feeling indisposed, had kept to his apartment for forty-eight hours, and that neither he nor Dr. O'Meara had been able to see him, he grew restless and decided to try himself. On April 30, at four o'clock in the afternoon, he came to Longwood and asked to see Napoleon. The Emperor had a severe cold, but ordered that he be admitted.

He found Napoleon seated on the couch, in his dressing gown. The Emperor did not rise, but motioned him to a chair. The governor opened the conversation by saying that having heard of his indisposition he had come to offer the services of Dr. Baxter, a very capable medical officer. "I want no doctors," the Emperor replied curtly, then launched into a denunciation of the manner in which he had been treated. "The allies," he said, "have made a convention declaring me their prisoner. I gave myself up to England and to no other power. I misjudged the character of the English people. I should have surrendered myself to the Emperor of Russia, who was my friend, or to the Emperor of Austria, who was related to me. If caring only about my own interest, I had persisted in defending them in France by force of arms, there is no doubt that the allies would have granted me important concessions, perhaps even territory."

Lowe nodded a polite assent and said that every effort would be made to make him comfortable. A vessel carrying furniture, and material to build a new house, was momentarily expected.

"Let them send me a coffin!" Napoleon ejaculated. "A couple of balls in the head is all that is required. What does it matter to me whether I lie on a velvet couch or on fustian? I am a soldier and accustomed to everything." What he needed, he said, was more space for exercise without being attended by an English officer. Lowe said that the range was greater at Longwood than anywhere else on the island. "Perhaps so," the Emperor replied, "but there is a camp on part of it. I cannot ride where the camp is located. If you cannot give me a greater range, then you can do nothing for me." The governor thereupon made the following astonishing remark: "This is the consequence of giving instructions at so great a distance and concerning a person of whom those who make them know so little." The insincerity of the remark may be judged from the fact that only a few days before he had suggested to Lord Bathurst that Napoleon be deprived of all his officers, with the possible exception of Las Cases.

Napoleon pondered Lowe's remark for a moment, then observed that the admiral had found it possible to modify the instructions. To this Lowe made no reply. He disapproved of the modifications, and was to say to Marshal Bertrand that he himself would have never dared to give Napoleon so wide a range over which he could roam unattended by a British officer —that, in fact, the instructions required that he be accompanied by the orderly officer even when walking in the garden. He did not, however, depart from the role of wolf in sheep's clothing it had pleased him to adopt for the interview, and meekly asked if since his arrival he had been unconsciously guilty of any shortcoming. "No, sir," the Emperor replied. "We have nothing to complain of since your arrival except your questioning of the servants, but that is over and done with." Before leaving the governor again offered the services of Dr. Baxter, and once more received the reply: "I want no doctors."

The interview had been more friendly than otherwise; yet O'Meara informs us that, on May 6, the Emperor said to him: "I never saw such a horrid countenance. He sat on a chair opposite to my sofa, and on the little table between us there was a cup of coffee. His physiognomy made such an unfavorable impression upon me that I thought his looks had poisoned it, and I ordered Marchand to throw it out of the window; I could not have swallowed it for the world."

SIX

Napoleon continued to keep to his apartment. Neither Captain Poppleton nor Dr. O'Meara were able to catch a glimpse of him. When he was well he saw O'Meara every day for the sake of the gossip, but when indisposed he preferred to be left alone and to doctor himself with dieting, barley water, and hot baths. He found it impossible to go riding or driving. Spring in the Northern hemisphere meant autumn at St. Helena, and autumnal weather on Longwood plateau was a succession of rain, fog, and high wind. He spent the days reading, seated on the sofa in his dressing gown, by the fireplace, in which a wood fire was blazing. Occasionally he sent for Las Cases, but did not keep him long. He rather enjoyed the solitude, deriving satisfaction from his ability to dispense with company.

While Napoleon spent his time not unpleasantly, Sir Hudson was in a fever of unrest. Captain Poppleton had reported to him that he was continually prowling around the house in the rain, vainly trying to catch a glimpse of Bonaparte. Occasionally he heard the tinkle of a bell when Napoleon rang for his valet, but there was no certainty that it was he who did the ringing. Yet certainty was what Lowe craved. What if Bonaparte were no longer at Longwood? What if he had taken advantage of the fog to escape? Reason told him that this was impossible; emotionally he was not so sure. Escaping from St. Helena when every possible landing-place was being watched and armed brigs were constantly cruising around the island would be no more extraordinary than his march from Cannes to Paris without firing a shot. If Bonaparte had escaped, he, Lowe, would be ruined. He would be a laughingstock. Perspiration glistened on his forehead as he paced back and forth in his study, his index finger in a corner of his mouth.

Nor was Napoleon's failure to show himself Lowe's only worry. Wilks had told him that Bertrand had tried to have him convey a packet to England. The French made frequent purchases at Jamestown. Even though accompanied by an English officer or sergeant, it would not be difficult for them to slip a letter to an obliging shopkeeper to be forwarded to Europe. This must be stopped. Henceforth, if they wanted anything, they must send their orders to him or to Balcombe. The shopkeepers must be told that anyone caught selling to the French would be deported. Then there was the question of passes. He had learned that Bertrand was issuing passes to whomever Bonaparte cared to receive. How could Cockburn have tolerated such a thing? Well, as long as he, Lowe, remained governor, Bertrand would issue no more passes except to persons who had received official approval. Officers of the garrison would moreover be told that he regarded any social intercourse between them and the French with disfavor. Madame Bertrand was a beautiful woman and spoke English fluently. Who could tell what use Bonaparte was making of her to corrupt his officers? Reade had already told him what he had heard concerning her and Captain Hamilton. As for the civil population, there must be no correspondence or communication whatever with them, except through the medium of the governor.

He rang for Gorrequer and dictated his orders to him. They were sent to Reade with instructions that they be carried out immediately. But there was no order concerning what to do if Napoleon persisted in remaining in his apartment without even giving Dr. O'Meara the opportunity to see him. Should he order Reade to pound on the door and demand admittance? If Bonaparte refused, should the door be forced? Admiral Cockburn had returned the exile's pistols to him. What if he fired and a man was killed? What if Napoleon himself were killed in the fray? News would spread throughout the world that he had been slain by the British. He, Lowe, would be regarded as an assassin by many of his own countrymen. No explanation he could make would avail. No, that would never do. He must wait.

SEVEN

When six days had passed without Napoleon having left his apartment, and neither Captain Poppleton nor Dr. O'Meara was able to vouch for his presence at Longwood House, the governor could bear it no longer. On May 4, accompanied by Reade, he called on Marshal Bertrand. Visibly agitated and speaking very rapidly, he told Bertrand that General Bonaparte evidently did not know his place and imagined he could do as he pleased. The orderly officer was under instructions to assure himself of his presence every morning and evening. It was the General's duty to show himself, or at least to admit Dr. O'Meara, so he could report concerning him. He said much more to the same effect. When finally the grand marshal was able to interrupt the flow of words, he stunned the governor with the information that if there was such a rule neither the Emperor nor he had ever heard of it. Lowe was taken aback. "What! Never heard of it? Astonishing! Unbelievable!" Then, reflecting that this might well be another of the admiral's modifications of the instructions, his tone softened and he said that such were the government's orders and that he hoped Bertrand would oblige by informing General Bonaparte.

Bertrand now asked why an order had been issued forbidding shopkeepers at Jamestown to sell to the French. Madame Bertrand had wished to purchase a bottle of rosewater and had been refused. Lowe replied that it was not a new order. It was his understanding that Admiral Cockburn had issued such an order some time ago, but that it had not been enforced. Bertrand declared that to the best of his knowledge no such order had ever been issued by the admiral. This was corroborated the following day by Glover, Admiral Cockburn's secretary. He said the shopkeepers had been informed that if they sold to the French on credit they did so at their own risk, as the government was only responsible for its own purchases. At no time had the admiral issued an order not to sell to the French. He was, however, not there to confront the governor, who said he had the information from the admiral himself. Anyway, if the French were in want of anything they must henceforth send their orders to him or to Balcombe.

The governor then took up the question of passes issued by the grand marshal. Bertrand said the matter had been arranged at an interview between the Emperor and the admiral. Lowe did not dispute this, but said that if the arrangement were to be maintained then he might as well resign as governor and turn the job over to Bertrand. So as not to make too radical a change he was willing that the grand marshal should continue to issue passes to persons who had received official approval for a visit on a previous occasion, but to none other. The interview terminated on a tart note. The French, the governor remarked, were hard to please. They had been granted privileges in violation of several of the government's instructions, yet were still dissatisfied. He saluted curtly and rode off, followed by Reade, who had not uttered a word during the interview, but had never ceased to smile.

EIGHT

When the grand marshal communicated to Napoleon what had taken place during the interview, he at first took it calmly. It was not until the following day that his anger burst forth. He sent for O'Meara. "Are you to be my surgeon," he asked, "or surgeon of a galley; and are you expected to report what you observe and hear?" At that time O'Meara was not only giving an account of all that happened at Longwood to his friend Finlaison, at the admiralty, but was also furnishing such information to Reade; nevertheless he replied: "I am your surgeon and not a spy, and one in whom I hope you may place confidence. I do not consider it imperative on me to report anything which is not contrary to my allegiance as a British officer."

This apparently satisfied Napoleon, for he was quite outspoken in telling O'Meara what he meant to do if the governor made an attempt to violate his privacy. "I understand," he said, "that he proposed an officer should enter my chamber to see me, if I did not stir out. Any person who endeavors to force his way into my apartment shall be a corpse the moment he enters it. This I am determined on. I know that I shall be killed afterwards. I have faced death too many times to fear it." Reverting to Sir Hudson Lowe he said: "I have seen Prussians, Tartars, Cossacks, Calmucks, but never before have I beheld so ill-favored and so forbidding a countenance. He carries the imprint of crime upon his face. I had reason to complain of the admiral, but though he treated me roughly, he never behaved in such a manner as this *Prussian*."

Napoleon's determination to defend his privacy was not put to the test either then or at any other time. The weather being much improved he again went out riding, which gave the orderly officer the opportunity to report that he had seen him. Nevertheless throughout his captivity he continued to defy the governor on this matter, but no attempt was ever made to force an entry into his apartment—although Reade once pounded on the door bellowing: "Come out, Bonaparte!" On January 20, 1819, Sir Hudson wrote to Lord Bathurst: "It is consideration *alone* for the feelings of General Bonaparte himself that has prevented personal intrusion upon him." It appears more likely that it was the conviction that Napoleon meant what he said. He kept four loaded pistols in his apartment with which to defend his privacy. Not until he was at death's door, and could not possibly have carried out his threat, did the governor make serious preparations to force an entry.

NINE

A week after his interview with Marshal Bertrand, the governor played host to a distinguished guest—Lady Loudon and Moira, wife of the governor-general of India. She was on her way to England with her children and was staying at Plantation House. Naturally she wished to meet Napoleon. This would have been a simple enough matter for one of her rank had she paid a visit to the Bertrands and asked the grand marshal to arrange an interview. She probably would have done so had not Sir Hudson, with his usual lack of tact, proposed to invite Napoleon to dinner.

There were excellent reasons why such an invitation should not have been sent. Common sense should have warned the governor that Napoleon must be smarting from the account Marshal Bertrand had given him of the changes Sir Hudson was making in the regulations. Plantation House, moreover, was outside the limits, and even if he had not already made up his mind not to go anywhere attended by an English officer, he assuredly would have objected to going to dinner under guard. Last, but not least, Napoleon would hardly have cared to be addressed as "General Bonaparte" in the presence of Lady Loudon. But, as the Duke of Wellington was to remark, Lowe was "a stupid man" and "knew nothing of the world." There can be no doubt that he sincerely believed he was conferring a favor on the Emperor and was employing Chesterfieldian nicety when he sent a polite note to Marshal Bertrand inviting "General Bonaparte" to meet the countess at dinner at Plantation House. Bertrand dutifully showed the note to Napoleon, who glanced at it and handed it back with the words: "This is too absurd; make no reply."

Since the note was addressed to the grand marshal, the latter acknowledged its receipt and wrote: "Count Bertrand has communicated the note of Sir Hudson Lowe to the Emperor, who has not made any reply to it." So obtuse was Sir Hudson that he was astounded. He thought there must be some mistake, and a few days later questioned the grand marshal concerning the details of the presentation of the note and the exact wording of Napoleon's reply. When the information was given him he was more perplexed than ever and, shaking his head, muttered: "It's extraordinary. At least an answer should have been given. It's not polite. What a strange way to act."

Napoleon had his confectioner prepare sweetmeats for Lady Loudon's children, and sent Marshal Bertrand to present his compliments to the countess and to assure her that had Plantation House been within the limits it would have given him great pleasure to pay his respects to her in person. The reception he gave Sir Hudson a few days later makes it appear highly improbable that he would have gone to the governor's residence under any circumstances.

TEN

On May 16, Sir Hudson Lowe paid another visit to Longwood, this time in the company of Colonel Wynyard, a new member of his staff who had arrived ten days before on the *Adamant*. His mission was a conciliatory one. He wished to see Napoleon to inform him that the *Adamant* had brought new furniture and material for the house, and to discuss with him whether he preferred Longwood House to be repaired and enlarged or a new house erected, either at Longwood or on some other suitable site. Confident that the Emperor would be pleased with the news he looked forward to an agreeable visit. It apparently never occurred to him that the new regulations might have offended the exile. On his arrival at Longwood House he asked for Count Las Cases, whom at that time he seemed to have preferred to any of Napoleon's attendants. The chamberlain went to notify the Emperor of the governor's arrival, and after a little while ushered Sir Hudson into the drawing room.

If Lowe had not given a thought to the changes in the regulations as a possible cause of friction between himself and the exile, Napoleon had not forgotten. The demand that he show himself twice daily to the orderly officer; the order to the merchants at Jamestown not to sell to the French; the curtailment of the privilege granted by Admiral Cockburn to Bertrand to issue passes to visitors; the order to civilians not to communicate with the exiles except through the medium of the governor; the suggestion to the officers of the garrison to have no social intercourse with the French; and, topping it all, the humiliating invitation to dine at Plantation House, to be shown off to Lady Loudon and be addressed as "General Bonaparte" after having arrived under guard—all this during one month of Sir Hudson's stewardship! If the governor did not have to wait long before being received by the Emperor, it was because the latter was seething within and was anxious to tell him what he thought of him. Everybody at Longwood knew that a quarrel was impending. Servants were eavesdropping at the door leading to the dining room, while in the billiard-room Las Cases was straining his ears to hear what was being said.

Lowe had no sooner entered than he realized the interview was not likely to be a pleasant one. Napoleon stood erect, his hat under his arm. His classical features, so charming when he was in a pleasant mood, were clouded by ill humor. He frowned and his lips were tightly compressed. He did not utter a word but glowered at the visitor. Sir Hudson broke the silence. Las Cases, who was able to overhear some of the conversation, has written that the governor spoke haltingly, as one embarrassed or confused. Lowe said that Napoleon had no doubt seen by the papers that it was the government's intention to build a new house for him. Furniture and material for the house had arrived.

"I have conceived, Sir, that possibly the addition of two or three good rooms to your present house, with other improvements to it, might add to your convenience in less time than by constructing a new building."

When the Emperor spoke his voice was fraught with anger. He later told Las Cases: "My anger must have been powerfully excited, for I felt a vibration in the calf of my left leg. This is always a sure sign with me. I had not felt it for a long time." Looking sternly at the governor, he said: "I ask you for nothing and will accept nothing from you. All I ask of you is to leave me in peace. I can't understand the conduct of your government toward me. Do they want to kill me? Are you come here to be my executioner, my jailer? Posterity will judge of the way in which I have been treated. The sufferings I experience will recoil upon your country. No, sir, I will not allow any one to enter the interior of my house, to penetrate into the privacy of my bed-chamber. If you order the gallant soldiers of the 53rd to do so, they will enter only over my dead body. When I heard of your arrival on the island, I thought that as an army officer I should find you possessed of more cultivated manners than the admiral's, who, being a naval officer, could be expected to be a little uncouth. I do not accuse him of lack of heart. But how are you treating me? It was an insult to invite me to dinner and to call me General Bonaparte. I am not General Bonaparte; I am the Emperor Napoleon! During the one month you have been here you have given me more cause for vexation than I have had during the preceding six months."

"Sir, I did not come here to receive a lesson," the governor retorted.

"That's no proof that you don't need one. Shall I tell you the truth, sir? Yes, sir, shall I tell you the truth? I believe you have received orders to do away with me—yes, to kill me! If Lord Castlereagh has given you such orders, then carry them out as speedily as possible. I know that those in power can find men for any kind of assignment, dishonorable as well as honorable."

"You remarked, Sir, at the last interview I had with you," the governor replied, "that you had misjudged the character of the English people. You now equally misconstrue that of an English soldier."

There was a moment's silence; then the governor said: "Sir, I have brought with me an officer of my staff, whom I should like to present to you. He is a lieutenant colonel of the King's Guard."

"I cannot see anyone at present," Napoleon said petulantly. "When one is insulted, one is in no mood to see anybody."

Napoleon was to regret having lost his temper. Throughout his career he had occasionally *pretended* to lose it when it suited his purpose, but to lose actual control over himself was a different matter. It hurt his pride. On May 31, speaking about the incident to Las Cases, he said: "I behaved very badly to him, no doubt, and nothing but my present situation could excuse me. But I was in a bad temper and could not help it. I should blush for it in any other situation. Had such a scene taken place at the Tuileries, I should have felt myself bound in conscience to make some atonement. Never during the period of my power did I speak harshly to any one without afterwards saying something to make amends. But this time I did not utter a conciliatory syllable and had no wish to do so. However, the governor proved himself very insensible to my wrath. His feelings did not seem hurt. I should have liked, for his sake, to have seen him show a little anger, or slam the door violently after him when he went away. This would at least have shown that there was some elasticity about him, but I found nothing of the kind."

To what extent Sir Hudson was given to self-delusion is evident from the report of the interview he sent to Lord Bathurst. It contains the following statement, so contrary to truth as to pass understanding: "It has been very remote indeed from either my intention or practice to give him any additional motive of irritation. *The precautions for his security are precisely the same as those established by Sir George Cockburn.*"

When out riding Napoleon had hitherto carefully avoided going past Deadwood Camp, where some five hundred soldiers of the 53rd regiment were quartered. On May 28, however, when returning from a ride with Las Cases and Gourgaud, he went past the encampment. Few of the soldiers had ever seen him. To them he was an almost legendary figure—a great captain for whom they had profound respect, as had many of their officers. So, when in gray surtout and cocked hat he suddenly appeared on horseback, followed by two of his officers, what wonder that the news spread through the encampment like a prairie fire, that soldiers came running from all directions, and that, spontaneously, they fell into line and stood at attention.

When Lowe heard about the incident he issued an order that henceforth any soldier who saluted Napoleon should be flogged.

XIII. The Commissioners

On the morning of June 17, 1816, the *Newcastle*, with Rear Admiral Sir Pulteney Malcolm and the commissioners of the allied powers on board, hove into sight. When told about this Napoleon went into the garden and watched the vessel through a field telescope. The air was balmy and little wisps of cloud lazed in an azure sky. The sea, on which the ship was slowly becoming more distinct, shimmered in the sun. Diana's Peak, usually shrouded in vapors at that season of the year, seemed to look down benevolently on the scene.

On June 18, Madame Montholon gave birth to a daughter. There being no Roman Catholic priest on the island, the Reverend Vernon, junior chaplain at Jamestown, baptized the child.

That same day Admiral Malcolm and the Russian and French commissioners—Count Balmain and the Marquis de Montchenu —set foot on St. Helena. The Austrian commissioner, Baron Stürmer, who had made the journey on the *Orontes*, did not land until a day later. The Prussian government had decided not to send a commissioner, apparently for reasons of economy. The new arrivals were greeted with a salute of thirteen guns and conducted to the Castle, where they were received by the governor and his staff and by Admiral Cockburn. O'Meara, who had gone to Jamestown that day, had the opportunity to meet the French commissioner and gave the following account to Napoleon: "He is an old *émigré* named the Marquis de Montchenu, extremely fond of talking. While I was standing in a group of officers on the terrace opposite the admiral's house, he came out and, addressing himself to me, said in French, 'If any of you speak French, for the love of God make it known to me, for I do not speak a word of English. I have arrived here to finish my days amongst these rocks, and I cannot speak a word of the language.'"

The Emperor laughed. The marquis was not altogether a stranger to him. "I know that Montchenu," he said. "He is an old fool, a gossip, an armchair general who has never smelt powder. What folly to send these commissioners here. Without charge or responsibility, they will have nothing to do but walk about the streets and clamber up the rocks. The Prussian government has shown better judgment and saved its money."

TWO

Claude Marin Henri de Montchenu could hardly be said to have contributed to French prestige at St. Helena. His appointment had been the last official act of Prince Talleyrand as minister of foreign affairs in the King's cabinet. Montchenu's Austrian colleague, Baron Stürmer, was to say that if the prince had deliberately tried to cast ridicule on those of the King's subjects who belonged to the old nobility, he could have done nothing more effective. Although belonging to a family whose genealogy dated back to the crusades, Montchenu had no valid claim to the title of marquis. He had substituted it for the legitimate one of "*seigneur,*" with which his ancestors had contented themselves, as more suitable to a man of his attainments. He was very proud of his descent, which constituted his principal topic of conversation. "In that booby's eyes," Napoleon was to say, "belonging to an old family is the only source of merit. He despises everybody who has not as many hundred years of nobility to boast of as himself. It was such as Montchenu who were the chief cause of the Revolution. Before it, such a man as Bertrand, who is worth an army of Montchenus, could not even be a *sous lieutenant,* while *vieux enfants* like him would be generals. God help the nation that is governed by such."

The marquis was fifty-nine when he came to St. Helena. As a boy he had been a page at the court of Louis XV, then, successively, a member of the King's guard, a lieutenant of dragoons, a captain, and a lieutenant colonel. In 1792, he had emigrated, returning to France shortly after Napoleon's *coup d'état* of the 18th Brumaire, toward the end of 1799. Having little or nothing to do, he had spent his time in the cafés, first in Paris, then in Lyon. He hated Napoleon, whom he called *"le petit monstre,"* and was in the habit of saying: "When that man has fallen I will beseech the King, my master, to make me his jailer." After the restoration he wrote innumerable letters to Louis and his ministers, vaunting his ancestry and his loyalty and soliciting an appointment, but without effect. When Napoleon returned from Elba, Montchenu followed the King to Ghent. Finally, thanks to Talleyrand, he was appointed commissioner and promoted to *maréchal de camp,* giving him the right to wear a general's uniform.

The Russian and Austrian commissioners went to live at Rosemary Hall, near Plantation House; Montchenu, however, remained at Jamestown, at Porteous' inn, where Napoleon had spent his first night on the island, then moved to the lodging house of a Mrs. Martin, a gaunt middle-aged puritanical widow. Being a devil with the ladies—in fact with any woman who happened to come his way—it was not long before he tried to embrace and kiss her. She uttered such piercing shrieks that people ran to her rescue and the affair became the talk of the island. Equally well advertised was an eight-page letter he wrote to Lady Lowe in which he expressed his undying devotion. He once boasted that no less than four thousand daughters of Albion had succumbed to his amatory impetuosity. In his general's uniform with huge gold epaulets, his sword, which sometimes threatened to trip him up, his rotund belly, his rubicund face, his powdered periwig, he looked for all the world like a travesty of the *ancien régime.* Sailors on the *Newcastle* had named him "Old Munch-Enough," because of his voracious appetite. People at Jamestown referred to him as "the French hairdresser." Among the comfortable class he became known as *"Marquis de Monter-Chez-Nous,"* for he was an inveterate sponger who never neglected an opportunity to dine at other people's expense and seldom reciprocated. Even the surly governor could not help being amused by him. The only witty remark to be found in Sir Hudson's humorless correspondence concerns Montchenu. He wrote to Sir Henry Bunbury: "The French Marquis says that the Revolution was caused by *les gens d'esprit,* which makes it evident that he had no hand in it."

Montchenu came to St. Helena accompanied by a secretary, whom he called his aide-de-camp. He was a tall young man of twenty-five named Jean Claude de Gors—the *particule nobiliaire* having been conferred upon him by his chief as indispensable to one attached to so important a personage. Gors had little respect for his chief and used to write letters to the Duc de Richelieu, minister of foreign affairs, criticizing his behavior. Richelieu, who was far from pleased with Montchenu's appointment, did not rebuke Gors, and it has been suspected that it may have been part of the young man's duty to keep an eye on the erratic marquis.

THREE

The Russian commissioner, Count Alexander Antonovich de Balmain, was thirty-five, a diplomat of distinction, cultured, able, witty, and accustomed to shine in society. "He enjoyed in anticipation the pleasure he would have from his intimate conversations with that genius [Napoleon] and also the stories he would afterwards be able to relate," Aldanov has written.[1] He was descended from a Ramsay of Balmain who had left Scotland with James II in 1685, and had settled in Russia, where the family had prospered. Balmain's father, who died when his son was nine, had held the important office of governor-general of Kursk and Orel. In 1801, when twenty and a captain in the imperial guard, Balmain struck a commissioner of police during a quarrel, and by order of Czar Paul was demoted to private in

[1] M. A. Aldanov, *Saint Helena, Little Island.* New York, 1924.

an infantry regiment. The demotion lasted only three days, for that same month Paul was assassinated and his successor Alexander restored the young man's rank.

Balmain, however, had decided that a diplomatic career would suit him better. After having served as attaché of legation to the Kingdoms of Sardinia and of Naples, he became secretary of the embassy in Vienna. In 1813, when secretary of the embassy in London, he rejoined the army with the rank of lieutenant colonel and took part in the campaign in Germany. When Napoleon returned from Elba, Balmain was attached to Wellington's staff as liaison officer. After Waterloo he fulfilled several diplomatic missions before being appointed commissioner at St. Helena. He was the Czar's personal choice for the office, for Alexander's ambivalent interest in Napoleon had not waned and he considered Balmain particularly qualified to keep him informed. The commissioner disapproved of Sir Hudson Lowe almost from the beginning and said so unequivocally. His attitude changed somewhat when he fell in love with Charlotte Johnson, the governor's stepdaughter, whom he married before leaving St. Helena.[2] After his recall the Czar appointed him his aide-de-camp, and he remained a favorite at court until his retirement in 1837.

Sir Hudson realized that Balmain would have to be reckoned with. In his letter to Sir Henry Bunbury concerning the commissioners he wrote: "The Russian appears to laugh at the other two, and really appears to have much more in him than the other two."

Balmain was to laugh at the governor even more than at Montchenu, but it was sardonic laughter.

The Austrian commissioner, Baron Barthelemy Von Stürmer was a young man of twenty-nine. Montchenu would have sneered at his title of nobility, for his father, whose knowledge of oriental languages had secured him the post of internuncio at Constantinople, had been ennobled as recently as 1813. The young man had been a dragoman at Constantinople and had

---

[2] Frédéric Masson has him marry her sister Susanna Johnson. The same error is made by Aldanov.

risen to secretary of the legation. In 1814, he was appointed secretary to Prince Schwartzenberg, in which capacity he had attended the Congress at Châtillon, where Napoleon so rashly cast away the opportunity to remain on the throne. Lowe wrote about Stürmer to Sir Henry Bunbury that he appeared to be a "gentlemanly, pleasant, and well-informed man," which, however, did not deter him from driving him almost to distraction with his unjustified suspicion.

Stürmer was with Prince Schwartzenberg in the French capital when the treaty of Paris was being negotiated. While there he met Mademoiselle Boutet, a girl of seventeen, plump and pretty, whose father, a minor official at the war office, found it necessary to augment his meager salary by tutoring young gentlemen. They fell in love and were married. It so happened that Las Cases' son Emanuel had been one of Boutet's pupils. Moreover, Madame Las Cases had befriended his daughter who was seeking employment as a governess. She had invited her to the house on several occasions and had introduced her to friends and acquaintances in the hope that this might help her find suitable employment. No sooner therefore had her identity become known to Las Cases than his hopes soared. "I am then about to have, I said to myself, positive, particular, and even secret information respecting everything that interests me," he wrote in his diary. He had expected that she would get in touch with him immediately after her arrival, but when day after day passed and he heard nothing, he sent her a message. The bearer, a young mulatto servant he had hired, returned with the information that the baroness had said she did not know the person who had sent it. Her husband, obeying instructions he had received from his government, turned the note over to the governor. Soon after Las Cases received a warning from Lowe not to attempt to communicate with any person on the island without his intervention.

When the chamberlain—who had hoped to be able to surprise Napoleon with news about the unrivaled source of information that was to be theirs—told him about his disappointment, the Emperor laughed heartily. "How little you know human nature," he said. "So her father was your son's tutor! So your wife befriended her when she needed it! My dear Las Cases, she is now a baroness, and you are the person she most dreads to meet—whose presence is most embarrassing to her."

FOUR

The instructions given to Montchenu by the Duc de Richelieu and to Stürmer by Prince Metternich did not differ essentially. Both were warned that the British government having assumed responsibility for the security of the prisoner, they must not interfere with the governor's regulations. Their duty consisted in assuring themselves *with their own eyes* and at regular intervals of the presence of Bonaparte, and sending reports whenever there was anything of interest to communicate. They were to have no relations of any kind with the prisoner or members of his suite and were to inform the governor of any attempt made by him or his followers to establish contact with them.

The instructions given by Count Nesselrode to Balmain differed materially from those of his two colleagues. "Your role," they read, "will be purely passive. You will observe everything and report everything. . . . In your relations with Bonaparte you will exhibit the consideration and the propriety which so delicate a situation demands, *and the personal regards which are his due.*" The last sentence had been added by order of the Czar, who had underscored the last part with his own hand. There is reason to believe it was intended less as an order to Balmain, who, he knew, did not need such a reminder, than as a hint to Sir Hudson Lowe.

Still another part of Balmain's instructions differed considerably from those of his colleagues. While they were ordered to assure themselves with their own eyes of the presence of Napoleon on the island and were forbidden to have any intercourse with the prisoner or his suite, Balmain's instructions read: "You will not avoid, nor will you seek, opportunities of seeing him, and you will conform in this respect strictly to the regulations which will be made by the governor. But you will keep a daily record of all that you may learn about him; you will above all apply yourself to write everything that may be of interest in conversations, whether with yourself, or with the Commissioners of the other Powers, or with other persons."

This can have no other meaning than that the Czar did not disapprove of contacts his commissioner might establish with Napoleon and his suite, provided the governor did not object.

The British government was not particularly happy with the arrival of the commissioners on the island. Lord Liverpool had written to Lord Castlereagh that having nothing to do, the commissioners would probably quarrel. If it was considered necessary to establish the principle that Bonaparte was the prisoner not merely of England but of Europe, then, he opined, it would have been wiser and more economical for the allied powers each to have sent a commissioner alternately for one year. Lord Bathurst wrote to Sir Hudson Lowe that they would have "too little to do not to be tempted to do a little mischief," and advised him to encourage them "to amuse themselves by going to the Cape by way of a change of scene." Sir Hudson felt annoyed by their arrival. In his letter to Sir Henry Bunbury, he expressed the hope that the high cost of living at St. Helena would soon drive them from the island.

In fixing the salaries of the commissioners the allied powers had indeed failed to take into account that prices at St. Helena were about four times as high as in London, which were the highest in Europe. The commissioners all received £1,200 per year, while Gors received £240. It was impossible for them to live on this in a manner commensurate with the dignity of their office. All went heavily into debt. Stürmer nearly ruined himself, spending £4,000 during his first year on the island. After much correspondence Balmain's salary was raised to £2,000 a year, and he received an allowance of £1,600 with which to pay debts he had contracted. Montchenu's salary was doubled, while Gors had to be content with £360.

FIVE

Immediately after his arrival at St. Helena, Montchenu asked to be taken to Longwood so he might assure himself "with his own eyes" of the presence of the prisoner. He wished to send a report with the *Northumberland,* due to sail for England the following day. Great was his disappointment when the governor told him that gaining access to Bonaparte was no easy matter and that he must wait.

On June 20, Sir Hudson personally informed Bertrand of the arrival of the commissioners and asked when Napoleon would be able to receive them. The grand marshal inquired if they had brought letters from their sovereigns addressed to the Emperor, and wanted to know the object of their mission. Lowe replied that they had brought no letters and were not authorized to interfere with regulations established by him, but were instructed to assure themselves of Bonaparte's presence on the island and to ascertain if he was properly guarded. Bertrand promised to take the matter up with Napoleon.

Eventually the governor was informed that if the gentlemen wished to see the Emperor as private persons they need but apply to the grand marshal, who would arrange their presentation. If, however, they wished to see him as commissioners, they should forward a copy of the convention of August 2, 1815, by virtue of which they were on the island, and which he had not seen. When he had read it he would decide.

It so happened that neither the commissioners nor the governor possessed a copy of the document. After a frantic search an old number of the *Journal des Débats* containing the text of the convention was found, and Sir Hudson arranged a conference to discuss the situation. Montchenu and Stürmer declared that they could not see Bonaparte except as commissioners. Balmain said that he could accomplish all his government wished him to accomplish by meeting Napoleon informally, but that he would not do so unless his colleagues were willing to do the same. It was finally agreed that the commissioners were to submit their demands to the governor in writing. They did so, and on July 23, 1816, copies were sent to Bertrand together with a copy of the convention and a letter of Sir Hudson again asking when it would be convenient for Napoleon to receive the commissioners.

The reply did not come until a month later, in a long letter

signed by Montholon, but dictated by Napoleon. It became
known as the "Remonstrance." The Emperor wrote: "In point
of fact the person of the Emperor Napoleon is in the power of
the English nation, but neither in point of fact nor of right has
he ever been, nor is he now, in the power of Austria, of Russia,
or of Prussia. . . . The convention of the 2nd August . . . cannot by right have any effect." Then followed a detailed discussion of his grievances.

Balmain sent a copy of the letter to Count Nesselrode together
with his comments. Some of the principal grievances he considered justified. So, for example, when Napoleon writes: "The
Emperor has been established in a place called Longwood, exposed to every wind, a barren spot, uninhabited, without water
or verdure," Balmain comments: "This passage from Count
Montholon's letter is absolutely true. Plantation House is a mag-
nificent place, well situated, with gardens and fountains; Longwood is only a hovel, buffeted by the wind, surrounded with
gumtrees—a wretched tree which gives no shade. The English
treat Bonaparte very shabbily. He has only the necessities. That
enormous expense which so aroused Parliament is wholly for
the maintenance of the troops and guard-ships, and a numerous
and more or less useless staff." When Napoleon writes: "You have
forbidden all communication between us and the inhabitants of
the island," Balmain comments: "This is also true. Since the departure of Admiral Cockburn, Sir Hudson Lowe has increased
the measures of surveillance to an incredible extent. There is no
extravagance of which he is not capable to assure himself of the
safekeeping of his prisoner."

After the receipt of the letter another conference was held.
Montchenu exclaimed: "Give me a company of grenadiers and
I'll know how to force an entrance!" Then, turning to his colleagues, he said: "Gentlemen, I count on your support if I am
obliged to use force." But neither Balmain nor Stürmer would
agree to this, nor for that matter would the governor. The lines
in Balmain's instructions concerning the way Napoleon should
be treated had had their effect upon him. He said: "You must
consider, gentlemen, whether such an act against the very per-

son of Bonaparte would secure the approbation of your governments. There is no doubt that all the Powers are in agreement
that he should be treated with the greatest respect."

It was decided that the French and Austrian commissioners
should ask their governments for further instructions. The reply
did not arrive until June, 1817.

SIX

While refusing to receive the commissioners except as private
persons, Napoleon was even more eager to see them than they
were to see him. This was especially true of Balmain. News had
reached him about that part of the count's instructions justifying
the assumption that the Czar was not altogether indifferent toward him. He hoped to be able to persuade Balmain to put him
in contact with his former friend. We do not know if in his
eagerness to see the count he went so far as to enlist the aid of
his friend Betsy, or whether the little minx, having heard the
matter discussed on a visit to the Bertrands, herself had decided
it was time for her to do something about it. Anyway, on September 10, 1816, Balmain reported to Nesselrode: "Little Betsy
Balcombe's letters assured me that her friend Boney was quite
eager to talk to me." He was almost equally impatient to see the
Austrian commissioner. Stürmer might be able to give him news
about his wife and child and inform him if there was any change
in the disposition of the Emperor Francis toward him. And
while he felt nothing but contempt for Montchenu he was not
averse to getting what information he could from him about the
situation in France. In the back of his mind there still lingered
the hope that England, if not her allies, might consider restoring him to the throne if it became evident that Louis could not
control the situation and Jacobinism threatened to gain the upper hand.

Montchenu had brought with him from France a letter for
Madame Bertrand from her mother, and another for Las Cases
from his wife. He had delivered both to the governor, who forwarded them to Longwood after having opened and read them.
It occurred to Napoleon that Las Cases, a member of the old no-

bility and an *émigré,* should not find it difficult to establish friendly relations with the marquis. So he asked Madame Bertrand to communicate with the commissioner. She would have done so anyway, for on June 21, three days after the commissioner set foot at St. Helena, Gourgaud had been at Porteous' inn where he had met Montchenu and his secretary. The marquis told him that he had seen his mother and sister and that both were well. He said he felt like an "oral letter," having been asked to communicate such a variety of things to Madame Bertrand and Madame Montholon. It would have been strange indeed if, after hearing of this and knowing her mother to be in delicate health, Madame Bertrand had not tried to get in touch with him. She wrote to Montchenu that having heard he had seen her mother, she would appreciate it if he would pay her a visit. She added that Las Cases would be present as he was anxious for more news about his family. She sealed the letter and entrusted it to Porteous for delivery to the marquis. Mindful of the governor's regulations, Porteous delivered it at Plantation House.

Sir Hudson already knew about the letter, as O'Meara had sent a note to Reade informing him that Madame Bertrand had told him she had written it at Napoleon's request. The governor now wrote to Bertrand, calling his attention to the fact that his wife's letter had been sent in violation of the regulation prohibiting communication either written or verbal, between Napoleon's household and persons on the island without the intervention of the governor. In his reply the grand marshal pointed out to Sir Hudson to what extent he had strayed, not only from the indulgence shown by Admiral Cockburn, but even from his own policy at the beginning of his administration: "During nine months that we have been here we have constantly carried on correspondence in the island, with the knowledge of the admiral, your predecessor, and even with your own knowledge since you have been here. The former governor and his wife, the lieutenant governor and his wife, General Bingham,[3] the captain of the *Northumberland,* the officers of the navy—in a word, all the of-

[3] Colonel Bingham had been promoted to brigadier general.

ficers and other persons residing here—have written to us and have received letters from us." To this the governor replied that if the grand marshal did not like the control "which my duty compels me to place you under," he was at liberty to leave. As a result of this correspondence, relations between Lowe and Bertrand became strained.

Lowe's attempt to isolate the French from all intercourse with the inhabitants without subjecting them to close confinement created a fantastic situation. When Bertrand's servant became ill and Dr. O'Meara sent over a bottle of medicine on the label of which he had inscribed directions in French, the soldier who delivered it removed the label, lest he be punished for delivering a clandestine message. The butcher's boy refused to hand over the meat at the gate, but threw it over the garden wall, lest he be accused of delivering a verbal communication.

SEVEN

The Stürmers had come to St. Helena accompanied by four servants and a young botanist, Philippe Welle. The Emperor Francis was the proud possessor of a large collection of exotic animals and plants, and Welle had been sent to find additional specimens for the collection. Before leaving Schönbrunn the young man had received a small packet from Herr Boos, director of the imperial gardens, which he had been asked to deliver to Napoleon's valet Marchand. The packet was unsealed and contained a lock of silky blond hair and a slip of paper on which was written: "Enclosed you will find a lock of my hair. If you have the opportunity to have your portrait painted, send it to me. Your mother Marchand." It will be remembered that Marchand's mother was nurse to the King of Rome. The lock of hair was not hers but the child's.

When Welle reached Paris another packet was entrusted to him, this time through the intermediary of an Austrian officer, for delivery to Gourgaud. It contained a letter from Gourgaud's mother and sister and a silk handkerchief. Of all this the commissioner knew nothing.

Soon after his arrival at St. Helena Welle asked a man named

Richard Prince, who, he was told, had business at Longwood, to tell Marchand that he had a message for him. It was not long before Marchand, accompanied by a soldier, came to Porteous' inn, where all the commissioners were then staying. While his escort remained outside, the valet went to Welle's room and was given both packets.

Such was what one of Lowe's apologists has termed "the underhand intrigue the governor had to unravel." Sir Hudson, having spies throughout the island, soon learned about the matter, at least as far as the packet containing the lock of hair was concerned. He demanded an explanation from the commissioner. Stürmer questioned Welle who related all he knew about the packet and said that he had not told the commissioner about it because he considered the matter too trivial. When he had sent the message to Longwood he had had no inkling of the existence of a regulation that forbade it. The commissioner had him make a sworn statement of the facts in the case and forwarded it to the governor.

Sir Hudson was not satisfied with the explanation furnished by the botanist. We have seen what absurd conclusions his tortured brain was able to draw from the most commonplace occurrences. He now reached the conclusion that Welle was an agent of Metternich sent over to assist Stürmer in reaching a secret understanding with Napoleon. Metternich, he was to write to his friend Thornton at Rio de Janeiro, had a "Napoleonic bias." During a conference with the commissioner he said: "It is alleged that you had knowledge of it."

"Any one who says that is a coward and a rascal!" Stürmer retorted.

Lowe insisted on questioning Welle, which Stürmer regarded as an affront to his government and to himself. The governor had his way, but learned nothing new.

Welle and Richard Prince were ordered to leave the island, and Lowe wrote to Bathurst suggesting that Welle's baggage be searched on his arrival in England, as he suspected him of carrying clandestine correspondence from Longwood. That not only Stürmer and his fellow-commissioners, but the admiral of the squadron, were out of sympathy with the governor's action in the case is evident from the following message Reade sent to Plantation House the day of Welle's departure: "All the commissioners, with the Baroness Stürmer *and Sir P. and Lady Malcolm,* accompanied Mr. Welle to the place of embarkment." Napoleon, who was under the erroneous impression that Welle had seen his wife and child and had spoken with them, and that he had asked permission to visit him and had been refused, was especially incensed.

XIV. Final Break
with the Governor

On June 20, 1816, at about two in the afternoon, Rear Admiral Sir Pulteney Malcolm was presented to Napoleon. Admiral Cockburn had told him that he could not introduce him and suggested that if he wished to be well received he should apply to Bertrand without the intervention of the governor, as Napoleon did not like Sir Hudson. Cockburn had a poor opinion of Lowe; when O'Meara published his *Voice from St. Helena* he found little fault with what the surgeon had to say about the governor. Lord Dudley (in *Dudley's Letters*) tells of an interview he had with Cockburn shortly after the publication of the book, and writes: "He defends Sir Hudson Lowe only just as far as precedence and decorum oblige an official man to do so. Indeed, he acknowledged that with respect to what passed in St. Helena, he was disposed to take O'Meara's part." Malcolm, however, thought that to bypass the governor in such a matter would be improper. At his request Sir Hudson wrote to Bertrand that he should like to present the admiral to General Bonaparte. He received the reply that the Emperor would receive him.

Malcolm took with him Captain Meynel of the *Newcastle*, Captain Cochrane of the *Orontes*, his secretary Mr. Irving, and Mr. Wright, his flag-lieutenant. Sir Hudson was accompanied by Colonel Wynyard, his military secretary, whom he had vainly tried to introduce to Napoleon on a previous occasion. The governor and the admiral were ushered into the drawing room, while the others remained in the billiard-room with Las Cases, Montholon, and Gourgaud. Admiral Malcolm was a solidly built, pleasant-featured man whose manners were impeccable, and Napoleon took to him instantly. He was to say: "Ah, there is a man with a countenance really pleasing, open, intelligent, frank, and sincere. There is the face of a true Englishman. His countenance bespeaks his heart, and I am sure he is a good man. I never yet beheld a man of whom I so immediately formed a good opinion as of that fine soldier-like man."

Although his hair was prematurely gray, Malcolm was only a year older than Napoleon. He was the only Englishman with whom the Emperor came in contact at St. Helena for whom he developed a feeling of friendship. Malcolm, on his part, felt a profound sympathy for the fallen monarch. As relations between Napoleon and Sir Hudson became increasingly strained, the admiral was caught in the middle. While disapproving of most of the measures taken by Sir Hudson, he yet thought it his duty to defend the governor whenever Napoleon criticized him in his presence. At times, however—as in the affair of Welle, when he and Lady Malcolm joined the commissioners on the quay in bidding farewell to the botanist—he openly showed his disapproval, which Lowe was quick to resent. They clashed on various other matters, and when in July, 1817, he was succeeded by Admiral Plampin, they were far from being on a friendly footing.

The satisfaction Napoleon derived from the presence of the admiral affected his attitude toward the governor. "After speaking a few words to the admiral, Bonaparte addressed to me several polite and attentive inquiries respecting myself and Lady Lowe," Sir Hudson wrote to Lord Bathurst. Malcolm was pleased with this. He wished nothing better than to be the means of establishing a better understanding between the two men. There followed a conversation about ships and about British admirals. Napoleon believed British sailors were too harshly treated and on a later occasion mentioned this to Malcolm, but he had great admiration for the British navy. When the conversation had lasted an hour, the officers waiting in the ante-room were admitted and Napoleon exchanged a few words with each. The visitors departed well content with the interview.

On June 25, the admiral called again, accompanied by Lady Malcolm. The road from Plantation House, where they were temporarily housed, being too rough for a carriage, they went on horseback as far as Hutt's Gate. Here Napoleon's barouche with six horses, driven by two postilions, was waiting for them. Lady Malcolm and Madame Bertrand were assisted into the carriage, which set off at a gallop, followed by the admiral and Bertrand on horseback. It was a wild ride, and, when they skirted the yawning Punch Bowl at full speed, Lady Malcolm felt it might well be her last. She was a gaunt little woman, deformed by curvature of the spine, and made too liberal a use of cosmetics; but her eyes were appealing, her smile pleasant, and she was lively, good-natured, and an excellent conversationalist. Her interest in Napoleon had a personal touch, for she was a sister of Captain Elphinstone whose life the Emperor had saved at Belle Alliance. Napoleon had ordered the captain, who lay bleeding on the battlefield, taken to a cottage and cared for by his personal physician. She felt a little nervous about meeting the great man, but Madame Bertrand reassured her by telling her the Emperor "was so good—was so kind."

The visit was a pleasant one. Las Cases, his son, Montholon, and Gourgaud were introduced to Lady Malcolm. Napoleon asked her to seat herself beside him on the sofa and invited the others to be seated. There followed a lively conversation. He inquired after Lord Keith, who was Lady Malcolm's uncle. When she told him that she was Scotch they talked about Ossian. She shared his admiration for the Gaelic poet, but said he was better known on the continent than in Britain. "It was I —I who made him the fashion," the Emperor said. "I have even been accused of having my head filled with Ossian's clouds." Napoleon, who under the Consulate had restored slavery in the French colonies, but who on his return from Elba had issued a decree abolishing it, asked Malcolm why England tolerated it at St. Helena. The admiral replied that he did not know, but that he considered its existence a disgrace. Lady Malcolm was to write in her diary that she was "struck with the kindness of his [Napoleon's] expression, so contrary to the fierceness she had expected." She saw in his face "no trace of ability; his countenance seemed rather to indicate goodness." Before leaving Longwood she called on Madame Montholon, not yet recovered from her confinement.

The admiral, having noticed that the tent which afforded the only shade near the house was badly worn, had a new tent set up by sailors from the *Newcastle*. Napoleon had Montholon give a gold piece to each of the men. The naval officer in charge did not object. Had it come to the ears of Lowe it would have been the subject of querulous letters to the admiral and to Bathurst.

The better understanding between the Emperor and the governor did not last, for soon after the visit Bertrand told him about Lowe's letter regarding Madame Bertrand's note to Montchenu and the governor's peremptory reply to his protest. Moreover, something else happened that convinced Napoleon there would be no let-up in the petty annoyances the infliction of which Lowe considered a part of his duty.

The *Newcastle*, which had brought some thirteen cases of books for Napoleon, had also brought him a present from an admirer—Mr. J. C. Hobhouse, the future Lord Broughton. It was a two-volume compilation of letters, written by the donor from Paris to his friend Lord Byron after Napoleon's return from Elba. The volumes were handsomely bound in dark blue morocco, and on the cover of the first volume, stamped in gold, was a flattering dedication in Latin, beginning with the words *Imperatori Neapoleoni*. The books were delivered to the governor with a letter in which the author said that if Sir Hudson found it improper to give them to the person for whom they were intended, he was authorized to give them a place in his own library.

There was at that time nothing in the governor's instructions that would have prevented him from delivering a book to Napoleon inscribed with the imperial title. There were hundreds of books published during Bonaparte's reign dedicated to the

Emperor Napoleon. Lowe, however, considered the inscription a sufficient reason for nondelivery. Napoleon first heard about the matter from Colonel Keating, governor of Mauritius, who had paid him a visit, and who, the Emperor claimed, told him that Lowe had "boasted" to him about having withheld the book.[1]

TWO

Having never received an answer to his query whether Bonaparte wished to have Longwood House repaired and enlarged or a new house built, Sir Hudson wrote to Montholon regarding the matter. Montholon referred him to Bertrand, who did not reply, having made up his mind to have as little as possible to do with the governor. So Sir Hudson again wrote to Montholon. In the letter he received in reply, dated July 8, 1816, Montholon quoted the Emperor as having said of the governor's communication: "This letter is written with the intention of being amiable. It presents a contrast to the ignoble vexations that are daily contrived." He hinted that the decent thing for the government to have done was to have lodged the Emperor at Plantation House, and said that to add more rooms to Longwood House "would be merely enlarging a ruin" besides inflicting on Napoleon the annoyance of having workmen around for five or six months. The sensible thing to do, he wrote, was to make the necessary repairs. If a new house was to be built "it would be desirable to do so in the cultivated part of the island, where there are trees, water, and vegetation."

As far as Napoleon's objections to Longwood House were concerned, the governor could not help agreeing with him. He wrote to Lord Bathurst: "The objections against Longwood House appear but too well founded. In proposing additions to it, I was rather guided by its situation than by its actual state; for to make a good permanent residence it would almost require

---

[1] Colonel Keating was to deny that he had ever said this, but disclaimers by men in public office of things said in private should be viewed with a good deal of skepticism.

to be rebuilt." The house had, he wrote, "so many defects as to stand in need of continued reparations."

Regarding Plantation House he told Montholon that the court of directors of the East India Company had informed Admiral Cockburn that he was at liberty to assign to Napoleon as a residence any building belonging to the Company except Plantation House. Under these circumstances Lowe could obviously not have turned over Plantation House to the Emperor even had he been so inclined; but it is difficult to believe that the British government was equally helpless in the matter and could not have prevailed upon the East India Company to rescind its prohibition. To house the imperial exile in a building about which the Russian commissioner was to report to Count Nesselrode that it was little more than a "hovel," and of which the governor himself said that it was "unfit for permanent habitation," was unworthy of the government of a great nation. True that the government offered to build him—and did build him—a new house, but it should have known that with the facilities existing at St. Helena and with a Sir Hudson Lowe in charge, it would take years to complete. It was not completed until the beginning of 1821, when Napoleon was mortally ill, and he never set foot in it. Lord Liverpool had at one time suggested that Napoleon be housed at the Castle in Jamestown, but this was considered impractical as it would have given him too great an opportunity for escape. But it would not have been impractical to have had the governor reside at the Castle and Napoleon at Plantation House, which was three miles inland. From the national and historical viewpoints it was far more important to make Napoleon than to make Sir Hudson Lowe comfortable. Had he been given Plantation House as a residence and permitted the freedom of the island and of correspondence, as suggested by the Duke of Wellington, a Lord Chief Justice of England, Lord Campbell, would have found no occasion to write: "As things were managed, I am afraid it will be said that he [Napoleon] was treated in the eighteenth century, with the same cruel spirit as the maid of Orleans was in the fourteenth." [2]

[2] *Lives of the Chancellors*, Vol. VI, p. 31.

THREE

On July 16, the governor decided to make another attempt to confer with Napoleon in person about the housing situation. He arrived at Longwood House at about two in the afternoon and was promptly admitted. Unfortunately his peremptory letter to Bertrand and the Hobhouse incident had freshly aroused Napoleon's ire, and he felt far more inclined to talk about his grievances than about the new house. This time, however, he kept himself well under control. He made the following statement concerning the house: "If I had to answer you officially, I would have said that a new house be constructed for me; but it would take six years building. In a couple of years there will be a change of ministry in England, or a new government in France, and I shall no longer be here. If, however, I were obliged to remain at this place, I could not live in this house; it would be necessary to build another for me in a more agreeable part of the island."

All the rest was a recapitulation of his grievances. He reproached the governor for having discarded Cockburn's liberal policy. Sir Hudson replied that he had done nothing "but what was in strict conformity with Sir George Cockburn's written instructions." He chose to overlook the fact that the government did not object to the responsible official on the island not following instructions blindly and making regulations "in accordance with circumstances." When former governor Wilks had suggested to Cockburn that Napoleon be given the freedom of Longwood plateau, it was equivalent to proposing the nonenforcement of Bathurst's instruction that the prisoner "must be *always* attended by an officer appointed by the admiral or by the governor." Cockburn had not only given him the freedom of the plateau but of some of the adjacent territory as well. Bathurst had been informed of this and had not objected. As a matter of fact, Lowe himself refrained from carrying out that particular order, though he undoubtedly would have done so had he been in charge from the beginning. He told Bertrand that he would never have dared to give Napoleon the freedom of movement the admiral had allowed him.

During the interview Napoleon paced up and down the room, his hat under his arm. He reproached Sir Hudson for his conduct toward Bertrand, for the irksome precautions he was taking to prevent an escape which was manifestly impossible without the connivance of the governor or the admiral, if not of both. "But you keep sticking pins into us," he told him. "There is no way of coming to an understanding with you. You are a lieutenant general—you should not perform your duty like a sentinel. You ought to consider your reputation, which is bound to suffer from the way you conduct yourself toward us." Lowe replied: "I did not come here in search of glory, nor did I solicit the appointment; but being here I must do my duty, which I esteem above glory." Napoleon retorted: "It is always with you as with the wolf in the fable: one cannot be in the right with you." Finally he bowed, and Lowe, having bowed in return, retired.

On July 4, Admiral Malcolm had called, accompanied by the officers of the *Newcastle* whom he presented to Napoleon at the conclusion of the visit. On July 25, he came again, this time remaining all afternoon. As the Emperor did not seat himself but walked to and fro during the conversation, the admiral did the same, thus avoiding his predecessor's mistake, which had so irritated the fallen monarch, of seating himself without having been invited to do so. During the conversation Sir Hudson was frequently mentioned. "His manners are so displeasing to me," Napoleon said, "that if he were to come to tell me that a frigate was ready to take me to France, and I was at liberty to go where I pleased, he could not give me pleasure. Call it *enfantillage*, or what you will, so it is."

That same day Napoleon had received letters from his mother, his brother Lucien, his sister Pauline, and some English newspapers sent over by the governor. There was bad news for the Bertrands. On May 7, 1816, the grand marshal had been condemned to death in absentia for high treason. The paper containing the news was sent by Lowe to Bertrand under separate cover, so it might not fall into the hands of Madame Bertrand. It was accompanied by a note in which the governor said with one of his occasional flashes of friendliness: "It is with infinite pain that I am the organ of this communication in regard both to yourself and your family." Napoleon learned about Bertrand's conviction from O'Meara, who had heard the news at Jamestown. He was at first gravely concerned, but after thinking the matter over came to the conclusion that Bertrand had not much to worry about. French law required that if he returned to France he must be tried over again. When this happened he would have no difficulty in proving that he had never sworn fealty to the King.

FOUR

Having been disappointed in his expectation that expenses at Longwood could be reduced by requiring Napoleon's retinue to sign an agreement to remain on the island for the duration of the captivity—which, he believed, would result in the exodus of many of its members—Bathurst had decided on a more direct approach. On April 15, 1816, he had written a letter to Sir Hudson—which arrived at St. Helena in June by the *Newcastle* —instructing him to inform Napoleon that henceforth the government would allow him only £8,000 yearly for the maintenance of his household. If he wished to spend more he must pay the difference himself. This meant that while Lowe was receiving £12,000 annually and numerous perquisites for his family of four; while Stürmer found it necessary to expend £4,000 annually for his household consisting of himself, his wife, and four servants; while Balmain, a bachelor, informed his government that the cost of provisions at St. Helena was such as to make it impossible for him to live "with an entire absence of luxury" on less than £2,000 annually—Napoleon was to be allowed £8,000 a year for the maintenance of himself, two married couples with children, four other members of his suite, two British officers stationed at Longwood, and numerous servants! That with careful management a considerable saving could have been made admits of no doubt, but "to abridge the expenditures of Bonaparte's table and household, so that the annual cost may not exceed £8,000, including wines and extraordinaries of every kind," was niggardly to the point of absurdity.

On August 16, the governor, accompanied by Major Gor-requer, called to confer with Napoleon about the government's retrenchment order. He was told that the Emperor was in his bath—his usual excuse to unwelcome visitors—and was asked if he would be good enough to take the matter up with the grand marshal. Bertrand was at luncheon when the governor and his secretary were announced. He presently entered the drawing room into which they had been ushered and begged them to be seated. Sir Hudson sat down on the sofa, in the opposite cor-ner of which the grand marshal seated himself. The governor had brought with him an estimate of the annual expenses at Longwood, which he handed to Bertrand, saying they amounted to about £18,000 a year and that the government wished to have them reduced very considerably.[3] Bertrand asked how much the government would allow, and Lowe said they would allow £8,000, adding that he doubted they would consent to a larger expenditure unless financed by General Bonaparte himself. The grand marshal studied the paper Lowe had given him, then said: "Very well. I'll speak to the Emperor about it and tell him what you have said." Then, in a tone not free from irony, he remarked that if the English government could not afford the expense, he had no doubt that the Emperor's friends in Europe would be willing to assist him; but since he was prohibited to correspond with them by means of sealed letters—the only way he cared to correspond—it was impossible to inform them.

Apart from the irony, which was not without justification, there was nothing in Bertrand's statement that should have ex-cited the ire of a man fitted for the delicate post Sir Hudson occupied. For a great nation to quibble about the expenditure of a few thousand pounds for the living expenses of a man who had ruled half Europe, had made and unmade kings, and was still considered so important that a quarter of a million pounds

[3] Lowe's estimate included the constant repairs on the house, amounting to about £1,000 annually, and the transport of the supplies, costing about £600.

was annually expended to guard him, might well have provoked the irony of any man. Moreover, what the grand marshal had mentioned was precisely the point at issue. It was upon that, and upon nothing else, that an understanding had to be reached. But so lacking in tact was Hudson Lowe, that while Bertrand was still speaking he rudely interrupted him, saying: "Sir, I did not come here to enter into details. I have had a conversation on the subject of the expenses in question with General Bonaparte himself, and also with Count Montholon, and neither the one nor the other has made any difficulty about the mode of obtaining funds."

This was an untruth. What they had told him was what the grand marshal had just said: that there would be no difficulty in obtaining the money, provided the Emperor was permitted to correspond by sealed letters with those who were to furnish it. Since Lowe dismissed this as a detail he did not care to discuss, there remained nothing more to confer about; and Bertrand, who had somewhat of a temper himself, rose and handing the estimate of expenses back to the governor said curtly: "Very well. You can give this paper to Count Montholon. As for me, *Monsieur le Gouverneur*, I desire to have as little communication with you as possible, personally or in writing." Lowe and Gorrequer had also risen, and the former retorted: "And I can assure you, sir, that wish is quite reciprocal on my part." The two officers left the house, mounted their horses, and rode back to Longwood, Lowe being anxious to tell his side of the story to Napoleon before Bertrand had been able to tell his. He did not succeed: the Emperor again excused himself.

That same day Bertrand's house was surrounded by sentries. No one was permitted to leave or to enter. A soldier who allowed Dr. O'Meara to pass so he might minister to Bertrand's servant, who was gravely ill, was placed under arrest. Thomas Brooke, secretary and member of the council of St. Helena, who had come to see the grand marshal, was turned away. This points to a vindictive streak in the character of Sir Hudson which was to manifest itself repeatedly, not only in his dealings with the French, but with anyone on the island who incurred his displeasure. Dr. Stokoe, Lieutenant Reardon, Major Pritchard, Mr. Breame (the company farmer) were some of his victims. In the case of the last two he overreached himself and received a letter from the court of directors of the East India Company, rebuking him for his conduct toward the two men and his insolence toward the court.[4]

The next day the governor wrote to Montholon asking to be informed if Napoleon was content to have him reduce the provisions furnished to Longwood to come within the £8,000 allowed by the government, or "if he is willing to place at my command sufficient funds to meet the extra charges which must otherwise be unavoidably incurred."

FIVE

On August 18, Lowe went to Longwood to complain to Napoleon about Bertrand and to inquire with whom in the future Bonaparte wished him to deal. He took with him Reade and Gorrequer, and, fearing Napoleon might refuse to see him, had made arrangements with Sir Pulteney Malcolm to meet him at Hutt's Gate, feeling certain the admiral's presence would assure his reception.

The Emperor was walking in the garden with Madame Montholon and Las Cases when the cavalcade appeared in the avenue. Recognizing Lowe among the horsemen he quickly turned into a side lane with his companions. It was not long, however, before Montholon came and told him that the admiral and the governor requested the privilege of seeing him. He met them in the avenue, greeted the admiral affably and the governor with a curt nod. He knew about Bertrand's house arrest and had learned the details of the quarrel from O'Meara. The three men —Napoleon in the center—now walked up and down the avenue, their attendants remaining respectfully out of earshot.

At first the Emperor did nearly all the talking, addressing himself to the admiral, who interjected a sentence now and then. What they said had no relation to the Bertrand affair. Finally, taking advantage of a hiatus in their conversation, Sir Hudson

[4] Arnold Chaplin, *A St. Helena Who's Who*, pp. 176-86.

made his complaint and asked with whom in the future Napoleon wished him to confer. In justice to him it should be said that his account of what had occurred was fairly accurate, which may or may not have been due to the fact that he realized Napoleon already knew. The Emperor listened without uttering a word, and when he finished remained silent for so long a time that Lowe came to the conclusion he meant to make no reply. Suddenly, however, he turned to the admiral and said in a voice that betrayed suppressed emotion:

"General Bertrand is a man who has commanded armies, and *he* treats him as if he were a corporal. General Bertrand is a man well known throughout Europe, and *he* has no right to insult him. The marshal did perfectly right in speaking about the prohibition against sending letters and was justified in engaging in a discussion on that subject. *He* treats us all as if we were deserters from the Royal Corsican regiment. *He* has insulted Marshal Bertrand, and he deserved what the marshal said to him."

Lowe interrupted, saying that the marshal had first insulted him, but Napoleon went on:

"There are two kinds of people employed by governments—those whom they honor and those whom they dishonor. *He* is one of the latter. The situation they have given him is that of an executioner. But though my body is in the power of evil-minded men, my soul is as free and independent as when I was at the head of an army of three hundred thousand men."

"I am perfectly indifferent to all that," the governor said. "I did not seek my present employment. But it being offered to me I considered it my duty to accept it."

"Then," said Napoleon, "if the order were given you to assassinate me you would carry it out?"

"I would not. My countrymen do not assassinate."

"Since your arrival here," the Emperor went on, "we have experienced nothing but vexations. Your instructions are the same as Sir George Cockburn's—he himself told me so—but you execute them with fifty times more rigor. He never vexed us with trifles; you vex us hourly with your petty ways. You do not know how to conduct yourself toward men of honor: your soul is too vile. You treat us like Botany Bay convicts. You take all sorts of useless precautions for fear I shall escape. Why do you not tie me hand and foot, then you will be tranquil."

The admiral tried to calm him, saying he knew Sir Hudson was anxious to please him as much as it lay in his power to do so. The trouble was that they misunderstood each other. He was certain, he said, that much of the misunderstanding was due to the fact that there was so little direct intercourse between them and reports reached them in a distorted form. But Napoleon would not be calmed and resumed:

"He has insulted General Bertrand, put him under arrest in his own house! He has no feeling. Even the soldiers of the 53rd look upon me with compassion and weep when they pass me. Do you know that he had the meanness to keep from me a book because on its cover I was referred to as Emperor, and then boasted of having done so?"

"Boasted of it?" Lowe exclaimed.

"Yes, Colonel Keating told me so. Yet you have delivered letters to me addressed to the Emperor."

"But they came from the Secretary of State's office and were from your relatives or former subjects, not from Englishmen," Lowe replied.

"And who gave *you* the right of disputing that title?" Napoleon cried. "In a few years your Lord Castlereagh, your Lord Bathurst, you who speak to me, the whole pack of you, will be buried in the dust of oblivion. Or, if your names are remembered, it will be only on account of the indignity with which you have treated me. But the Emperor Napoleon will continue forever to be the subject, the ornament of history. You ask me for money to pay my living expenses. I have none. But I have plenty of friends who would send me whatever sum is required if I could write to them. Put me on rations if you wish. I can dine with the officers of the 53rd, and if not with them, then with the soldiers. I shall go and seat myself at the grenadiers' table. I am confident they will not drive away the first, the oldest soldier of

Europe.[5] You had no right to put Bertrand under arrest. You never commanded armies. You were nothing but a scribe of an *État Major*. I had imagined I should be well among the English, but you are not an Englishman."

"You make me smile, Sir," Lowe remarked.

"How, smile?"

"Yes, Sir, you make me smile. Your misconception of my character and your rudeness excite my pity. I wish you good day." So saying, he turned on his heel and walked away. The admiral saluted by raising his hat and followed him.

Later the Emperor said to Las Cases: "I must see him no more. He makes me fly into a passion. It is beneath my dignity. Words escape me that would have been unforgivable at the Tuileries. Their only excuse here is that I am in his power." The following day he added: "It would have been more worthy of me, more in keeping with my dignity, to have said all that with perfect composure; it would besides have been more impressive."

Such was Napoleon's last interview with Sir Hudson.

[5] Lowe has denied that Napoleon said anything about dining with the officers or soldiers of the 53rd. He has denied many things. It is not only his word against Napoleon's, who told Bertrand, Las Cases, Montholon, and O'Meara, but his word against Malcolm's. See Lady Malcolm's *A Diary of St. Helena*, p. 62.

XV. Lowe's Revenge

Partisans of Sir Hudson Lowe have severely criticized Napoleon for his angry outburst in the presence of Admiral Malcolm, but Sir Hudson was far from blameless. By his blunt refusal to discuss the question at issue during his interview with Bertrand, he had provoked the grand marshal. Placing him and his family under house arrest was a vindictive act which did him little credit. It was this that was mainly responsible for Napoleon's outburst. That Lowe's defenders knew this is evident from the fact that they have carefully abstained from making any mention of the house arrest, although Napoleon referred to it twice during the quarrel.

The relationship between Napoleon and Lowe was not improved by the "Remonstrance" which the former sent to Plantation House five days after the stormy interview. This famous document, signed by Montholon but dictated by Napoleon, has already been mentioned in the chapter dealing with the commissioners. It not only informed Lowe that the Emperor could not receive the commissioners in their official capacity, but discussed in detail all his grievances against the British government and its representative at St. Helena. In connection with the "Remonstrance" the following remarks exchanged during Lowe's interview with Napoleon on May 17, 1816, take on peculiar significance:

LOWE: If you think you have any cause to complain, you have but to write, and I will transmit your representation to England by the first opportunity.

NAPOLEON: What will be the use of sending it to your government? It will not be attended to there any more than here.

LOWE: I will have it published in all the papers of the Continent, if you wish it.

The "Remonstrance" was published in English newspapers and those on the Continent, but not by courtesy of Sir Hudson or Lord Bathurst. Napoleon managed to smuggle copies of the document to Lord Holland and other leaders of the Opposition after Lowe and Bathurst had done everything in their power to keep it secret. How anxious Lowe was that the document should *not* become public is evident from a conversation he had with O'Meara, who had received a copy from Montholon and had sent it to the admiralty. On October 10, 1816, the surgeon wrote to his friend Finlaison: "He was very much displeased at the idea of its being made known, and also with me for reading it, and said that the admiralty had nothing to do with what took place respecting him; that it ought not even to be made known to any of the Cabinet Ministers, except the Secretary of State [Lord Bathurst] with whom he corresponded himself."

TWO

A few days after sending the "Remonstrance" Napoleon committed a serious tactical blunder. On August 28, the governor received a letter from Montholon informing him that if he intended to persist in his policy that only those provided with a pass issued by him were to be admitted to Longwood, then the Emperor would be obliged if he would cease to give out passes altogether, "either to residents of the island, to officers, or to strangers," except to people "necessary for the service of the establishment." As things were now, wrote Montholon, persons provided with passes "wander round the house at Longwood, to the great discomfort of the Emperor in his walks."

Napoleon's decision in this matter appears to have been made on impulse. His valet Marchand criticises it in his memoirs, saying it played into the hands of Sir Hudson Lowe, whose aim it had been from the beginning to isolate the inhabitants of Longwood House. Two days after the letter was sent the Emperor had cause to regret it. News reached him that the officers of the 53rd, so well disposed toward him, felt hurt at the intimation that their visits to Longwood were an intrusion on his privacy. He sent for Captain Poppleton and asked him to assure the officers that they had been misinformed. "I am no old woman," he said. "I love a good soldier who has undergone the baptism of fire, no matter what country he belongs to."

On September 21, Admiral Malcolm called. He had not visited Napoleon since the disagreeable scene of which he had been an unwilling witness, considering it his duty to demonstrate his disapproval of the Emperor's conduct on that occasion. As, however, he was about to sail for the Cape, where he expected to remain for some time, he did not wish to depart without paying a visit to the captive. He had told Lowe of his intention, saying that if he did not do so Bonaparte would be certain to believe the governor had influenced him, which would still further envenom the situation. Moreover, by remaining on good terms with Bonaparte, he hoped to be able to act as a peacemaker. Sir Hudson did not ask him to abandon his plan, but showed unmistakably that he did not approve. It was the beginning of a coolness between them, which rapidly ripened into enmity. The admiral's visit to Napoleon was brief—scarcely twenty minutes —and both avoided any mention of the governor.

THREE

On October 1, a cavalcade of English officers and their attendants came riding up the avenue toward Longwood House. It consisted of the governor, Sir Thomas Reade, Colonel Wynyard, Major Gorrequer, Major Pritchard, two dragoons, and a servant. Obviously something important was afoot. The riders dismounted in front of the house, and, Montholon having been called, Sir Hudson demanded to see General Bonaparte. Napoleon, who had been peering through the opening carved in one of the Venetian blinds, had instructed Montholon to say that he was indisposed. The governor insisted, saying he had something of great importance to communicate which could not be handled through an intermediary. He was told a second time that the Emperor could not see him.

That afternoon Napoleon sent for O'Meara. He told him about the governor's insistence on seeing him and said: "I am sure he has nothing good to communicate, or he would not be so anxious to deliver it himself. Go to him and tell him that if he has anything to communicate, he had better send it to Bertrand, or Bertrand will go to his house. Or let him send Colonel Reade to me to explain what he has to say. I will receive and hear him, because he will be only the bearer of orders and not the giver of them."

O'Meara's visit to the governor resulted in Colonel Reade's appearance at Longwood on October 4. He came provided with a statement, written in English, which he had been instructed to read to Napoleon. The Emperor was in the garden when Lowe's emissary was announced. O'Meara presented him and then went to call Las Cases to act as interpreter. The statement informed Napoleon that the declarations signed by his followers in April, expressing their intent to remain on the island and to submit to the restrictions imposed upon their chief, had been rejected by the government, the signers having departed from the official formula. They must sign the declaration as originally presented. Those unwilling to comply would be sent to the Cape, where facilities would be provided for their return to Europe. The government, moreover, found it necessary to reduce General Bonaparte's retinue by four persons, who were to be sent to the Cape and thence to Europe. Those remaining must in the future abstain from criticizing the government or its representatives at St. Helena on pain of being deported to the Cape, where they would have to make what arrangements they could for transportation elsewhere. The government wished to have it understood, however, that those signing the declaration would not be "irrevocably bound" to remain on the island for the duration of the captivity. Facilities would be provided for departure to Europe, by way of the Cape, within a reasonable time after application had been made.

The reason Lord Bathurst no longer insisted that the signers bind themselves to remain on the island for the duration of the captivity obviously was due to the fact that more effective means had been found to reduce expenses at Longwood.

FOUR

The following day Bertrand swallowed his pride and went to Plantation House to learn the identity of those who would have to leave, and the exact wording of the declaration the others would have to sign. Napoleon told O'Meara: "We are in the power of that *boja* (hangman). They will send away all the rest by degrees, and it may as well be now as later. What shall I gain by having them here until the arrival of the next ship from England, or until that animal finds some new pretext for sending them away?"

The declaration Napoleon's followers were required to sign read: "I, the undersigned, do hereby declare that it is my desire to remain on the Island of St. Helena, and to participate in the restrictions imposed upon Napoleon Bonaparte personally." The document they had been asked to sign in April, but for which they had substituted their own versions, had referred to the Emperor as "General" Bonaparte.

Napoleon did not encourage his officers to sign. On October 10, O'Meara wrote to Reade: "Bonaparte told me this morning that he had recommended strongly to the French officers to go away, that he would be more independent without them." However, on October 14, he drafted a declaration which did not differ materially from the official version, except that "the Emperor Napoleon" was substituted for "Napoleon Bonaparte." He gave it to Bertrand, who signed it and asked all the others to do the same. It was forwarded to the governor who returned it that same evening with a note to the effect that the declaration was unacceptable in any but its official form.

Napoleon forbade his officers to sign the government's version, so, on the morning of October 15, Bertrand wrote to the governor that he and his colleagues felt it would be failing in respect to the Emperor to sign the document. That afternoon Sir Hudson came to Longwood, and having established himself in the new house of the Bertrands, which was nearing completion, summoned the officers one after another to come and explain themselves. He listened patiently to their arguments. Bertrand said that historical precedent justified Napoleon in clinging to the imperial title. Las Cases was grandiloquent and proved worthy of the nickname *l'Extase* which Gourgaud had given him by saying: "*Monsieur le Gouverneur,* you talk of us revering the Emperor as our Sovereign; we do more—we worship him!" Montholon—according to Lowe's report to Bathurst—spoke "with great plausibility and moderation," due, no doubt, to his training in diplomacy. Of Gourgaud's argument the governor wrote that "he commanded attention by his candor and sincerity." When, however, one reads Gourgaud's explanation, as reported by himself in his journal, one finds that he spoke mostly about himself, his sacrifices, his tribulations, his sufferings—intimating that the latter were due to Napoleon's treatment of him.[1] All finished by saying that the Emperor having forbidden them to sign, they had no choice in the matter.

That evening, after dinner, all, with the exception of the Bertrands, were assembled in the drawing room. Napoleon was reading aloud from *Don Quixote*. A servant entered with a letter from the grand marshal containing a note from the governor which the Emperor read to his companions. Unlike Lowe's usual epistles, it was short and to the point. With the exception of the

---

[1] Sir Hudson's favorable opinion of Gourgaud, expressed on several occasions, was due to the fact that in his letters home, which went through Lowe's hands, he represented St. Helena as a terrestrial paradise, and Longwood House, of which the governor himself found nothing good to say, as a "pretty country house." In some way Napoleon found out about it and asked him why he was doing this. He explained that he did it so his mother and sister should not be worried about him. Soon after he had written his mother about the salubrity of St. Helena he became gravely ill with dysentery.

Bertrands and four servants all would be embarked for the Cape. A temporary exception would be made of the grand marshal because of Madame Bertrand's pregnancy.

Consternation! Madame Montholon burst into tears. The Emperor appeared unconcerned and picked up the book as if he meant to resume reading. Instead of doing so, however, he shut it with a bang, saying: "One must be more cold-blooded than I am to be amused by such trifles in circumstances like the present." Gourgaud rose and exclaimed: "I'm going to sign!" Montholon followed suit, and after some hesitation Las Cases did the same.

It was almost midnight when Captain Poppleton, who had gone to bed, was awakened by a loud knocking. He had been entertaining some friends and was a little tipsy. When he opened the door he was confronted by the three officers, one of whom handed him four sheets of paper. Three were copies of the declaration, signed by the officers; the fourth was signed by the servants, with the exception of Santini. Las Cases made a little speech. He said that they were determined, if possible, not to abandon the Emperor. They had signed the declaration out of regard for him, but not by his order and even unknown to him. Poppleton remarked that Bertrand had not signed and was told that his declaration would be ready in the morning.

FIVE

On October 18, Sir Hudson notified Bertrand that the four persons he intended to send away were Captain Piontkowski, Rousseau, Santini, and one of the Archambaults. The removal of Piontkowski had been ordered by Lord Bathurst. He had incurred the latter's displeasure with his April declaration, in which he had said that St. Helena was a "horrible" place and that its climate—fog and rain alternating with scorching heat—was bound to shorten the lives of Napoleon and his suite. From a man for whom an exception had been made by allowing him to rejoin Napoleon this was more than Lord Bathurst was willing to tolerate. However, Lowe would have chosen him even without Bathurst's order, for it had been discovered that he had tried to persuade Lieutenant Nagle of the 53rd, who was about to return to England, to take with him a copy of the "Remonstrance."

As for Santini, Napoleon himself engineered his departure by prevailing upon him not to sign the declaration, thus making sure that he would be one of the four to be sent away. The young Corsican was intensely loyal to Napoleon and just as intensely hated Sir Hudson Lowe. In the vendetta spirit of his homeland he had decided to free the Emperor of the governor's hateful presence. He possessed a double-barreled fowling-piece with which he hunted pigeons and partridges. It was his intention to hide in a thicket Lowe had to pass when leaving after a visit, shoot him, and then kill himself. He made the mistake, however, of telling Cipriani about his plan. The *maître d'hôtel*, a Corsican himself, understood perfectly but, being older and wiser, realized what trouble this would bring on the Emperor and his suite. He tried to persuade Santini to abandon his intention, and finally told Napoleon, who summoned the young man to his apartment. "It was only by imperial, by pontifical authority that I finally succeeded in making the rascal abandon his project," the Emperor told Las Cases. However, he decided to take no chances. He told Santini not to sign the declaration as he needed him for an important mission in England. He had Saint-Denis write out the "Remonstrance" on a piece of white satin, which Santini sewed into the lining of his coat.

The governor had informed Bertrand that the four must be at Jamestown in the early afternoon of the following day, ready to depart. Each was given a booklet containing a request by Napoleon to his relatives and friends to pay the bearer two years' wages and a pension of one third his annual salary. Piontkowski was moreover promoted to *chef d'escadron*—cavalry major. Madame Bertrand presented him with a gold chain and the grand marshal gave him a personal letter of introduction. They sailed to the Cape on the *David* where, thanks to the intervention of Admiral Malcolm, they were kept only about a month instead of the six months Lowe had intended for them. They arrived at Spithead on February 15, 1817.

Rousseau and Archambault secured passage for the United States, where they entered the service of Napoleon's brother Joseph. Piontkowski and Santini were allowed to go to London and promptly made contact with Lord Holland, Sir Robert Wilson, and other leaders of the Whig party. The result was that on March 13, 1817, an English translation of the "Remonstrance" appeared in the *Morning Chronicle*. That same day Ridgway published a pamphlet in English and French entitled *An Appeal to the British Nation*. It had been written by Colonel Maceroni, who had served under Murat, from material furnished by Santini, in whose name it was published. The young Corsican meant well, but overemphasized the inadequacy and inferior quality of supplies furnished for the Emperor's table, which to a domestic might well have appeared the most serious grievance. Napoleon, however, considered this hardly worth mentioning, and when toward the end of May a copy of the pamphlet came into his hands, he pronounced it "a foolish production, exaggerated, full of trash, and some lies." Yet so great was the interest in the imperial captive in England that edition followed edition.

SIX

It would have been surprising if the man who was to hound Admiral Malcolm with vindictive epistles long after he had left St. Helena—who was to try to break Captain Poppleton for accepting a snuff-box from Napoleon when leaving the island—whom the court of directors of the East India Company found it necessary to rebuke for his unjust behavior toward Major Pritchard and his vindictive persecution of Thomas Breame, the Company farmer—who vented his spite on Lieutenant Reardon, Major Emmett, Captain Lutyens, Colonel Lascelles, Dr. Stokoe, in fact on anyone who showed the least sympathy with the exiles at Longwood—should have made no attempt to retaliate for the tongue-lashing he had received on August 18. If retaliation did not follow immediately, as in the case of Bertrand, it must have been because Lowe realized that where Napoleon personally was concerned it would not do to make it too obvious that he was trying to avenge himself. He must wait for a favorable opportunity.

The letter he had received from Bathurst on September 29, instructing him to remove Piontkowski and three others, furnished that opportunity. It contained this sentence: "The conduct of General Bonaparte and his followers, the information which I have from time to time directed to be forwarded to you, and many concurring circumstances cannot fail of impressing you with an expectation of some attempt being made to effect his escape; and it is to be apprehended that he may be much assisted in such an undertaking by the number and character of the persons who are with him."

This was as vague as it was illogical. If Napoleon had been making preparations to escape, he and his followers would have tried to lull the governor into security by making it appear that they had become reconciled to their lot. They were doing the exact opposite. As for the rumors of preparations being made in Brazil for an expedition to free Napoleon, this was nothing new. A little over two weeks after Lowe's arrival on the island, Bathurst's assistant, Sir Henry Bunbury, had written him a letter containing much more precise information. He had replied on July 29: "Every step has been taken that depends on me to counteract the effects of the plotting which you give me reason to apprehend, by your letter of the 4th of May, is going on at the Brazils for the attempted liberation of the prisoner; but it is by an additional number of small cruising vessels, rather than by any other means, the projects of the persons you mention are most likely to be defeated, and I believe Sir Pulteney Malcolm writes to this effect."

Nothing could be clearer. All that could be done on land to safeguard the security of the prisoner had been done. The rest depended upon the admiral. Then why the new regulations of October 9, 1816, so much more severe than those already in force? The answer: they were purely retaliatory—the result of the quarrel of August 18.

It appears that in framing the new regulations Lowe had

hoped to kill two birds with one stone. He would have liked to send away three of Napoleon's officers instead of three of his servants. This, however, would have aroused the Opposition in Parliament and the Whig press. But if he made a new set of regulations sufficiently severe, might not the officers leave of their own accord? He was to explain to Lord Bathurst: "It was a particular request of Count Bertrand to me that I would give him in writing an abstract of the several regulations to which he and the other persons who might subscribe to the declarations would be subject. . . . I framed in consequence the Regulations of the 9th of October."

SEVEN

The regulations of October 9, 1816, contained restrictions already in force—such as the one providing that no one could visit Napoleon without a pass from the governor and forbidding all correspondence between the inhabitants of Longwood and the people on the island without his intervention. To these were now added several new restrictions which seemed particularly designed to plague the captive and his companions in exile. The four principal ones were as follows:

The territory in which Napoleon and his suite were allowed to walk, ride, or drive without being accompanied by an English officer was reduced by one third—from a circumference of twelve miles to one of eight. All the pleasant shady places adjoining Longwood plateau—Fisher's Valley (which Napoleon had named the Valley of the Nymph), Woody Ridge, Miss Mason's cottage and lovely garden, Prospect House and grounds (the property of Mr. Brooke), Geranium Valley—were now outside the limits. There remained only the bleak plateau with a forlorn gumwood tree here and there, not unlike a ragged scarecrow. Sir Hudson was to give as an excuse that since he had been on the island, Napoleon had not gone down into the valley anyway. The fact was that since Lowe had been on St. Helena it had been the rainy season, when riding in the valley was well-nigh impossible, as the ground became marshy and horses were liable to become hopelessly mired.

The new regulations further provided that when Napoleon went out riding he must "abstain from entering into conversation (except such as the interchange of customary salutation may demand) with the persons whom he may happen to meet, unless in the presence of an English officer." Thus, if he wished to talk to someone he met on the plateau he would have to send an attendant to Longwood House to fetch Captain Poppleton, who might or might not be there. In the meantime he and his chance acquaintance must remain silent. If they engaged in conversation and one of the sentries placed around the limits happened to be near, they were liable to be arrested, or he might even fire at them. "This," commented Napoleon, "is a moral annulment of the circuit allowed us. It is so extraordinary that we are now actually induced to believe, what many persons have already suspected, that Sir Hudson Lowe is occasionally subject to fits of lunacy."

If Napoleon consented to receive someone to whom Lowe had granted a pass, the visitor was not allowed to speak to any other member of the establishment, nor were they allowed to speak to him. Obedience to the letter of this instruction would have meant that Napoleon would have had to open his own front door, and if the visitor did not speak French they could only look at each other, as no member of the establishment could have acted as interpreter.

Sunset at St. Helena varied with the seasons from 5:30 to 6:30. Hitherto the sentries stationed around Longwood Estate had been drawn in around the house at 9 P.M., after which no one could enter or leave the house. Admiral Cockburn had appointed that hour notwithstanding the fact that on St. Helena it grows dark almost immediately after sunset. He had done this because he realized that on the shadeless Longwood plateau it was only after sunset that in summer Napoleon would enjoy walking in the garden. The prisoner had never abused the privilege. Lowe's new regulations, however, called for the sentries to be drawn in around the house immediately after sunset. Thus, in summer, Napoleon would no longer be able to walk or ride by day where there was shade, and after sunset would be prevented from walking in the garden. This meant that during the only season of the year when the plateau was relatively free of fog, wind, and rain, he would have to remain indoors.

Lord Bathurst had at no time instructed Lowe to make these absurd and sadistic regulations. They were entirely his own invention. They were retaliatory and would not have been formulated had there been no quarrel. That Lord Bathurst doubted their wisdom is evident from his letter to Lowe of January 1, 1818, in which he says that such embarrassing questions might be asked in Parliament as "Why should you prohibit him from those places within the original limits, to which he never went, as his never going there shows he could not have made a bad use of them." Walter Scott, in his *The Life of Napoleon*, appears to have no doubt that Lowe's motive was revenge. He has written: "We are inclined from a review of his conduct, divesting it of the exaggerations of his personal enemies, to think there remain traces of a warm and irritable temper, which seems sometimes to have overborne his discretion, and induced him to forget that his prisoner was in a situation where he ought not, even when his conduct seemed most unreasonable and most provoking, to be considered as an object of resentment, or being subject, like other men, to retort and retaliation."

EIGHT

Since August 17, the day before the quarrel, when Lowe had notified Montholon that the government had directed him "to limit the expenditure of General Bonaparte's establishment to £8,000 per annum," but gave him liberty to permit further expenses being incurred "provided he furnishes the funds whereby the surplus charges may be defrayed," Montholon, manager of Napoleon's establishment, had pondered the problem without arriving at a solution. The Emperor, he knew, still had most of the money he had brought with him from France, but apparently had no intention of stripping himself of ready cash for the benefit of the British government. As for limiting expenses to what the government was willing to allow, considering the size of the household and prices at St. Helena, a far more able manager than Montholon might well have despaired. In the meantime, however, the governor had done some figuring. He, too, realized the impossibility of reducing expenses at Longwood to £8,000 per annum unless many more of Bonaparte's followers were sent away. He considered it unlikely that the captive would supply the money with which to pay the deficit unless permitted to correspond by sealed letter concerning the matter. Sending away Napoleon's officers for no other reason than that the government was unwilling to pay their keep, might result in an uproar in Parliament and produce an unfavorable impression throughout Europe. So he took a bold step. On September 5, he sent Gorrequer to Longwood to inform Montholon that the governor, *on his own responsibility,* would allow £1,000 monthly for the maintenance of the household.[2]

When told about the governor's concession Napoleon was amused. He ordered that the wine be rationed, but agreed with Montholon that no reduction worth mentioning could be made in the amount expended for food and other necessities. With prices what they were at St. Helena, Lowe's concession did not suffice. So, when on the 7th of September Gorrequer called again, Montholon informed him that the Emperor had said he would be obliged to sell his silver tableware to meet the monthly deficit.

Sir Hudson did not relish the news and felt sure Lord Bathurst would relish it even less. The government would be excoriated by the Opposition press for its pettiness and parsimony. There would be speeches in Parliament. All Europe would be talking. A month went by and nothing happened. But toward the middle of October, when Lowe made a demand for money to cover the monthly deficit, Cipriani appeared at the office of Balcombe, Cole, & Company, at Jamestown, with a quantity of silver. It was some of the Emperor's tableware hammered into a shapeless mass after the imperial eagles which adorned it had been re-

[2] This is further proof that Sir Hudson had the power to change instructions to Napoleon's advantage, if he felt so inclined, as well as to his disadvantage, his usual procedure. Frédéric Masson is therefore mistaken when he holds Lord Bathurst principally responsible for what went on at St. Helena

moved. There were some dozen people in the office, including several officers of a frigate about to depart for England. They watched the silver being weighed and one of them asked Cipriani if the Emperor was well. "As well as a man can be who has to sell his tableware in order to live," the Corsican replied. The silver brought £240.

There were further sales in November and December. The first brought £309, the second £516. Napoleon had ordered twelve covers to be left intact, but to dramatize the situation further he had Cipriani buy cheap earthen tableware at Jamestown and send it to Longwood. Tongues were wagging all over the island. Never had Lowe so anxiously awaited a letter from Bathurst. Finally it came. In a dispatch dated November 22, 1816, Bathurst authorized Lowe to permit Napoleon to send sealed letters to a London banking house. The Emperor's stepson Eugene, who had married the daughter of the King of Bavaria and with whom Napoleon had 800,000 francs, made arrangements with Andrews, Street, & Parker of London, so drafts signed by Bertrand should be honored. In October, 1817, Bathurst made a further concession. He wrote to Lowe: "If you should consider the sum of £12,000 a year not to be adequate to maintain such an establishment as would be requisite for a general officer of his distinction, you will have no difficulty in making what you deem to be a requisite addition."

A victory? Yes; but what a victory for the hero of Austerlitz and Jena! "It is but a step from the sublime to the ridiculous," he himself had said once.

4

XVI. Las Cases Deported

Las Cases was dissatisfied and unhappy. It was after the removal to Longwood that his real troubles had begun. For reasons already noted he had remained the Emperor's favorite companion, but he was now constantly exposed to the jealous resentment of Gourgaud and of Montholon. It expressed itself in slighting remarks and in innuendoes. Montholon had taken advantage of his appointment to manager of the Longwood establishment to assign to him and to his son Emanuel three little connecting rooms worse than those occupied by some of the servants. Emanuel wrote to his mother: "They are so low that you can touch the ceilings with your hands; they are covered with tar-paper. When the sun shines we are almost suffocated; when it rains we are almost drowned." Small of stature, elderly, unaggressive, Las Cases was no match for his tormentors. He suffered in silence, but his health became affected. His eyes troubled him, and he was compelled to tell Napoleon that he could no longer see well enough to take dictation. When not in the Emperor's company he spent his time dictating to his son all Napoleon told him about his career and those associated with it, interspersing it with rhetorical outbursts about his hero and fulminations against the governor. Saint-Denis, with the Emperor's permission, did the transcribing. Toward the end of November, 1816, the manuscript consisted of 925 closely written pages.[1]

[1] The Garner edition has over 2,000 printed pages.

The ill will of Las Cases' colleagues increased in intensity as time progressed. A two days' record of the discord, as given by Gourgaud in his journal, is sufficiently revealing. In the afternoon of November 16, 1816, according to his account, Napoleon, accompanied by Gourgaud and the Montholons, went walking in the garden. After a while they called on the Bertrands, who, since October 20, had been living in their new house, about 120 yards from the Emperor's establishment. While Napoleon was conversing with Madame Bertrand, Montholon said to the others that Las Cases was about to lose his private servant. "However, one need not feel sorry for him," he added with a smirk. "He is going to have the services of Gentilini. The Emperor's valet will be emptying the Jesuit's chamberpot."

That evening, when Napoleon, the Montholons, and Gourgaud were assembled in the drawing room, Emanuel entered and said his father was ill and would be unable to appear for dinner. While they were at table the Emperor sent Saint-Denis to see how the sick man was faring. The servant returned and reported that Las Cases was in bed, but had said he could eat some soup and some breast of chicken. "Oh, the poor man!" Montholon exclaimed sarcastically. Napoleon glanced at him but said nothing. When they had returned to the drawing room he remarked that the annoyance the governor was causing Las Cases about his servant might well be responsible for his illness. Gourgaud bristled and said: "I had to put up with far greater annoyance when they took away my servant. For three days I had nobody to wait on me."

The Emperor spoke to Bertrand about Gourgaud's behavior, and, on November 18, the grand marshal reasoned with the young man, trying to convince him that Las Cases, a chamberlain, had a right to precedence over him. Gourgaud replied with some heat that he had been His Majesty's chief ordnance officer at an annual salary of 32,000 francs, had taken orders from no one but him, and had had entry to his cabinet at all times. He, a general officer, was not going to have a chamberlain, a mere titled valet, take precedence over him.

That same day the Emperor summoned Montholon and Gour-

gaud to his apartment. He spoke to them about Las Cases, trying to convince them that he was a man of great merit, a "little
Talleyrand." They were wrong, he said, in being jealous of him.
True that he sometimes laid himself open to ridicule, as when
he claimed that his family tree was second only to that of the
Bourbons, "but I find his conversation entertaining. He knows a
great deal about England, where all of us may be living some
day, and is giving me much useful information about that country." Turning to Gourgaud, he added: "I speak to you as I would
to a son, and beg you to be friends with him."

Gourgaud replied that Las Cases was too much of a Jesuit to
suit him as a friend and appealed to Montholon for support,
whereupon the latter put forth his own claims. He had, he said,
been minister to Würzburg, had served his country for seventeen years, had been a general as well as a chamberlain, was as
well descended as Las Cases, and would under no circumstances
allow him to take precedence over him.

The man who had made and unmade kings and had laid the
law down to emperors keenly felt the absurdity of this petty
quarrel about who should have precedence at his shabby little
imitation court. Waxing somewhat impatient, he reproached
Montholon for encouraging Gourgaud in his stand. Then, turning to the latter, he said: "You not only want precedence over
Las Cases, but also over Montholon." The young general drew
himself up and said with apparent conviction: "Nothing can disturb the friendship between myself and Montholon."

That evening Las Cases had sufficiently recovered from his
indisposition to appear in the drawing room. When Cipriani
opened the door leading to the dining room and announced,
"His Majesty is served," and the Emperor, having offered his
arm to Madame Montholon, walked toward the door, Gourgaud
quickly fell in behind Montholon, in front of Las Cases.

TWO

There came a time when Las Cases had to confess to himself that
the privilege of being Napoleon's favorite companion in exile
did not compensate for the enmity, humiliation, and discom-

fort to which he was daily subjected. Moreover, he began to wonder if his presence at Longwood did not make things worse rather than better for the captive. Now that he no longer took the Emperor's dictation, might he not be more useful to him as his representative in Europe? As for the memoirs he was writing, it was Napoleon's reminiscences of his astounding career in which the world was primarily interested, and what the Emperor had already told him covered all the main events of that career and would fill several volumes. Napoleon's existence at St. Helena was not likely to differ much from one year to another, so that, too, was sufficiently covered. He thus reached the conclusion that it would be to the Emperor's advantage as well as his own if he were to leave.

But how could he leave of his own volition—he who had said in the May declaration he had sent to Lowe: "I mean to share the fate of the Emperor Napoleon; to accompany him, to follow him, and to alleviate as much as I can the unjust treatment he experiences"; who had exclaimed within the hearing of his colleagues: "The Emperor is my god, the object of my veneration and adoration!"? Would not people say what Montholon and Gourgaud had clearly intimated, that he had come to St. Helena not from devotion to Napoleon but to collect material for a book? He saw only one solution: to get himself deported.

He may have driven the thought away as unworthy when it had first obtruded itself, for he had by this time become devoted to Napoleon. Where does egotism end and devotion begin? He hardly knew the Emperor when he offered to follow him to St. Helena, and there is reason to believe that the desire to write a first-hand account of his career, gleaned from his conversation, had been his predominating motive at that time. But Bonaparte was a man of exceptional charm and possessed a streak of innate kindness that shone forth from his face and manifested itself throughout his life on numerous occasions. We have seen that Lady Malcolm has written she was "struck with the kindness of his expression," that "seemed to indicate goodness." The Englishman Basil Hall, who visited him at St. Helena on August 13, 1817, wrote: "It is impossible to imagine an expression of more entire mildness, I may almost call it benignity and kindliness, than that which played over his features during the whole interview." He had been kind to Las Cases, and they had been in almost daily communication for months. Impressionable as was the chamberlain, he could hardly have helped becoming devoted to him. Yet the thought that getting himself deported was the only way out of his dilemma kept intruding and influenced his actions. It manifested itself in his correspondence. The Bertrands, the Montholons, knowing their letters were read by the governor, were circumspect when writing to relatives and friends. Gourgaud, not wishing to cause anxiety to his mother and sister, managed to make his exile appear almost enviable. Las Cases, on the other hand, faithfully echoed Napoleon, and to the man who had had all Europe for a playground and a score of palaces to live in, Longwood and Sir Hudson's restrictions were worse than stone walls and iron bars to the ordinary mortal.

One cannot help wondering if Las Cases' note to the Baroness Stürmer—a bold infraction of the regulation forbidding any communication with persons on the island without the intervention of the governor—was not sent as much in the hope that it would fall into the hands of Sir Hudson as for the purpose of establishing contact with the baroness. It did fall into Lowe's hands, but Las Cases got only a warning. His next move was to invite two officers, who had visited with the Emperor, to his room for the purpose of reading Napoleon's "Remonstrance" to them. It was well known that Lowe was in the habit of questioning visitors to Longwood, so Las Cases knew that the governor would learn about the matter. That Lowe was becoming seriously aroused against him is evident from his letter to Lord Bathurst of July 27, 1816, in which he wrote, speaking of Napoleon's officers: "There is not one of them who has not shown a disposition to elude the execution of the established regulations, and abuse the indulgences granted them—but none more so than the one from whom I least expected it, the Count Las Cases."

While Las Cases therefore was anxious to be deported, the governor was no less anxious to get rid of him. But Sir Hudson felt that to deprive Napoleon of his favorite he needed a more flagrant breach of the regulations than any of which the chamberlain had thus far been guilty.

THREE

During Admiral Cockburn's administration Las Cases had hired a personal servant—a slave named James Scott belonging to a white man who had fathered him. It was Scott who had delivered Las Cases' note to the Baroness Stürmer. This having attracted the governor's attention to him, it was discovered that no permission had been asked to hire him. So Lowe demanded that he be dismissed and offered to send a soldier to take his place, which offer Las Cases declined.

Scott left on November 17, but a day or two later eluded the sentries during the night and reappeared at his former employer's quarters at Longwood. Las Cases was with the Emperor, who was having one of his sleepless nights. Scott waited a considerable time and finally departed, but not before having told young Emanuel that he had obtained a situation "with a person going to London," was leaving in a few days, and had come "to offer his services without reserve." He promised to return.

Las Cases told the Emperor about the visit and suggested that advantage be taken of this opportunity to send letters to London. Napoleon was at first interested, but reconsidered. He was to say later that he did not think it prudent to entrust letters to a slave already suspect to the governor.

Las Cases, however, decided to go ahead anyway. When on Friday night of that same week the servant reappeared, he told him that he meant to take advantage of his offer and that letters would be prepared to be delivered by him to a person in London. Scott promised to call for them on Sunday night, which, he said, "would in all probability be the eve of his sailing." Las Cases had his son copy two letters in minute script on strips of white satin. One was addressed to his friend Lady Clavering in London, the other to Napoleon's brother Lucien at Rome. Both were to be delivered to Lady Clavering, who was requested to forward Lucien's letter and to give Scott five louis for his trouble. Lucien's letter was long and required two strips of satin. When on Sunday night Scott put in an appearance, he sewed Lady Clavering's letter and one strip of Lucien's into the lining of his waistcoat. The third strip he put into his pocket, apparently with the intention of secreting it later in some other garment. He was likewise given a testimonial concerning his reliability as a servant and a slip of paper with Lady Clavering's address. It developed that before leaving Longwood Scott hid the strip he had put in his pocket under a stone, which suggests that he had no intention of delivering the letters.

FOUR

On November 25, 1816, Admiral Malcolm, back from his sojourn at the Cape, called on the Emperor. When he had departed Napoleon went walking in the garden with Las Cases and Gourgaud. A servant appeared with a tray on which were five oranges, a sugar bowl, and eating utensils. The Emperor seated himself on a log and, having given one of the oranges to Las Cases for his son, peeled and sliced the others, powdered them over with sugar, and invited his companions to help themselves.

Soon after a cold wind sprang up and the Emperor and Las Cases went to the billiard-room. While they were conversing, Napoleon, happening to glance toward a window, saw a number of officers, headed by the governor, enter at the gate and advance toward the house. A short time later a servant appeared and said that Colonel Reade was in Las Cases' apartment and wished to speak to him. The thought flashed through Las Cases' mind that the visit might have some connection with his clandestine correspondence. He hesitated. The Emperor, noticing his hesitation, said: "Go and see what that animal wants," then added: "*And come back soon.*" These were the last words the favorite was fated to hear Napoleon utter.

Several dragoons with plumed hats were stationed about the door of Las Cases' living quarters. Inside were Colonel Reade and Emanuel. The boy was pale and frightened, the colonel suave and smiling as usual. He greeted the little man with apparent cordiality, asked about his health, and made a few other commonplace remarks. Suddenly, however, his face hardened and his voice grew harsh as he said: "By order of His Excellency the Governor I arrest you both on information furnished by your former servant James Scott concerning unauthorized correspondence." Las Cases, who had regained his self-possession, asked permission to see the Emperor, which was refused. Rainsford, an inspector of police, recently arrived from England, entered, as did Captains Blakeney and Poppleton. Emanuel was ordered to remain to assist in sealing his father's papers, while the latter was led away surrounded by dragoons.

Father and son were at first housed in Major Harrison's cottage, near the one formerly occupied by the Bertrands. After a couple of days they were transferred to Ross Cottage, belonging to Balcombe, in the garden of which the purveyor raised poultry for Napoleon's household. They were closely guarded and not permitted to have visitors, but were free to walk in the garden. Their meals were brought to them from Plantation House, which had the disadvantage that they often arrived cold.

FIVE

From what has been said it would be natural to infer that Las Cases had given the letters to Scott in the hope that when the servant was searched before his departure, they would be discovered, giving the governor an opportunity to deport him and his son. What makes it appear highly improbable that on this occasion the chamberlain had that end in view is the nature of his letter to Lady Clavering. Las Cases wrote: "Please oblige by letting me know if Lord Holland has received the packet I sent him." (No packet had been sent him through official channels.) He reveals that a note she had secreted in clothing she had sent had reached its destination, and suggests that articles be inserted in the *Times* and the *Morning Chronicle* containing some phrases "the reading of which makes it plain that my letter has been received."

Why should Las Cases have written such a letter if it was his intention that it should fall into the hands of Sir Hudson? He could have written one that would have aroused the governor's ire sufficiently to deport him without throwing suspicion on Lord Holland and Lady Clavering and putting the government on its guard against clandestine correspondence conducted through the newspapers. It was, moreover, his intention—to which he remained faithful on his return to Europe—to make use of his own and Napoleon's friends for the benefit of the captive. Involving them in possible difficulties with the authorities would hardly have served that purpose.

When, however, we consider that Lowe was just as anxious to find a pretext to deport Las Cases as the latter was to be deported, we are on firmer ground. Why, one wonders, was James Scott not arrested and punished for delivering the note to the Baroness Stürmer? May it not have been because it was intended to make use of him to entrap Las Cases into a more serious breach of the regulations? Lowe has claimed that John Scott, father of James, appeared at Plantation House on November 25, 1816, and laid before him the two strips of satin, the testimonial Las Cases had given his son, and a slip of paper with Lady Clavering's address, all of which, he said, James had shown to him. The young man was placed under arrest, but while in the case of the botanist Welle and the case of Captain Lamb and Radowitch (discussed in a future chapter) the parties concerned were questioned under oath and their sworn statements are available to historians, there exists no legal document showing what questions were asked Scott and what answers were given. The name of the person supposed to have hired him to accompany him to London is nowhere mentioned. No explanation is given why, if James had acted in good faith, he hid one of the strips of satin under a stone at Longwood. A slave could not leave the island without a permit from the governor, yet there is no evidence that Scott had received or had even applied for a permit. Another question that presents itself is how did Scott manage to get through the line of sentries, drawn closely around the house after dark, six times, coming and going? And how does it happen that there is no mention anywhere of an investigation having been made of the malfunctioning of the sentry system? Scott's punishment for the serious offense of aiding the French in clandestine correspondence was confinement for a time to his father's farm. For far less serious offenses slaves were inhumanly flogged. All this seems to justify the conclusion that after Scott had delivered the note to the Baroness Stürmer a deal was made with his father to use him to entrap his former employer, in consideration of which he would be let off with a light punishment.

SIX

From a window in the billiard-room Napoleon had watched Las Cases being led away. He was to write to his favorite: "A numerous staff was prancing around the house; methought I saw the inhabitants of some island in the Pacific dancing around the prisoner they are about to devour." Major Gorrequer, one of the party of officers who had invaded the premises, told Montholon the reason for the arrest and he hastened to inform Napoleon. Gourgaud, Bertrand, and Madame Montholon had joined the Emperor in the billiard-room. Gourgaud has written: "The Emperor does not appear particularly disturbed by the occurrence and plays with the billiard balls. The grand marshal seems in a bad humor. The Montholons have difficulty to hide their satisfaction. I seem to be the only one who is painfully affected." The impulsive young man appears to have had a twinge of conscience, but not for long. He asked Bertrand, whom the Emperor had instructed to try to see the prisoner, to tell him that "although I am his enemy, I am sorry about what has befallen him."

Early the following morning Napoleon sent a note to Bertrand asking him to go to Plantation House and try to obtain Las Cases' release. He was further instructed to ask for the return of all papers found in Las Cases' rooms that were the property of the Emperor. Among the papers so designated were chapters of his memoirs he had dictated to the chamberlain and Las Cases' own memoirs, which, he said, had been written by his order. He may have claimed the latter as his property in the hope that if he did so Sir Hudson would refrain from reading them. Papers which obviously belonged to him were returned to him unread;

Las Cases' memoirs, however, were eventually sent to England after having been read by the governor. Sir Hudson declined to permit Las Cases to return to Longwood, saying that his "instructions would not permit it."

Napoleon was somewhat uneasy about the effect a reading of Las Cases' journal might have upon the governor. Since Saint-Denis had done the transcribing he called him in and questioned him.

"How is Sir George Cockburn treated in the memoirs?" he queried.

"So-so, Sire," the valet replied.

"Did he write that I called him a shark?"

"Yes, Sire."

"And Sir George Bingham?"

"He is very well spoken of, and so is Colonel Wilks."

"Is there anything in it that might compromise anybody?"

"No, Sire."

"Anything about Admiral Malcolm? Does it say that I remarked once, 'There is the face of a true Englishman'?"

"Yes, Sire, he is very well treated."

"Anything about the governor?"

Ali could not help smiling, then said: "A great deal, Sire."

"Does it mention that I said he was a villainous wretch?"

"It does, Sire."

"Does it say that his is the most ignoble face I ever beheld?"

"Yes, Sire, but at times it tones down Your Majesty's remarks about him."

"Does it say that I called him a *sbirro Siciliano* (a Sicilian spy)?"

"It does, Sire."

"Well, that's precisely what he is."

Montholon and Gourgaud soon noted with mounting displeasure that the Emperor was taking the loss of his favorite far more to heart than they had hoped. A week after the arrest Gourgaud wrote in his diary that he and Montholon were unhappy, as the Emperor hardly noticed them, "all because they have taken away his Las Cases." Three days later Montholon confided to his colleague that he believed the Emperor meant to strike a bargain with the governor by offering to ask them to leave provided Las Cases was returned. Gourgaud wrote in his journal: "I have seen Lannes, Bessières, Duroc die. They were the Emperor's devoted servitors, his disciples, yet he mourned them less than he now does Las Cases."

SEVEN

On December 11, Napoleon dictated to Marchand a letter to Las Cases in which praise for his favorite alternated with condemnation of the British authorities. It read, in part: "Your conduct at St. Helena has been like the whole of your life, honorable and irreproachable. Your letter to one of your friends in London contains nothing reprehensible; you merely unburden your heart in the bosom of friendship. . . . Your presence was necessary to me. You are the only one that can read, speak, and understand English. How many nights have you not watched over me when I was ill! . . . Once in Europe, whether you proceed to England or return home, endeavor to forget what you have been made to suffer and pride yourself on your loyalty to me and the affection I cherish for you. If you should, some day or other, see my wife and son, embrace them for me. . . . As there is every reason to believe that you will not be allowed to come and see me before your departure, receive my embraces and the assurance of my esteem and friendship. May you be happy."

The following evening the Emperor and his three dinner companions—all that now remained of the seven that had graced his board at the beginning of his captivity at Longwood—remained for a while at table when they had finished eating. Napoleon related that he had written a letter to Las Cases, which, he felt certain, the governor would find sufficiently embarrassing. He asked Gourgaud to fetch it from his study, and on his return told him to read it aloud. When the reading was concluded he asked him what he thought of it. The young general, who had not yet learned that, as Bertrand was to say, "when the Emperor asks for someone's opinion it is only to have his own confirmed," said he considered it too laudatory and too effusive. Las Cases, he said, had known the Emperor only eighteen months. He, Gourgaud, knew of no sacrifices the chamberlain had made, or of any real danger he had incurred for the sake of the Emperor. His Majesty had never written a letter like that even to old and tried friends like Duroc and Lannes, so why to Las Cases?

Napoleon said with a show of temper that he had not asked his advice, but had merely wished to know whether he thought the letter would have a desirable effect on Hudson Lowe. Before Gourgaud could reply, Madame Montholon said that Gourgaud was wrong, that the letter was very good indeed. The young general, his eyes blazing, told her that when His Majesty did him the honor of addressing him, he would thank her if she would refrain from interrupting. She, however, paid no heed but continued speaking, while he subsided into a morose silence. Such was the beginning of the feud that was to erupt between him and the Montholons.

The Emperor, whose anger had not yet cooled, took the letter, rose, and went to the drawing room. He called for pen and ink, sat down at the Pembroke table, and signed: "Your devoted, Napoleon." Gourgaud was to confide to his diary that if Napoleon had not been angry he would not have made use of the term "Your devoted."

When all were assembled in the drawing room, Napoleon, whose anger was usually short-lived, invited Gourgaud to a game of chess. "It will calm you down," he said. "Why do you always carry a chip on your shoulder?" Gourgaud replied that if the Emperor thought he was jealous of Las Cases, he was mistaken. But he had considered it his duty to point out that the letter was unworthy of His Majesty. It made it appear as if having lost Las Cases, he was forsaken—as if those who remained counted for nothing. He knew, he said, of no time when Las Cases had watched over the Emperor in his illness. He was beginning to understand, he said, that it did not pay to tell the truth to sovereigns. Napoleon interrupted him and said: "What I should like is that some day you should consider Las Cases your best friend." The young general exclaimed with passion: "Never! I detest him!"

225

"Ah, Gourgaud," said the Emperor, "that is unkind."

"I never did him any harm," the young man resumed, "and now that he is no longer here I have no intention of doing so. But if circumstances had been different I would have avenged myself on that Tartufe! Some day Your Majesty will realize how right I was."

"So you think he will betray me, speak ill of me?" Napoleon said with a touch of bitterness. "Ah, my God! Berthier, Marmont, whom I loaded with honors and favors, how have *they* behaved? I defy anybody to disappoint me. Men would have to be evil indeed to behave as I believe them capable of behaving."

"No, Sire," Gourgaud replied, "I don't think he will betray you. But he has made no sacrifices. If he came with us it was not from devotion for Your Majesty, it was to get himself talked about, to get material for a book, to make money."

"And what if he did?" the Emperor said. "Do you believe Drouot, who always wanted to be with the most exposed battery, did so out of devotion to me, or because he wanted to be talked about?"

Napoleon's letter to his favorite was returned, it having been delivered sealed to Poppleton. The Emperor ordered that the seal be broken.

EIGHT

On November 31, shortly after Las Cases and his son had been transferred to Balcombe's cottage, the chamberlain wrote a letter to the governor which began with the words: "In consequence of a snare, according to all appearances, laid by my servant, I was on the 25th instant removed from Longwood, and all my papers were seized." Further in the letter he says that the governor could not possibly avail himself of the opportunity to read the papers he had seized "lest you expose yourself to the conclusion that will be drawn from this abuse of your power and the circumstance be connected with the trap laid for me." This was an unmistakable accusation that Lowe had made use of James Scott as an *agent provocateur*.

On December 4, the governor came to the cottage and pro-tested against the accusation. Gorrequer, who was present, wrote in a memorandum: "The governor observed, that to accuse the servant was making him a party in it, as the servant could not have run the risk of carrying into effect such a design without his knowledge." This, of course, was what Las Cases had meant to imply. But he, his son, and his cherished memoirs being at the mercy of the governor, he replied that "he certainly had consid-ered it as a snare laid for him, that it had all the appearance of it, but that he had been very careful in the wording of the para-graph of the letter, and had made use of the words 'according to all appearances'; that it only implicated the servant, and would not be considered as alluding to the governor's being privy to such a design."

When Las Cases published the letter in his memoirs he omitted the qualifying words.

There can be no doubt that the chamberlain was pained and chagrined at having allowed himself to be fooled, with the result that a letter compromising to Lady Clavering and to Lord Holland had fallen into the governor's hands. Nevertheless he decided to take advantage of the situation to escape from his tormentors at Longwood. He feared that the governor might yield to pressure from Napoleon to have him sent back to Long-wood, at least until Lord Bathurst had been heard from, which might not be for five or six months. He decided to make it plain to the governor that he would refuse to return. But what reason could he give? Sir Hudson undoubtedly knew what he had had to endure from Gourgaud and Montholon, but he had no intention of confessing this to him. So, in his letter of Novem-ber 30, he wrote: "But a few days ago you could have made me submit to any sacrifice by the fear of being separated from the Emperor. Today it is no longer in your power to restore me to him. A brand of iniquity has been inflicted upon me by arresting me before his eyes. I can no longer be a source of consolation to him. He would see in me only a dishonored being whose pres-ence would evoke painful recollections."

By making it plain that he would refuse to return if the opportunity offered, he was inviting the very thing he sought to avoid. What an opportunity for Lowe to divert suspicion from himself and fasten it upon Las Cases! What an opportunity to appear magnanimous with the practical certainty of not being called upon to pay the price of that magnanimity!

NINE

Las Cases spent his time at Ross Cottage writing letters to the governor, dictating an account (many times the length of the Emperor's "Remonstrance") of all Napoleon's grievances since the beginning of Lowe's administration, and kept adding to his memoirs. Little wonder that Emanuel, who besides taking down the dictation now also did the transcribing, broke under the strain. Dr. Baxter was sent for and reported that the boy was suffering from "an organic affection of the heart, or large blood vessels in its vicinity," and added that the complaint was "in no way connected with the climate . . . nor is it likely to derive any benefit from a change." O'Meara, who examined the boy a week later, made a similar diagnosis, but recommended "the removal of the young gentleman to Europe," which suited Las Cases much better.

On December 17, Las Cases, who never missed an opportunity for declamatory self-expression, wrote a reproachful letter to the governor. He pointed out that had he and his son been at Longwood, O'Meara could have given the boy his immediate attention. When Bertrand had called at Plantation House to request that Las Cases be returned to Longwood, Lowe had replied that his "instructions would not permit it." But that was before he had received Las Cases' letter which made it obvious that if he was offered the opportunity to return he would refuse. That same day, accompanied by Gorrequer, he went to Ross Cottage and told Las Cases that considering his son's health, and the fact that his presence would be gratifying to Bonaparte, he had decided to allow him to return to Longwood until the arrival of the government's instructions. Las Cases was taken aback, and according to Gorrequer's memorandum replied that "the governor had misunderstood him if he considered he meant by his letter to solicit his return to Longwood." He added, however, that "if the Emperor made known to him the slightest wish for his return, he would immediately go back; his will was law to him, and he would waive all personal considerations." He apparently believed that the Emperor would understand and would not ask him to return.

On December 23, Sir Hudson, accompanied by Major Gorrequer and Colonel Wynyard, went to see Bertrand to tell him about Las Cases' refusal. "What do you think of it?" he asked. Bertrand was noncommittal. He knew the reason and was fully aware that the governor also knew. It did not surprise him that Las Cases should have decided to take advantage of this opportunity to escape from the jealousy, hatred, and persecution to which he had been subjected. As for Napoleon, when told by O'Meara that Las Cases had refused to return to Longwood unless the Emperor asked him to do so, he was painfully affected, but he, too, understood. He later told O'Meara that "if Las Cases returned he would receive him with pleasure; if he went away he would also view that with pleasure, but would wish to see him before he went."

That same day, December 23, Balcombe came to Longwood House and handed Napoleon the girdle containing Hortense's diamond necklace which the Emperor had entrusted to Las Cases on the *Bellerophon*. He related that he had been at Ross Cottage, looking after his poultry, and that Sir Hudson and Major Gorrequer had also been there. As he was leaving Las Cases had followed and had said: "I think you are a man of principle and I am going to put it to the test. It is nothing injurious or contrary to your honor, merely a valuable object to be restored to Napoleon. If you accept, my son will put it in your pocket." For sole answer he had slackened his pace and the boy had caught up with him and had stuck the girdle in his pocket "almost in sight of the military attendants." [2]

[2] All who have written on the subject have accepted Montholon's version that Las Cases slipped the girdle into Bertrand's hand on December 30, before boarding the vessel that was to take him and his son to the Cape. Bertrand, however, says in his journal that Napoleon showed the necklace to

TEN

Napoleon had Bertrand write to Sir Hudson asking that Las Cases be permitted to proceed directly to Europe, and that he be allowed to make a parting visit to Longwood. Lowe rejected the first request and said he could grant the second only provided an English officer was present during the visit. Considering that he had offered to have Las Cases remain at Longwood until Lord Bathurst had been heard from, this confirms the suspicion that he had not made that offer in good faith, but merely because Las Cases had made it plain in his letter of the 30th of November that he would refuse to return. If he could see no harm in having Las Cases confer with Napoleon for five or six months, what objection could there have been to his seeing him alone for one hour?

Las Cases and his son had been transferred with their belongings to the Castle at Jamestown in preparation for their departure to the Cape. Except for being closely guarded they had no reason to complain. "Ask for whatever you want, the Honorable East India Company pays for everything," the major-domo had told them. The rooms were spacious and well furnished. The windows of the salon gave out upon the quay and the harbor. One of the ships at anchor in the harbor at that time was the *Orontes*, which was returning to England from the Cape with Piontkowski and three of Napoleon's servants on board. They had not been allowed to go ashore, but Archambault's brother had been permitted to visit him and had brought them a basket of provisions, a gift from their former master.

On December 29, Bertrand called on Las Cases and was allowed to converse with him in the presence of Major Gorrequer. He was shocked at the chamberlain's altered appearance. He had grown a beard, his face was haggard, his eyes had a wild and tormented look. He was exceedingly nervous and became

Madame Bertrand in the billiard-room on December 24. The manner in which the necklace was returned is told by Las Cases in his memoirs. Arnold Chaplin in his *St. Helena Who's Who* lists Balcombe as having visited Napoleon on December 23, the only visitor during that entire month.

even more so when Bertrand urged him to reconsider and await the government's instructions at Longwood.[3] "There are victories which can only be won by flight; the victory I am pursuing is of that kind," he said enigmatically. "What if the Emperor asked you to stay?" Bertrand queried. "Then I should remain, for that would be law to me," he replied.

He and his son were to depart for the Cape the following day in the sloop of war the *Griffin*, which Admiral Malcolm had placed at their disposal so the boy, who was far from well, would not have to travel on a transport with no doctor on board. In a letter to Bertrand at the beginning of December, Las Cases had written that he had £4,000 in a London bank and that the money was at the Emperor's disposal. The grand marshal now inquired if he was sure he would not need the money for some time, and having received an affirmative reply requested that he have Balcombe draw up thirteen bills of exchange for £300 each, payable monthly to his (Bertrand's) order. He would come on the morrow and fetch them.

The following morning, when Bertrand, escorted by Poppleton, was ready to go to Jamestown, Gourgaud asked the Emperor's permission to accompany them, so he could bid farewell to Las Cases. He was undoubtedly as sincere in this as he had been two weeks before when he told Napoleon that he "detested" Las Cases, who, he said, was a "Tartufe." He himself tells us that tears welled into his eyes as he embraced the chamberlain and his son at the moment of parting. His conduct toward Las Cases gives us a clue to his subsequent behavior toward Napoleon.

Bertrand and Gourgaud were allowed to lunch with Las Cases and his son. Captain Poppleton was with them at table. After lunch the chamberlain and his visitors went to the *salon*—a spacious chamber about fifty by twenty feet. Colonel Wynyard and Major Gorrequer were there, but remained discreetly at a distance. O'Meara has written: "Las Cases might just as well have been permitted to come to Longwood, and thereby a refusal,

[3] Lord Bathurst was to write that Las Cases could return to Longwood, but that if he did so he must remain there for the duration of the captivity.

which was considered as an insult, would have been spared Napoleon." Lowe's talent for making restrictions that served to irritate but had no practical value was inexhaustible. Las Cases handed Bertrand the bills of exchange Balcombe had drawn up and was given a receipt signed by Napoleon. He was to return the receipt, with the signature snipped off, soon after his arrival at the Cape.

Finally the time of parting came. Sir Hudson, who felt uneasy about what Las Cases, whose ability he did not underrate, might write about him after his arrival in Europe, continued his efforts to placate him by presenting him with several letters of recommendation to friends at the Cape. Las Cases thanked him, but does not appear to have made use of them. Lowe personally escorted him to the gate and ordered his officers to attend him to the place of embarkation, "as a mark of respect." As the chamberlain and his son were being rowed to the *Griffin,* Piontkowski and the three French servants waved to them from the deck of the *Orontes.*

Father and son were to remain at the Cape nearly eight months, until August 20, 1817, before being allowed to depart. On their arrival in Europe Las Cases was not permitted to reside in England and was barred from France and from the Low Countries. In December, 1817, he found a refuge at Frankfort. From that city he conducted an unremitting campaign in the interest of the exile of St. Helena. He wrote letters to Marie Louise, to Napoleon's relatives, to the allied sovereigns, to Lord Bathurst, to Lord Liverpool, to Prince Metternich, and sent a lengthy petition to the British Parliament. Indeed, it can be said that he left nothing undone to try to ameliorate the situation of his idol. Whatever his original motive in following Napoleon to St. Helena, he served the fallen monarch with ability and devotion.

XVII. Lowe Quarrels with Malcolm

Before issuing his regulations of October 9, Sir Hudson had shown them to Admiral Malcolm and had asked his opinion. The admiral had confined himself to saying that some of the new regulations would be impossible to enforce and "would give cause for much irritation." The governor promised to modify them, and Malcolm assures us that he kept his promise, which means that, as originally conceived, the new regulations had been even more senseless than when finally issued. Lowe himself soon came to realize that they were unenforceable and might bring down ridicule not only upon him but upon the government of his country. On December 26, 1816, he abandoned the regulation requiring the house to be surrounded by sentries immediately after sunset. Napoleon and his suite were again able to remain in the garden until nine o'clock. He moreover made it known that he did not mean to enforce the regulation forbidding Napoleon to converse with persons he met when out riding or driving. We shall see, however, that this was not the end of the matter; for, as Balmain had remarked, he had a veritable mania for "doing, undoing, and redoing."

These concessions and a visit paid by Lady Lowe to Madame Bertrand—the first since Sir Hudson's arrival on the island—made it appear to Napoleon that the governor was seeking an accommodation. He decided to meet him half way. He asked

O'Meara to call on Sir Hudson and to tell him that "he desired nothing more than to have matters put on the same footing they were some months past, or nearly equivalent to it, and that he conceived the best method to accomplish the business would be for you to authorize the admiral to act as an intermediator; that by so doing he thought it would be easy to come to a right understanding."

Lowe asked O'Meara to put in writing what Bonaparte had said and the doctor complied with the request.

On receipt of O'Meara's written statement Lowe sent him a memorandum in which he said: "The governor is not conscious of having ever willfully given to General Bonaparte any just cause of offense or disagreement. . . . Any channel by which he may think such misunderstandings may be removed the governor is perfectly ready and willing to avail himself of." But a few days later we find him saying to O'Meara: "What can he want a mediator for? What necessity is there for one? Answer me. Do you not think that he asked the admiral for a mediator because he thinks he can *humbug him*, which he cannot do me?" O'Meara replied that he did not think so, that Napoleon had told him he felt he could talk things over with the admiral calmly and reasonably, but would find it difficult to negotiate with the governor without losing his temper. Sir Hudson conceded that this might well be his reason, but when, on January 17, O'Meara told him that Bonaparte had expressed his surprise that the governor had not yet authorized the admiral to begin negotiations, Lowe observed that he considered the negotiations broken off because of the strictures regarding the regulations of the 9th of October sent him by Bertrand—that "the frequent use of the word '*emperor*' in the strictures . . . was sufficient for him to break off the affair." On January 30, Napoleon charged O'Meara to inform the governor that "in consequence of his conduct in having accepted the proposed intermediation of the admiral, declaring that he would charge the admiral with it and afterwards doing nothing, I conceive him to be a man without word and without faith. That he has broken his word with me, broken a compact which is held sacred by robbers and Bedouin Arabs, but not by the agents of the British ministers."

TWO

William Forsyth has written: "It is, I think, much to be regretted that Sir Hudson Lowe did not take advantage of the admiral's willingness to act as mediator between him and Bonaparte. . . . Few more likely to succeed in such a mission than Sir Pulteney Malcolm, whose countenance irresistibly inspired confidence, and whose manner won respect from all who knew him. But unfortunately before this time a coolness had arisen between him and the governor, the precise origin of which is difficult to discover."

That so able a barrister as Forsyth should have been unable to discover the reasons for the differences between the governor and the admiral is difficult to believe. What appears more probable is that he chose to ignore them, as they do not reflect credit on the man whom he had undertaken to rehabilitate.

The differences between the governor and the admiral began toward the end of September, 1816, when Sir Pulteney, about to sail for the Cape, decided to pay a visit to Napoleon. He had not visited him since the painful scene between the governor and the captive on August 18, of which he had been an unwilling witness, wishing to make it clear to Napoleon that he disapproved of his conduct on that occasion. He told Lowe that he considered it advisable to remain on friendly terms with the prisoner so as to be in a position to act as intermediary whenever Sir Hudson considered it advisable to make use of his services for that purpose. Lowe, however, felt chagrined.

When Malcolm arrived at the Cape he discovered that half the garrison—the 1st battalion of the 60th regiment—was entirely composed of foreigners, mostly Poles, who had served in Napoleon's army. Yet it was here that Lowe had sent a Polish officer who had been with the Emperor on Elba and at St. Helena, and three of Bonaparte's devoted servants, with the request that they not be allowed to depart for England for at least six months, as he feared that on their arrival there they might indulge in propaganda. Why a six months' stay at the Cape should have dispelled their inclination to indulge in propaganda is not clear. Malcolm rightly considered that under the circumstances to keep the four men at the Cape was to run a far greater risk, and advised Lord Charles Somerset, governor of the colony, to send them away as speedily as possible. Somerset had already written to Lowe informing him of the composition of the garrison and had added: "From this circumstance Your Excellency will perceive that an evil-disposed person has a fair field here for forwarding his views." He decided to heed Malcolm's advice, and the four departed on the *Orontes,* which, as we have seen, arrived at Jamestown on its way to England before Las Cases' departure for the Cape. Lowe, unwilling to acknowledge his mistake, wrote a spiteful letter to Bathurst complaining about the admiral's "officious interference."

Another bone of contention between the governor and the admiral was the allotment of space on transports for the shipment of provisions to St. Helena, mostly from the Cape. Balmain has written: "The apparent cause of the quarrel is that the admiral has taken the wrong course with regard to the provisioning of St. Helena, with the result that we have been in want of wine, flour, and meat; and that the horses on the island, not excepting those at Longwood, are on half rations, for all of which the governor is being blamed." It did not take the Russian commissioner long to discover that not the admiral but the governor and the English government were to blame—the first for failing to build a storehouse, the second for not providing sufficient transports. On September 10, 1816, Balmain wrote: "As for provisions, there is no storehouse on this rock, and the English government is unwilling to go to the expense of four or five transports to establish regular communication with the Cape, the African coast, or Brazil. It is therefore impossible to have provisions of good quality." On October 1, 1817, he reported to his government: "It is quite true that the meat is tough, the fowl lean, the vegetables watery, all the provisions poor. But there are no others. . . . There are 3,000 men to feed and only two transports to carry rations, when there should be at least six." And on January 30, 1819: "There is again a great want of provisions, forage, and other necessities at St. Helena. It is the seventh or eighth time this has happened since I have been here, nor will it be the last. The reason is that Sir Hudson is not an administrator. He digs trenches, constructs parapets, is always getting ready for battle, but fails to build a storehouse."

Still another grievance Lowe had against Malcolm was that the admiral was in the habit of giving newspapers to O'Meara for Napoleon. In this Sir Pulteney merely followed the example of Admiral Cockburn, a man infinitely more capable than Lowe, who considered this quite in keeping with his instructions.

Nothing was too petty for Lowe with which to harass the admiral. Malcolm had given orders that when Las Cases ultimately was allowed to leave the Cape he should be put on a ship that did not touch at St. Helena. "Sometime afterwards," he has written, "it came to Sir Hudson's knowledge . . . that such an order had been given, which occasioned another long and more disagreeable correspondence than that which had passed and was still going on respecting the transport." To Lowe's discomfiture Bathurst fully approved the admiral's instructions concerning the matter.

THREE

It has been charged that Malcolm schemed to have Lowe recalled and himself appointed in his place. It is possible that compassion for the exiles may have betrayed him into expressing such a wish to one of the commissioners. But the fact is that while Lowe wrote numerous letters to Bathurst denouncing Malcolm, the latter, according to Bathurst's own statement, did not make a single complaint about the governor. Indeed, after his return to England he did what so many men in public life are in the habit of doing: praised officially what he condemned unofficially. Before he left St. Helena Sir Hudson had proposed to him that they destroy their mutual correspondence, with the exception of one letter. Malcolm's answer was: "All or none." Lowe thereupon sent the correspondence to Bathurst, together with a letter complaining about the admiral. For once Lord Bathurst lost patience with him. In a letter marked "Private and Confidential" he wrote to the governor: "As Sir Pulteney has not, in any of his communications with me, referred to the differences which you state have existed between you and him, I have neither begun the conversation with him, nor have I thought it necessary to open the cover which contained the correspondence which has taken place between you. You will judge of the disposition which he has on this subject when I tell you that, in his audience with the Prince Regent, he expressed himself in terms of great commendation of your conduct."

Unmerited as was the "commendation" it was in keeping with what, during his stay at St. Helena, Malcolm had been in the habit of saying to Napoleon whenever the latter assailed Lowe in his presence. Considering it his duty to uphold the governor, he had always managed to find excuses for him. On January 31, 1817, when Napoleon accused Lowe of having broken his word regarding mediation, Malcolm advised him to be patient as Sir Hudson was undoubtedly awaiting instructions from England. On March 7, he told Napoleon that he was mistaken in Lowe's character, that the governor was perhaps "a little too quick in temper," [1] but that he "had a good heart." At another time Malcolm chided the Emperor for the tone of the letters he had sent to Sir Hudson.[2] When Lord Amherst, ambassador to China, was expected at St. Helena he urged Napoleon to consent to have the governor present his lordship to him: "All these misunderstandings might be obviated on the arrival of Lord Amherst—forget the past, and you will go on better in future." The Emperor replied: "You are so much of an Englishman there is no reasoning with you; like all Englishmen you think everything your countrymen do must be right, and a foreigner must be wrong."

---

[1] In the United Service Magazine (June, 1844) Lowe's son concedes that his father's temper was "naturally violent and hasty enough."

[2] Malcolm found, however, occasion to chide Sir Hudson for the tone of the letters the latter was sending to him in the dispute about the transports and other matters, as for example: "Your style of writing to me for a considerable time has been repugnant."

For these constant attempts to smooth the way for the governor he was rewarded with suspicion and insult. One day, in the presence of Reade, Lowe said to him: "At your last interview with Bonaparte, did anything occur of which His Majesty's government should be informed?" His tone and manner were so offensive that the admiral curtly replied, "Nothing!" In the diary, which he dictated to his wife in the third person, he has written: "Had Sir Hudson expressed a desire to be informed of the conversation, the admiral would have had much pleasure in detailing it to him; but to be interrogated in that mode was repugnant to his feelings." Before he left St. Helena he was to discover that he was constantly being spied on by the governor's agents.

Forsyth, who could find no reason for the "coolness that had arisen between the two men," nevertheless put his finger on what may well have been the principal reason for Lowe's dislike of Sir Pulteney when he wrote: "We can easily conceive that he may have felt some little jealousy at finding Sir Pulteney Malcolm admitted to easy and familiar intercourse with Napoleon, while he himself was treated with contumely and insult, and denied even an interview." It was not "some little jealousy," but a considerable feeling of envy Lowe appears to have developed toward the man who was everything he himself was not. No one could have said of Sir Hudson that he "irresistibly inspired confidence." The opposite was true. He had neither looks, nor tact, nor breeding. In the language of Professor William Henry Hudson (no admirer of Napoleon), he was "a tactless, fussy, interfering, indiscreet, and thoroughly disagreeable man—in fact, the very last man in the world who should have been entrusted with responsibilities demanding precisely the qualities which he did not possess." [3]

Sir Pulteney Malcolm can, however, not escape censure. He was to blame for not giving the government a truthful account of Lowe's maladministration. Most of all he was to blame for misleading the Prince Regent by speaking "in terms of great commendation" of a man whose conduct, as he must have known, would ultimately be a reproach to his country.

[3] *The Man Napoleon*, London, 1915, p. 202.

FOUR

The governor had in the meantime still further modified the regulations of October 9. He had told O'Meara to inform Bertrand that he had no objection to Bonaparte's riding in the valley, alone or with his generals, unaccompanied by an English officer, but that if any of the generals went there without him they must be so accompanied. He likewise specified what houses Napoleon was permitted to enter. The Emperor replied that his generals had signed an agreement with the English government to submit to all regulations imposed upon their chief, not to any special regulations applying to them alone. As for entering houses along the way, if the governor furnished him a list of houses he desired him *not* to enter he would abstain from doing so. On March 14, Lowe, however, again changed his mind. He issued a regulation that when riding in the valley Napoleon and his officers must not leave the road, either to one side or the other.

The upshot of it all was that Napoleon persisted in not leaving the house except for an occasional airing in the garden. This worried Lowe whom O'Meara had warned that lack of exercise had a harmful effect on Bonaparte's health. Although Napoleon often claimed to be convinced that Lowe was under orders to shorten his life by harassing him with oppressive measures, he must have known this to be untrue, since he used the threat of shortening his life as a weapon to have those measures abolished. Sir Hudson was far from indifferent to the health of the captive. The post he occupied was by far the most important and remunerative he had ever held or was ever destined to hold. He knew that if Napoleon died he would lose it, and the threat had its effect upon him. It was largely responsible for his hesitancy, his "doing, undoing, and redoing."

XVIII. The Struggle with Lowe Continues

Months after the departure of Las Cases, Napoleon exclaimed one evening, after a dinner during which hardly a word had been spoken: "Poor Las Cases! Where is he? He at least entertained me with his stories. The rest of you are so many nightcaps." Bertrand noted in his journal that the Emperor had lost "all desire to work, to dictate." If the days dragged on monotonous, melancholy, the nights were even harder to bear. He slept badly and would lie for hours on his camp-bed staring into space, upon which, as upon a screen, his mind projected images of people and events. One night he rose, went to the billiard-room, had Marchand light a couple of candles, and walked restlessly back and forth, casting a huge shadow upon the wall. But he could not rid himself of his thoughts any more than he could have driven away the shadow. "The thoughts one has at night are not cheerful thoughts," he told Bertrand.

On January 17, Madame Bertrand gave birth to a boy. Dr. Livingstone, superintendent of the East India Company's medical establishment at St. Helena, delivered the child. A week later the Reverend Vernon came to baptize the boy, who was named Arthur, after his maternal grandfather. The Emperor, who had not stirred from the house since November 20, went to visit Madame Bertrand nine days after her confinement. She proudly showed him the child, saying: "I have the honor to present to Your Majesty the first Frenchman who since your arrival has entered Longwood without Lord Bathurst's permission."

TWO

On February 12, Mrs. Balcombe and her two daughters came to visit the Bertrands, whose guests they remained until the afternoon of the 14th. When Napoleon learned about their presence at Longwood he sent Gourgaud to invite them over.

He was pleased to see Betsy. She was now a young lady, even prettier than she had been when he had first met her, if not quite as mischievous. There was hardly a young officer on the island who had not lost his heart to her. Colonel Reade and Major Fehrzen were among her suitors. Napoleon twitted her about Reade and felt relieved when she told him that she was not interested in him. She was not so sure about Fehrzen—a dashing young officer of thirty, well-born and well-bred, who had been a frequent visitor at Longwood in the days of Cockburn. The girls played the piano in the billiard-room and danced with Montholon and Gourgaud. The following evening they came again. This time when Gourgaud escorted them to the Bertrands they were stopped by a sentry, and it took some arguing before they could proceed. Lowe was to say that they had had no business to go to see Bonaparte, their pass being good only for a visit to the Bertrands.

During her stay at Longwood Mrs. Balcombe accompanied Madame Montholon on a visit to Lady Lowe. They went on horseback, escorted by Reade, who had dropped in to pay court to Betsy. Lady Lowe received them courteously. While Madame Montholon played with the Lowe baby, the governor's wife confided to Mrs. Balcombe that Bonaparte could not so much as drink a glass of water without it being reported to the governor. She thought such spying ridiculous, she said. A few days later Reade attempted to interrogate Mrs. Balcombe and the girls about what had been said during their visit to Bonaparte. Mrs. Balcombe indignantly replied that they had not gone there to spy on anybody. She told Bertrand about the experience and he in turn told Napoleon. Gourgaud suspected O'Meara, but Napoleon did not follow up the matter.

Early in March Lowe sent Napoleon a copy of Dr. Warden's book *Letters Written on board His Majesty's Ship the Northumberland and at St. Helena.* The Emperor read it with the assistance of Bertrand. He told O'Meara: "Warden is a man of good intentions, and the foundation of his work is true; but many of the circumstances are incorrectly stated. . . . He has put in my mouth expressions unworthy of me, and not in my style." The author speaks sympathetically about Napoleon and the members of his suite, with the exception of Gourgaud, whom he considers a coxcomb. Gourgaud was furious, but the Emperor advised him to calm down. He himself, he said, had been called a poisoner, an assassin, a violator, a monster guilty of incest and every other horrid crime, but had remained unruffled. "It is only the truth that hurts," he had once said to Las Cases.

He decided, however, to correct some of Warden's statements, and dictated a series of letters to Bertrand and to Montholon, supposedly written by Las Cases from the Cape. Madame Bertrand translated them into English, and despite Lowe's elaborate precautions against clandestine correspondence, Napoleon had no difficulty getting the manuscript to England, where it was published under the title *Letters from the Cape of Good Hope.*

THREE

Toward the end of March Mr. Churchill, an official of the East India Company, his wife, and two daughters, arrived from India on the *Tortoise*, on their homeward journey to England. The young ladies were charming, and Reade was delighted to be their cicerone when they went out riding, while their mother had herself carried about the island in a palankeen by Indian servants. The girls, who spoke French fluently, were anxious to meet the Emperor. As a necessary preliminary, Reade took them to Longwood and introduced them to the Bertrands. It was here that, on April 1, Gourgaud made their acquaintance and immediately lost his heart to Amelia, the younger of the two. That evening he gave the Emperor an enthusiastic description of the young lady. Napoleon was amused, pinched his ear, and said: "We will marry you. I won't be here over three years. You will marry a French or an English girl."

When Gourgaud went out riding the following afternoon he met the girls again. They were returning from an excursion to Diana's Peak, in the company of their father, Reade, and Balcombe. Not being accompanied by the orderly officer, Gourgaud could go no farther than Alarm House, but he was riding beside Amelia and was happy—at least until she told him that they were leaving the following day. They had not heard from Marshal Bertrand, she said, and she would be forever grateful to him if he could arrange an interview, and if that proved impossible obtain for her a specimen of the Emperor's handwriting. He promised to do his utmost.

That evening after dinner he asked Napoleon for a few words written by him. The Emperor refused. He then proposed that they play three games of chess, the stake to be an audience for the two young ladies and a specimen of his handwriting. Napoleon agreed provided Gourgaud would stake four pigeons, shot by himself. The young general, who had no fear of Napoleon at an opponent at chess, said he would stake eight. So they played, and Gourgaud won all three games. But then the Emperor said they must play two more. The young man won both, which should convince anyone that a great military strategist need not necessarily be an expert at chess, or vice versa. When, however, it came to taking the consequences of his defeat, Napoleon welshed. He said that to receive the Churchills would be contrary to the policy he had adopted of remaining in seclusion. Such a policy would, he believed, make an impression in England. As for a specimen of his handwriting, that, too, he would not give. "We will marry you; we will marry you," he said laughing as he retired to his private quarters.

The following morning Bertrand gave Gourgaud two slips of paper, one with "*Français*," the other with "*disaient*" written upon it in the Emperor's well-nigh illegible hand. To this the young man was able to add "*combattre*" and "*Lyon*," clipped from a manuscript page the Emperor had entrusted to him. He made a neat package of these treasures, which he tied with a ribbon and put in a briefcase. Poppleton went with him to Jamestown.

Several notables accompanied the Churchills to the place of embarkation. The governor offered his arm to Mrs. Churchill; Gourgaud, his to Amelia. She asked him coyly if he had anything for her. He opened his briefcase and handed her the package, which she received with a gasp of delight. Fortunately Lowe did not notice. Had he done so he assuredly would have demanded that it be opened. *"Français," "disaient," "combattre," "Lyon"!* The man who was to read a sinister meaning into a picture in Madame Bertrand's living room, and into the words "upon this rock" uttered by Count Balmain, would undoubtedly have regarded it as a code message Gourgaud had persuaded the young girl to forward to some agent of Bonaparte.

FOUR

On April 7, there were to be races at Deadwood Camp. Gourgaud had been invited by Sir George Bingham to attend, but had little inclination to do so. Napoleon urged him to go, so he might meet the commissioners. He went on horseback and received a friendly reception from the notables present, among whom were Sir Hudson and Lady Lowe, Sir Pulteney and Lady Malcolm, Sir George and Lady Bingham, Sir Thomas Reade, Colonel Wynyard, Count Balmain, Baron and Baroness Stürmer, the Marquis de Montchenu, and his aide-de-camp Gors. Lady Lowe was particularly nice to him, and he thought her a charming woman. She introduced him to Count Balmain, whom he had not yet had the opportunity to meet. The Marquis de Montchenu gave an exhibition of how coarse and ill-mannered a member of the old nobility could be on occasion. When a sudden breeze lifted the skirt of one of the ladies, displaying a shapely calf, he remarked to Lady Lowe that hers must be lacking in shapeliness as otherwise she would have found an opportunity to show them.

Major Fehrzen, who had joined them, invited Gourgaud and the commissioners to his quarters for refreshments. Reade was

furious when told about this, but the conversation was innocent
enough. Gourgaud and Balmain conversed about the war of
1812. On two occasions the count forgot himself, referring to
Bonaparte as "the Emperor," and as "that great man." Montchenu had made a similar slip in the presence of Lady Lowe,
which, however, had not shocked her in the least. Balmain told
Gourgaud that he would gladly have called on Bonaparte in his
private capacity, but that the governor objected. Besides, he
wanted to act in concert with his two colleagues, who were expecting instructions from their governments. However, the *Conqueror* was momentarily expected and might bring dispatches
that would change the situation. Then they heard the firing of a
gun announcing the commencement of the races, and went to
take the seats reserved for them in the grandstand.

When the races were over Gourgaud assisted the Baroness
Stürmer to mount her horse, and she chided him for not coming
to see her. He rode beside her husband, who remarked: "Do you
know who is raging mad about you having conversed with us?"
The young general replied: "Hudson Lowe, I presume."

"No, the admiral."

"What!"

"Yes, he is an Englishman to his fingertips, and thinks you
have told us about the way the Emperor is being treated. He
is afraid it might injure his country's reputation."

Napoleon had been standing at an open window in the upper
story of Bertrand's house and had watched the races through a
spyglass.

FIVE

On March 17, 1817, Lord Holland made a speech in the House
of Lords and moved "the production of papers that may serve
to make known the treatment of Bonaparte." Lord Bathurst opposed the proposal and managed to have it tabled. Toward the
end of May copies of *The Times* and of the *Morning Chronicle*
giving accounts of the speeches were delivered at Longwood.
Napoleon asked the Bertrands to make a faithful translation of
the accounts. The grand marshal noted in his journal that hav-

ing read the translations, the Emperor said he was glad to notice that the English minister had found it necessary to resort to falsehood to justify his conduct toward him.

Lord Bathurst's speech may not have contained twenty untruths, as claimed by Napoleon, but it contained several statements that were obviously false. When he said that since his arrival at St. Helena Napoleon had received "only one letter" from members of his family, he must have known that he was not telling the truth, as letters addressed to Bonaparte were read by him personally. On May 1, 1817, Napoleon's mother wrote to him protesting against that untruth. When he denied that the house at Longwood was "unpleasant and unwholesome," he was in possession of Lowe's letter of July 9, 1816, in which the governor admits that complaints about the house "appear to be well founded." In view of Lowe's Draconian regulations of October 9, 1816, of which he had received a copy, the following statement made by him is truly astonishing: "When Admiral Cockburn went out to St. Helena, instructions were given him which would apply to him while he remained there, and which would also apply to his successor after his departure. Up to this moment I am prepared to state there has been no substantive alteration of these instructions. Whatever changes have taken place either in the explanation of the instructions, or the execution of them, were for the benefit of the person subjected to them"! Little wonder that he should have objected to submitting his correspondence with Lowe to the scrutiny of a committee.

Napoleon dictated a reply to Bathurst's speech, which he revised repeatedly and which was not completed until October 5. It is known as *Observations sur le Discours de Lord Bathurst*. He offered an early version of the document to Malcolm, but the admiral declined to accept it or even to read it, saying it would serve no purpose as it was not in his power to do anything about the matter. Unknown to him, however, his secretary Irving accepted a copy and took it with him to England. On October 7, 1817, Bertrand gave a copy of the final version to Lowe in a sealed envelope addressed to Lord Liverpool. The governor forwarded it without breaking the seal, thus again proving that he could modify the government's instructions in Napoleon's favor if he chose. That same month Baron Stürmer sent a copy to Metternich, which Napoleon had managed to get into his hands. Count Balmain likewise obtained a copy which he sent to Nesselrode with the remark: "These observations are too long and too rhetorical; everything is exaggerated and excessive. Yet they are basically true."

SIX

In June, 1817, the serio-comic affair of the marble bust of Napoleon's son, the King of Rome, served to dispel the monotony of life at Longwood. On May 28, the storeship *Baring* had arrived from England. Its captain, a naval officer on half pay, had learned that one of his men, an Italian named Radowitch, former gunner in the British navy, had brought aboard a marble bust of the King of Rome for delivery to Napoleon. A letter in Italian in possession of Radowitch showed that the bust had been entrusted to him by Messrs. M. & G. Beaggini of London, and related that it was one of an identical pair made by a sculptor of note from a portrait painted the previous summer at Leghorn, where the boy had been with his mother. One had been sent to the former Empress, who had generously rewarded the sculptor, the other had come into possession of the Beagginis. The gunner was to leave it to the Emperor's generosity how much he wished to pay, but if he wanted to know the price, 100 louis should be asked, "such being about what it cost us in remuneration to the talented artist and for other contingent expenses."

The letter contained hardly a word of truth. Napoleon's son had not left Vienna since his arrival in that city in 1814. The bust was not the work of a "talented artist" but the mediocre production of a statuary of little talent. It was about half-size and pleasant enough to look at—a rounded, smiling, boyish face framed by long locks falling upon the shoulders. On the breast was the plaque of the Legion of Honor. The unscrupulous Beagginis had had it made with the object of extracting money from a doting father.

When, on May 28, the *Baring* arrived at Jamestown, Rado-witch who had suffered an apoplectic stroke was delirious and remained in that condition for a couple of weeks. Captain Lamb, the commander of the vessel, informed Sir Thomas Reade of the presence of the bust on board. A rumor spread through town, and quickly reached the ears of Napoleon, that Reade had told the captain to throw the bust overboard. Another version had it that he told him to break it into fragments and throw these overboard. When questioned by Lowe the captain denied that Reade had said this, and when at Bertrand's request he was allowed to call on the grand marshal he reiterated the denial. But on June 29, Bertrand wrote in his journal that Captain Johnson of the *Ocean,* whom Napoleon received in the garden, told the Emperor that what he had heard was true; and on July 2, Bertrand wrote that Johnson's statement had been corroborated by Captain Davie of the *Conqueror,* the admiral's flagship, who told Napoleon that he and Captain Johnson had the story from Captain Lamb himself. Davie added that Lamb had later asked him not to mention it to anyone. He had replied that he had already spoken about the matter to some fifty persons.

If Sir Hudson had wished to get at the truth in the matter he would have confronted Captain Lamb with the two captains. No such confrontation took place; but, on July 24, he had Captain Lamb make a sworn statement before a justice of the peace. The captain swore that "no directions or intimation of any design or intention for breaking the bust into pieces had been given him." However, nowhere in the sworn statement is there any mention of the charge that he had been advised to throw the bust overboard. The omission is significant. On August 18, O'Meara wrote to Finlaison: "Although to tell you the truth, I did then, and do now, believe that such counsel was really given—though I acquitted Sir Hudson Lowe *himself* of knowing anything about it—yet I was extremely anxious, from obvious reasons, to convince Bonaparte that it was false." The truth appears to have been that Reade had *not* told Captain Lamb to break the bust into fragments, but *had* told him to throw it overboard.

Captain Lamb had not heeded Reade's advice. He had had the box containing the bust carried to his own cabin and had notified the governor of its presence on board. It took Lowe from the 29th of May to the 10th of June to make up his mind what to do with it. Although the bust was made of a single piece of white marble, he feared it might contain clandestine correspondence. On June 10, he finally made a decision, went to see Bertrand, told him about the arrival of the bust, said it was "a *mauvais* piece of cut stone, not worth the hundred pounds the man asked for it," but that if Napoleon wanted it he would have it delivered. Bertrand, who had known about its arrival almost as soon as the governor, asked him to do so with as little delay as possible. It was delivered the following day.

Napoleon, who believed the bust had been ordered sent to him by Marie Louise and was prepared to admire it no matter what its defects, had in the meantime been seething with rage. When it finally arrived he had it placed on the chimney-piece in the drawing room and looked at it adoringly. The only defect he would concede was an excessive depression about the neck. He told O'Meara: "I do not know what he [Lowe] meant by saying that a hundred guineas was too much for the bust. Surely no sum could be too much for a father to pay under similar circumstances. But this man has no feeling. . . . If it had not been delivered I would have told a tale which would have made the mothers of England execrate him as a monster in human shape." He instructed Bertrand to pay Radowitch three hundred napoleons and to send him a letter of thanks. On his return to England the gunner carefully avoided the Beagginis and kept the money. They wrote to Bertrand, soliciting indemnification, but received no reply.

SEVEN

Admiral Sir Pulteney Malcolm was to return to England on July 4, 1817, Rear Admiral Robert Plampin being momentarily expected to arrive on the *Conqueror* to relieve him. On June 19, he and Lady Malcolm came to Longwood to pay a farewell visit to Napoleon. The admiral spoke to the Emperor about the expected arrival of Lord Amherst, ambassador extraordinary returning from China. He begged him to seize the opportunity to have Amherst act as mediator and to make a conciliatory gesture by consenting to have the governor introduce the visitor.

He was poorly rewarded for his pains. He and Lady Malcolm had been accompanied to Longwood by Captain Jones of the *Julia* and Major Boyer of the marines, both of whom he introduced to the Emperor at the conclusion of the visit. When he sent a report of the visit to Lowe, he toned down the uncomplimentary remarks Napoleon had made about him, but on the way back to Jamestown mentioned some of them to Captain Jones. This was imprudent as he should have known that the captain would be questioned by Reade. When Lowe had read the admiral's report, he wrote to him: "Some of the observations, I have reason to believe, were expressed with much more violence and embraced a greater variety of remarks than what your note conveyed to me." Malcolm made the dignified rejoinder: "Whatever impressions may be in your mind and however much I may regret our differences of opinion, I feel satisfied my conduct on this and on every other occasion has been actuated by a sincere desire to promote the public good." To this Lowe replied with his customary boorishness: "I am not aware in what respect the public service has been benefited by your visits to General Bonaparte." Thereupon Malcolm informed him that he considered his way of writing "repugnant."

During the visit Napoleon called Lady Malcolm's attention to the bust on the chimney piece. She admired the curls framing the boyish face, and he said: "He has fair hair, like a Scotchman." Shortly before the visitors left he took from the table a cup and saucer, decorated with Cleopatra's needle, belonging to his exquisite Sèvres set, and presented them to Lady Malcolm. When she thanked him he remarked that the admiral would get no parting present because he was a man who would not listen to reason. "Ladies have more compassion for those who have fallen into misfortune," he said; then added: "I have worn the imperial crown of France, the iron crown of Italy; England has now given me a greater and more glorious crown, such as was worn by the Savior of the world—a crown of thorns. It is to the persecutions of England that I shall owe the brightest part of my fame." He thanked the admiral and Lady Malcolm for their kindness to him. "You wanted nothing from me," he said. "I have no longer the power to do any person a service. You came from the goodness of your hearts."

EIGHT

On June 27, Lord Amherst arrived at St. Helena. He had been sent to China as ambassador extraordinary, but the Emperor of that country had refused to receive him because he would not agree to prostrate himself before him, as required by Chinese court etiquette. Admiral Malcolm had, as has been mentioned, urged Napoleon to consent to have the governor present the ambassador to him, but the Emperor would not hear of this. He told O'Meara that he would not receive his own son if he came accompanied by Sir Hudson. He had in fact difficulty making up his mind whether to receive the visitor at all, but finally consented provided application for the visit were made to the grand marshal. The governor bowed to his wishes and sent a message to Bertrand informing him that Lord Amherst and he would call at his house on the 28th, at three in the afternoon, to make arrangements for the ambassador's visit to Napoleon. The Emperor instructed the grand marshal to inform Lord Amherst that he would receive him on the 1st of July at three o'clock.

When, on July 1, the hour of the visit approached Napoleon grew uncommonly restless. He went to the billiard-room a half hour before the ambassador's arrival, reproached Montholon for not wearing his dress uniform, and scolded Noverraz for having no buckles on his shoes. He had, in fact, come to the conclusion that Malcolm's proposal to have Amherst serve as mediator was not devoid of merit, and had decided to acquaint the visitor with all his grievances.

Lord Amherst appeared at Bertrand's house shortly before

three, accompanied by a suite of nine, among whom were Henry Ellis, secretary of the embassy; Hayne, the ambassador's private secretary; Maxwell, the naval captain; Dr. Abel, a naturalist; Lord Amherst's adolescent son; and others. The grand marshal accompanied the visitors to Longwood House, where Montholon and Gourgaud received them in the billiard-room, while he went to the drawing room, where the Emperor was already waiting. Presently he reappeared and asked Lord Amherst to come with him.

On entering the drawing room the ambassador bowed to Napoleon and said: "My great desire for twenty years has been to meet you." Napoleon acknowledged this with a nod and a smile. They remained in conversation for over an hour. The Emperor complained about the governor's arbitrary behavior and the needless and vexatious restrictions to which he and his suite were subjected. He later told O'Meara that he had asked the ambassador: "Would you, my lord, go out under the restriction of not saying more than 'How do you do?' to any person you met unless in the presence of a British officer? True that he has removed that prohibition, but he may impose it again as his caprice dictates. Would you go out if you were obliged to come in again promptly at six o'clock in the evening, on pain of being stopped by sentries at the gate?" Lord Amherst replied: "No, I would do as you do; I would remain in my room."

When, in 1822, O'Meara's *Napoleon in Exile* was published in London and Lowe was making preparations to sue the author, Lord Amherst, at Sir Hudson's request, wrote him a letter in which he said: "I did not use the expression nor anything like the expression attributed to me in the conversation." Apart from the fact that O'Meara's statement is corroborated in Bertrand's journal, what is the value of such official denials of statements made in private? No one can read Admiral Malcolm's correspondence with Lowe, or the diary he published under his wife's name, without being convinced that he thoroughly disapproved of the governor. Yet on his return to England he praised him to the Prince Regent. We shall see that the Duke of Wellington was equally inconsistent.

NINE

When Lord Amherst's audience had been concluded, Henry
Ellis was admitted and was presented by the ambassador. Like
most of those privileged to obtain an audience with the exiled
monarch, Ellis was favorably impressed. He wrote: "Bonaparte's
manner was throughout dignified, affable, and pleasing. In person he was not by any means overgrown, and then appeared in
good health. He expressed himself with great fluency and
strength, the sentences short and epigrammatic. . . . Had he
been in the plenitude of his powers, his manner could not have
been more dignified or more calculated to command respect."

The remaining members of Amherst's party were then admitted, ranged by Bertrand in a half circle around Napoleon, and
presented by the ambassador. The Emperor exchanged a few
words with each. One of the visitors, Dr. Abel, has written:
"Bonaparte's person has nothing of that morbid fulness which I
had been led to look for. On the contrary, I scarcely recollect to
have seen a form more expressive of strength and even of vigor.
It is true that he was very large, considering his height, 5 feet,
7 inches; but his largeness had nothing of unwieldiness. . . .
His whole form, indeed, was so closely knit, that firmness might
be said to be its striking characteristic."

Gourgaud has written that when Lord Amherst and his party
had left, Napoleon expressed the conviction that as a result of
the interview "he would postpone his departure and try to reconcile us with the governor." After dinner he remarked that
"there would be some new development on the morrow."

After the visit Lord Amherst went to dine at the Malcolms'.
If he had any intention of acting as mediator it was natural that
having heard Lowe's and Napoleon's side of the controversy he
wanted to obtain Malcolm's. What could the admiral have told
him except that when he had tried to smooth the way for him to
act as mediator Lowe had written him in a manner which he felt
justified in labeling as "repugnant"? Not unlikely he also told him
about his advice to Lord Somerset not to keep Piontkowski and
Napoleon's three servants at the Cape six months, since his gar-

rison was largely composed of Poles who had served under Bonaparte, and about Lowe's reaction to that advice. He must have told him about Lowe's "system of spies," about which he says in his diary that it "must cause incalculable evil." Little wonder that Lord Amherst decided not to become involved and departed the following day.

TEN

On June 29, Rear Admiral Robert Plampin arrived at St. Helena on the *Conqueror*, and was presented to Napoleon by Admiral Malcolm the day before the latter's departure for Europe. The fact that Sir Pulteney's successor spoke French fluently, having lived in France for over a year, did not dispose the Emperor favorably toward him. "He reminds me," he told O'Meara, "of one of those little, drunken Dutch *schippers*, that I have seen in Holland, sitting at a table with a pipe in his mouth and a bottle of gin before him." Plampin was to become a pliant tool of the governor, to whom he was greatly obligated for the following reason:

The admiral, who was fifty-five, had brought with him a young trollop, who, it was said, bestowed her favors not only on him but on his orderly officer and several of his midshipmen. It was not long before the irregularity of the relationship became known. The inhabitants of what has sometimes been called the "abandoned and profligate isle" would not have cared, had it not been for the Reverend Richard Boys, "chaplain of the Honorable East India Company in St. Helena." The chaplain was a stickler for morality, especially among those highly placed, who, he believed, should set an example to the community. When called upon to record the birth of an illegitimate child born to a slave woman, he never failed to put down in large letters the name and position of the father—be he the leading merchant or planter on the island, a member of the council, or one of Lowe's most trusted lieutenants. He no sooner heard of Plampin's irregular relationship than he called upon him from the pulpit to flee from the wrath to come by putting away the "accursed woman." Nor was he a man to remain silent if his admonitions were not heeded. How Lowe managed to silence him is somewhat of a mystery, for he was as fearless and incorruptible as he was narrow-minded and tactless.

The chaplain did not forget. On July 8, 1821, a few days before the governor left the island, he preached a sermon in which he spoke his mind. Sir Hudson, Lady Lowe, members of the governor's staff and officers of the Company's civil service and their ladies were present, as well as the whole of Reverend Boys's congregation. Addressing himself to the notables he said that they were self-righteous formalists, possessed no other morality than what the world called morality, and that their religion was nothing more than a specious appearance. "Verily I say unto you that publicans and harlots go into the Kingdom of God before you."

During Plampin's three years' stay at St. Helena (he left the island in July, 1820) he saw Napoleon only one other time, on September 5, 1817. Lowe had asked him to deliver a book to Bonaparte, sent by Lord Bathurst, entitled *Manuscrit venu de Sainte-Hélène d'une Manière Inconnue*. It was purported to have been written by Napoleon, and it created a sensation throughout Europe. Some ascribed it to Madame de Staël, others to Benjamin Constant. Napoleon believed it to be the work of Roederer. It has since been established that the literary hoax was perpetrated by Lullien de Châteauvieux, a talented citizen of Geneva.

ELEVEN

The Honorable John Elphinstone, brother of the officer whose life Napoleon had saved at Belle Alliance, was in charge of the East India Company's affairs in China. He had already once sent a chest filled with valuable gifts to the exile at St. Helena. In July, 1817, another shipment arrived, accompanied by a letter which Lowe forwarded to Bertrand with the information that the chest would follow promptly. Among the many beautiful products of Chinese handicraft it contained was an exquisitely wrought ivory chess game and a tea chest of the same material which, when opened, disclosed a tray embossed with a representation of the city of Canton. Underneath the tray were packets of fragrant tea.

When Lowe examined the contents he came upon a box of ivory counters embossed with the letter N surmounted by the imperial crown. Then he noticed to his horror that most of the other articles were similarly initialed. He must have sat for a long time with his finger in his mouth pondering the dilemma. If he sent the presents to Longwood, would it not imply recognition of Bonaparte's right to the imperial title? He finally called the admiral into consultation. Plampin had at that time not yet run afoul of the terrible Reverend Boys, so did not feel under obligation to agree with the governor. He thought Lowe's reasoning rather silly. "If the crowned N bothers you," he told him, "all you have to do is not to look at it." He expressed the opinion that the shipment should be sent to Longwood without any comment. This, however, was beyond Lowe's ability at self-control. "He is like a man afflicted with a perpetual itch," the Emperor said of him once. He might have added that Lowe did most of his scratching on paper. He wrote to Bertrand that having promised to forward the shipment promptly, he was doing so, but that "if I acted in perfect conformity with the established rules, I ought to delay sending it."

When Napoleon had inspected the contents of the chest and had read Lowe's letter, he had no difficulty divining the reason for the remark. He dictated an answer, which Bertrand signed, making it plain that he considered Lowe's objection to the shipment puerile, and added: "The Emperor will not accept of favors from anybody, nor be indebted for anything to the caprice of anyone." This was all Lowe required to set him to penning page after page of argument, explanation, protest. One would have thought that the safety of Europe had been endangered by the presence of a crowned N on ivory counters. Soon the whole island was talking about the matter. Count Balmain wrote to Nesselrode: "His conduct toward them is a little crazy, even the English are beginning to say so."

TWELVE

On July 14, Napoleon received the officers of the 53rd regiment, which was leaving the island. They had demonstrated their sympathy and respect for him on numerous occasions, and he was sorry to see them go. They stood lined up in the drawing room and were presented by Sir George Bingham. The Emperor exchanged a few words with each: "How many years of service?" "In what battles did you take part?" "Were you ever wounded?" "Are you married?" "Any children?" and so forth. He then addressed them collectively, saying he had been very pleased with the conduct of the 53rd toward him and would always be glad to hear that its officers and men were doing well. He told Sir George that he must feel he was losing his children and that he should compensate himself by having his lady present him with a little Bingham. The general blushed, then joined in the general laughter.

The departure of the 53rd meant the departure of Captain Poppleton. He was as sorry to leave as Napoleon and his suite were sorry to see him go. He had asked permission to remain, but it was refused. The Emperor asked Gourgaud what he thought of his intention to present Poppleton with a gold snuff-box. The young general replied that the captain fully deserved it: "He has done his duty with all possible tact. He could have tormented us, but has been as considerate as he possibly could be without being disloyal to his government." So Napoleon gave a gold snuff-box to Bertrand, to be presented to Poppleton the day of his departure, together with a letter expressing the Emperor's appreciation of his conduct. Before leaving, Poppleton presented his successor, Captain Blakeney, to Napoleon.

Lowe recommended Poppleton for promotion to major, lauding his "prudence, firmness, and moderation." This, however, was before Gourgaud left Longwood and told Gorrequer about the snuff-box. Lowe no sooner learned about this than he tried to break Poppleton. But the captain's prudence had served him well. Upon his arrival in England he had immediately informed the colonial secretary about the present he had received.

Bathurst could see nothing wrong with his acceptance of such a gift when leaving the island, so Lowe got snubbed for his pains, as he had in the case of Malcolm.

Poppleton's wife died in 1818 and he went to live with her relatives at Ross, County Galway. His great niece, Mrs. Callwell, has written in her *Old Irish Life:* "Throughout our childhood, the gold snuff-box always stood upon the dining room chimney-piece, and every visitor to the house was offered a pinch out of Napoleon's box. It was kept well filled therefore, white snuff at one end, black snuff at the other, and underneath lay a piece of white paper. . . . Many years afterwards when snuff taking had ceased to be the fashion and the box was only a curiosity, a gentleman to whom it was shown asked the reason of the white paper. 'To keep the fingers of the snuff-takers from scratching the box,' he was told. More inquisitive, however, than all who had gone before him, he prized up the bit of paper, and underneath lay another closely folded paper—a letter from Napoleon himself to the Count of Las Cases, sending messages to his adherents in France, and his wishes for the bringing up of the King of Rome. It had lain there for forty years. Louis Napoleon reigned at the Tuileries. The Count Las Cases' son, however, was alive, and to him the long-concealed letter, destined for his father, was sent."

On Poppleton's tombstone appear the words: "He was honored by the esteem of Napoleon."

XIX. Gourgaud's Departure

One might have expected Las Cases' departure to have eased the situation at Longwood. This was far from being the case. His presence had kept in abeyance the enmity between Gourgaud and Montholon, united as they were in their hatred of the favorite. Even before his departure from the island relations between the two generals had become strained. Gourgaud had always been jealous of Montholon as well as of Las Cases. We have seen that as early as December, 1815, he had threatened to fight Montholon rather than have the latter take precedence over him at the dinner table. It will likewise be remembered that when Napoleon had had Gourgaud read aloud the letter he had written to Las Cases and the young general had expressed the opinion that it was too laudatory, Madame Montholon had interrupted, saying he was wrong and that the letter was just right. He had resented the interruption, and the following day asked Montholon to speak to his wife about the matter. Montholon had been conciliatory and Gourgaud's anger had subsided.

Five days later, however, we find him saying to his colleague: "Tomorrow, if you wish, with pistols, at the corner of the plowed field. I'll ask Bertrand to be my second." What had happened? Two days earlier Gourgaud had played chess with the Emperor and they had parted on the best of terms. The following day, however, at 7:30 in the morning, when Napoleon was hardly out of bed, Madame Montholon had gone to the Emperor's apartment and Napoleon had not sent for Gourgaud since. From this the young general concluded that she had spoken ill of him during the visit, and considered himself justified to ask satisfaction from her husband. Again Montholon had managed to pacify him, but that same day Gourgaud wrote in his journal: "Let the Emperor have mistresses if he feels like it, but I am not going to humiliate myself before them."

Obviously Gourgaud believed Madame Montholon had become Napoleon's mistress, and to this might be added that he was convinced the relationship existed with her husband's knowledge and consent. Madame Bertrand was of the same opinion, and when in January, 1818, Madame Montholon gave birth to her second daughter, christened Napoléone Joséphine, she remarked that the child resembled neither Montholon nor his wife, but did resemble the Emperor. On March 3, of that same year, Baron Stürmer reported to Prince Metternich: "Madame Montholon was able to triumph over her rivals and to climb into the imperial bed." Montchenu sent a similar report, adding that Madame Montholon's wishes were law at Longwood. Gourgaud wrote in his journal that while the Emperor economized on fodder for the horses, a cow was being kept because Madame Montholon liked cream, and that Napoleon had changed the dinner hour from nine in the evening to three in the afternoon to suit her convenience. On September 3, 1817, he wrote that at 2:30 in the afternoon the Emperor went to the Montholons and half an hour later returned with Madame Montholon whom he led to his apartment. On November 5, he recorded that Madame Montholon, dressed in her best, went to Napoleon's apartment while he was in his bath. Her husband was with the Emperor at that time and immediately left when she entered. Gourgaud remarked sarcastically: "So they chase you when she visits him," to which Montholon gave an embarrassed reply.

TWO

Five days before Las Cases sailed for the Cape, the Emperor, apparently worried about the renewed discord in his household, made a little speech. It was after dinner, the table had been cleared, the servants had left the room, but he, the Montholons, and Gourgaud remained at table, as they now often did. He told them that all things considered his generals did not have much to complain about. They were free to ride anywhere on the island accompanied by a British officer. They could visit Plantation House and General Bingham. They could leave St. Helena whenever they chose. They had had a glorious past and there was hardly a sovereign in Europe who would not be glad to avail himself of their services. They had participated in stirring events, enough to serve them as topics of conversation for the rest of their lives. They had therefore every reason to be happy in the present and need not worry about the future. He alone, he said, had reason to be unhappy. To have fallen from so high a state! He could not, like them, leave St. Helena, and it was out of the question for him to ride about the island escorted by a British officer. He was moreover constantly being spied on, even in his own house. If a woman entered his room there was jealousy, talk of dueling. Becoming animated he exclaimed, fixing Gourgaud with his eye: "No consideration for me! What right has anyone to object to my receiving this or that person? What business has anybody to mix in my personal affairs?"

Gourgaud tried to explain. Never before, he said, had he challenged any man to a duel, but he had been driven to the verge of despair.

The Emperor said sternly: "What right have you to object if Madame Montholon comes to visit me?"

Again Gourgaud tried to explain, but the Emperor interrupted him, saying: "Braggadocio! What you deserve is a good lesson—a bullet."

"Sire, it would not be the first one I've stopped."

"You were jealous of Las Cases. You thought that by coming here you would be my pal. I am nobody's pal. Nobody can gain influence over me. Ever since we have been here you have given me nothing but headaches. Had I known it would turn out like this I would have brought only servants along. I can live very well alone. If one gets tired of life the thrust of a stiletto brings quick relief. If you don't like it here, don't quarrel with Montholon—leave!"

THREE

A couple of weeks went by. The Emperor tried kindness. He would pinch Gourgaud's ear and call him "my son Gourgaud," "Gorgo," "Gorgotto," "my little Gourgaud." But relations between the young man and the Montholons remained strained. On January 20, 1817, Napoleon summoned him to his apartment and said firmly, but not unkindly: "It's time for the bickering between you and the Montholons to stop. Your conduct worries me. Outwardly at least you must live at peace with them, go to see them occasionally, lunch with them sometimes."

The young man replied that he used to like Montholon, but that his colleague had behaved treacherously by misrepresenting him to the Emperor. He had been reading the New Testament in the hope that this would dispel his resentment, but it was too strong for him. He could not bear the idea of seeing the Montholons preferred to him.

Napoleon said what he needed at St. Helena was someone to comfort and to cheer him, and that Gourgaud was always moping. "What matters it to me what a man's hidden sentiments are, provided he is good company? I can hear what men say, I can't read their hearts."

They spoke about Gourgaud's mother. The young man's affection for his mother seemed quite extraordinary. He seldom mentioned her without tears gathering in his eyes. Lord Bathurst was touched by the letters he wrote her, which passed through his hands. Napoleon thought his feeling for his mother exaggerated, and once, losing patience, had said to him: "You are crazy to rave about your mother like that. Do you think I don't love mine? But one should be reasonable about it." Gourgaud had burst into tears. The Emperor, a little conscience-stricken, had said to Las Cases: "Is this peculiar to him or do people in general feel like that? Am I unnatural in that respect? I certainly love my mother with all my heart, but if I were to hear that she had died, I doubt if I would shed a single tear. If, however, it was my

263

wife or child, I probably would. Is this because my reason has prepared me to expect her death in the course of time, or is it egoism? For, you see, I belong to my mother, but my wife and child belong to me."

Soon after their arrival at St. Helena Gourgaud had told the Emperor that his mother had only a small pension to live on, insufficient to enable her and her unmarried daughter to live in comfort. Napoleon had told him to write a note to Prince Eugene instructing him to pay Madame Gourgaud an annual pension of 12,000 francs from funds on deposit with him, and bring the note to him to sign. On various pretexts Gourgaud had delayed writing the note. It was not sent until the middle of July, 1817, and then only over his protest. What was the reason for this? The note had to be sent clandestinely as Napoleon did not want his enemies to know the whereabouts of his deposits. Gourgaud, who cherished the hope of sooner or later being able to return to France, did not wish to run the risk of it being intercepted by the British. He wanted his record at St. Helena to be such as to facilitate his rehabilitation by the Bourbons. For this reason he also managed to avoid signing any letter or document dictated by Napoleon that might offend the British authorities. All such papers were signed by Montholon or Bertrand. It may well be that the letters he sent home, which represented St. Helena in such glowing colors, were written with an eye on the effect they would have on the British authorities as much as with the intention of comforting his mother. Certain it is that when his mother's interests clashed with his own, it was the former that had to yield. One is forced to believe that the tears he shed when he spoke of her were due to sentimentalism rather than sentiment.

It was Napoleon who brought up the subject of Gourgaud's mother. He had been wondering why the young man had not written the note regarding his mother's pension. Turning the matter over in his mind he had found the answer, but believed the time had not yet come to tell him what he thought of it. He only said: "As for your mother, you only had to write the lines— 'My dear Eugene, be so kind as to forward to Madame Gourgaud 12,000 francs annually, retroactive to January 1, 1815.' I would have signed them, as I told you I would. But you did not write them."

Gourgaud gave the following confused and disingenuous reply: "Ah, if you had only told me! How could I have feared to compromise myself for my mother? Your Majesty did tell me, but did not mention it again. Could I have importuned Your Majesty? Being poor makes me very reserved in such matters."

After this conversation he still did not write the note, although the Emperor assured him that he would be incurring no obligation, as granting his mother the pension would not inconvenience him in the least.

The following morning Napoleon summoned Montholon and Gourgaud to his apartment and managed to prevail upon them to embrace in his presence.

FOUR

For some time there was comparative peace. On February 12, 1817, the Emperor invited Gourgaud to his study, told him to be seated, called for a bottle of champagne, and they drank together. Under the influence of the wine he became more than ordinarily communicative. He said he was fully aware that the Montholons were principally concerned with their own interests and comfort. They had appropriated the Venetian blinds from his drawing room for their own apartment. He had pretended not to notice. Gourgaud, too, should try to live at peace with them. He was wrong in thinking that he (Napoleon) had taken a fancy to Madame Montholon. There had been too many gracious women in his life for him not to notice her lack of good manners and her ludicrous behavior. But on St. Helena one would make a companion of a parakeet for lack of anything better. There was no choice. All the same the Montholons were always on hand when he needed them and never gave him any trouble. If he had to choose between the Bertrands and the Montholons, he would take the latter. He still had a few millions, and when he died they would be his principal heirs. He knew that Madame Montholon had come to St. Helena because her reputation in Paris was somewhat spotted and she hoped that her stay on the island would improve her social standing. "But what do I care about motives? They help me pass the time, and if she were better looking I would profit of her in every way."

On March 20, the Emperor reproached Gourgaud for refusing to accept the monthly stipend of 500 francs Bertrand had been instructed to pay him. The general replied that he did so because Montholon received more than double that amount. Napoleon said angrily that he would do with his money as he pleased. He was paying Madame Montholon as well as her husband. If Gourgaud refused to accept the money he had better leave. "Before we came to St. Helena I liked you better than Montholon. We had gone through military campaigns together and had more in common. That was the reason I chose you at Rochefort to deliver the letter to the Prince Regent. Now I prefer him to you." Gourgaud left the room, choked with tears.

He hurried to Bertrand's house. He wanted to know, he told the grand marshal, if the Emperor were serious in wanting him to leave. "If he does, he need not fear that I shall say anything that might be harmful to him. I am too honorable a man for that." Bertrand sought to reassure him and finally persuaded him to take the money.

Relations between Bertrand and Gourgaud were now beginning to spoil. The grand marshal disliked the Montholons, whom he considered unscrupulous intriguers, but the complaints of the temperamental Madame Bertrand were a drain on his patience, and when Gourgaud came to pour out his heart to him he found him increasingly indifferent. When in June of that year Napoleon asked Gourgaud if he had seen Bertrand, the young man replied: "No, Sire. A coolness has arisen between us. I believed him to be a sincere friend, and find I was mistaken. I asked him for advice and he answered me in a ministerial fashion—me who would have gone through a fire for him! It's a trying apprenticeship I am serving at Longwood. Here the motto is: Everyone for himself."

When in July, 1817, the 53rd regiment was preparing to depart, Bertrand reminded Gourgaud that he had not yet written the note regarding his mother's annuity. The departure of the regiment furnished an excellent opportunity to entrust it to one of the officers. Gourgaud again found excuses. If the Emperor had really meant to give his mother a pension, he said, he would have inquired about the note. He (Gourgaud) was not the man to importune him to bestow something he did not really care to bestow. But when toward five o'clock that afternoon the Emperor invited him to his study and they were sipping tea together, he weakened and mentioned the matter to him. Napoleon looked at him quizzically, then picked up a pencil, wrote a note to Eugene, told Gourgaud to transcribe it, and then said: "It is doing me an injustice to believe that this matters anything to me. But this is not what troubles you. My having written this note will not stop you from looking morose. You are afraid, as always, of compromising yourself. Would you have signed the Remonstrance, which Montholon signed? Would you have signed my reply to Bathurst? You think yourself shrewd. Your imagination is playing you false. What is occupying your thoughts should not so much as have entered your mind."

He got up and with hands clasped behind his back walked several times up and down the room, then, looking fixedly at Gourgaud, said: "You have forfeited a good deal of my friendship."

"Ah, Sire, what have I done to be treated like that? Your Majesty is very unjust to me."

FIVE

On July 15, four days after the above scene, the note to Prince Eugene had not yet been entrusted to the British officer who had promised to forward it. It occurred to Napoleon that he might as well take advantage of the opportunity to instruct Eugene to open a monthly credit of £500 for him with Messrs. Andrews, Street & Parker of London, on which Bertrand would be able to draw for their household expenses. He asked Gourgaud to bring the letter to him, opened it, and scribbled the additional instructions on a piece of paper, together with the remark that they "lacked the barest necessities." He handed the paper to Gourgaud and told him to transcribe what he had written on the back of the note concerning the pension. Gourgaud did so, and the Emperor signed. Having invited the young man to lunch he could not help noticing that he seemed greatly troubled and hardly ate at all. He guessed the reason: Gourgaud feared that the additional instructions to Eugene and the remark about the lack of the barest necessities would make the letter, if intercepted by the British, even more compromising as far as he was concerned.

That afternoon Napoleon went to the billiard-room and strode meditatively back and forth. Finally he rang and when Ali came told him to call General Gourgaud. When the general entered the Emperor looked at him fixedly, then said: "How changed you look! Shall I tell you what is the matter with you? You lack courage. Look at the Montholons. They do not mope, yet he signed the Remonstrance and is begging me to let him sign my reply to Bathurst, but I won't let him."

"But, Sire, they have a fortune to fall back upon; I have none. He is like a man wearing armor; I am exposed. He runs no risk; I, who have lost all by following Your Majesty, risk everything. If I were to be deported to the Cape . . ."

"We are here on a battlefield," Napoleon interrupted. "A man who leaves a battle because he has no fortune to fall back upon is a coward. Yes, this is more than you can bear. You lack courage."

"I admit, Sire, that when you told me I had lost your friendship, it was more than I could bear. Your Majesty is taking an unfair advantage of my situation. How could I leave? People would say I left because I lacked stamina. All the same, if Your Majesty desires me to leave, I'll go."

"Yes, I know. You can't bear this, that, and the other." O'Meara entered, but the Emperor went on: "You're getting on everybody's nerves—mine, Bertrand's, Montholon's."

Gourgaud withdrew and went to see the grand marshal. He gave him the letter to Eugene and said he would accept nothing from the Emperor. He was going to see the governor. He was leaving. Bertrand persuaded him to defer his decision until the following day. He went to his room, lay down on the bed, and did not get up for dinner. "How can I leave with honor?" he wrote that evening in his journal. "I cannot publish all that has happened. People would say I was libeling the Emperor. Yet if I leave without any explanation to the public, they will say my courage had failed me."

He did not go to see the governor, and, on July 22, the Emperor sent for him and asked what he had done with the letter to Prince Eugene. He replied that he had given it to Bertrand. Napoleon said: "Whatever differences may have arisen between us, you have no right to refuse what I wish to do for your mother. What I do for her is in recognition of your past services and does not obligate you in the least. You can always leave whenever you feel like it. Think of how you would reproach yourself if your mother were to fall into want, when she could have had security for the rest of her days."

The 53rd regiment had already departed, but he told Gourgaud to get the letter from Bertrand and give it to O'Meara, who was going to Jamestown and would see to it that it was sent. Even if it were to fall into the hands of the British, he told him, it would not compromise him. The instruction to Eugene to open up a credit for him with a London banking house would merely serve to convince the British authorities that he had no treasure hidden at St. Helena. The argument apparently appealed to Gourgaud, for he did as he was told and the letter was sent.

SIX

Throughout the month of August there was no clash worth mentioning between the Emperor and Gourgaud, and outwardly at least relations between the latter and the Montholons appeared improved. But the young man had in the meantime managed to pick a quarrel with Cipriani. Napoleon seldom saw him. The Emperor now dined alone in his apartment. It was far from pleasant to sit at table with three people, one of whom detested the other two and was detested by them. Except for an occasional fine day, fog and rain shrouded the landscape and Gourgaud did not care to go out riding. There was nothing for him to do except to sit with a book in the drawing room or visit the Bertrands, whose reception of him was not what it had been once. He had not seen the Emperor for three days, when on the evening of the 4th of September Ali came and told him that His Majesty wished to speak to him.

Napoleon appeared in a bad humor and demanded to know what was the trouble between him and Cipriani. The reply was unsatisfactory, and the Emperor said it was his misfortune to have Lowe as governor of the island and him as a member of his suite. Gourgaud replied that he had too many enemies at Longwood to make life bearable. He would prove his attachment to His Majesty by leaving. Napoleon remarked curtly that that was the best thing he could do. "Go and write libels about me," he added. Gourgaud said that he had no intention to wreak vengeance upon his enemies or to dishonor himself. The rupture seemed definite. Gourgaud bowed and turned to go, then abruptly wheeled about and seizing the Emperor's hand tried to bring it to his lips. Napoleon withdrew his hand, but he was touched. "You are a good son," he said, "a good brother. But you have a terrible disposition. Go now and have a good sleep."

It would have been better for both had this been their final parting, but it was not. The unhappy young man hurried over to the Bertrands, where he sank down upon a couch, covered his face with his hands, and wept. The Emperor, he said, was driving him away. Bertrand must go with him tomorrow to see the governor. This was the end! The grand marshal spent that evening and part of the two succeeding days in trying to calm him. His Majesty did not mean all he said, he assured him. Montholon, too, tried. He told Gourgaud that he was very useful to the Emperor, that being an artillery officer he could discuss with him many things he and Bertrand knew little about. On the evening of the 6th he had dinner with the Bertrands. The food and the wine were excellent and put Gourgaud in good spirits.

After dinner he and Bertrand had an animated conversation about the campaign of 1813. When he returned home he felt at peace with the world and decided to forget about leaving.

SEVEN

Gourgaud was not the only one of the Emperor's following to whom life at Longwood was becoming a burden. The new favorite, Montholon, was far from happy, but had the good sense to be always cheerful and obliging in the Emperor's presence. On September 16, he confided to Gourgaud that "everybody wants to leave," that his wife had not seen the Emperor for a long time, that His Majesty now listened only to the servants, that he seemed determined to dine alone. Three days later he told him that he had not come to St. Helena to dine with Tristan, that he would be glad of an opportunity to depart, that he should have listened to the Duke of Vicenza (Caulaincourt) who had advised him not to go. Since misery loves company this information so mollified Gourgaud that he paid a visit to Madame Montholon, who regaled him with gossip about Madame Bertrand and tried to get him to agree with her. But the following day Bertrand told him that Montholon was undermining him with the Emperor.

Whether the Montholons sought to ruin Gourgaud's reputation with Napoleon is a moot question. Montholon swore that they did not, but his reputation for veracity is far from unblemished. It is likewise a moot question if, had they tried, they would have succeeded. Napoleon once told Gourgaud that when ill was spoken to him about someone he liked, it merely served to stimulate his liking and to put him on his guard against the traducers. Judging by his unswerving loyalty to Las Cases, whom the generals had represented to him in the worst possible light, this may well have been true. He had at the beginning of the captivity liked Gourgaud. It was the young man's habit of contradicting him, his unreasonable attempt to monopolize him, his splenetic disposition, his foolish pride, his fear to do anything that might compromise him with the British authorities which were responsible for Napoleon's irritation with him. Something pathological in Gourgaud's attachment added to this irritation. Balmain and Stürmer have both reported that after Gourgaud left Longwood, Napoleon told Bertrand: "Speak to me no more of that man. He is mad. He was jealous, in love with me. What the devil! I am not his wife and can't sleep with him. I know he will write libels about me, but I don't care. If he returns to France he will be locked up, hanged, or shot."

The fact that Napoleon was becoming increasingly irascible and determined to isolate himself aggravated the situation. Toward September, 1817, his health was beginning to fail. He complained about pain in his right side, and his legs had swelled. His sedentary existence and lack of social intercourse contributed to his irascibility.

EIGHT

On January 26, 1818, when Madame Montholon gave birth to a daughter, Madame Bertrand was to ask Gourgaud if he had noticed how uneasy His Majesty had been when she was in labor. Gourgaud told her he had definitely made up his mind to send a formal challenge to Montholon as soon as his wife had recovered. Madame Bertrand volunteered the suggestion that they fight with swords, not with pistols. They spoke about Dr. Livingstone, who had delivered Madame Montholon, and agreed laughingly that he would not get 100,000 francs from the Emperor, as had Dr. Dubois for delivering Marie Louise.

Things were shaping toward a crisis. It came the evening of February 2. Napoleon was in the drawing room playing chess with Bertrand; Montholon stood watching the moves. Gourgaud entered, looking glum as usual. The Emperor glanced at him and remarked: "Why so sad? Cheer up!"

"Your Majesty knows I have no reason to be cheerful."

"Why not?"

"Because of the way I am being treated."

The Emperor frowned and told Montholon to go and see how many sentries there were around the house—a stratagem to get him out of the room. When the door had closed behind him, he rose and said in a tone of voice which suggested that he had reached the limit of his endurance. "What exactly do you want?"

"I beg Your Majesty to permit me to leave. I can no longer bear the humiliations to which I am subjected. I have always done my duty, but have the misfortune of displeasing Your Majesty. I don't want to be a burden to anyone."

The Emperor replied that if it was his relations with the Montholons that were troubling him, he had better understand it was none of his business. "Supposing I were to go to bed with Madame Montholon, what harm would there be in that?"

"None, Sire, but I have never said anything about that to Your Majesty. I did not believe Your Majesty's taste was so depraved."

Napoleon's temper rose. "If you threaten Montholon you are a brigand, an assassin!" he cried.

Gourgaud pointed to his longish hair and said: "I haven't had my hair trimmed for several months, and don't intend having it trimmed until I have avenged myself on the scoundrel who has driven me to the verge of despair. Your Majesty calls me a brigand, an assassin. I have not assassinated anybody. It is I who am being assassinated, whom they are killing with vexation."

"I forbid you to threaten Montholon. If you do my curse will be upon you. If you fight him he will kill you."

"I have always thought, Sire, that it is better to die with honor, than to live in disgrace."

All this while Bertrand stood leaning against the wall and remained silent. Gourgaud now appealed to him to tell the Emperor how often he had asked him to intervene on his behalf, to point out to His Majesty that it was not right he should be treated in such a way, that he would be compelled to hold Montholon responsible. The grand marshal made no reply. The Emperor, however, said: "What do you want? To have precedence over Montholon? To dine with me? To see me every day?"

"An assassin, a brigand can have no pretensions to ask for anything," Gourgaud replied.

Napoleon, whose anger waned as quickly as it flared up, and who even at the height of his power always regretted losing his temper, said almost humbly: "Forget the expressions that escaped me."

Gourgaud, too, had calmed down, and said that if the Emperor would give him a written order not to call out Montholon, he would obey it. Napoleon agreed, and asked him if he realized that if he left, the governor might think he was being sent on a secret mission. Then he added bitterly: "I'm sure you will be well received. Lord Bathurst loves you. He has read your letters and found them very much to his liking."

Gourgaud replied he had always written that all was well with him so his mother should not worry about him, and had nothing to reproach himself with.

"The grand marshal will make all necessary arrangements for your departure," Napoleon said. "It will be best to say that you are leaving for reasons of health. I shall have O'Meara give you a certificate to that effect. Take my advice: do not complain to anybody and don't talk about me. Once back in France you will be able to judge what course you should take." Having said this he left the room.

NINE

On February 3, the day after the scene just described, the *Cambridge* dropped anchor at Jamestown, bringing news of the death of Princess Charlotte, heir presumptive to the throne. Before leaving the island Gourgaud was to say to Stürmer: "Everybody knows that the Princess of Wales has for him an almost fanatical admiration. He hoped that when her daughter mounted the throne, she would take advantage of the influence she has over her to have him taken to England. 'Once there,' said he, 'I am saved.'"

It appears probable that preoccupation with Charlotte's death was responsible for Napoleon's neglect to dictate the promised note to Gourgaud. So, on February 4, the latter sent a formal challenge to Montholon, leaving the choice of weapons to his adversary and demanding an interview to arrange details. Montholon wrote in reply that the Emperor had exacted from him his word of honor not to fight a duel as long as he was with him. He added that a duel between them would raise a great scandal and could not but be painful and embarrassing to

His Majesty. When no longer with the Emperor he would give Gourgaud the satisfaction he demanded. Gourgaud considered this unacceptable and insisted on an interview. When he received no answer he said within the hearing of others that he would horsewhip Montholon. Lowe heard about this and instructed Captain Blakeney to take whatever measures were necessary to prevent a clash between the two generals.

On February 6, Gourgaud had dinner at the Bertrands. The grand marshal suggested that he write a letter to the Emperor asking permission to leave for reasons of health. "Nobody will believe it, but it will be a decent excuse," he said. Gourgaud replied that if he wrote to His Majesty at all, it would be to tell him that he was tired of being at the orders of his paramour. Having been treated as he was, he felt, he said, released from any obligation toward him.

The following day he went on horseback to Plantation House to see the governor. He asked to be removed from Longwood as speedily as possible. "I can no longer live there with honor," he said. "I have been treated like a dog. He [Napoleon] had wished me to do things contrary to my honor, or force me by bad treatment to leave him."

Sir Hudson was not in the least surprised at the visit. He had been expecting it for a long time. As early as the 5th of August of the previous year he had written to Lord Bathurst: "General Bonaparte and one of his officers, Baron Gourgaud, are at present on very bad terms. They have not seen or spoken to each other this fortnight. Gourgaud has addressed a letter to me requesting to be sent to the Cape, but was advised by the Bertrands to recall it." He did not encourage Gourgaud's defection and pointed out to him that his departure might be misconstrued. Some would say that he was abandoning Bonaparte, others that he was being sent on a secret mission. However, if he was determined to leave he should write him a letter to that effect.

Gourgaud wrote to Sir Hudson the following day that since his illness of two years ago he had been periodically plagued by attacks of dysentery and liver complaint. To this had recently been added afflictions of a "moral" nature. He therefore asked to be allowed to depart and to be permitted to live in some other part of the island while awaiting departure. Lowe replied that he would be happy to facilitate his journey and that in the meantime arrangements would be made to enable him to live away from Longwood.

TEN

On February 11, Bertrand came to Gourgaud's room and told him that the Emperor wanted to see him. Gourgaud went to Napoleon's apartment, dressed in mufti. The Emperor was seated on the couch. He looked up and said: "So you are leaving?"

"Tomorrow, Sire."

"It is well. You will be sent to the Cape, then to England. A new national army is being formed in France. I can already see you in command of the artillery against the English. You are a good officer. You have served me well. I am sorry to see you go. I was able to discuss with you things the others know little about—our campaigns, science. Let us hope . . ." He broke off, then added: "But there is the Princess Charlotte, on whom we counted so much . . ." He rose and gave Gourgaud a tap on the cheek. "We may meet again in another world. Well, adieu. . . . The grand marshal will help you write your farewell letter. . . . Embrace me. . . ."

The emotional young man burst into tears, threw his arms about the Emperor, then quickly left the room.

The letter which Gourgaud had vowed he would not write reads as follows:

Longwood, February 11

SIRE,

Now that I am about to depart the most painful feelings assail me. I forget all and am solely occupied with the thought that I am about to separate myself forever from him to whom I have consecrated all my existence. That thought overwhelms me. My only consolation is the conviction that I have always done my duty. I yield to fate. In my misfortune I still cherish the hope, Sire, that you will retain some recollection of my services and of my attachment, that you may even do justice to the sentiments and the motives that have led to my departure, and that, if I have lost your good will, I have not forfeited your esteem. Deign, Sire, to accept my farewell and the wishes I entertain for your happiness. Have compassion for my lot, and sometimes, when thinking of me, may Your Majesty say "He at least had a good heart."

I am, etc.,
General Gourgaud.

Napoleon replied:

February 12

GENERAL BARON GOURGAUD,

I thank you for the sentiments expressed in your letter of yesterday. I regret that the disease of the liver, so injurious in this climate, necessitated your departure. You are young, you have ability, a long career lies before you. May it be a happy one. Never doubt the interest I take in you.

Napoleon.

The previous day Bertrand, on behalf of the Emperor, had offered Gourgaud 12,000 francs, which the latter declined to accept, saying he meant to make his living by teaching mathematics. Two other incidents served to mar his departure from Longwood. Gourgaud had in his possession several manuscripts dictated by Napoleon, among which was an account of the campaign of 1815 in Belgium. When Bertrand came to fetch them Gourgaud refused to surrender them.[1] Another unpleasant incident resulted from a mistake made by Ali. Napoleon had told him to give Gourgaud all duplicate copies of books in the library, taking it for granted that if a copy bore the imperial arms and its duplicate did not, Ali would pick the latter. When he learned that several books bearing his arms had been given to Gourgaud, he was vexed, having intended to leave all such books to his son. He told Ali to explain this to the general and to

---

[1] He was to publish the story of the campaign under his own name. Napoleon dictated another version which he gave to O'Meara when the latter left for England.

ask for the return of such copies. Gourgaud took the request as an insult and returned all the books. He left Longwood in a huff, accompanied by Lieutenant Basil Jackson, who was to live with him at Beale's cottage which the governor had rented for him.

ELEVEN

Lowe did his utmost to make Gourgaud's stay at Beale's cottage a pleasant one. The place was well furnished, situated in agreeable surroundings and within walking distance of Plantation House. Servants and horses were placed at his and Jackson's disposal. While the lieutenant never left him he proved an agreeable companion. They dined almost nightly at Plantation House with Sir Hudson and Lady Lowe, or at Rosemary Hall with the Stürmers and Balmain. Gourgaud's papers underwent only the most cursory examination. Lowe did not read his journal, as he had that of Las Cases. The governor judged rightly that Gourgaud's ego having been wounded, the surest way to get valuable information from him was to cater to his vanity and self-importance.

On December 12, 1816, Gourgaud had written in his journal: "I have one great fault, and that is that I always tell the truth." On March 20, 1817, he told Bertrand that the Emperor need not fear anything he might say about him if he decided to leave. "I am too honorable a man for that." But, it has been said that "Heaven has no rage like love to hatred turned." Gourgaud's pathological love for Napoleon having, for the present at least, turned to hatred made him forget all about honor and truth. He made revelations which no honorable man would have made and, when he ran out of facts, resorted to shameless invention.

He told Stürmer that Napoleon's illness was feigned and that O'Meara was his dupe: "He will bury us all; he has a constitution of iron. His swelling of the legs dates from Moscow. As for his insomnia, since I have known him, he has never slept several hours in succession. As for his pain in the side, nobody has been able to make out what it is." The fact that the swelling of the legs dated from Moscow merely proves that he was in poor health even then. Dr. Baxter, in a report to Lowe, diagnosed it as a "tendency to dropsy." It is not true that nobody could make out the reason for the pain in the side. O'Meara felt sure that his liver was affected . . . noted that "the right side felt firmer to pressure than the left" and that if he pressed harder the patient winced with pain. He diagnosed it as "chronic hepatitis."

Gourgaud told Major Gorrequer that there was no difficulty whatever in sending clandestine letters and parcels to Europe from Longwood. The truth of this cannot be denied. But it was hardly honorable to reveal that it was Prince Eugene who had arranged the monthly drawing account for Napoleon with Andrews, Street & Parker of London—all the more so as the letter instructing Eugene to do so at the same time instructed him to pay 12,000 francs annually to Gourgaud's mother.

He told Stürmer that Napoleon "had had ten times the opportunity to escape and has so still at the present moment." When the commissioner expressed his disbelief, Gourgaud replied: "Eh! what cannot be done when one has millions at one's disposal!" It was, he explained, not necessary for Napoleon to have the money at St. Helena to help him escape. A draft signed by him would be honored by members of his family. Balmain has written that he told him an escape might be effected in a beer barrel, a basket of dirty linen, or a case used to transport sugar, and that the matter had been discussed at Longwood. "He has repeated that nonsense on every street corner at Jamestown, always adding that he would never betray the Emperor," the Russian wrote. Asked by Stürmer why Napoleon had not escaped, Gourgaud replied: "However miserable he may be here, he secretly enjoys the importance attached to his detention, the interest taken by all the Powers of Europe, the care with which his smallest remarks are reported, and so on. He has said many times to us, 'I can no longer live as a private person; I prefer being a prisoner here than living free in the United States.'"

He told Lowe that Poppleton, before his departure, had received a gold snuff-box from Napoleon. The captain had been uncommonly kind to Gourgaud and the latter must have known that the governor would try to have Poppleton demoted or worse for having accepted the gift. The governor, as we have seen, tried to do so but did not succeed. Gourgaud's revelation about Poppleton was especially treacherous since he himself had advised Napoleon to give him the snuff-box.

Among the absurdities he told which did not contain a particle of truth was that Santini's pamphlet had been written by Napoleon; that Dr. Warden's book had been composed under the Emperor's supervision; that when the silverware was broken up and sold Napoleon had just received a large sum of money in gold; that Las Cases had received a draft for 200,000 francs for the 100,000 he had loaned Napoleon. Uncorroborated by any entry in his journal is his fantastic story that Napoleon and Bertrand had both urged him to commit suicide, and that he had made the counter proposal that they all gather in the Emperor's study around a brazier with burning charcoal, close all doors and windows, and die together while drinking champagne!

Count Balmain, by far the most intelligent of the commissioners, listened to Gourgaud's revelations with considerable skepticism. He considered Gourgaud a vain braggart, "jealous of Napoleon as of a mistress," in whose veracity no reliance could be placed. On February 27, 1818, he wrote to Count Nesselrode: "The governor talks in pompous praise of Gourgaud; he lauds him to the skies as a man of good judgment who has never violated the regulations. Why does he not add: 'A man who, having quarreled with Bonaparte and with his compatriots, appears to approve my ungenerous conduct toward him, thinks I am right about everything, and who, in fact, is my creature'? That, at bottom, is what makes him like, esteem, and extol this general."

Lowe assured Gourgaud that he would not be sent to the Cape, but would be allowed to sail directly for England; and that he would send a report about him to Lord Bathurst that would guarantee him a good reception. As Gourgaud cherished the hope of returning to France and being restored in the good graces of the Bourbons, it was important for him to be recommended by the French commissioner to the Marquis d'Osmond, French ambassador in London, and to the Duc de Richelieu.

Montchenu, however, had had his doubts about Gourgaud. It was not that he believed his disagreement with Napoleon to be feigned and that he was being sent on a secret mission. All the commissioners agreed that he was too much lacking in balance and judgment to be employed for such a purpose. But seeing Gourgaud change sides again he doubted his dependability. He forwarded the laudatory letter Lowe had written him concerning Gourgaud to Osmond with a few noncommittal remarks of his own, and wrote to Richelieu that to employ Gourgaud was not devoid of risk. Balmain gave Gourgaud an introduction to Count Lieven, the Russian ambassador, equally noncommittal.

TWELVE

While defaming his former associates, Gourgaud was nevertheless indignant that Napoleon and Bertrand took no further notice of him. When, on March 8, O'Meara came to see him, he complained bitterly about this, saying he was without funds and totally abandoned by them. He particularly asked O'Meara to make it known at Longwood that he would "publish everywhere that Montholon was a scoundrel and his wife a whore." He had written a letter to Bertrand asking him for a loan. When he received no reply, he went, on the day before his departure, to the outer barrier at Longwood. Remaining at the barrier, he asked Jackson, who had accompanied him, to tell Bertrand that he wished to speak to him. The grand marshal refused to see him. He told Jackson that he had three times offered Gourgaud 12,000 francs on behalf of the Emperor. The money had been placed on deposit with Balcombe, where it was at Gourgaud's disposal. If he found the sum inadequate for his needs, he would gladly make him a loan; but to do so when the Emperor's help was being spurned would be an affront to the latter.

Gourgaud delayed calling on Balcombe until about an hour before he embarked on the *Campden*. He did not find the purveyor in his office and after vainly trying to locate him borrowed £100 from Sir Hudson, who promised to forward the deposit and did so the following day. Before going aboard the vessel Gourgaud entrusted Balmain with the following minatory message for the grand marshal: "Remind Bertrand that I am in a position to make it very unpleasant for the Emperor by revealing his secrets; that my journal of Longwood is worth twelve thousand pounds in London; and that he had better not drive me to extremities."

On May 8, he arrived in England and before the month was over had had interviews with Bathurst's assistant Henry Goulburn and with the French and Russian ambassadors. He gave them approximately the same information he had given at St. Helena to Lowe, Gorrequer, and the commissioners. He told Osmond that before leaving Longwood he had said to Bonaparte: "If destiny were to inflict upon France the awful misfortune of seeing you again, you will find me fully armed in the ranks of your enemies." Needless to say he had made no such statement at Longwood but had told something similar to Montchenu. During his conversation with Osmond he clearly implied that O'Meara and Balcombe had been helpful in transmitting clandestine correspondence.

His treachery availed him nothing. Weeks passed and the hoped-for permission to return to France and the assurance of being restored to the favor of the Bourbons did not come. Fortunately for him nothing about the charges and revelations he had made—true as well as false—had appeared in print. The public knew that there had been a disagreement among members of Napoleon's suite and that Gourgaud had left as a consequence, nothing more. It was not until 1827—six years after the Emperor's death—that Goulburn's report to Bathurst was discovered by Walter Scott and published in his *The Life of Napoleon*. English liberals and Bonapartist refugees living in London, anxious for first-hand information about the Emperor, called on Gourgaud. He began to waver. Napoleon's enemies had used him but did not appear to trust him and did nothing for him; Napoleon's partisans were ready to receive him with open arms. Had he not made a mistake? In the fall of the year representatives of the allied powers were to meet at Aix-la-Chapelle. On August 25, he sent a long letter to "the Empress Marie Louise," which soon after appeared in the newspapers.

The Emperor, whom he had represented to Lowe, to Gorrequer, to Balmain, to Stürmer, to Montchenu, to Goulburn, to Osmond, to Lieven as having nothing much the matter with him, he now described as "dying in the most frightful torments and the most prolonged agony." He appealed to Marie Louise to use her influence with the allied sovereigns to save him from a "martyrdom which might still last a long time." The emotional epistle, which one acquainted with his conduct cannot read without distaste, was followed, on October 2, by a letter to Czar Alexander and, on October 25, by another to the Emperor of Austria. He had given a signed statement to Hudson Lowe pledging his word of honor not to write anything either against him or the allied powers, which, however, did not prevent him from writing to the Czar: "He [Napoleon] has been placed under the surveillance of an official whose unique occupation is to invent every day some new restriction and humiliation. . . . Napoleon is wasting away; he is rapidly approaching the grave." To the Emperor Francis: "Sire, the Emperor Napoleon is dying the most agonizing of deaths. . . . Perhaps it is not yet too late to save him. The climate of Europe might bring him back to life. In another year even that will no longer avail."

As a result of this new about-face he was ordered to leave England and went to Hamburg. For the next few years he lived on the pension Napoleon had granted his mother, which Napoleon's stepson paid to him.

After Napoleon's death, when Bertrand and Montholon were able to return to France, and Gourgaud likewise received permission to do so, it was decided that mutual recriminations would lower the prestige of all and that the common interest required a reconciliation. When, in 1827, Walter Scott published the account of Goulburn's interview with Gourgaud, together with some uncomplimentary remarks of his own about the general's conduct, Gourgaud challenged him to a duel and claimed that Goulburn's inadequate knowledge of French was responsible for his having misunderstood him. The correspondence of Osmond, Lieven, and the commissioners invalidates that claim. The fable was invented that Gourgaud had been sent by Napoleon on a secret mission to Czar Alexander, and that his revelations were made for the purpose of gaining the confidence of those without whose aid it would be impossible for him to carry out his assignment. To lend verisimilitude to this, Montholon fabricated a letter, dated Longwood, February 19, 1818, beginning with the sentence: "The Emperor, my dear Gourgaud, considers that you are overplaying your role."

THIRTEEN

While Gourgaud was still at Beale's cottage, the Emperor lost a far more valuable member of his household—Cipriani, his *maître d'hôtel* and, with the exception of Marchand, his most devoted servitor. On February 23, he became suddenly ill and fell to the floor of the dining room writhing with pain. He was carried to his room, and O'Meara called into consultation Dr. Baxter and Dr. Henry. All three diagnosed the disease as inflammation of the intestines. Modern pathologists have claimed the symptoms point to acute appendicitis followed by a perforation. The pain abated somewhat on the 25th, but the condition of the patient was such that O'Meara believed the end to be approaching. He had been reporting Cipriani's condition to the Emperor after every visit, and at midnight of the 25th Napoleon sent for him and asked if it might not benefit the patient if he were to visit him. O'Meara advised against it, saying that the resulting shock might be fatal. The patient died on February 27, at four in the afternoon.

Cipriani was buried in the country church yard, close to Plantation House, on the morning of the 28th. His remains were followed to the grave by Counts Bertrand and Montholon, Sir Thomas Reade, several officers of the 66th, all male servants at Longwood that could be spared, and many of the inhabitants. The Emperor told O'Meara that if he had been buried within the limits, he would have attended too. That he mourned Cipriani sincerely there can be no doubt. On the 27th Dr. Baxter reported to Lowe that Napoleon "is low-spirited and looks ill today, probably owing to the approaching death of his faithful servant Cipriani." Balmain reported to Count Nesselrode:

"Bonaparte is extremely affected, for he was greatly attached to him." Stürmer wrote to Prince Metternich: "He spent the day of his burial at Bertrand's house, walking up and down from one room to another, and appeared to be in a state of agitation."

There being no Catholic priest on the island, Reverend Boys, assisted by Reverend Vernon, conducted the services at the grave. Judging by a letter Bertrand wrote to Cardinal Fesch, informing him of the death of the major-domo, whose son was in the cardinal's service, the fact that a Protestant clergyman officiated at the grave appears to have worried the grand marshal. The dead man would probably have preferred the absence of all religious ceremony, for he was a confirmed unbeliever. Dr. Henry who had several conversations with him has written that he was "very ferocious in his anti-religious sentiments."

Napoleon was to present the Reverend Boys with a silver snuff-box as a token of his appreciation.

XX. O'Meara's Dismissal

On March 18, 1818, Balcombe and his family left St. Helena for England. Having become aware that Sir Hudson suspected him of aiding Napoleon in his clandestine correspondence, he had thought it expedient to ask for a six months' leave, giving his wife's health as a pretext. He had suggested to the governor that his partner, Joseph Cole, be appointed purveyor to Longwood. Lowe ignored the suggestion and appointed Denzil Ibbetson, the army commissary. St. Helena never saw Balcombe again.

Before his departure he came to Longwood with his two daughters to bid farewell to Napoleon and to borrow money from him. He obtained a draft on Laffite for 75,000 francs. He promised to get in touch with Letizia and with Eugene, to send French books and papers, and to exert every possible effort to get the governor recalled. In his own interest even more than Napoleon's he was to join forces with those who wished to see Lowe removed, and he sent a small quantity of books to Longwood but did not contact any of the Emperor's relatives.

Betsy has written that during the visit Napoleon went walking with her in the garden and said, pointing to the sea: "Soon you will be sailing away to England, leaving me to die on this miserable rock. Look at those dreadful mountains—they are my prison walls. You will soon hear that the Emperor Napoleon is dead." She began to cry, and as she had left her handkerchief in the pocket of her side-saddle Napoleon produced his own, wiped away her tears, and told her to keep the handkerchief. The girls and their father remained for dinner. Before they departed the Emperor asked Betsy what she would like as a remembrance. She said that a lock of his hair would please her best. He had a servant fetch a pair of scissors and snipped off two locks, one for her, the other for her sister. "I still possess that lock of hair," Betsy wrote in 1844.

In 1823, Balcombe, having been approached by Lowe, filed an affidavit in his favor in the case of Lowe vs. O'Meara. No value can be attached to the document, filed by Balcombe for the purpose of clearing his record by having Lowe withdraw charges against him. In a letter to Lowe he says significantly that he hopes Sir Hudson will now overlook differences that may have arisen between them. Soon after he was appointed to the lucrative post of colonial treasurer of New South Wales, where he died in 1829. His family returned to England, and in 1832 Betsy married a Mr. Abell, by whom she had a daughter. Napoleon's brother Joseph and his nephew Louis Napoleon were among her callers. After her husband's death, having become impoverished, she appealed to Napoleon's nephew for assistance. He was then Napoleon III, Emperor of France, and presented her with a large tract of land in Algiers. She died in 1871, at the age of sixty-nine.

In June, 1818, six of Napoleon's people left Longwood: the cook Lepage, his wife and baby daughter; Bertrand's servant Bernard Heymann, his wife and fifteen year old son. Two years before, Lepage had injured his hand and was unable to attend to his duties. At Montholon's request that a cook be sent who understood French cuisine, Sir Hudson had sent Jeannette Sablon, a Belgian woman employed in his own kitchen. Lepage married her, and in September, 1817, she gave birth to a daughter. Both wished to return to Europe, and Lepage had asked Montholon to obtain permission for them from the governor. When months passed and they heard nothing they went one day together to Plantation House to inquire about the matter. When

Napoleon heard that they had been to see Sir Hudson without his permission, he ordered their dismissal. Bertrand dismissed Bernard Heymann because of the latter's inability to keep sober. All were permitted to sail directly to Europe.

The Lepages were not allowed to remain in England and were barred from France until February, 1819. They went to live in Hamburg, where they were interrogated by the French consul-general, Baron de Marandet. Part of their testimony, as recorded by Marandet, reads: "He, Bonaparte, has since his arrival on the island grown far more corpulent than he had been when leaving Europe. His legs are always swollen; his complexion is livid. He takes very little exercise, and his disposition has become unbearable. At the slightest provocation he flies into a fit of passion. At such times he wanders through the rooms of the house, a billiard cue in his hand, swearing and striking at anybody who happens to be near. When not in that condition, he is taciturn. It has, for that matter, become his habit to remain in bed a good part of the day."

If one can believe this testimony, then the change must have taken place shortly after the departure of Gourgaud, who makes no mention of such scenes in his journal. Indeed, when asked by Baron Stürmer: "What is his conduct in the house?" Gourgaud replied: "He is excellent with the domestics, trying to make everything agreeable for them, fostering the small talents of those who possess any, and trying to develop them in those who have none."

TWO

On September 28, 1917, the Emperor said: "O'Meara has taken my part against Hudson Lowe and has declared it to be his opinion that I would not live over six months. It's good to have a witness like him." On October 4, we find him saying: "The doctor is good to me only since I give him my money. Ah! of him I'm pretty sure." This leaves little doubt that O'Meara had allowed himself to be bribed, which must have taken place some time in September of that year. However, as far as his medical reports were concerned, the only way in which he tried to please

Napoleon was by stressing the necessity of exercise on horse-back and by claiming that lack of such exercise might have fatal consequences. Bertrand co-operated by trying to impress Sir Hudson with the seriousness of the situation in language far from conciliatory. On September 30, 1817, he wrote: "I have, sir, always spoken to you to this effect more or less forcibly. I shall speak to you of it no more, for denials, subtleties, and arguments are useless. The question is: do you or do you not wish to kill the Emperor? If you persist in your conduct you will have answered in the affirmative; and, unhappily, the object will probably be attained after some months' agony."

Sir Hudson was not insensible to the barrage from Longwood. It was to his interest to keep Napoleon alive as long as possible. So lucrative and important a post was not likely to drop into his lap a second time. If Bonaparte were seriously ill something must be done about it. He offered the services of Dr. Baxter as a consultant. O'Meara had no objection, but the fact that Baxter was Lowe's favorite physician disqualified him with Napoleon. A few days before he had received Bertrand's letter, Lowe had offered to build a wooden barrack, seventy by twenty feet, in which Napoleon could promenade when it was impossible to do so elsewhere on the shadeless plateau. The Emperor did not consider the offer worthy of a reply and none was sent. Sir Hudson next asked Miss Mason if she would be willing to rent her house, where there was shade and water, to serve as Bonaparte's summer residence. She said she would for £100 per month. As Lowe expected Napoleon to pay the rent himself, that offer, too, remained unanswered.

The Emperor did not lack ingenuity in going after what he wanted. We have seen how he had shamed the government into increasing the allowance for the upkeep of the Longwood establishment by making it appear that he had to break up and sell his silverware in order to exist. Longwood House, humid and buffeted by wind and rain in its exposed situation, needed a great deal of fuel for its fourteen fireplaces. Napoleon was sensitive to the odor of burning coal and, in the part of the house inhabited by him, tolerated only wood fires. In May, 1817, Montholon had asked O'Meara to inform the governor that they needed a far greater supply of fuel. Wood being scarce on the island, Lowe had Gorrequer write that the supply of coal would be doubled, but that the quantity of wood furnished would have to remain the same. When in September Montholon informed the Emperor that they were running out of wood, Napoleon ordered a servant to break up a bedstead and some shelving with which to feed the fire in the drawing room. The following day the news was all about Jamestown that being denied firewood, the Emperor was burning his furniture. A supply of wood was promptly forthcoming.

So also Napoleon's refusal to take exercise on horseback was bearing fruit. One after another Lowe was to drop nearly all the restrictions of October 9, 1816, as well as his order of March 14, 1817, that when riding on the new road at Woody Ridge he must not deviate to either side. No longer were his visitors forbidden to speak to members of his household. No longer was he forbidden to converse with persons he met when out riding. The former limits were restored and he could enter the houses of inhabitants in the valley. More than that! In a letter to Bertrand, October 26, 1817, Sir Hudson wrote that if Napoleon wished to extend his rides west of Hutt's Gate, he could do so without being accompanied by a British officer, provided he informed the governor the previous day where he wished to go.

As for the demand that Napoleon and his followers be allowed to remain away from home until nine in the evening, as had been the case under Cockburn, Lowe would not agree to this. Sentries, however, were to be placed at six o'clock not around the house but around the garden enclosure, and were to be kept out of sight as much as possible. This would enable the French to remain outdoors long after dark. He would not concede the demand that passes issued by Bertrand should suffice to admit visitors, but a compromise proposal made by the grand marshal was forwarded to Bathurst, who on January 1, 1818, wrote to the governor: "You will consider yourself at liberty to accede to the suggestion of Count Bertrand, and you will for this purpose direct him to present to you for your approbation a list of persons, not exceeding fifty in number, resident in the island, who may be admitted to Longwood at seasonable hours without any other pass than the invitation of General Bonaparte."

THREE

Thus Napoleon's stubbornness appeared to have paid off handsomely, but he did not take advantage of the changed situation. This may have been partly due to the fact that he was unwell, believed this to be due to the climate, and wished to put pressure on the government to change his place of exile. His main reason, however, appears to have been that he did not trust Sir Hudson. He told O'Meara that he wanted assurance from the government that "no changes would be made unless ordered by His Royal Highness the Prince Regent or by the privy council, as otherwise he would have no guarantee that restrictions taken off today might not be laid on tomorrow." His distrust was justified. Lowe was expert at evading his commitments by devious means. So, for example, after having made the concession that sentries were to be posted at sunset around the garden enclosure instead of around the house, he at the same time appointed a couple of gardeners who turned out to be sergeants with power to arrest anyone whose actions appeared to them in the least suspect. Thus the "concession" really meant that the French could no longer walk in the garden at any hour of the day without being under surveillance.

When Napoleon discovered this, he ceased walking in the garden. In his letter to Lowe of July 20, 1818, complaining about the matter, Bertrand wrote that Napoleon "had not left the house for one hundred days."

As for Bathurst's instruction that a list be drawn up by the French of not exceeding fifty persons resident on the island, who would be allowed to visit Napoleon without any other formalities except his invitation, Lowe, so punctilious in carrying out instructions obnoxious to the French, managed to avoid carrying out this one altogether. Bathurst's letter containing the instruction must have reached him sometime in March, yet on the 26th of July Count Balmain reported to Count Nesselrode that "under a thousand false pretenses" Lowe failed to obey the order, and added: "I am ready to certify to this and prove it to all Europe." On March 1, 1819, he wrote that he had asked the governor when, finally, he meant to put Bathurst's instruction into effect. Lowe replied that "the French had not drawn up the list of people of the island who were to be admitted to their society." Balmain knew this to be a falsehood, for the list had been shown to him in June of the previous year. When Sir Hudson told him that he himself had drawn up a list, had presented it to the French, and "was waiting for it to be approved or rejected," the commissioner, having sought confirmation from Bertrand and Montholon, reported to Nesselrode: "They tell me positively that he has not presented anything of the kind."

Far from obeying Bathurst's order, Lowe issued on May 16, 1818, a proclamation forbidding anyone on the island "from holding any correspondence or communication" with the French or "receiving [from them] any communication whatsoever . . . without his express authorization." He went so far as to have the orderly officer read the proclamation to the English servants at Longwood. Strictly interpreted the order would have meant that if Napoleon or any member of his suite wished to communicate with one of the English servants, they would have to ask the orderly officer to semaphore to Plantation House for permission to do so! The Emperor promptly ordered Montholon to dismiss all the English servants.

FOUR

Soon after his arrival on the island it had been Sir Hudson's intention to substitute Dr. Baxter for O'Meara as Bonaparte's personal physician. In a letter to Lord Bathurst, January 20, 1818, he was to explain that the opinion given him by Admiral Cockburn of O'Meara was "very much in his favor," but that "certain views which I had taken of his character were responsible for this decision." Until the middle of 1817, he had, however, no reason to complain about O'Meara. The prisoner's health had not yet taken a turn for the worse, and the doctor's medical bulletins contained nothing alarming. He volunteered moreover in letters to Reade a good deal of information about life at Longwood, which the governor found useful and entertaining, but which O'Meara, in his capacity of trusted personal physician, had no business to divulge.

He has claimed that he finally broke with the governor because of the restrictions of October 9, 1816, which he considered outrageous. The fact is, however, that fully half of his confidential letters to Reade were written after that date. His quarrel with Sir Hudson dated from May 23, 1817, when the latter summoned him to Plantation House and in the presence of Reade asked him gruffly if the postmaster, Mr. Cole, had not loaned him some English newspapers. He replied in the affirmative. Had O'Meara passed on the newspapers to Bonaparte? He replied that he had. "It's against the Act of Parliament!" the governor ejaculated. O'Meara said that Admiral Cockburn had often given him newspapers for Napoleon, sometimes before having read them himself. Lowe shouted again that it was against the Act of Parliament, and said he wanted it understood that in the future he was not to lend General Bonaparte any newspaper or give him any information without the governor's permission. When a ship arrived he should not even leave Longwood. When sufficient time had elapsed after its arrival, he could come to Plantation House and would be told what news it was proper for him to communicate to Bonaparte. O'Meara replied that if an order were issued to that effect he would immediately resign.

To what petty malice Lowe was capable of resorting may be judged from the following incident which O'Meara reported to the admiralty after his departure from the island and to which Lowe was given an opportunity to reply:

"On the 3rd of February, 1818, Mr. Barber, supercargo of the *Cambridge* store-ship, arrived at St. Helena, where he opened a shop. He brought with him two beautiful portraits of young Napoleon, which he had bought in some of the print-shops in London, for the purpose of selling them to some of the inhabitants of Longwood. Sir Hudson, informed of this, caused both to be delivered to him, pretending that it was for the purpose of sending them directly to the father, but in reality to deprive him of them, as neither of them ever have been sent to Longwood since."

Lowe's comment on O'Meara's statement is as follows:

"It is false that Sir Hudson Lowe ever caused the prints to be brought to him, or pretended to offer them to the father. They had been sent up to him as common prints to look at, without his having had any previous communication either with the captain of the vessel or the purser, and he was never informed or ever understood that they were to be sold at Longwood. As Governor of St. Helena it was not for him to be sending up prints of Napoleon II, with tricolor decorations on them. Napoleon Bonaparte had besides already several portraits of his son."

The insincerity of Lowe's statement is obvious. If the supercargo sent the engravings to Plantation House, it was assuredly not so the governor could feast his eyes upon them, but to obtain permission to sell them to someone from Longwood. What did the governor do with the engravings? Since he did not return them and they are not among his papers, he undoubtedly destroyed them.

The clue to what probably happened can be found in the affair of the telescope, related by Balmain. Shortly before the departure of O'Meara from the island, the captain of a trading vessel offered a particularly fine telescope for sale. O'Meara saw it and said he felt sure Bonaparte would want it. He would let the captain know the following morning. Reade heard about it and semaphored the news to Lowe, who instructed him to snap up the instrument. When O'Meara came to buy it, it was gone. Sir Hudson showed the telescope to Balmain and boasted gleefully about his clever maneuver. The commissioner raised his eyebrows and said: "But surely you wouldn't prevent Bonaparte from having a telescope?" Lowe felt embarrassed and stammered: "Was he [Napoleon] to have the best telescope on the island? Surely it was for the governor to be able to discover the approach of ships before any other person, not for Bonaparte."

FIVE

On May 27, 1817, O'Meara received a letter from Finlaison informing him that Lord Bathurst had wished to have him removed, but that Lord Melville, first lord of the admiralty, had intervened. Since their quarrel the doctor had given Lowe information only about Napoleon's health. When asked if he had nothing else to communicate he invariably replied that there was nothing of importance. Having Lord Melville as a protector he apparently felt secure and, on June 29, 1817, sent a letter to Finlaison in which, for the first time, he ventured to criticize the governor.

Lowe, jealous of his power, resented O'Meara's defiant attitude. He began to find fault with him whenever he saw him. On July 17, 1817, he reproached him for not standing up for him sufficiently when Napoleon assailed him. The following day he upbraided him again, and O'Meara, emboldened by Finlaison's letter, said: "Put yourself, sir, in Bonaparte's situation. Would you have availed yourself of the permission to ride out coupled with the restrictions imposed upon him?" Lowe lost his temper and said that henceforth O'Meara was to have no conversations with Napoleon except on matters of health, and was to report to him every Monday and Thursday about the prisoner's health and behavior. On the 21st there was another verbal clash that terminated in O'Meara's offering to resign. This had a sobering effect on the governor. He knew that Napoleon would refuse to consult any other physician on the island. It was not a risk he cared to run. So, for over a month, he managed to restrain himself. But, on August 24, he told O'Meara again that unless he communicated to him the particulars of his conversations with Bonaparte, he must confine himself entirely to medical matters and must decline to answer any questions put to him by Napoleon not related to the prisoner's health. This time O'Meara boldly replied that he could not obey such an order, which left the governor speechless with rage and undecided what to do.

SIX

On October 14, 1817, Napoleon, having discovered that O'Meara
was sending reports of the state of his health to the governor in
which he referred to him as "General Bonaparte," told him that
in the future he must refer to him as "the Emperor Napoleon"
and leave the original copy of each report with Marshal Bertrand. Copies of the reports were, he said, furnished by the governor to the commissioners; hence they were read by the allied
sovereigns and their cabinets and published in the allied press.
When his personal physician referred to him as "General Bonaparte" it left the impression that he acquiesced in the appellation. The surgeon replied that it would be impossible for him to
use the term "the Emperor Napoleon," and suggested "Napoleon" or "Napoleon Bonaparte." The prisoner would not consent,
but said he would agree to "the patient," to which, however,
the governor objected. Napoleon then told him that if he wished
to give oral reports of the state of his health he did not care
what he called him. It was therefore agreed that O'Meara
should report orally to Dr. Baxter, who would relay the information to the governor.

The relationship between Sir Hudson and O'Meara was becoming progressively worse. The former still insisted that the
latter must keep him informed about conversations he had with
the prisoner and, finding himself unable to enforce obedience,
became abusive. On October 28, he told O'Meara that he was "a
jackal running about in search of news for General Bonaparte,"
and for the third time forbade him to converse with Napoleon
except on matters pertaining to his profession. The surgeon
asked a written order to that effect. Lowe refused, flew into a
rage, and ordered O'Meara to leave the house. On November 25, when in answer to a demand for information, O'Meara
replied that he had discussed nothing of any importance with
Napoleon, the governor cried: "You are no judge, sir, of the importance of the conversations you may have with General Bonaparte. I might consider several subjects of great importance
which you consider as trifling or of no consequence." O'Meara

retorted that he was not a *"mouton"* (stool pigeon), where-upon Lowe heaped insults upon him and again showed him the door.

On December 18, when the governor attempted to question him again, O'Meara told him that in May, 1816, he had pledged himself to Bonaparte "not to reveal the conversations that passed between them, except they had a tendency to his [Napoleon's] escape."

After Lowe had exclaimed, "You do not blush to avow this!" and had otherwise given vent to his indignation, it occurred to him to ask the surgeon a question which was very much to the point: If he had given such a pledge to Bonaparte, how was it that in the past he had furnished the information? O'Meara gave this unconvincing reply: "Because you had asked me, and I thought it might be interesting to the government. But though I told you some parts, I did not tell you all; besides, I thought I might in some things depart from the promise without impropriety."

Lowe's behavior on this occasion must have been particularly violent, since, on December 23, O'Meara could not refrain from writing him a letter of protest such as a superior officer seldom receives from a subordinate. That when Lowe lost his temper, which was rather often, he behaved in a manner hardly becoming an officer and a gentleman is evident from the reports of all three commissioners. Montchenu in his reports to the Duc de Richelieu of May 22 and June 2, 1818, has written: "He has disgusted two excellent colonels, who have left under the pretext of their health. . . . All the servants the governor brought over with him from Europe have left him, and his household staff has already been renewed twice. He has been extremely rude to Count Balmain. . . . With Baron von Stürmer he had a scene fit for a cabdriver."

SEVEN

Cipriani had died toward the end of February, 1818, but it was not until the 2nd of April that the Reverend Boys, who had officiated at the funeral, was presented on behalf of Napoleon with a silver snuff-box, purchased at Solomon's. The reason for the delay was that Boys was to leave St. Helena on the 3rd of April for a sojourn in England, and the Emperor believed that if the present were given him the day before his departure, the matter would escape the vigilance of Reade. It was O'Meara who made the presentation. Boys accepted the gift, but when cautioned by his colleague, the Reverend Vernon, that acceptance without the governor's intervention might get him into difficulties, he deposited the box at Solomon's and wrote to O'Meara that for his sake as well as his own it would be advisable if he were to receive it "through the *unobjectionable* channel."

Napoleon had underestimated the efficiency of Reade's system of espionage. Soon after Boys's departure, Lowe learned about the matter. O'Meara had broken the regulations! What a golden opportunity to make him pay for his insolence! On April 10, 1818, the surgeon received a letter from Reade informing him, by order of the governor, that pending instructions from Lord Bathurst he was forbidden to leave Longwood. But O'Meara was not easily intimidated. He began by writing to Count Bertrand that he could not sacrifice his rights as a British subject to the desire of being of service to "the chief personage at Longwood," and had decided to return to England. He then sent his resignation to Sir Hudson and asked permission to leave. Ignoring Lowe's order not to go beyond the confines of Longwood, he went to see Admiral Plampin, who lived with his inamorata at *The Briars*, which he had leased from Balcombe. The admiral refused to see him. Napoleon, however, put pressure on Lowe, who had provisionally accepted O'Meara's resignation, by telling the doctor that since he was no longer a free agent he must dispense with his services. O'Meara promptly informed Gorrequer who gave the news to Lowe.

It is interesting to note that in his letter of the 10th of April Reade makes no mention of the supposed reason for the governor's order—the presentation of the snuff-box. Forsyth has written: "It is quite true that the letter contains no allusion to the present of the snuff-box, nor can I explain the reason"—an astonishing lack of insight on the part of so prominent a barris-

ter. The reason is obvious. As the Reverend Boys was to write to
the Reverend Vernon, on August 6, 1818: "The whole business
from beginning to end will be deemed by everybody in England
a complete bagatelle." That for such a "bagatelle" Lowe should
have initiated an action to deprive Napoleon of his personal physician would have aroused indignation in England. Lowe was sufficiently shrewd not to put such a weapon into O'Meara's hands.

EIGHT

When, on April 14, the Emperor had told O'Meara that he could
no longer avail himself of his services as the doctor had lost his
independence, he had handed him a letter addressed to Prince
Eugene. It was an order to pay O'Meara 100,000 francs. Was it
part of the bargain he had made with him in September of the
previous year, or was it given in the hope that the doctor would
continue to be active in his cause after his return to England?

Three days after the doctor had been ordered to remain within
the limits of Longwood, Bertrand wrote a letter of protest to the
governor. He told him that the Emperor was determined not to
accept the services of any other English doctor, no matter what
the consequences. On April 24, he wrote to him again informing
him that the Emperor had been quite ill on the night of the 18th
and again on the night of the 24th, that Count Montholon had
watched by his bed, helpless to aid him, and asked that the order of the 10th of April be revoked. Three days later he sent
him a note written by Napoleon, reading: "I bequeath the op-
probrium of my death to the Reigning House of England." On
May 5, O'Meara wrote to the governor: "His excellency may perhaps reflect on the terrible responsibility which weighs upon him
if (as is possible and very probable) Napoleon Bonaparte,
deprived of assistance, was to die before the expiration of the
five or six months required to obtain an answer from England."
As a result of all this and of advice given him by Balmain, Lowe
revoked his order of April 10.

Vindictive by nature, he could, however, not forego the satisfaction of evening up scores with O'Meara. The surgeon had
been elected by the officers of the 53rd as honorary member of

299

their mess. When that regiment had departed and the 66th had taken its place, its officers had done the same. Lowe had Reade call on Lieutenant Colonel Lascelles, who commanded the regiment in the absence of Colonel Nicol who had gone to England for his health,[1] to explain to him why O'Meara was not fit to associate with the officers and to ask that he be no longer received at the mess. Since Lowe knew nothing about the money the surgeon had accepted from Napoleon, the reasons Reade was able to offer were not very convincing. The officers knew all about the snuff-box O'Meara had given to the Reverend Boys and thought the governor a fool for making a fuss about the matter. Lowe's request could, however, not be ignored, so the colonel asked Lieutenant Reardon, a particular friend of the surgeon, to suggest to him that he voluntarily withdraw from the mess. O'Meara replied that he never would renounce the honor the officers of the 66th had conferred upon him in granting him a seat at their table "unless (according to the custom of the army) by a vote of the mess, or by an order from the governor." That same evening he appeared at the mess, and although the officers were acquainted with Lowe's wishes in the matter, no one objected to his presence.

The governor now commanded General Bingham to order Colonel Lascelles to bar O'Meara from the officers' mess. Lascelles obeyed the order but made it plain in his letter to O'Meara that he was acting from expediency. The surgeon addressed a letter to the officers thanking them for their hospitality and expressing his regret that "orders emanating from a superior power" prohibited him any longer to enjoy their society. He received a reply in which the writer, Lieutenant McCarthy, wrote that he had been "directed by the commanding officer and officers composing the mess to say it is with much regret they hear of your departure as an honorary member of the mess, and to assure you they always conceived your conduct, while with them, to be perfectly consistent in every respect with that of a gentleman."

[1] Montchenu has claimed that he left because he could not get along with the governor.

When as a result of the affair Colonel Lascelles and Lieutenant Reardon were ordered to return to England, the officers were sufficiently intimidated to repudiate their testimonial to O'Meara. He did not deserve such a testimonial, but the affair leaves no doubt concerning Lowe's unpopularity with the officers.

NINE

On July 16, 1818, Captain Blakeney, who had been orderly officer at Longwood for a year, asked to be relieved. Balmain has written that he wished to leave because Lowe wanted him to act as a "salaried spy" and demanded that he examine the dirty linen lest it contain clandestine correspondence. The story about the linen has been confirmed in unsavory detail by Montholon in a letter to the governor, but has been denied by the captain in a communication to that official. It has been charged that the denial was dictated to him by Sir Hudson.

Lowe appointed as orderly officer Thomas Lyster, inspector of the island militia with the rank of lieutenant colonel, and gave him Lieutenant Basil Jackson as assistant. It had been customary for the doctor to have some of his meals with the orderly officer, but Lyster refused to have O'Meara as a table companion. O'Meara retaliated by refusing to give him any information about the prisoner, whom Lyster never saw.

Napoleon regarded the slight to his doctor as a personal insult and forbade his generals to have any dealings with Lyster. On July 20, 1818, he dictated a letter to Lowe in which he said that Lyster was the same officer whom he had refused to receive during the three years he had been on the island because he had commanded at Ajaccio during the occupation of Corsica by the British, and whom he regarded as a personal enemy. "Hitherto the orderly officer has been a captain of high standing in his regiment. When the 53rd left the island, Captain Poppleton was replaced by Captain Blakeney, who enjoyed an excellent reputation. I beg you, sir, if you do not wish to make the situation here even worse than it already is, to appoint an officer equally honorable." The letter was signed by Bertrand. Lowe replied that Lyster had never commanded at Ajaccio, but did not deny that he had served there. He further wrote that as no immediate objection had been raised to the appointment, it was too late to recall it. That, of course, was a mistake, but to have aggravated an already strained situation by letting Lyster—a coarse-mannered, ill-tempered old man—read the letter signed by Bertrand is further proof of the governor's lack of qualification for the post he occupied. The colonel wrote a letter to Bertrand in which he heaped insults not only on him but on Napoleon, and challenged him to a duel. Bertrand ignored a challenge coming from such a source, whereupon Lyster wrote him a second letter threatening to horsewhip him. The grand marshal sent the first letter to the governor with a note in which he said that since "the demented old man" could not have seen the letter concerning him unless the governor had shown it to him, he must regard Sir Hudson as the principal in the affair and would be pleased to accommodate him if he demanded satisfaction.

Lowe recalled Lyster from Longwood and apologized for his conduct, but ordered the officers of the 66th to ostracize the Bertrands. When on September 25, 1818, he appointed Captain Nicholls to succeed Blakeney—temporarily restored to his former post—and Bertrand made a formal visit to the new orderly officer, he ordered him not to return the visit.

TEN

In a letter dated April 29, 1818, Lord Bathurst had refused permission for the removal of O'Meara, but in July Lowe received two letters from him—one dated May 16, the other two days later—in which he took a different stand. In the first he notified Lowe that there was no longer any objection to O'Meara's removal, as information given by General Gourgaud had convinced him (and apparently also Lord Melville) that O'Meara's reports concerning the state of Napoleon's health were "very fallacious." Bonaparte's refusal "to admit the visit of any medical person on whose ability and integrity a reliance could be placed . . . strongly confirms the truth of General Gourgaud's intelligence." In the second letter he said he hoped Sir Hudson had not yet completed the purchase of Rosemary Hall to serve as Bonaparte's future residence, as "General Gourgaud considers Longwood as the situation best adopted for 'surveillance.'"

To deprive Bonaparte of the services of a doctor in whom he had faith on the testimony of a layman who had developed a grudge against him was an astonishing procedure. That the prisoner was really ill had become obvious even to Montchenu who, knowing his aversion to any kind of medicine, wrote to the Duc de Richelieu: "Bonaparte is really ill. It appears that he suffers from an obstruction of the liver. The proof is that he has finally decided to take mercury in such large doses that his nerves are affected."

Lowe was only too eager to carry out Bathurst's instructions. The letter reached him on July 23. Two days later he sent his military secretary Colonel Wynyard to notify O'Meara that he must leave Longwood with the least possible delay "without holding any further communication whatever with its inmates," and that Admiral Plampin had been instructed by the admiralty to make all necessary arrangements for his removal from the island. O'Meara told his servant to pack his belongings, but disregarded the order of holding no further communication with Napoleon. He went to the Emperor's apartment and conferred with him for over two hours. Napoleon gave him the manuscript of the campaign of 1815, a letter to his mother—which ultimately resulted in an annual pension of £320—two gold snuff-boxes, and a bronze statuette showing him in his greatcoat and cocked hat with arms crossed. The manuscript was published in England in 1820 and later also in Paris and Philadelphia, and must have netted O'Meara a tidy sum. When the doctor returned to his own quarters he found Colonel Wynyard waiting for him. The colonel asked him why he had disobeyed the governor's order, to which O'Meara blandly replied that he did not recognize Sir Hudson's authority. Wynyard thereupon conducted him to Jamestown, where the following day he was taken by the marshal of the island aboard the *Griffin*.

O'Meara has charged that his desk was broken open and several valuable pieces of jewelry were stolen. An investigation by

Sir George Bingham produced no result. Lowe sent Dr. Baxter to see him and to ask that in the interest of the patient he surrender the medical journal regarding Napoleon's illness. O'Meara replied: "I would not think it consistent with propriety, with the respect due to the patient, or with the rules of the profession, to deliver it up into the hands of a strange surgeon not called in by him, without having obtained his consent." The *Griffin* left St. Helena on August 2, 1818.

Soon after his arrival in England, O'Meara sent a lengthy report of his experiences at St. Helena to the admiralty. Among the charges he made against the governor was that when he and Sir Hudson were still on good terms, the latter "made to me observations upon the benefit which would result to Europe from the death of Napoleon Bonaparte, of which event he spoke in a manner which, considering his situation and mine, was peculiarly distressing to me." This is an insinuation that the governor desired him to kill Napoleon, presumably by poison. That Sir Hudson made some such remark is more than probable. The man who showed Bertrand's letter to Lyster and issued some of the restrictions of October 9, 1816, was fully capable of such a *faux pas*. But from this to conclude that he wished to have Napoleon assassinated is absurd. Lowe may have been as "stupid" as the Duke of Wellington believed him to be, but hardly sufficiently so not to have realized that it was to his interest to keep Napoleon alive as long as possible. If, however, the opinion of pathologists who believe Napoleon did not die of cancer of the stomach but of perforation of the pylorus by a peptic ulcer is accepted, then Lowe may well have hastened the Emperor's death. Physicians are agreed that the growth of such ulcers is accelerated by irritation of any kind, and Lowe administered a plentiful supply of that kind of poison to his prisoner.

The government took a serious view of O'Meara's accusation. According to Dr. Walter Henry, Lord Melville, who apparently had no liking for Lowe, still tried to protect the surgeon, but was overruled by Lord Liverpool, the prime minister. On November 2, 1818, Mr. Croker, secretary of the admiralty, wrote to O'Meara: "Either the charge is in the last degree false and calumnious, or you can have no possible excuse for having hitherto suppressed it. In either case, and without adverting to the general tenor of your conduct as stated in your letter, my Lords consider you to be an improper person to continue in His Majesty's service, and they have directed your name to be erased from the list of naval surgeons accordingly."

XXI. Napoleon Woos
the Commissioners

Sir Hudson had been far from happy about Gourgaud's meeting with the commissioners at the races on April 7, 1817. He did not want the representatives of the allied powers to establish friendly relations with the French. This was especially true of the Russian and the Austrian commissioner through whom Bonaparte might attempt to appeal to their sovereigns to intervene.

On April 25, Poppleton reported to him that he had seen Gourgaud riding with Balmain and Gors on the road to Alarm House. Three days later, when riding along the same road, Gourgaud saw Balmain and Gors at a distance on horseback. They no sooner saw him than they turned the heads of their horses and started in the opposite direction, then thought better of it, wheeled about, and rode to meet him. When greetings had been exchanged, Balmain said he hoped Gourgaud would not be offended, but that the governor had heard about their last meeting and had expressed his displeasure. However, when the *Conqueror* had arrived with new instructions for his colleagues, he had every intention of calling on Bertrand and asking to be presented to Napoleon. Altogether accidental these meetings were not. Napoleon had instructed Gourgaud to try to contact Balmain and Stürmer as often as possible and assure them that he would always be glad to receive them as persons of distinction.

The *Conqueror*, flying the pavilion of Admiral Plampin, arrived at St. Helena on June 29, 1817. The new instructions it brought for Stürmer and Montchenu were that they could visit Bonaparte unofficially, but should not insist on doing so. Both decided to abstain from making any further attempt to visit him.

Balmain had expected his colleagues to join forces with him in a demand on the governor to be presented to Napoleon. For him to do so alone would be awkward and not likely to succeed. He found it, however, equally awkward to withstand Gourgaud's importunities. On July 8, he wrote to Count Nesselrode that the general was following him everywhere, urging him to visit Bonaparte, while Bertrand was laying siege to Madame Stürmer. He told about an incident that had taken place at Rosemary Hall, where he lived with the Stürmers. The grand marshal had called and had seated himself close to the baroness. When she happened to drop her handkerchief, he picked it up, at the same time whispering to her: "Madame, in the name of Heaven, come and see the Emperor. He expects you. He constantly speaks about you. He needs company. Only Englishmen ever come to see him. He is quite melancholy."

On July 20, the Russian commissioner finally went to Plantation House and handed a note to the governor in which he said that since there now existed no valid reason why the commissioners should not visit Bonaparte in their private capacity, he begged leave to be authorized to call on Count Bertrand and ask to be presented to Napoleon. He called attention to the fact that Lord Amherst and many others had been permitted to do so. He received in reply a long rambling letter, teeming with contradictions and sophistical reasoning, in which the governor informed him that under no circumstances could he acquiesce in his being presented by Count Bertrand. Balmain annotated the letter, demolishing the governor's arguments in a thoroughgoing fashion, and sent it to Nesselrode. He decided, however, not to pursue the matter further.

A few days later he met Gourgaud, who reminded him of his promise to call on Bertrand to make arrangements for the presentation. He replied that he had written to the governor concerning the matter, but had met with such stubborn resistance as to make it impossible for him to carry out his intention.

"What!" exclaimed Gourgaud. "Not even a little greeting for Madame Bertrand?"

"No. As long as Longwood remains at war with Plantation House and Bonaparte's door is closed to Sir Hudson Lowe, not even a little greeting for Madame Bertrand. Make your peace with him. He is not a bad fellow. He means well. Nothing would suit him better than to be on friendly terms with you. He will invite you to his dinners, his social functions; he and Lady Lowe will call on you sometimes. Time will not drag as it does now."

Gourgaud sighed and said: "He made a false start. It can now no longer be remedied."

TWO

On September 9, there were races at Deadwood. No one from Longwood attended, but Napoleon watched the proceedings through a spyglass from an upper window of Bertrand's home. When the races were over, Balmain and the Stürmers decided to walk to the outer barrier of Longwood estate and take a look at the grounds. Napoleon, who had returned home, saw them and asked Gourgaud and the Montholons to go and engage them in conversation. The commissioners did not beat a retreat, and soon the Bertrands, too, joined the group at the barrier. Finally Gourgaud offered his arm to Madame Stürmer, her husband did the same with Madame Bertrand, and all strolled leisurely toward Hutt's Gate.

In the meantime someone had told the governor, who was still at Deadwood, that Balmain and the Stürmers had been seen walking toward Longwood House. Convinced of their intention to visit Bonaparte, he hastily mounted his horse and set off for the house at a gallop. He felt vastly relieved when a servant told him that the commissioners were not with Napoleon, but had conversed with his followers at the barrier. Further reassurance was given him the following day by Balmain, who told him that he and Gourgaud had discussed the battle of Waterloo and that the conversation of the others had been equally innocent. Although far from pleased he managed to control himself and merely remarked that Gourgaud was a good fellow who never gave any trouble, but that Bertrand and Montholon were intriguers.

On September 29, Balmain and the Stürmers came again to Longwood, this time penetrating as far as the grounds of the estate, and conversed with the Bertrands and Montholon. The following day the grand marshal met Balmain at Hutt's Gate by appointment. Both were on horseback, and Bertrand slipped to the commissioner a copy of Napoleon's "Observations on Lord Bathurst's Speech." A day or two later Montholon had a chance meeting with Balmain and Stürmer, during which the following conversation took place:

"Why don't you come to see the Emperor? He has been expecting you for a long time. It would give him great pleasure to see you."

"Does that include the marquis?" Stürmer asked with a smile.

"Certainly. Come! You will be well received—not as commissioners, but as illustrious strangers."

"You know that the governor insists that he alone can present us," Stürmer remarked, "and Napoleon won't receive him. However, there is a way out of the difficulty. Let him invite us to dinner and we will come."

"But will the marquis accept the invitation?"

"I think I can promise you that he will."

It was agreed that they were to come on October 5, which was a Sunday, toward four in the afternoon. Montholon was to let them know if this met with Napoleon's approval. Notwithstanding his dislike for Montchenu, the Emperor approved.

So, on October 5, the man in whose antechamber kings had waited for the privilege of being received eagerly awaited the visit of three men and a young woman not one of whom would at one time have found it easy to penetrate to his august presence. And what a stir their expected visit created at Longwood! Montholon rose at five o'clock in the morning to see to it that nothing went amiss. Madame Bertrand and Madame Montholon brought forth their somewhat outmoded finery; the generals, their dress uniforms. The children were made to look their best. Napoleon had Pierron prepare a quantity of dainties he knew so well how to make and they were carefully arranged in a basket the Emperor meant to present to Madame Stürmer. He himself dressed with care. Toward four o'clock he went to the billiard-room, where the others joined him, and watched the road through his spyglass. At half past four the Bertrands and Gourgaud went to see if there was any sign of the expected visitors. They returned disappointed. The Emperor from time to time went to the window and scanned the road. It was after five when a horseman was seen approaching. It turned out to be Archambault. Napoleon put away his spyglass and arranged to have the children draw lots for the dainties. Hortense received the basket.

"It's the governor's doing," he said. "But for him they would have come."

Later Balmain was to offer his excuses, saying it was fear of arousing the governor's ire and its effect on Napoleon and his suite that had decided them not to keep the engagement. On November 10, he wrote to Count Nesselrode: "They do not want me to have a close view at things for fear national pride will suffer."

THREE

Early in January, 1818, Lowe received a letter from Bathurst which confirmed him in his determination not to permit the commissioners to be presented to Napoleon in their private capacity. They were to be presented only as commissioners of the allied powers and "introduced by you in your official character as Governor of St. Helena." Napoleon, however, had no intention of giving up the struggle. It was, after all, not so much the commissioners he cared about—welcome as their visits would have been as a diversion—but the possibility of establishing contact with the Czar of Russia and the Emperor of Austria. On April 10, Balmain reported to Nesselrode:

"The other day Count Bertrand made me a strange proposal. While telling me about the sufferings and misfortunes of Bonaparte, he suddenly said: "The Emperor, bored unto death, treated inhumanly on this rock, abandoned by all the world, wants to send a letter to the Emperor Alexander, to whom alone he feels he can appeal. I implore you to forward the letter.

"He made a movement as if to draw the epistle from his pocket, but I said: 'No, I cannot do it. I would be failing in my duty.'

"'Not at all,' he said, 'for the Emperor Napoleon makes important revelations to the Emperor Alexander. It is not merely a question of aiding a great man against oppression, but of serving Russia. He will read the letter with interest and pleasure. He will be delighted with it. Not to send it to your court is to neglect its interests, to sacrifice them to the English. I must tell you moreover that in it you are spoken of in a manner that cannot help being of advantage to you.'

"'I promise you,' I told him, 'to report faithfully to my court all that you wish to communicate to me verbally. But I cannot forward any letter. I have not the right to do it, and would be disavowed if I did.'

"'Nonsense!' he replied. 'They might disavow you for form's sake at St. Helena, but once back in Russia you will be rewarded. I am sure of it. Anyway, think it over carefully.'"

While unwilling to forward a letter from Napoleon to his sovereign, Balmain did his best to get his colleagues to make common cause with him in calling on Napoleon in defiance of the governor's wishes. It seemed to him a breach of the convention of August 2, 1815, that the commissioners of the allied powers should be denied a privilege that had been granted to Lord Amherst and to many other persons who had no official standing. By prearrangement with Bertrand he asked his colleagues to accompany him on a ride to the Company garden at Longwood. It was a pleasant spot planted with trees, shrubs, and flowers and hidden in a swale of the bleak plateau. None of the commissioners had yet visited it. Montchenu and Gors accepted, but the Stürmers excused themselves. So, on May 3, the two commissioners and the aide-de-camp arrived in the garden in the early afternoon. They had hardly been there half an hour when the Bertrands and the Montholons came with their children. Montchenu was not displeased. He found himself chatting with Bertrand as if the latter were a knight of the Order of St. Louis, not a Bonapartist condemned to death *in absentia* for treason to the King. Soon servants arrived from Longwood House carrying a large wicker basket, which proved to contain a collation such as Montchenu vowed he had not tasted since he had left France. It was served on silver plates and coffee was poured from a gold coffee pot into Sèvres coffee cups. After this it was not difficult to get Montchenu to promise to come to dinner at Longwood House the following Sunday with his secretary. Balmain, also invited, said he would try to get the Stürmers to be of the party.

Napoleon felt confident that this time the commissioners would not fail him. Lepage has related that the Emperor summoned him to his private apartment and helped him prepare the menu for the repast, saying: "I want it to be good, very good. Those poor unfortunates don't get anything but salted meat. The two Frenchmen will be especially happy to eat something that will remind them of their country." But, alas! the guests again failed to put in an appearance. Montchenu's courage had failed him; Stürmer, who had been censured by his government in the affair of the botanist, had not cared to risk further censure; while Balmain felt it would be unwise to defy Lowe unsupported by his colleagues.

FOUR

In June, 1818, Stürmer was recalled from his post and notified of his appointment as consul-general to the United States. The Austrian government had apparently reached the conclusion that no one they could send would be able to get along with the governor, for instead of appointing a successor they asked Montchenu to represent Austria as well as France. Balmain envied Stürmer his good fortune. On May 28, he wrote to Count Nesselrode: "Since the three [?] years of my residence at St. Helena expire on the 18th of June, 1818, I think it fit to make use of the first opportunity available to return to Europe, and cannot refrain from informing Your Excellency, that far from becoming acclimated on this dreadful rock I suffer constantly from my nerves." Stürmer, before leaving, asked Sir Hudson to allow him to be presented to Napoleon. The governor consented on condition that the presentation be made not by Bertrand but by Gorrequer, and that the major should be present at the interview. When this was communicated to the Emperor he had Montholon write to the governor that hitherto every presentation, *including his own,* had been made by the grand marshal. As for a British officer being present at the interview, he would deprive himself of the happiness of seeing his mother, wife, or son on such terms. Stürmer left St. Helena on July 3, 1818, without having seen Napoleon except once through a field telescope.

What made Balmain's situation increasingly embarrassing were the attempts Napoleon now repeatedly made to get him to accept a letter addressed to the Emperor Alexander. Why he should have refused to do so is not quite clear, since he had accepted a copy of the "Observations on Lord Bathurst's Speech" and had forwarded it to his government. Bertrand having failed in getting him to accept the letter, Montholon was entrusted with the task. He made several attempts, the boldest of which took place in the early part of August, 1818. The commissioner gave an account of this to Nesselrode the 14th of that month.

Montholon began by telling Balmain it was his duty to accept the letter and that it would be of great personal advantage to him. When this apparently made no impression, he spoke about Stürmer. Had the baron conducted himself differently, he said, the Emperor would have gladly loaned him 100,000 francs and would have given him historical memoirs he could have easily sold for six or seven thousand pound sterling. "We now have a very valuable manuscript that we should like to have published. Do you want it? It is offered to you wholeheartedly." The Russian smiled and said that if such a manuscript came into his possession, he would send it promptly to the Emperor Alexander, which again raises the question why he declined to send the letter.

To escape reproaches from Plantation House on the one hand, and pressure from Longwood on the other, Balmain decided to take a vacation in the hope that things would calm down a bit during his absence. Four days after his conversation with Montholon, he wrote to Count Lieven, Russian Ambassador in London, describing the difficulties of his position, telling him of his plan, and requesting that he inform Count Nesselrode. On August 22, 1818, he and Gors sailed on the *David* to Rio de Janeiro. He did not return to St. Helena until December 3. After his return Reade wrote to Lowe that Balmain "had quite altered his opinion in regard to the French people at Longwood. He now thought them a 'curious set' (this was his expression), but particularly Count Montholon, whom he described as a very intriguing character." If his opinion in regard to the French had altered, his opinion of the treatment Napoleon was receiving apparently had not, for on March 1, 1819, we find him writing to Nesselrode: "In one of his notes, the governor maintains that the various complaints of Bertrand and the other Frenchmen are calumnies. In my opinion they are not, for nothing could be more absurd, more impolitic, and less generous than the treatment of Napoleon by the English."

FIVE

A congress of the allied powers was to meet at Aix-la-Chapelle in November, 1818. It was the first of several such congresses that followed the defeat of Napoleon at Waterloo. To obtain the support of the populace in their struggle against Napoleon in 1814 and 1815, the oligarchies that ruled Europe had been forced to make promises of reform which they had failed to keep. The result was unrest in practically every European country. The allied powers had to find ways to stem the tide. England's representatives to the congress were to be Lord Castlereagh and the Duke of Wellington. It appeared certain that the treatment accorded Napoleon at St. Helena would come up for discussion, for had he not been "the power of the French Revolution, concentrated in one man" (as the Russian note to the congress was to refer to him), hence responsible for the difficulties that beset the rulers of Europe? It was necessary to supply the English representatives with material to combat the charges that would be made by the Bonapartists. So, on September 25, 1818, Lord Bathurst wrote to Lord Castlereagh:

"It appears to be the intention of Las Cases and certain other friends of General Bonaparte to call the attention of the sovereigns assembled at Aix-la-Chapelle to the treatment he is receiving at St. Helena. I believe it therefore to be desirable that you should be in possession of some documents which will enable you to refute the gross inexactitudes which are circulating on the subject. The first of these documents gives the regulations which are in existence. . . ."

The document made no mention of the regulations of October 9, 1816, which Lowe had initiated and Bathurst had approved, and which, but for Napoleon's resistance to them, would undoubtedly have remained in force.

"The second document," Bathurst wrote, "contains the statements made by General Gourgaud on his arrival from St. Helena. I regret that he could not have been induced to say more, which, I imagine, he could have been easily persuaded to do if it had been possible to hold out the hope to him that the French government would pardon him."

While Bathurst was thus engaged in trying to maintain the *status quo* at St. Helena, Napoleon's relatives and sympathizers were not idle. Pope Pius VII wrote to the British cabinet: "Napoleon is very unhappy. We have forgotten his mistakes; the Church must never forget his services. . . . The knowledge that this unfortunate suffers is almost a torment to us. . . . We will not, we cannot share in the responsibility for the hardships he is made to endure. On the contrary, we wish from the bottom of our heart that they be lightened and his existence be made more bearable." Napoleon's mother sent a moving letter to the sovereigns through the intermediary of Cardinal Fesch. Las Cases, too, tried. But all this could not prevail against the testimony Gourgaud had given. It must have been particularly painful to Napoleon that the note—based mainly on Gourgaud's testimony, which asked stricter surveillance of the prisoner—should have been presented by the Russians. The congress concurred and issued a protocol to that effect. It put an end to Napoleon's hopes that Czar Alexander might intervene in his favor.

XXII. Vicissitudes of Dr. Stokoe

When Cipriani died the absence of a Catholic priest had been keenly felt by Napoleon's following. Shortly after his death Bertrand had written to Cardinal Fesch: "You are our bishop; we wish that you would send a French or Italian priest. Be so good as to select a well-informed man under the age of forty." He had likewise asked that a *maître d'hôtel* be sent to take the place of Cipriani, and a cook to replace Lepage. When O'Meara's resignation was provisionally accepted by the governor, a formal request had been made to the latter that a French doctor be also sent. Lowe forwarded the request to Lord Bathurst, who left it to Cardinal Fesch to select all the persons desired. Those chosen did not, however, arrive at St. Helena until September 21, 1819.

When Lord Bathurst had written to the governor giving him permission to remove O'Meara, he at the same time instructed him to place the services of Dr. Baxter at Napoleon's disposal, but added that should Bonaparte prefer the services "of any other professional man on the island, you are perfectly prepared to acquiesce in his wish on the subject." Lowe knew that Napoleon would under no circumstances accept Baxter. It would have been tactful as well as in conformity with Bathurst's instructions to have asked Napoleon what doctor he preferred. But with his customary lack of tact Lowe failed to do so; he appointed Dr. Verling, assistant surgeon of the royal artillery, resident physician at Longwood. Verling was as competent as most men of his profession at that time. He had an engaging personality, and the Emperor, who had met him on the *Northumberland*, liked him. But he considered the manner of his appointment a gratuitous insult and refused to see him. The Bertrands and the Montholons, however, made frequent use of his services.

While there can be no doubt that Napoleon suffered from a liver complaint long before he succumbed to the perforation of the pylorus by a peptic ulcer, there can likewise be no doubt that he tried to make the most of his affliction in the hope that it would result in his removal from the island. He wished to have a doctor who, like O'Meara, would lend himself to furthering that design, and in April, 1819, had Montholon make the following proposal to Dr. Verling:

Napoleon would give him 12,000 francs per annum, payable monthly. He would not be required to do anything that "might compromise him with his government, with any tribunal or even with public opinion." He must, however, pledge himself never to make a written report concerning the state of the Emperor's health without giving the original to Bertrand, and never to report conversations he might have or might overhear at Longwood, unless they were of a nature which duty to his government required him to divulge. In his reports he "might lean rather to an augmentation than a diminution of the disease— draw the line rather above than below." To protect Verling against any such misadventure as had befallen O'Meara, the Emperor would deposit with the banking house of Baring in London a sum sufficiently large so the interest thereof would pay him an amount equal to the salary he was receiving from the government.

Dr. Verling rejected the offer and considered it his duty to report it to the governor. Most men would have considered this proof of the doctor's loyalty and sense of duty; not so Sir Hudson. He reasoned that the offer would not have been made if Verling had not been on intimate terms with the French. He had the doctor closely watched and made an inquiry into his antecedents and family connections. He soon found a peg on which to hang his suspicions: some of Verling's relatives were Roman Catholics! He promptly communicated this momentous discovery to Lord Bathurst. The colonial secretary had Goulburn write to him: "Lord Bathurst cannot permit any circumstance of that nature to invalidate the confidence to which his [Dr. Verling's] uniform discretion and propriety of conduct, up to the date of your last communication, so justly entitle him."

TWO

The reason the governor had not obeyed Lord Bathurst's instruction to let Napoleon decide what doctor should take O'Meara's place at Longwood may well have been that he believed Bonaparte would choose John Stokoe, surgeon of the admiral's flagship the *Conqueror*, whom Lowe considered suspect for a variety of reasons.

Admiral Malcolm had presented his officers to Napoleon; his successor, lacking his tactfulness and kindly disposition and anxious to please the governor, had refrained from doing so. He had moreover issued an order forbidding any naval officer to go to Longwood without his permission. On October 10, 1817, Stokoe had obtained permission to visit O'Meara, with whom he had struck up a friendship. They were conversing in the garden when Napoleon accompanied by the Montholons, came from the billiard-room and seated himself on the steps of the veranda. Seeing O'Meara with a naval officer, he asked the count to inquire to what ship he belonged and, having received that information, had the two surgeons called. When O'Meara had presented his friend, Napoleon tried his English on him, saying: "Surgeon *Conqueror*, man of war, fine ship!" When told that Stokoe spoke Italian, there followed the usual series of questions.

Stokoe dutifully reported his unsolicited interview with Napoleon to the admiral and was severely reprimanded for having allowed himself to be presented to him. When he objected that he could not have declined without being discourteous, Plampin retorted: "You needn't have bothered being polite to him. I

319

have enough trouble with the governor as it is." Reade's spy system promptly informed the governor of the presentation, and Stokoe was summoned to Plantation House where he was subjected to a humiliating interrogatory.

The next incident occurred in July, 1818, a short time before O'Meara left Longwood. The Emperor had contracted bronchitis and was running a fever. His legs were swollen, the pain in the side had become acute, and his gums bled at the slightest touch. O'Meara became alarmed and told Napoleon he should like to have another doctor examine him, so they might have a consultation. The fact that Napoleon consented makes it evident that he must have felt uncommonly wretched. He would, however, have neither Verling nor Baxter, but suggested Stokoe. With Lowe's permission the surgeon of the *Conqueror* was called, but declined to examine the patient unless a third doctor was present. He said that since O'Meara and he were known to be friends and O'Meara had quarreled with the governor, the latter might suspect collusion on their part if they happened to agree in their diagnosis. O'Meara had no objection to the presence of a third doctor but Napoleon would not hear of it. Stokoe departed without seeing the patient.

Two days later he was asked to drop in at Reade's office at Jamestown. He did so and found there the governor as well as Reade. Lowe asked him why no consultation had taken place. He replied that he had considered the responsibility too great unless a third doctor was present, this being customary when the patient was a person of note. Sir Hudson asked him to write him a letter stating his reasons, but not to send it to Plantation House without first showing it to him. Stokoe left and a short time later returned with the letter. He found Sir Hudson alone in the office. The governor read the letter, then took pen and paper and wrote that he had seen the surgeon of the *Conqueror* and had questioned him. "Mr. Stokoe had declared that he would not go to Longwood without a formal order to do so, in which case he wished to be assisted by others of his profession, but not by General Bonaparte's personal physician." Countersigned by Stokoe this was to take the place of the letter. The surgeon remarked that the governor's version was a reflection on O'Meara's ability and professional integrity, with which he could not associate himself. Lowe, his face flushed with anger and embarrassment, made a few minor changes, then pushed the paper from him impatiently, said: "You may send your letter, sir," and stalked out of the office.

Still another incident was the result of Balcombe's arrival in London, where he met O'Meara's friend and business agent William Holmes. The latter had had difficulty communicating with O'Meara. Some of his letters never arrived at their destination, while others were delivered after having been opened. Balcombe suggested that he address his letters to Stokoe, who was O'Meara's friend and would not mind delivering them to him. When O'Meara left the island Stokoe was ordered to open all letters or shipments addressed to him in the presence of the admiral. Thus it happened that in September, 1818, the surgeon of the *Conqueror* received a package from Holmes, which he took to Plampin's office. It contained books and pamphlets and two sealed envelopes. One, addressed to Stokoe, contained a letter to Bertrand and a note in which the surgeon was asked to deliver the letter to the grand marshal together with the books. In the letter to Bertrand, Holmes gave details about various financial transactions. The second envelope, addressed to O'Meara, contained a letter from Balcombe. "Holmes," it read, "is indefatigable in your cause, and all my friends . . . are of the same opinion with us . . . A change in the administration is expected."

Stokoe was not acquainted with Holmes and had never corresponded with him. Holmes later wrote to him apologizing for having involved him in his affairs without his consent. He also wrote to Lord Bathurst explaining why he happened to send the books and the letters to Stokoe, saying that Lowe had unlawfully meddled with his correspondence. All this, however, availed Stokoe little. As far as Sir Hudson and the admiral were concerned, he was suspect.

THREE

On January 6, 1819, Napoleon had an attack of vertigo. Ten days later, between midnight and one o'clock, while dictating to Montholon, he had a syncope and lost consciousness. Montholon sent for Bertrand. When the grand marshal arrived the Emperor had somewhat recovered, and it was decided not to irritate him by asking him to receive Dr. Verling. Bertrand, however, penned a note to Stokoe, telling him that Napoleon was gravely ill and asking him to come with the least possible delay. The note was given to the orderly officer at 1 A.M., and he immediately sent a dragoon to deliver it; but since it had to pass through the hands of the governor, the admiral, the harbor master, and the captain of the *Conqueror* before reaching Stokoe, it was not until 7 A.M. that the surgeon arrived at Bertrand's house.

The patient had in the meantime recovered from what may have been an attack of apoplexy, had taken a hot bath, and had fallen asleep on the couch. Stokoe had breakfast with the Bertrands and agreed to wait until the Emperor had awakened. After breakfast Montholon came, and the surgeon got what information he could from the two generals about the nature of the attack and the state of Napoleon's health. In the course of the conversation Montholon asked him if he would be willing to take O'Meara's place at Longwood, provided permission could be obtained from the governor and the admiral. Remembering O'Meara's difficulties he gave no definite reply. Montholon left, but an hour later returned with a document, apparently dictated by Napoleon, and asked him to read it. It contained the following proposal, which he was asked to accept provisionally, subject to approval by his superiors:

He was to become Napoleon's personal physician and was to live at Longwood. During that time he was to be relieved of all military discipline and duty, but was not to be deprived of any of his rights as a British subject and an officer in the royal navy. He was to receive the same remuneration from his government as his predecessor. He was to draw up daily reports concerning Napoleon's health, the originals of which were to be left with Marshal Bertrand. He was not to be required to furnish any other information concerning the French, unless it was of a nature which it was his duty to his country and to his sovereign to reveal. Stokoe has written that he saw nothing in the agreement "incompatible with the honor of an officer and a gentleman" and, after some reflection, said he would be willing to accept the post on the terms specified provided the governor and the admiral gave their consent. A short time later he was admitted to the chamber where the Emperor lay on the sofa. Napoleon submitted to an examination, after which Stokoe drew up a report ending with the words: "From the evident tendency of a determination of blood to the head, it will be highly necessary that a medical man should be near the patient, in order that immediate assistance may be afforded in case of a recurrence of the above alarming symptoms, as well as for the daily treatment of chronic hepatitis which the above symptoms indicate."

FOUR

Stokoe did not leave Longwood until two in the afternoon of January 17. He stopped at The Briars to report to Admiral Plampin, whom he gave a copy of his medical report and of the agreement dictated by Napoleon. The admiral read both and said he would take the matter up with the governor. Bertrand had in the meantime sent a copy of the document to Sir Hudson, together with a letter to the effect that Dr. Stokoe had expressed his willingness to accept the post if permitted to do so by his superiors. Lowe sent a letter to Plampin expressing his surprise and displeasure that Stokoe "should have given his assent to a proposal of such a nature . . . without, it appears, any previous reference to, or consultation with, either Your Excellency or me." Plampin who had previously found no fault either with the terms of the agreement or with Stokoe's provisional assent immediately adopted the governor's viewpoint.

In the evening of that same day Napoleon showed signs of a renewal of the attack of the previous night. Montholon became alarmed and at nine o'clock set out on horseback for Plantation House in a driving rain, accompanied by Captain Nicholls and two dragoons carrying lanterns. He begged the governor to permit Stokoe to remain at Longwood while the question of his permanent establishment there was being considered. Lowe replied that he had no objection, but that "Mr. Stokoe was under the admiral's authority, and that he could not dispose of his services." He promised, however, to confer with the admiral on the matter.

Before Montholon returned from Plantation House, Napoleon's condition had worsened and Bertrand sent a dragoon with a note to Stokoe asking him to hasten to Longwood. The surgeon arrived at Napoleon's bedside at six in the morning of January 18. His second health bulletin read, in part:

"It appears from the symptoms of chronic hepatitis (the first appearance of which he experienced sixteen months ago) that this is the principal cause of the present derangement in his health, and although they are described as having increased considerably of late, yet, judging from present appearances, I do not apprehend any immediate danger; although it must be presumed that in a climate where the above disease is so prevalent, it will eventually shorten his life.

"The more alarming symptom is that which was experienced on the night of the 16th, a recurrence of which may soon prove fatal, particularly if medical assistance is not at hand."

That Stokoe should have adopted O'Meara's view regarding the nature of Napoleon's illness is not surprising. In the course of eighteen months over 100 of the *Conqueror*'s crew of 600 had died of what he and other doctors on the island believed to be hepatitis. Smaller vessels stationed at St. Helena had suffered as much or more. The *Mosquito* had lost 24 out of 100; the *Racoon*, 16 out of 100; the *Griffin*, 15 out of 85; the *Leveret*, 11 out of 65. But the view adopted by Stokoe conflicted with Gourgaud's testimony, which the government considered unimpeachable, even though he himself had repudiated it. The surgeon of the *Conqueror* was therefore bound to incur the displeasure of the government's representatives on the island. When on the afternoon of the 18th he called at Plampin's office to report, the admiral, after reading his health bulletin, subjected him to a severe interrogatory, at the conclusion of which he told him that no matter how great the emergency he was not to go to Longwood without a pass. That same evening Montholon received a letter from the governor informing him that the admiral "could not dispense with the services of Dr. Stokoe," but that there was no objection to his being summoned to Longwood when needed. The governor was desirous, however, that henceforth "his visits should be made in conjunction with Dr. Verling."

FIVE

In the afternoon of the 19th of January Stokoe again received a message from Longwood. Napoleon was very ill; he had not left his bed for twenty-four hours; the surgeon's presence was urgently required. He went to the admiral's office and showed him the message. Plampin asked a number of questions, among which was why, in his medical bulletins, he referred to the prisoner as "the patient" instead of as "General Bonaparte." Stokoe replied that it was his understanding the latter mode of address had been discarded by the governor. Plampin replied that Lord Bathurst used it when writing to the governor. Lord Melville used it when writing to him. He himself never employed any other and failed to see why Stokoe should permit himself to do otherwise. He finally gave him a pass, and the surgeon departed for Longwood, where he arrived at six in the evening.

Captain Nicholls met him and showed him a copy of the governor's letter in which Sir Hudson said that he desired Stokoe to visit the patient in conjunction with Dr. Verling. The surgeon and the captain went together to Bertrand's house, and Stokoe asked the grand marshal to attempt to persuade Napoleon to receive his colleague. Bertrand replied that this would merely irritate the patient and produce no result. Nicholls departed and for a moment Stokoe considered doing the same. He reflected, however, that to fail to see Napoleon involved as great a risk as seeing him. If after his departure Bonaparte were to die, Lowe would say that he had merely expressed a desire but had not given an order and that the surgeon had failed in his duty.

He found Napoleon stretched on the couch in his study. He

325

had fever and his face looked congested. He breathed with difficulty and complained of a splitting headache. Stokoe suggested bleeding, but Napoleon would not hear of it—not even when the doctor warned him that he was risking an attack of apoplexy. The surgeon remained at Longwood overnight. Toward five in the morning the Emperor's headache became so unbearable that he consented to be bled and experienced some relief. Stokoe drew up his third medical report, concluding with the words: "I took this opportunity of more particularly examining the liver, and am fully persuaded of the diseased state of that viscus, having distinctly felt a degree of hardness. . . . I therefore advised the immediate adoption of a course of mercury, with other medicines in such form as best suited the constitution of the patient."

The surgeon believed Bonaparte's condition required his remaining at Longwood the rest of the day, but toward noon he received an order to report at The Briars. He found the admiral in a belligerent mood. Having read the report, Plampin asked if Stokoe had told Bertrand about Lord Bathurst and Lord Melville referring to the prisoner in their correspondence as "General Bonaparte." Stokoe replied that he had found it necessary to do so when explaining why he could no longer refer to him in his medical reports as "the patient." Plampin flew into a rage and shouted: "You are a dangerous man! One can't say anything in your presence without it being reported at Longwood!" He went on in this fashion for some time, and Stokoe realized that unless he severed relations with the French he was headed for serious trouble. As soon as he reached his cabin on the *Conqueror* he wrote a letter to the admiral in which he said: "The experience of today points to the necessity of my declining all further communication with Longwood." He requested that the admiral notify Bertrand to that effect.

He had hardly finished when a message was delivered to him asking him to return to Longwood immediately. Sorely perplexed, the harassed man took the message to The Briars together with the letter he had written. The admiral refused to read the letter and ordered him peremptorily to return to Longwood. He could remain there overnight, but must report at the admiral's office at half past ten the following morning.

In his medical bulletin of the 21st of January Stokoe reported that General Bonaparte's fever had been slight, but that he had complained increasingly about pain in the side. He had, he wrote, told Napoleon that he could not continue to be of service to him "under the unpleasant circumstances to which I am exposed," and had already asked to be relieved of that duty. When he left Longwood that day he carried with him a note from Napoleon to his brother Joseph, dated January 21, 1819, reading: "I beg you to pay Dr. Stokoe one thousand pound sterling, which I owe him. When he sends you this note he will supply you with all the information concerning me you might desire. Napoleon."

That Stokoe had been promised a monetary reward for stating in his medical reports that Napoleon was suffering from hepatitis is unlikely. Had such a reward been promised he would not have written a letter to the admiral asking to be excused from returning to Longwood before he had collected it. Napoleon apparently felt that having confirmed O'Meara's diagnosis, Stokoe stood in danger of meeting the same fate as his friend and wished to compensate him for having placed his career in jeopardy. Whether under the circumstances Stokoe was justified in accepting the gift is debatable.

SIX

The admiral had ordered Stokoe to report to him not later than 10:30 in the forenoon of January 21. The surgeon did not arrive at The Briars until noon. This was partly due to a fall from his horse, but mainly to his having lingered too long at Longwood. Plampin upbraided him severely for having disobeyed his order and would listen to no excuse. In the meantime Lowe had reached the decision that something must be done about Stokoe. Since his medical reports corroborated O'Meara's he must be discredited. Apart from Napoleon's note to Joseph—of which Lowe had no knowledge and which was not to come to light until 1912, when it was found and published by Frédéric Masson—

there was nothing on which to base a court-martial; yet it was not long before Stokoe heard that such a move was intended. Believing that what Lowe and Plampin principally desired was to be rid of him, he asked and obtained a leave of absence for reasons of health. He left St. Helena for Portsmouth on January 30, 1819, on the *Trincomalee*, unaware that with the same vessel Admiral Plampin was sending a report to the admiralty recommending a court-martial.

On April 4, he arrived at Portsmouth and thence traveled to London. When he reported at the admiralty he was informed that it had been decided to have him return forthwith to St. Helena. No reason was given, and he suspected nothing. One of his friends congratulated him, believing the admiralty's action to be a sign that his conduct at St. Helena had been fully approved. He left Portsmouth on the 19th of April on the *Abundance*, which sailed for St. Helena by way of the Cape. When he arrived on the island on August 21, he was arrested and brought before a court-martial.

Some of the charges brought against him were so frivolous that Lowe's apologists have thought it best not to mention them. One was that in his earliest medical reports he had referred to the prisoner as "the patient" instead of as "General Bonaparte" —this notwithstanding the fact that Lowe himself had discarded the latter appellation and called him Napoleon Bonaparte. Another was that, on January 21, he had been an hour and a half late in reporting to the admiral. Still another was that he had discussed matters at Longwood not pertaining to Bonaparte's illness. To have a medical officer travel a total of 188 days to be tried on such charges must have been something novel in the annals of the royal navy. Almost equally trivial was the charge that he had left copies of his medical reports with Bonaparte, which Lowe considered a breach of the regulation forbidding any written communication with the people at Longwood; and the charge of having provisionally agreed, subject to approval by his superiors, to the terms of the proposal made him by Napoleon to become his personal physician. The principal charge against him was that he had "stated facts relative to the health of General Bonaparte which did not fall under his observation, and which, as he later admitted, were dictated or suggested to him by members of his suite." This referred to his statement that the first appearance of chronic hepatitis was experienced by Napoleon sixteen months ago, and that he had had a syncope.

Stokoe was found guilty on all counts of the indictment and his name ordered stricken from the list of naval surgeons. In consideration of his many years of service he was, however, to receive an annual pension of £100. In the difficult financial circumstances in which he found himself he was generously aided by members of the Bonaparte family.

XXIII. Napoleon's Inconclusive Victory

Napoleon was officially notified of the action of the Congress of Aix-la-Chapelle on May 26, 1819. Long before that time the proceedings of the congress had been reported in the English newspapers and had been translated for him by Bertrand. His disappointment was profound. So he was doomed to spend the remainder of his life on the "accursed rock." A new house was being built for him on the plateau, a stone's throw from the old. Lowe had had a sod wall erected to shield him from the prying eyes of the workmen. He knew that its grounds were treeless and that he would be unable to stir out without seeing the red uniforms of the British at Deadwood Camp. This was all he had to look forward to. "Why live?" he asked himself. "Why live? For what purpose?" The thought of suicide intruded occasionally, but was always followed by the thought that it would please the British—save them a lot of expense.

He knew that there was not a member of his household who was not anxious to leave—anxious for him to die undoubtedly, for if they delayed their going it was because they expected to be remembered in his will. All the same, in December, 1818, Pierron and Ali had gone to Plantation House to ask permission to leave. A few months before he had dismissed Lepage for doing so; now he no longer cared. Madame Bertrand was worrying her husband that they should return to Europe. Madame Montholon was speaking of leaving for reasons of health. Her husband had dropped the remark that it might be necessary for him to accompany her. They had better wait: he still had a few million francs to distribute.

TWO

While O'Meara had been at Longwood he had daily reported to the orderly officer that he had seen Bonaparte. The surgeon being a British officer, Sir Hudson had stopped insisting that the orderly officer must himself see the prisoner. Now that O'Meara had departed, he thought it imperative that Captain Nicholls should assure himself at least once a day of Napoleon's presence at Longwood. But unless force were used this was almost impossible to accomplish. Napoleon now rarely went into the garden. It was only by accident that Nicholls sometimes managed to catch a glimpse of him. Lowe had spoken about it repeatedly to Montholon, but always received the answer that the Emperor was unwell and did not leave his bed more than two or three hours a day. It was not that the count did not try to be helpful. Since he was seriously considering returning to Europe, he thought it expedient to gain Lowe's good will, so he could go directly to England and not be forced to spend months at the Cape. But he got no co-operation from Napoleon. On several occasions he got the children to play in front of the Emperor's bedroom windows. This usually drew him to the window to chat with them, giving Nicholls an opportunity to catch a glimpse of him. The ruse, however, could only be used sparingly and did not always have the desired effect.

Lowe wrote to Lord Bathurst concerning the matter. On September 28, 1818, the colonial secretary sent him new instructions, which reached him in December of that year but which he did not communicate to Bonaparte or to the commissioners until the end of March, 1819. From this it may be inferred that they were not to his liking.

Lord Bathurst wrote that he had received Lowe's letter containing the memorandum of a conversation that had taken place between Count Montholon and Dr. Verling, and went on to say:

"I was particularly struck with that part of the conversation in which Count Montholon states that General Bonaparte is never seen and that he defies the governor to say that he knows for certain that General Bonaparte is at Longwood or has been there for the last two months. . . . I confess that it appears to me so essential to the security of his person that the fact of his being actually at Longwood should be regularly and daily ascertained, that if this were daily enforced I should have less objection to dispense with some of the instructions of which General Bonaparte has complained."

He therefore instructed Lowe to inform Napoleon that if he would agree to admit the orderly officer to a daily interview between the hours of nine and eleven every morning and evening—"leaving it to his discretion each day to select within the time limit the precise moment at which he may prefer admitting the officer"—he would be authorized to walk, ride, or drive on the island unattended by a British officer: "I should hope that with the exception of the immediate neighborhood of Jamestown and two or three other places, he may be permitted under this regulation *to range through the whole of the island in what manner he may think proper.*[1]

"You will point out to General Bonaparte that, in leaving it to him to fix the time within the limits assigned at which he will admit the orderly officer to a personal interview, and directing him that until such interview the sentries shall not be placed round his house, whatever inconvenience he may have occasionally complained of by the early posting of the sentries will in future be entirely removed." This involved sentence meant that Napoleon could remain away from Longwood until shortly before eleven o'clock in the evening, unaccompanied by a British officer, provided he showed himself to the orderly officer on his return.

It is hardly necessary to point out that this was the plan the Duke of Wellington had wished the government to adopt from the beginning of the captivity, except that he also favored that Napoleon should be allowed "to receive or send as many letters

---

[1] Italics are the author's.

as he chose." He must have meant uncensored letters, for no limit had ever been placed on the number of letters the prisoner could receive or send. Indeed, once he was given the freedom of the island, censorship would have been impossible to enforce. Even with all the precautions taken by Lowe, the latter had to acknowledge that clandestine correspondence could not be stopped.

It is to be noted that in Bathurst's new instructions there is no mention of Bonaparte's not being permitted to converse with persons he met while riding or driving, or to visit at the houses of the inhabitants. Yet, if allowed to do so, what possible purpose could it have served to forbid Bertrand to issue passes to those whom Napoleon wished to receive? Thus Bathurst's new regulations, if enforced without quibbling, would have swept away Lowe's entire system of surveillance and espionage. It would have been the business of the admiral to keep any ship that appeared in the least suspect from approaching the island, and the business of the governor to have the few existing landing-places carefully guarded. For the rest Napoleon would have been almost as free as any other inhabitant of St. Helena.

Bathurst's new instructions were equivalent to an admission that those he had previously given—and even more so Lowe's regulations of October 9, 1816—were in no way necessary to keep Bonaparte in safe custody. They proved moreover that Napoleon had not miscalculated when he began his campaign of passive resistance. He had gained a sweeping victory, but like all the victories he had won during his astounding career it proved inconclusive.

THREE

On April 2, 1819, toward four in the afternoon, Napoleon received the last visitor he was to receive at St. Helena—Mr. Ricketts, a cousin of Lord Liverpool, the prime minister, who was on his way to England from Calcutta. The Emperor had heard about his arrival and had Bertrand send him an invitation to call. Ricketts had accepted, and Sir Hudson knew better than to raise his usual objection against a visitor being presented to Napoleon by Marshal Bertrand. In a report of the visit Ricketts wrote: "I was ushered into a very small room where Napoleon was lying in a camp-bed with only his shirt on, with a colored handkerchief round his head, and with his beard of three or four days' growth. The room admitted so little light that I could not at first discern his features, though subsequent introduction of candles gave me a tolerable view of them. He resembled the picture of his leaning on the capstan of the *Northumberland*, and a French picture with laurel round his head."

The Emperor asked Ricketts and Bertrand to be seated, and the three remained in the stuffy little room for four hours. Bonaparte did not appear seriously ill to the visitor, who, however, noted that his complexion was sallow and that, whenever he brought his arm round the metal post of the camp-bed to raise himself on the pillow, his face became slightly contorted with pain. "He possessed a readiness of delivery and his sentences were epigrammatical and pithy. . . . In his conversation he was animated and sometimes facetious; quick of thought and rapidly changing his subject and renewing it. I had very few remarks to make, and not many questions put to me; but he frequently said to me, '*Comprenez vous?*' . . . He seemed to be a little deaf."

During the conversation Napoleon thought it advisable to exonerate Lord Liverpool from responsibility for the treatment he was receiving, saying that the prime minister undoubtedly had no knowledge of the persecution to which he was subjected. He mentioned the appalling death rate among the soldiers of the garrison and the crews of the squadron, which, like others of his time, he attributed to the climate. He assured Ricketts that if he were allowed to live in England the government would have no cause for regret: "I am a soldier, I keep my word." He rejected Lord Bathurst's latest offer in these words: "I will take no exercise, which I know to be indispensable to my health, so long as Sir Hudson Lowe remains here. I shall not expose myself to insult nor be the cause of expulsion from the island of persons with whom I happen to exchange a few words."

At first glance this may appear unreasonable, but only at first glance. It should be noted that Napoleon raised no objection to receiving the orderly officer twice daily for a few minutes in exchange for being allowed the freedom of the island. But he objected to having the execution of the plan entrusted to Sir Hudson Lowe. He was not alone in believing that if Sir Hudson remained in charge the only result of the new dispensation would be renewed squabbles and recriminations. When on March 29, 1819, Lowe finally communicated the plan to the commissioners, Balmain wrote to Count Nesselrode: "If the matter is handled tactlessly, as is usual at Plantation House, the result will be unfortunate." There can be no doubt that with an official in charge as suspicious, jealous of his authority, and fearful of mutiny as was Sir Hudson, the plan would not have worked. The governor was punctilious in executing orders that tended to increase his authority, but did not hesitate to resort to devious means to avoid executing those that tended to curtail it.

There was still another reason why Napoleon could not accept Lord Bathurst's proposal. While he was to be given the freedom of the island, his followers were not, except when in his company. This was a petty and needless vexation. They had, moreover, been made to sign an agreement that they were to be subject to the same restrictions as their chief. Napoleon had called this to the government's attention on a previous occasion, making it plain that he would accept no privilege that did not equally apply to them.

Ricketts had been exceedingly courteous and sympathetic, which aroused a hope in Napoleon and his suite that his visit might be fruitful. But like the Duke of Wellington, Sir Pulteney Malcolm, Sir George Cockburn, Lord Amherst, and others, what he said in private had little or no relation to what he said officially. When he reached England the report he made proved entirely satisfactory to Lord Bathurst, who wrote to Lowe: "Nothing could have been more fortunate than Mr. Ricketts' visit to St. Helena."

FOUR

William Forsyth has written: "Surely, there was something of childish obstinacy in the determination of the fallen Emperor not to submit to the requisition that his actual presence at Longwood should be daily ascertained by the orderly officer. Such conduct was neither dignified nor reasonable."

A man who finds himself in the power of his enemies and considers himself unjustly treated resists by whatever means are at his disposal. Napoleon's "childish obstinacy" in refusing to go riding or driving had resulted in the annulment of Lowe's regulations of October 9, 1816; and while it might have appeared "neither dignified nor reasonable" to refuse to show himself to the orderly officer, it had already wrung from Lord Bathurst the offer of freedom of the island on condition that he cease doing so. Realizing, however, that the offer was meaningless so long as Sir Hudson Lowe remained governor, Napoleon decided to continue, and even to intensify, his passive resistance in the hope that it might result in the removal of Sir Hudson or his own removal from the island. In this, however, he was doomed to disappointment.

It was regrettable that the victim of Napoleon's passive resistance was to be the well-meaning Captain Nicholls, whose duty it was to report daily to Plantation House that he had seen Bonaparte or at least had done his utmost to do so. All day long, no matter how inclement the weather, he wandered forlornly around the house and about the grounds in the hope of catching a glimpse of him. The French servants and the English gardeners and repairmen (the house had to be constantly repaired to remain habitable) amused themselves at his expense. Not only did they make jocular remarks, but took a mischievous pleasure in giving him misinformation about Napoleon's whereabouts. They had him running from the garden to the wood and vice-versa, from one window to another. Once he appealed to Montholon, who told him that the Emperor was in the billiard-room and that if he went on the veranda and peeked through the keyhole he might be able to see him. "I told him," Nicholls reported, "that I certainly would not adopt such a plan." Another time he reported to Gorrequer: "At this moment there is a person sitting in the General's dining room with a cocked hat on. I, however, can only see the hat moving about. If the French are accustomed to sit at dinner with a hat on, probably this is Napoleon Bonaparte at dinner." The major replied: "There is in fact no other person of the establishment at Longwood in the habit of wearing a cocked hat, and consequently it is more than probable that you did see him." On such questionable evidence as this Lowe had to rely that Napoleon was still at Longwood. On one occasion Bertrand took pity on the orderly officer and told him that if he looked in at the bathroom window he might see the Emperor in his bath. He hastened to the window, but steam had clouded it and he could see nothing. Another time, finding the window open, he was able to report: "I saw General Bonaparte this morning, quarter to eleven, up to his neck in water in a bath. He had a ghastly appearance. Marchand, his chief valet, attended him." The following, dated July 21, 1819, is a typical report: "Yesterday I was upon my feet at least *ten hours* walking about Longwood garden, but had no opportunity of seeing general Bonaparte. . . . The weather at present is so very bad that I fear my health will be greatly injured."

On August 4, Lowe himself accidentally saw Napoleon and reported to Bathurst: "I had on the 4th instant a most distinct view myself of his person. . . . He had his back turned to me, and he had a long stick like a wand in his hand, was dressed in his usual uniform, looked as lusty as I had ever seen him, but walked with a gait that bore somewhat the appearance of infirmity. The children of Count Bertrand were with him. The rencontre was wholly unexpected on my part." As soon as Napoleon became aware of the governor's presence he went up a side path. No sign of recognition passed between them.

FIVE

On May 26, 1819, Count Montholon called at Plantation House to ask permission for his wife to leave for Europe without being obliged to spend several months at the Cape. She had been

treated for a liver complaint by O'Meara, by Dr. Verling, and by
Dr. Livingstone. Major Gorrequer took notes of the conversation
between Montholon and the governor. Sir Hudson told the
count that he could not allow his wife to sail directly for Europe
unless he was able to produce a doctor's certificate. Montholon
replied that he had *frequently requested Dr. Verling and had
also applied to Dr. Livingstone to sign a certificate of her state
of health, but they had declined giving it, fearing, as it appeared
to him, that it might be considered a political question and that
they might compromise themselves.*

When, following her husband's visit, Lowe granted permission to the two doctors to give her a certificate they reported
that "Madame Montholon has suffered severely and for a long
time, in France, from a disease of the liver, and the functions of
the stomach and liver are much impaired." No evidence exists
that she suffered from the liver "in France." The words were undoubtedly inserted by order of the governor. Nor was this the
only falsification in the certificate. The document is dated January 7, 1819, notwithstanding the fact that documentary proof
exists that as late as May 26, 1819, Montholon complained that
the doctors had declined to give a certificate, "fearing, as it appeared to him, that . . . they might compromise themselves."
Apparently Lowe had insisted on the false dating so he might
be in possession of a document with which to disprove Montholon's damaging testimony if necessity arose. Madame Montholon's case proves conclusively that doctors at St. Helena were
so terrorized by Lowe that they did not dare tell the truth. If
Sir Hudson gave permission to Dr. Verling and Dr. Livingstone
to issue the certificate, it was because it would have been embarrassing for him not to have done so. Dr. Baxter, his favorite
medico, had asked and had received permission to leave the
island, because, as Balmain reported to Nesselrode on March
18, 1819: "He has been suffering for two years from a liver complaint and does not think he can recover at St. Helena."

The day after his visit to the governor Montholon told Gorrequer that it was his intention to ask Sir Hudson to permit him
to accompany his wife to Europe. He spoke about the daily

arguments he had with Napoleon, who tried to persuade him to remain, at least until someone could be found to replace him. He was to claim that his wife persuaded him to stay, which is more than probable as it is also more than probable that she originated the terms on which he would agree to remain, for she was what Bertrand called "a scheming woman." On June 15 and June 28, 1819, the Emperor signed documents specifying that Montholon was to receive an annual pension of 20,000 francs, payable by Prince Eugene, and an annual pension of 24,000 francs, payable by Napoleon's mother. He received moreover a draft on Joseph for 144,000 francs, and was to continue to draw 2,000 francs a month as long as he remained at St. Helena.

Before Madame Montholon's departure on July 2, the Emperor presented her with a jewel casket the cover of which was adorned with his miniature framed with diamonds, and entrusted her with the curiously wrought ivory chess game Elphinstone had sent him from China, which he bade her to forward to Marie Louise. Lady Lowe invited her and her husband to dinner, and on the day of her departure sent two carriages to take her, her three children, and three servants to the embarking place at Jamestown. Montholon followed on horseback. After she had boarded the ship he sent her a note reading: "The Emperor is desolate at your departure. He wept real tears for you, perhaps for the first time in his life."

SIX

On August 27, 1818, the Duc de Richelieu had sent a letter to the Marquis de Montchenu in which he said that since it was not possible for the commissioner to see Bonaparte personally, he wished him to multiply his meetings with members of Bonaparte's suite, as that was the only way the French government could keep informed about his physical and mental condition. In his report of March 18, 1819, Balmain writes that Richelieu's letter, written in cipher, had been "just received" by Montchenu, and remarks: "If such an order were sent to me, how I should make Mr. Lowe dance!"

Even before he received the letter Montchenu had begun to

seek Montholon's company. In December, 1818, he had a meeting with him during which the general regaled him with utterances supposedly made by Napoleon concerning affairs in France. What he said must have been music to the votary of the *ancien régime*. That Napoleon ever expressed such opinions is highly improbable. Montholon was following in Gourgaud's footsteps in trying to make himself agreeable with an eye on his ultimate return to France.

In May of that year a remarkable change came over Count Balmain. The month before he and the governor had quarreled bitterly about his consorting with Napoleon's generals, and he had told Lowe defiantly to complain about him to the British government if he chose. But, lo! by the middle of June he has become meek and tractable. No longer does he speak in his reports about making Lowe "dance." He writes that his "relations with the British authorities are peaceful and friendly," that he is a frequent visitor at Plantation House, "where they receive me with open arms." That he attends dinners, balls, soirées. He regrets to have to report, however, that he is completely ignorant about what goes on at Longwood, as he no longer sees either Bertrand or Montholon. What had happened? He had fallen in love with Charlotte Johnson, Lowe's elder stepdaughter. He was nearly forty; she was sixteen, blond, blue-eyed, and pretty. It has been claimed that she was poorly educated and a little stupid, but no matter! *Amantes, amentes.* According to Dr. Walter Henry he raved about her and would exclaim: "Look, my dear friend—what a neck!—what an exquisite bust—what a profile!—what an expression!—what an *ensemble* of charms!"

On May 30, 1819, Sir George and Lady Bingham departed for England. The general did not pay a farewell visit to Napoleon. The reason undoubtedly was that on three successive occasions the Emperor had failed to receive him, pleading indisposition. That Bonaparte felt far from well, and indeed believed his end to be approaching, is evident from the fact that in August, 1819, he dictated to Bertrand his last will and testament. All this while no doctor attended him. Montholon had made another attempt to get Verling to become Napoleon's personal physician, this time on the terms that had been proposed to Stokoe, but Lowe had refused to give his consent.

Relations between Longwood and Plantation House became still further strained when Lowe made it known that henceforth when he had anything to communicate he would address his letters not to Count Montholon but to "Napoleon Bonaparte." Napoleon instructed his following not to accept any letter or package not addressed to the "Emperor Napoleon." When Sir Hudson wrote to him concerning the difficulty the orderly officer had in seeing him, and entrusted the letter to Colonel Wynyard to be delivered, the colonel could find no one at Longwood willing to accept it. With Lowe's approval he thereupon issued an order to Nicholls to enter the house by the offices, proceed to whatever room where he believed Napoleon was to be found, and, if unable to enter, deposit the letter "on a table in the room nearest to him that you may be enabled to reach."

Napoleon, however, had taken the necessary precautions. When Nicholls, assisted by one of Lowe's staff officers, tried to enter the house, he found the doors locked. On August 16, the Emperor sent a protest to Sir Hudson, in which he said: "On the 11th, 12th, 13th, 14th, and 16th of August, 1819, attempts have been made for the first time to break into the apartments inhabited by the Emperor Napoleon, which had hitherto been respected. He has resisted these acts of violence by closing the doors and locking them, and thinks fit to repeat a protest already made on several occasions, that no intruder will cross his threshold except over his dead body." He added that any letter introduced into the house without his consent would be thrown unread into the fire. On August 19, Reade pounded on the door leading from Napoleon's private apartment to the garden and shouted "Come out, Napoleon Bonaparte!" but made no attempt to force the door.

5

XXIV. The Newcomers

On September 20, 1819, there arrived at Jamestown what Napoleon's half-uncle Cardinal Fesch was pleased to call a "little caravan," composed of a doctor, two priests, a major-domo, and a cook, to fill the gap in the Emperor's household. The request for a priest and the two servants had been made in March, 1818, and for a doctor a few months later. Why then this delay of over a year? Bathurst had left it to Cardinal Fesch to select the persons desired. Unfortunately, the cardinal and the Emperor's mother harbored the strange illusion that Napoleon was no longer at St. Helena. Prodded by Las Cases he finally made a choice but, in July, 1819, wrote to the former chamberlain: "There can be no doubt that the St. Helena jailer compels Count Bertrand to write to you as if Napoleon were still in custody, but we possess superior certitudes."

What were the "superior certitudes"? Fesch as well as Letizia had fallen under the spell of a German clairvoyant who had assured them that the Virgin appeared to her every night and gave her news about the captive. The woman had told them that the Emperor had been carried off by angels to a secret hiding place, where he was well and happy. That the cardinal—only six years older than Napoleon and apparently in full possession of his mental faculties—should have believed such a tale is extraordinary, but, as he wrote to Las Cases: "Everything in his [Napoleon's] life is miraculous, and I am inclined to believe in still another miracle."

Napoleon had asked for "a French or English civilian doctor of established reputation." A capable French doctor, Foureau de Beauregard, had been willing and even anxious to go. He had been the Emperor's physician at Elba and during the Hundred Days. The Sacred College, however, whose dictates Fesch found it necessary to obey, did not want him to appoint a Frenchman. It was the Vatican's policy to weaken, not to strengthen, Napoleon's ties with France. So the cardinal appointed a young Corsican, Francesco Antommarchi. It was said in those days of St. Andrew's College in Scotland that it "got rich by degrees." The University of Pisa appears to have followed a similar policy. At the age of eighteen Antommarchi had obtained a degree from the university of doctor of philosophy and medicine. He had become assistant to the famous Florentine anatomist Mascagni, under whose guidance he had become expert in dissecting corpses; but his experience as a physician and surgeon was negligible. His character, too, left much to be desired. He was vain, presumptuous, ill-mannered, and of questionable integrity.

Bertrand had asked Cardinal Fesch to send a "well-informed priest under the age of forty." The cardinal had sent two, neither of whom met these requirements. The Abbé Buonavita was a feeble, gouty old man of sixty-six and far from erudite. He had a defect of speech, the result of an apoplectic stroke. He had spent twenty-six years in Mexico as a civil servant and had been Letizia's chaplain at Elba and during the Hundred Days. When asked to go to St. Helena he was chaplain in Pauline's establishment at Rome. His assistant, the Abbé Vignali, was a young Corsican rustic, so poorly informed that he spoke of Alexander the Great as a Roman general. He had begun a course of studies in medicine, which had prompted Cardinal Fesch to write to Las Cases that he would be useful to Napoleon not only as a priest but as a medical consultant! It had been justly remarked that with Vignali to assist him, Antommarchi should have had no difficulty getting Napoleon ready for the dissecting table. However, the Emperor later took a liking to Vignali, who proved devoted and made himself useful in many ways.

Of the two servants, Coursot, who was to have filled Cipriani's place as major-domo, did not even know how to brew coffee. Chandelier, the cook, was a young man of twenty-one who as a boy of fifteen had been assistant to the chef at the Tuileries. Before leaving for St. Helena he had been chef in Pauline's establishment. He was devoted to Napoleon and, when asked if he was willing to go and serve him, replied that he would go anywhere on earth to do so. He was, however, in poor health and frequently unable to attend to his duties. Napoleon was to express the opinion that "it would have been impossible to have made a worse choice than the five persons they sent me."

TWO

It was tactless, to say the least, on the part of the governor to invite Antommarchi and the two priests to dinner at Plantation House before they had had the opportunity to be presented to Napoleon. When the latter learned that they had accepted the invitation he felt annoyed. He received the two servants the day of their arrival but deferred seeing the others until the following day, and then only after they had been questioned by Bertrand and Montholon. Buonavita was the first to be admitted to his presence. He found Napoleon lying in bed and, as Bertrand presented him, went down on one knee and kissed the Emperor's hand. Bonaparte was bitterly disappointed when he saw the decrepit old man. He had been expecting a theologian in the prime of life with whom he would be able to discuss Church doctrine and religion in general. Feeling sorry for the old priest, he hid his disappointment, spoke kindly to him, and inquired about Letizia and other members of his family residing at Rome. He next received Vignali and finally Antommarchi.

Bertrand had already given him an account of the doctor's education and experience, which the latter had presented to him in the most favorable light. His manner and his cocky self-assurance displeased the Emperor, and he later told Bertrand

347

that the very sound of his voice was irritating to him. Antommarchi told him that while in London he had conferred with O'Meara and Stokoe. O'Meara had allowed him to peruse his medical journal, and Stokoe had shown him copies of the medical reports he had submitted to Admiral Plampin. A couple of days later Antommarchi examined the patient and has written that "part of the left lobe of the liver which touches the epigastric region seemed to be hardened, and extremely painful to pressure."

Whatever the shortcomings of the two priests, their presence had a salutary effect upon the household. Their anticipated arrival had decided several of the servants who had been living in concubinage to regularize their relationship by having the Reverend Vernon marry them. Noverraz had married Josephine, Madame de Montholon's former maid; Archambault had married Mary, maid of the Bertrands; Saint-Denis had taken for wife Miss Mary Hall, governess to the Bertrand children. Napoleon, however, had forbidden Marchand to marry Esther Vesey, the mulatto by whom he had had a son. Buonavita gave the unions his blessing. As for Napoleon, he found his zest for life reviving. Buonavita had brought with him everything needful to outfit a chapel and conduct Mass. Every Sunday morning the dining room was transformed into a chapel. The walls were suitably decorated. The sideboard—elevated upon a carpeted platform, covered with a lace-fringed white cloth, and furnished with silver candelabra and vases filled with flowers—served as altar. Fronting it was an armchair and a prayer-stool for the Emperor and, a little farther back, chairs for the grand marshal, Madame Bertrand, and Montholon. Mass was said by Buonavita, assisted by Vignali and twelve-year-old Napoleon Bertrand, who served as choir boy. The whole household attended. There is no record of Napoleon ever having used the prayer-stool. He was in a vague way a deist, skeptical about the historic existence of Christ and a life after death, but he seemed to derive satisfaction from a ceremony familiar to him since childhood, besides finding it politically expedient.

THREE

Notwithstanding his inexperience Antommarchi did more to improve the state of Napoleon's health, at least temporarily, than either O'Meara or Stokoe. Like them he advised exercise on horseback but, finding Napoleon unresponsive, proposed gardening. Montholon seconded the proposal, and the Emperor began to reflect. It meant giving up his hide-and-seek with the orderly officer in the hope of obtaining the removal of Hudson Lowe or his own removal from the island; but he had almost come to the conclusion that that was a lost battle anyway. He decided to follow the advice and, having reached that decision, experienced a remarkable upsurge of energy. He had Marchand draw up plans for the embellishment of the garden, changed them to suit his fancy, and went to work with a will. He secured a large bell, and at six o'clock in the morning would go out into the garden and swing it vigorously. "Immediately upon this signal all the servants turn out to work in the garden," the orderly officer reported. Not only the servants turned out. Bertrand, Montholon, the doctor, the priests, the Bertrand children, all were expected to take part in the horticultural activities. The Emperor, in dressing gown and red morocco slippers, his balding head protected by a broad-brimmed planters' hat, directed the work. "The General was in his morning-gown amidst the people at work directing them," the delighted Captain Nicholls reported. "Takes a spade sometimes and begins to potter—sends messages to me for carts, shovels, and spades. God send he may always continue in this humor during my residence at Longwood!"

What made it possible for Napoleon to carry out his project was that Lowe had a reservoir constructed on Diana's Peak, from which water had been piped to Longwood and to Deadwood Camp. A stone reservoir was now built on the grounds of Longwood House, after which several small ponds were dug. When it was found that they would not retain water, the cooper was sent for and given instructions. On January 20, 1820, Nicholls reported: "This day the one-eyed cooper came up from

Jamestown with a large tub (twelve feet wide) for General Bonaparte's favorite garden. The cooper told me that the General was very much pleased with the tub, and gave him a glass of wine in consequence with his own hand. The old cooper seemed highly delighted." A great variety of flowers was planted; an aviary, a trellis walk, a fountain, a Chinese summer house were constructed. Sod walls were erected in various places to protect the house from the wind and to insure privacy. Napoleon purchased twenty-four large willows which were set up along the avenue. Oaks, orange trees, peach trees, and rose bushes were planted. To what extent his zest for life had revived may be judged from the fact that in March, 1820, which in the austral climate of St. Helena is the pleasantest month of the year, he called a couple of valets, removed his clothes, and dived into the reservoir. Refreshing as this must have been he apparently preferred hot baths, for he did not repeat the experiment.

The governor, vastly relieved, sent soldiers with ox-carts to help in the transplanting, and a wagon-load of garden furniture. He hastened to inform Lord Bathurst of the change that had taken place at Longwood, and his lordship wrote that if Bonaparte wanted seeds or plants from the Cape or Mauritius they would be promptly supplied. Captain Nicholls took advantage of the abatement of the tension, which he feared might not last long, to ask to be relieved. He left Longwood on February 9, 1820, and was replaced by Captain Lutyens.

FOUR

During this time Napoleon indulged in another, less harmless, activity. In his study at Malmaison he had kept a carbine with which he had been in the habit of shooting from the window at birds that came within range. Having now the further incentive of protecting his garden against intruding animals, he indulged himself to the full. In January a goat and two kids belonging to Madame Bertrand strayed into the garden and began nibbling the flowers. He called for his fowling-piece and shot one of the trio. A few days later he shot three hens and the day after a kid belonging to Archambault. When in February he killed three fowls belonging to Noverraz, his "Swiss bear" became so incensed that he went to Plantation House and asked to be allowed to leave the island but was dissuaded by the governor.

In April cattle from the nearby Company farm strayed into the garden where the Emperor and Montholon were taking an evening stroll. The fault was with one of the servants who had left the garden gate open. Napoleon, however, did not stop to consider this. Captain Lutyens reported: "He immediately ordered his two fowling-pieces to be brought, loaded with ball, both of which he fired, and killed one of the oxen. I believe there is another slightly wounded in the leg." Lutyens spoke to Montholon about the danger of firing with ball. What if one of the sentries had been hit? The count explained that the Emperor had taken the precaution of firing toward the house, but was determined to shoot with ball again if cattle strayed into the garden. Lowe wrote to Lord Bathurst asking what action he should take if Bonaparte's shooting proclivity resulted in the death of a person. The matter was submitted to the solicitor general for an opinion.

Napoleon now often breakfasted or dined in the garden with Montholon and in the evening sometimes called at the Bertrands, but refused to receive any visitors. When, on January 25, Lord Charles Somerset, governor of the Cape of Good Hope, came to St. Helena with his two daughters and expressed the desire to be presented to him, Sir Hudson informed Montholon, who relayed the message to the Emperor, but received no reply. The following day Lord Somerset and the two young ladies came to Longwood to have a look at the new house, which was nearing completion. The orderly officer reported to Gorrequer: "Bonaparte was at dinner in the garden under the oak trees with Count Montholon. The governor, Lord Charles Somerset, and the young ladies passed round the garden into the wood. As soon as they were perceived, the General rose from his dinner and ran into the house. The dinner was carried after him. After Lord Charles's party had left Longwood, General Bonaparte immediately came out."

FIVE

On December 31, 1819, Sir Hudson had considerably enlarged the limits within which Napoleon and his generals could ride without being escorted by the orderly officer. Montholon wrote to his wife: "All the territory between Longwood, Francis Plain, Plantation House, and Sandy Bay is now within our limits. This is a voluntary concession on the part of the governor and greatly ameliorates our situation." Sir Hudson, who seemed to have finally realized to what extent his own future depended on Napoleon's survival, did not stop there. Captain Nicholls having informed him that the horses in Napoleon's stable were mostly old and worn out, the pony he had been in the habit of riding was lame, the carriage dilapidated, and the harness poor, he proceeded to remedy the situation. He had Reade send his phaëton to Longwood and wrote to Lord Somerset at the Cape to send four good saddle horses. One of those that arrived was a shapely little horse with crimson housing, which immediately took the Emperor's fancy. But it was not until May 26, 1820, that he decided to make use of it. That day, at six in the morning, he took a leisurely ride within the four mile enclosure, attended by Archambault. After that he frequently went out riding or driving.

In March of that year Count Balmain married Lowe's stepdaughter Charlotte Johnson, and in May they departed for Europe. The Russian government decided not to send anyone to replace him, and the Marquis de Montchenu remained the only representative of England's allies on the island. In June Colonel Wynyard departed, and the following month Admiral Plampin left St. Helena with his inamorata. Plampin's successor, Admiral Robert Lambert, left his card at Longwood, but was not received by the Emperor. In August Brigadier General Pine Coffin arrived to fill the place left vacant by Sir George Bingham. Having leased land, he proceeded to raise poultry and cattle and went into competition with the butcher at Jamestown. Not finding business booming, he billed his subordinate officers for cuts of meat he had sent to them without an order. They avenged themselves by covering the walls at Jamestown with placards informing the public that bargains in meat could be obtained at General Coffin's. The prices quoted on the placards were so tempting that he was swamped with orders. This, together with a warning from the governor, put an end to the enterprise.

SIX

Less than a month after his wife's departure Montholon had written to her: "I await with impatience the arrival of the priests and the doctor the newspapers have been telling us about, and if they turn out to be as expected I'll leave this accursed Longwood." A fortnight later: "I believe that even your first letter will no longer find me here." And on October 31, 1819, after the priests and the doctor had arrived and had been found far from what had been expected: "If you haven't yet sent anybody to replace me, don't lose a moment. It does not matter much whom you send, provided it is one of his former officers, generals, or friends."

Did Madame Montholon really do her utmost to find a successor? There is reason to doubt it. Less than a week after her departure, Basil Jackson, the young lieutenant who had guarded Gourgaud, left for England. Montholon gave him a package of clothing she had overlooked for delivery to her and wrote to her about the matter. On September 8, 1819, she replied: "I have not seen Mr. Jackson, and he has not yet written to me, hence I have no news about you. I know his address and am going to write to him." She was not allowed to remain in England and departed with her children for Brussels. We hear no more about Basil Jackson from Madame Montholon, but a note from Reade to Sir Hudson reads: "A woman who accompanied Madame Montholon to Brussels says Basil Jackson is living in the same house with her."

Three days after Napoleon's death, Reade was to volunteer the information to Madame Bertrand that Basil Jackson had not been a lover of Madame Montholon but was an English spy. It was not for nothing, he said, that they had allowed him to become intimate with the Montholons and sometimes remain at their house until four o'clock in the morning. Jackson, he said, had followed Madame Montholon to England and thence to Brussels because he had been assigned to keep check on her activities.[1]

The news that his wife and Jackson were living in the same house at Brussels might well have reached Montholon's ears. Certain it is that he began to have serious doubts about his wife's zeal to find a successor for him. He wrote her a reproachful letter, to which she replied on June 12, 1820: "I do not deserve this. It is well known that I have been searching these ten months, but nobody has presented himself. I have written to the Princess Borghèse [Pauline] that she, too, should try. I am very sorry that your health might oblige you to leave Longwood, for I know that there you are free from worry, which perhaps might not be the case here."

This is hardly the language of a wife eager to be reunited with her husband. Montholon was right when he wrote to her: "I believe it should be easy for you to find someone. So many unfortunate companions of his past glory are wandering about that it should not be difficult to find quite a number who would consider themselves lucky to spend a few years here in honorable retirement." Colonel Planat de la Faye had been suggested to her before her departure, but she wrote to him only after she had received the count's reproachful letter. He had been one of the officers chosen by Napoleon on the *Bellerophon* to accompany him to St. Helena before Gourgaud's tearful insistence got the Emperor to change his mind. The colonel no sooner received her letter than he wrote: "I hope you have never doubted my unalterable devotion and my resolve to go and share the captivity of the greatest of men." In a letter to her husband, dated October 24, 1820, she makes the excuse that people had advised her not to contact Planat because his health was poor, but that she is now convinced the advice had been prompted by jealousy and intrigue. Yet she waited another couple of months before she

[1] Henri Gratien Bertrand, *Napoleon at St. Helena*. The Journal of General Bertrand. January-May, 1821. Copyright 1952 by Doubleday & Company, Inc. Quotations from the book by permission of the publisher.

wrote to Lord Bathurst asking permission for the colonel to join Napoleon. When it was finally granted, it was too late. If it was not infatuation with Basil Jackson that was responsible for the little effort she put forth to find a successor, then it must have been the fear that Montholon's premature departure might jeopardize the fortune she and her husband hoped to inherit.

SEVEN

Montholon in the meantime left nothing undone to prepare the way for his ultimate return to France. He now often visited Montchenu and made himself agreeable. The marquis, bored to distraction, welcomed his visits, especially since the Duc de Richelieu had written to him: "The King will be grateful to you if you will keep him informed of all the projects and hopes of the inhabitants of Longwood." Not that the information Montholon gave him was of much value. If the count is to be believed Napoleon had become an ultra-royalist, going even so far as to say: "It is a great misfortune for France that my son lives, for he has great rights." When news of the assassination of the King's nephew, the Duc de Berri—whose father, the Comte d'Artois, had had a hand in most of the attempts on Bonaparte's life— reached St. Helena, Montholon told the commissioner that Napoleon had been so shocked as to appear dazed and had repeated over and over again: "Poor France! Poor France!" He had shut himself up in his room and for twenty-four hours had refused to see anyone. The effect of this touching recital was somewhat spoilt by the behavior of young Napoleon Bertrand, who accompanied Montholon on the visit. The boy, looking at a portrait on the wall, asked: "Who is that fatty?" When told that it was the King, he remarked: "He is a great rascal." Then, having read the inscription under an engraved portrait of the Duc de Berri, he exclaimed: "Ah! they got that one! That makes one big rogue less!"

When speaking to the marquis about events in Bonaparte's life, Montholon was careful to call him "the Emperor" only when the event took place prior to 1815; otherwise he referred to him as "Napoleon." To impress the commissioner with his prospective importance, he told him that Napoleon meant to leave him a million pound sterling. When Montchenu expressed his surprise, he blandly assured him that Bonaparte had two hundred million pound sterling on deposit in various European banks, the annual revenue of which amounted to ten million pounds. He had little good to say about Bertrand, who, he claimed, was Napoleon's evil genius. According to him, whenever Napoleon felt inclined to come to an understanding with the governor, Bertrand would say: "Think of your glory, Sire."

Lowe was by no means pleased with the intimacy between Montchenu and Montholon, but having quarreled with Stürmer and with Balmain he thought it unwise to pick a quarrel with the only allied commissioner on the island. When, however, Montchenu informed him that he meant to visit Montholon at Longwood House—which Lowe interpreted to mean that he meant to establish direct contact with Napoleon—he put his foot down. The marquis—whose ego had swelled enormously after the departure of his two colleagues—replied that being ignorant of the English language, he would, when challenged by a sentry on his way to Longwood House, calmly pursue his way, and that if the soldier fired at him "the shot would echo throughout Europe." The governor did not weaken, and Montchenu did not carry out his threat. He did, however, decline Lady Lowe's invitations to dinner and wrote notes to Montholon—which he knew would be read by Sir Hudson—complaining about the insufferable boredom of what went by the name of society at St. Helena. He almost envied Montholon, he said, for living among Frenchmen, who alone understood the requirements of civilized behavior.

The quarrel between the commissioner and the governor lasted well-nigh three months and was considerably more trying to the former than to the latter. Montchenu missed Lady Lowe's dinners as well as her company. Had he not once written her a letter pledging his undying devotion? He finally decided to humble his pride and wrote a letter to the governor in which he said that it was all a misunderstanding and that he felt great respect and friendship for him. Sir Hudson was quite willing to end the feud and promptly invited him to dinner. He moreover thought of an excellent expedient to insure the commissioner's good behavior in the future. He proposed to the marquis that he come and live at Plantation House. Montchenu accepted with alacrity, and henceforth Montholon saw little of him.

XXV. Napoleon's
Fatal Illness

There is no certainty that Napoleon's father, Charles Bonaparte, died of cancer, and modern pathologists consider it practically certain that Napoleon did not. The fact that none of the doctors present at the autopsy noticed any evidence of metastasis—the spreading of the disease to any other bodily organ—virtually rules out the possibility that the peptic ulcer that perforated his pylorus was cancerous.[1] Napoleon, however, had been told that his father had died of cancer and had accepted the statement without questioning. As is common among those who believe themselves afflicted with cancer, he forebore to mention the name of the dread disease; but on November 16, 1819, he told Antommarchi about his father's ailment and asked if it was hereditary. The doctor replied that one could inherit a tendency to a disease, but not the disease itself. From that day on, however,

[1] In a lecture delivered before the Clinical Conference of the Chicago Medical Society, March 6, 1958, Dr. I. S. Ravdin, Professor of Surgery at the University of Pennsylvania School of Medicine, and Surgeon-in-Chief at the University Hospital of Pennsylvania, said: "The most experienced gastrointestinal surgeon is very often unable to tell with accuracy whether the lesion is benign or malignant even after he has exposed and palpated the lesion. Position, size, and the presence or absence of lymphadenopathy, or even induration of the gastric wall surrounding the lesion, frequently cannot create more than suspicion of its true character." (*Chicago Medical Society Bulletin*, September 13, 1958). If in 1958 gastrointestinal surgeons could not tell with accuracy the nature of an exposed lesion, how much less so in Napoleon's time.

358

Napoleon was haunted by the thought that in addition to his liver complaint he was suffering from the disease that had killed his father. From about the middle of October, 1819, to the middle of July of the following year, he felt, however, reasonably well and busied himself with beautifying the garden. But on July 19, Antommarchi wrote in his medical journal: "The Emperor experienced shivering, fever, pain in the head, nausea, dry and frequent coughing, and vomiting of a bilious quality, extremely bitter." It was the prelude to his last and fatal illness.

When the disease was dormant, his zest for life would revive. On the last day of July, 1820, we find him in the garden with the Bertrand children busy transferring goldfish that had arrived from Jamestown into one of the little ponds. This over, he took from his pocket a pair of coral earrings he had found among his effects and asked Hortense if she would not like to wear them. She would very much, she said, but her ears were not pierced. So the doctor was called and came accompanied by Montholon. All retired into the shade of a tree, the count put his arm about the girl, and Antommarchi got ready to operate, using a kitchen skewer as operating instrument. But they had counted without little Arthur, who stamped his feet and yelled that he would not allow his sister to be hurt. He was about to belabor the doctor with his fists when Napoleon caught him, saying: "If you don't behave, you little rascal, I'll have *your* ears pierced too." When the operation was over, the Emperor patted Hortense on the head, said she was a brave little girl, and adorned her ears with the earrings. "There!" he said. "Now go and show your mama, and if she does not like it tell her it wasn't I, but the *dottoracio* that did it."

Napoleon was fond of the Bertrand children, and when their parents spoke of leaving he sometimes wondered if he would not miss the children most. Little Arthur was his favorite. He was a spirited, determined little lad who reminded him of himself when he was a boy. One day little Arthur asked him to give him money so he could buy a Javanese pony, for sale at Jamestown. It cost twelve hundred francs. "Come and see me tomorrow, when the gun fires at noon," Napoleon said. The next day, long before noon, little Arthur sat on the steps of the veranda waiting for the firing of the gun. It had no sooner boomed than he climbed the steps and began kicking the door. Marchand opened and told him to go away and keep quiet: the Emperor was asleep. But he would not go away and would not keep quiet. The Emperor had told him to come "when gon fair" (when the gun fires), he said in his childish prattle.[2] The gun had been fired, and here he was and here he would stay until he had seen the Emperor. Marchand, in desperation, said he would admit him to the Emperor's chamber if he promised not to make any noise. He promised and was given a footstool to sit on. He sat still as a mouse, but the moment the Emperor awakened he ran to the bed and said he had come for the money to buy the pony. Napoleon told him to hold up his little apron and had Marchand put the money into it. The boy went riding nearly every day and never failed to rein in and salute when he saw the Emperor.

Napoleon continued to ride or drive whenever the weather permitted, but he felt far from well. Although by this time he must have known that the main seat of the trouble was in the stomach, he considered it expedient to cling to the theory that it was in the liver and that the climate was to blame. On September 2, he dictated a letter to Lord Liverpool, which Bertrand signed, asking to be permitted to leave the island as its climate was killing him and he needed to partake of mineral waters. Lowe returned the letter because Napoleon was referred to as "the Emperor" and wrote to his friend Thornton at Rio de Janeiro that the epistle had undoubtedly been intended to revive "the attempts which, I surmise, are again likely to be renewed to obtain Public Commiseration toward Bonaparte on account of his health." Yet, if in the past Napoleon had exaggerated his illness, he was not doing so now. He did what he could to combat it. Believing that vigorous exercise on horseback was the most efficacious remedy, he went riding nearly every day, although calculi in his bladder and the pain in his side made such exercise far from pleasant. On September 18, for the first

[2] Having an English mother and an English governess, the boy spoke an English jargon but little French.

time in four years, he made the round of the old limits of Longwood, a distance of twelve miles. He felt exhausted on his return,
but at the beginning of the following month went on another
long ride, this time to Sandy Bay, where he had been once with
Admiral Cockburn.

TWO

On October 4, 1820, soon after sunrise, Napoleon accompanied
by Bertrand, Montholon, and four servants set out on horseback
on the five-mile ride to Sandy Bay. They followed the Jamestown
road as far as the Devil's Punch Bowl, then turned into a lane
leading to the zigzag path that ascends the slope of Diana's Peak.
The summit of the mountain was bare, but the ascent led
through a lush growth of bracken, aloes, cabbage trees, and da-
turas with their large bell-shaped flowers. It was a fine day. Not
a cloud was in the sky. The air was perfumed with a spicy odor
emanating from some of the vegetation. When they had reached
the top, the whole island stretched beneath them on the vast ex-
panse of the sea. Napoleon on his sleek little horse and wearing
his cocked hat, outlined against the sky as he halted to overlook
the landscape, might have been taken for a statue, with the
mountain as its colossal pedestal.

Down below, in a wide fold of the mountains, was a fertile
green valley that sloped gently toward Sandy Bay and the sea.
At its highest point, amidst wide stretches of lawn, stood a cottage known as Mount Pleasant, belonging to Sir William Doveton, a septuagenarian retired member of the council of St.
Helena and one of the most respected citizens of the island. He
was taking his customary morning walk in the garden when he
saw the party of horsemen on the mountain road that zigzagged
toward the valley. He had no difficulty identifying Napoleon by
his green coat and cocked hat. One of the horsemen, who proved
to be Count Montholon, now galloped ahead and, having
reached the garden gate, dismounted and greeted Sir William,
who had gone toward the gate to meet him. Montholon said that
the Emperor presented his compliments and that being fatigued
he would be obliged if Sir William would allow him to rest him-

self at his house. Doveton, who considered it his duty to obey the regulation in the matter of the title, replied that he would feel honored to receive *General Bonaparte* and that his house was at the *General's* disposal. Montholon thanked him, mounted his horse, and rejoined the others. A short time later Napoleon and his two officers dismounted at the gate and were greeted by Doveton who conducted them to the house and ushered them into the drawing room, not without noticing that Napoleon leaned heavily on the grand marshal's arm as he ascended the steps.

The Emperor seated himself on the sofa and, with the assistance of Bertrand who translated what he said into halting English, conversed with their host. Doveton invited Napoleon and his officers to breakfast with him. The Emperor thanked him, but said that they had brought an abundant breakfast along of which they hoped to partake in his garden. Would he not do them the pleasure of breakfasting with them? He accepted, and Montholon left to direct the servants.

One of Doveton's grandchildren, a little girl of about seven, stood at a distance shyly eyeing the Emperor. He smiled and beckoned to her, and encouraged by her grandfather, she came. He took her hand and asked her name and age, then, extracting from his pocket the tortoise-shell box in which he kept the licorice he was in the habit of chewing, he took out a piece and stuck it into her mouth, while holding her nose between thumb and forefinger. She giggled and everybody smiled.

Sir William's daughter, Mrs. Greentree, came into the room carrying a baby in her arms and holding a little girl of about five by the hand. Napoleon rose and, when Sir William had presented her, asked her to sit beside him on the sofa. He tickled the baby under the chin, treated the little girl to a piece of licorice, complimented the mother on her lovely children, and asked about Mr. Greentree—a member of the St. Helena council. After a while Montholon came in and said that breakfast was ready. Napoleon got up, playfully pinched Sir William's ear, and arm in arm with his host went into the garden. Doveton who had contributed freshly made butter, a bottle of orange shrub—a specialty of his daughter—and other delicacies to the repast has written that the table was loaded with a variety of food, such as "cold pie, potted meat, cold turkey, curried fowl, ham or pork, I could not tell which; coffee, dates, almonds, oranges, and a very fine salad." He was given the place of honor on the Emperor's right, and after they had feasted on several of the dishes, Napoleon, with his own hand, filled two tumblers with champagne and they drank each other's health. Then everybody had a glass of Mrs. Greentree's shrub, which the Emperor pronounced excellent. When coffee was being served, he insisted that Mrs. Greentree must join them. She did so, and later headed the procession to the drawing room on Napoleon's arm.

Seated on the sofa with Mrs. Greentree beside him, the Emperor began his customary interrogatory. He asked Sir William the question he was in the habit of asking nearly every Englishman with whom he came into contact: "Do you ever get drunk?" [3] His host replied noncommittally: "I like a glass of wine sometimes." Turning to the young woman Napoleon pursued his inquiry: "How often does your husband get drunk? Once a week?" She laughed and replied: "No."

"Once a fortnight?"

"No."

"Once a month?"

"No, it is some years since I saw him so."

"Bah!" he exclaimed with a wave of the hand, as if feeling that such sobriety was unworthy of an Englishman. His apparent disappointment created general amusement.

Soon after, the visitors departed. Doveton has written: "From every appearance but his pale color, it might be concluded that General Bonaparte was in good health. He seemed as fat and round as a China pig." The appearance was deceiving. When the party reached Hutt's Gate he felt exhausted and saw with relief

[3] "It is little complimentary to our national character at that time that Napoleon so frequently asked the question, and it is humiliating to think that he was often justified in asking it." Forsyth III, p. 245.

that the phaëton was waiting for him. He had to be helped into the carriage, sank back into the seat with a profound sigh, and closed his eyes.

THREE

On October 10, when leaving his bath, Napoleon fainted. He was carried to his bed, and when revived complained of a pain in the side "like the stabbing of a knife" and of a headache. Antommarchi advised the application of a blistering plaster to each arm, but the Emperor would have none of it. Bertrand and Montholon, however, persuaded him to take the doctor's advice, and Antommarchi applied the blisters—but in such a manner as to make it impossible for the patient to bend his arms. When he had left and the Emperor realized his inability even to feed himself, he became angry and sent for him to come and correct this. The servant returned and said that the doctor had gone to Jamestown.

Napoleon had been dissatisfied with Antommarchi from the beginning. For several months the doctor had made his daily visits nonchalantly dressed, until Bertrand finally told him that this had to stop. Marchand had felt obliged to take him aside and tell him that, when speaking of Marshal Bertrand or Count Montholon, he must not say "Bertrand" or "Montholon." "The Emperor may do that, but you should not permit yourself to take that liberty." He was seldom at Longwood when his services were required, but spent most of his time at Jamestown with women of ill repute, getting himself talked about. It was, moreover, becoming increasingly evident that he lacked knowledge and experience. Realizing that if he were to dismiss him it might take a year or more before his successor arrived, the Emperor had restrained himself. This time, however, he lost patience with him; and when late that day Antommarchi came to see him and asked him how he felt, he upbraided him severely for the blundering way in which he had applied the blisters and finished by saying: "You are an ignoramus, and I a worse one for letting myself be treated by you."

His illness continued to have its ups and downs. One day he

felt better, the next day worse. Although the thought that he was suffering from the disease that had killed his father kept intruding, he refused to entertain it—protesting that his stomach had never given him any trouble, that it was the influence of the climate upon the liver that was to blame. Yet Las Cases has written that when he was at St. Helena Napoleon occasionally had had vomiting spells. These now became more and more frequent. He refused to take any medicine but tried salt baths, the water being brought up from the sea in barrels by ox-cart. Montholon told the governor: "You have no idea what a bad patient he is; he is worse than an infant two years old—one can do nothing with him." Lowe remained skeptical, and Antommarchi's behavior fed his incredulity. On November 16, 1820, he wrote to Bathurst: "That General Bonaparte cannot be in any very alarming state of illness is, however, sufficiently obvious from his physician taking daily rides at such a distance as would create a delay of an hour and a half before his assistance could be availed of." Napoleon still went out riding or driving nearly every day—more often the latter, as it was less fatiguing. Montholon accompanied him on the drives, which no longer were at top speed, but at a walking pace. On November 30, the postilion had to stop the carriage thrice for the Emperor to vomit. On December 4, he fainted after the drive.

He spent much time in the garden, sitting by the pond watching the movements of the goldfish. Little Arthur would come and help him feed them. One day when Napoleon came into the garden he found several of the fish floating about dead. The next day more had died. "Everything I love, everything that belongs to me is immediately struck," he remarked sadly. It was found that the paint with which the basin was coated had poisoned them. The remaining fish were saved by being taken from the pond.

Life at Longwood, which had never been cheerful, had become so depressing as to be almost unendurable. The Bertrands, Montholon, most of the servants were longing to leave. Madame Bertrand, whom since the Lyster affair nobody visited, wept and made scenes, declaring that if Bertrand insisted on remaining she would leave with the children. Gentilini, the Elban, left on October 4, the day of the picnic at Sandy Bay. He had implored Montholon for months to get him permission to leave and had gone into fits of weeping. In a letter to his wife dated November 6, 1820, Montholon gives the following melancholy description of existence at Longwood: "All the days here are much the same. At half past eight or nine the Emperor sends for me. I often breakfast with him, that is, if he feels like breakfasting. At half past eleven or twelve he returns to his bed. At one o'clock he receives Bertrand for a longer or shorter period, but seldom for more than two hours, after which the Grand Marshal comes to see me. At three o'clock I dress for the promenade and accompany the Emperor in the carriage, unless Madame Bertrand comes to take my place, which, however, has not happened more than three or four times during the last couple of months. At five the Emperor and I dine together, and I remain with him until nine o'clock. Three fourths of the time he dines in bed. If I leave him before half past nine, I go to the Bertrands for tea and return at half past ten to keep him company. Occasionally he has me called during the night. He has done no work for some time. His health is now so poor that he seldom leaves his bed or his couch. I have great difficulty getting him to go out for a ride or even for a walk in the garden. Horseback tires him so that he has well-nigh given it up. Last week he was very ill and for a couple of days had us greatly worried. Fortunately he is better now, but is extremely weak. He begs you to send him books. They are now his only consolation. He has to be read to, for he has hardly begun reading than his eyes give out."

On December 5, he wrote: "For several days now his stomach has failed to retain anything. His pulse can be felt only with the greatest difficulty. His gums, his lips, his nails are quite discolored. His feet and legs, although wrapped in flannel and hot towels, are ice-cold, as are his hands. I do my utmost to get him to go out into the fresh air every day, which the doctor considers essential. Often, however, it seems to do him more harm than good. When he says, 'There is no more oil in the lamp,' it is unfortunately but too true. I have become altogether a nurse."

The letter reveals the estrangement between Napoleon and the Bertrands, especially Madame Bertrand: "As for Bertrand, he never varies his mode of life. At a fixed hour he presents himself, and appears not to care particularly whether he is or is not received. As for his wife, once in a while she bestirs herself, and then for a month or two we see nothing of her. They are really strange people, absorbed in their egoism to an unbelievable degree. Although their jealousy of me increases daily we manage to get along."

Sir Hudson forwarded Montholon's letter to Bathurst with the comment: "Count Montholon's letter is calculated for effect in Paris." All the same he was worried. He wrote to the count, offering the services of Dr. Archibald Arnott, surgeon of the 20th foot regiment, but received no reply.

Toward the end of December, 1820, news reached Longwood that the Emperor's eldest sister Eliza had died. There had never been any intimacy between them, but her death saddened him. "Eliza has just shown us the way. Death, which seemed to have overlooked our family, now begins to strike it. My time cannot be far off," he mused.

FOUR

At the beginning of the new year the grand marshal called on the Emperor accompanied by Madame Bertrand, who told Napoleon that she had decided to leave St. Helena with her children. Bertrand is vague about the matter in his journal, but acknowledges that "the atmosphere grew somewhat tense." Montholon, present at the scene, wrote to his wife on January 19, 1821: "Beautiful Fanny would not for anything in the world consent to spend another spring on our mournful rock. She wants to spend what is left of her youth gaily in Paris." The Abbé Buonavita, who had suffered another stroke, likewise asked permission to leave. It was promptly granted. He had been of little use to Napoleon, who saw him only at Mass. On January 22, the

Emperor's mounting wrath against Antommarchi exploded, provoked by his frequent absences which were now due to the young doctor's growing interest in Madame Bertrand. He instructed Montholon to inform the governor that he wished the government to send him another doctor.

On January 27, the count had a long interview with Sir Hudson, whom he told that Napoleon had instructed him to request that a doctor and a priest be sent to replace Antommarchi and Buonavita and that successors be found for himself and Bertrand. Napoleon, he said, especially requested that no member of his family be consulted about the choice. He was willing to trust to the judgment of the King's ministers, most of whom had served under him and were acquainted with his habits and disposition. In a memorandum Montholon sent Lowe the following day he said the Emperor had suggested that doctors Desgenettes, Percy, and especially Larrey be consulted in the choice of a physician, and gave the names of some dozen notables who would be acceptable to Napoleon as successors to Bertrand and himself.

When the count had given the Emperor an account of his conversation with the governor, the latter told Antommarchi that he had asked that a doctor be sent to replace him and that he could depart with Buonavita or remain until his successor had arrived. The Corsican replied that he would do the latter.

Upsetting as all this must have been to one in Napoleon's condition, yet during January there was a marked improvement and with it a revival of energy. Having given up riding as too fatiguing, he had a seesaw constructed in the billiard-room with a saddle at one end and a heavy weight at the other. For about a fortnight he mounted the saddle every day and seesawed up and down in the belief that the exercise would do him good. Arthur Bertrand has written that Napoleon would sometimes amuse himself by having his brothers and sister serve as counterweight, and there were shrieks and laughter when with a vigorous upthrust he would send them sprawling on the floor. Montholon, however, was not deceived. He wrote to his wife: "I can't express my thoughts any better than by saying: it is a fire that is slowly going out; now and then it flares up, but this is always followed by a diminution of strength." He was right. The vomiting, which had abated for a while, now racked him several times a day and during the night and was more violent and exhausting. The pain in the side became more acute. His legs swelled and would become so cold that towels heated so Marchand could hardly hold them could not warm them. Unable to sleep at night, he spent most of the day in bed or on the couch. With the Venetian blinds tightly closed and the drapes drawn over them, the room was so dark that those entering had to feel their way.

Montholon, prompted by Antommarchi, who believed it to be essential for the patient to be out in the fresh air a little while every day, usually managed to persuade him to take a drive in the phaëton. Leaning on the count's arm, he would go with wavering steps toward the carriage and would be helped in by Archambault. Montholon would climb in beside him, and the phaëton would advance slowly down the road through the wood. Napoleon would sit slumped in the seat, sunk in somber thought. Sometimes the sound of a trumpet would be wafted toward them from Deadwood Camp, as if to mock the great captain whose trumpets had sounded from Madrid to Moscow.

On March 17, the Abbé Buonavita was to sail for Europe. Lowe had told him that he would send his carriage to take him to Jamestown and came to bid him farewell. He asked about Napoleon, and the old priest said solemnly: "He can't live much longer. If you could only see his face! I tell you this as a man of honor. He is not going to live. Remember what I tell you."

The Emperor was in bed when the abbé came to tell him good-by. They spoke about Napoleon's relatives living in Rome, and the sick man gave him a letter to his sister Pauline. Although dictated by himself it was signed by Montholon, and read, in part: "The Emperor counts upon Your Highness to make his real situation known to some influential Englishmen. He dies without succor on this awful rock. His agonies are frightful." Before leaving the sick room Buonavita went down on one knee and kissed the Emperor's hand. Tears coursed down his withered cheeks as he rejoined Antommarchi whom Napoleon had instructed to accompany him to the place of embarkation.

That day when Marchand helped the Emperor to dress for the daily outing in the carriage, and the latter, on Montholon's arm, went into the garden, he became so ill that the promenade had to be abandoned. In the evening of the 17th of March the count wrote to his wife: "St. Helena is coming to an end. He cannot possibly live much longer. Our doctor pretends that a change of climate might save him. I hope so, but I don't believe it. I have never seen anything more cadaverous than his appearance is at present."

The following day, March 18, 1821, Napoleon took his last drive in the carriage. After that he no longer left the house.

XXVI. Nearing the End

Although the sick man was throwing up nearly everything he ate, Antommarchi prescribed a daily emetic. Napoleon refused to take it, but Bertrand and Montholon joined forces to get him to obey the doctor's orders. He allowed himself to be persuaded and swallowed a dose on three successive days. On March 23, it produced violent convulsions. When the following day Antommarchi urged him to take it again, he cried: "Get out! Swallow it yourself!" Antommarchi, however, was so convinced of the merit of his treatment that he tried to persuade Marchand to put the emetic in a glass of lemonade he was going to serve the Emperor. The valet refused, and news of the matter having reached the Emperor's ears, the doctor received a severe tongue-lashing. He defended himself, saying he had acted in the Emperor's best interest—that by refusing to take the medicine His Majesty was jeopardizing his life. "And what if I am, do I owe you an accounting?" Napoleon retorted. "Don't you know, sir, that for me death would be a heavenly blessing? I will do nothing to hasten its coming, but I care not a straw about prolonging my existence."

That same day he was to say to Bertrand that it would be a great relief for him if he were to die within the next couple of weeks. He remained thoughtful for a while, then added: "I am very glad that I have no religion. I find it a great consolation, as I have no imaginary terrors and no fear of the future."[1]

Yet shortly before his death he was to take steps which made it appear that he still adhered to the faith of his ancestors. It may be that this had political, not religious, significance, but there can be no certainty in the matter. In June, 1816, he had said to Las Cases: "No man can say what his feelings will be when he is approaching the end nor answer for the lucidity of his mind at that awful moment. Who can say with any certainty that I shall not die in the arms of a confessor?" In August, 1817, when Gourgaud—with whom he often discussed religion—remarked that His Majesty might yet finish by being devout, he said with a laugh: "When the body is weakened, the mind ceases to function properly."

TWO

When Lowe had written to Bathurst about Montchenu's desire to visit Montholon at Longwood House—which the governor had interpreted to mean establishing relations with Napoleon himself—his lordship had replied on November 30, 1820, that he had done well to forbid it. "It is impossible," he wrote, "not to feel that the Allied Powers, however cordially united in interests and feelings at the present moment, may, from various circumstances, entertain hereafter different or contradictory political views, even with respect to the detention of General Bonaparte; nor is this less likely to originate in the instance of France than that of any other of the governments which were parties to the Treaty of Paris."

Had Lord Bathurst been able to see what remained of the great Emperor, he would have been less concerned; but Lowe, who still believed that Napoleon was malingering, was disturbed by the letter, which did not reach him until February. A week had now passed since the orderly officer had seen the prisoner. What if his followers were staging an elaborate conspiracy

[1] Bertrand, *op. cit.*, p. 125.

to cover up his escape? Had not the intimacy between Montholon and Montchenu and the latter's desire to visit Longwood House been a warning that something was afoot?

On March 29, Lowe had Reade write to Captain Lutyens: "If General Bonaparte is really so ill as Dr. Antommarchi and Count Montholon have represented him to be, it is an act of humanity on their part to insist upon calling in other medical advice. . . . It is your duty to insist, after what has been said to you of General Bonaparte's illness, upon having an opportunity afforded to you of seeing him, if an English medical person is not admitted to him."

The following day Lowe called on Montholon. He was in a belligerent mood, frowning and speaking in a staccato voice, like the cracking of a whiplash. No Englishman, he said, had seen General Bonaparte for twelve days. He did not doubt Montholon's word, but as a representative of the allied powers he must have certainty. Ships from India were waiting to depart. He had delayed their departure so they might carry a letter from him to his government. Either the orderly officer or an English medical officer must see the General that day or, much as he regretted it, he would have to use force.

"You would batter down the door?"

"Yes."

"That might kill him."

"I must do my duty."

Montholon asked and obtained a delay of twenty-four hours. Early the following morning he told Captain Lutyens that Napoleon was to be transferred from the cot in his bedroom to the one in his study. If the captain would stand by the window of the study he would be able to see him as he entered the room. Lutyens did as he was asked and was able to report to Sir Hudson that he had seen Bonaparte entering the room in his dressing gown, leaning on the arm of Dr. Antommarchi. That same day Bertrand and Montholon managed to prevail upon Napoleon to receive Dr. Arnott.

THREE

Frédéric Masson has written that "Napoleon died without any doctor about him." The eminent historian obviously had no high opinion of the attainments of either Dr. Antommarchi or Dr. Arnott. The former's scant knowledge and experience have already been noted; as for the latter, his reports to Lowe and to Reade leave no doubt that he was either incompetent or that his main concern was to ingratiate himself with the governor. Thus, on April 17, three weeks before Napoleon's death, Arnott reported that he was becoming "more and more confirmed in the opinion that the disease is hypochondriasis. . . . Anything occurring to break the present association of his ideas would doubtless have a good effect. If, for example, a 'seventy-four' was to arrive from England to take him away, I have no doubt he would soon recover. This would put him on his feet directly."

He was to publish his medical reports in 1822, in a volume entitled *An Account of the Last Illness of Napoleon*. A comparison of the reports in the volume with the originals in the Lowe Papers has shown that he made important changes.

Dr. Arnott, a man of fifty, had been educated at Edinburgh, and as a surgeon of the 20th regiment had served in the peninsular and the Egyptian campaigns. He made his first visit to Napoleon on April 1, 1821, at nine o'clock in the evening, accompanied by Dr. Antommarchi. Only a ghost of light from a shaded candelabrum in the adjoining chamber penetrated into the sick room. He has written: "The room was dark, so that I could not see him, but I felt him or *someone else*. I felt his pulse and state of skin. I perceived there was considerable debility, but nothing that indicated immediate danger."

At nine o'clock the following morning he called again, accompanied by Bertrand, who was to serve as interpreter, and by Antommarchi. Napoleon replied readily enough to the questions Arnott put to him, told him about the pain in the side, and gave him an invaluable hint by asking if the trouble might not be in the pylorus. His father, he said, had died at thirty-five from a tumor in that organ. Arnott, having palpated that part of his body, declared with assurance that there was nothing wrong with the pylorus or with the liver, that he was suffering from an "infection of the stomach," and that the pain was caused by "gas in the intestines." He prescribed a purgative pill, and it was agreed that he was to call every morning at nine and every afternoon at four, together with Dr. Antommarchi.

On April 6, when Napoleon had been under Arnott's care for nearly a week, Reade reported to Lowe: "From what I could learn generally, out of Dr. Arnott's conversation, he appears to think that General Bonaparte is not afflicted with any serious complaint, probably more mental than any other. Count Bertrand has asked him his opinion of General Bonaparte: he told him that he saw no danger whatever." If this was not what Walter Pater would have termed "sapient, instructed, shrewdly ascertaining ignorance," then it must have been servile desire to please the governor. Even Forsyth admits that it was "certainly strange."

FOUR

In the early morning of the 9th of April a scene took place in the sick room that did Napoleon little credit. Toward the end of January Madame Bertrand had had a miscarriage. Dr. Livingstone had taken care of her, assisted by Antommarchi. Since then the young Corsican had been frequently calling on her. That a liaison existed between them is highly improbable, but Napoleon appears to have thought so and to have resented it— his own advances after the departure of Madame Montholon having proved fruitless. His burst of temper on this particular morning must be ascribed to this, as it cannot be said that at that time Antommarchi had been neglectful of his duties.

In the evening of the 8th Napoleon had been quite ill, and at eleven o'clock Antommarchi was sent for. He remained until midnight and got the Emperor to swallow a pill and a dose of quinine. At one o'clock he had been called again, remaining until two. An hour later he was sent for a third time and did not leave until four. When at half past seven in the morning he entered the sick room, Napoleon received him with invectives. Now

375

that he was ill, he said, it was the doctor's duty to be at his bedside at six in the morning, not spend his time with Madame Bertrand. He ordered Marchand to call the grand marshal, whom he told in the presence of the doctor and the valet that all Antommarchi was interested in was whores, that Madame Bertrand was a whore, that he had made his will and had left Antommarchi twenty francs to buy a rope to hang himself with. At that point the doctor left the room, but the tirade continued. Antommarchi, he said, was Madame Bertrand's lover, which was as dishonorable to the grand marshal, as it was to her. Bertrand must tell Montholon that henceforth Arnott alone was to be his doctor. He was finished with Antommarchi.

That day the grand marshal and Montholon remonstrated with Antommarchi, urging him to devote himself entirely to the Emperor's care. He replied that he was not a nurse and could not properly function as a physician if he did what the Emperor demanded. He had, he said, decided to leave the island and was going to Plantation House to obtain the governor's permission.

He did, indeed, go to Plantation House and was received by Major Gorrequer who told him that the governor was at the Castle. When informed of the purpose of the visit, he offered to accompany him there. Arrived at the Castle at Jamestown, Antommarchi told the governor that he found he could be of no further service to Napoleon and had decided to leave. Lowe expressed his regret that he should think of doing so at a time when his and Dr. Arnott's combined efforts promised to be beneficial to Bonaparte. Anyway, he would have to submit the matter to his government before granting him permission to leave.

Antommarchi gave Bertrand an untruthful account of his visit to the governor, who, he said, had fully approved the step he meant to take and had promised to facilitate his departure. That evening Bertrand communicated this to Napoleon, pointing out moreover that the doctor had been called three times during the night, had had hardly any sleep, and that his Chinese servant had neglected to wake him. This, together with the fact that, as usual, Napoleon regretted having lost his temper brought about a reconciliation. On April 11, he sent for Antommarchi

and asked his opinion about medicaments Arnott had prescribed. Four days later Antommarchi moved his bed into the
library so as to be on hand when needed during the night.

FIVE

Great men often have great faults, but are rarely petty or mean.
Those qualities belong to men inherently shoddy. Few incidents
that took place at St. Helena are as revealing of Sir Hudson
Lowe's character as the one that had its beginning on April 13.

That day, when the doctors called at four o'clock, they found
Napoleon in a talkative mood. He castigated the ruling class of
Europe, that of England in particular. Then he spoke of the
Duke of Marlborough for whom he professed profound admiration. He considered him a farsighted statesman as well as a great
general. The previous October, the Honorable Robert Spencer,
a member of the liberal opposition, had visited St. Helena on
his way to England from India. Napoleon being too ill to receive
him, he had left with Bertrand a richly bound, inscribed copy
of Coxe's *Life of Marlborough*, which he asked the grand marshal to present to Napoleon with his compliments. The Emperor
now had Marchand fetch the two-volume work from the library
and handed it to Dr. Arnott with the words: "Here, doctor. I am
giving you this book to be placed in the library of the 20th regiment. I want them to know that I honor the brave men of all
nations."

Dr. Arnott expressed his appreciation but thought it prudent
to leave the book with Captain Lutyens, especially as he noticed
that *L'Empereur Napoleon* was written on the title page—Ali
being in the habit of putting that inscription on all books in the
library. Captain Lutyens sent the book to Major Jackson, his
commanding officer, so he might take the matter up with Sir
Hudson. On April 15, Lowe wrote to Arnott: "The attempt to
make you the channel of communication in such matters, *they
well know*, is foreign to your professional duties, and it will probably, therefore, not have been made without some ulterior design in view." He at the same time instructed Major Jackson to
order Captain Lutyens to return the book to Montholon.

Lutyens resigned in protest, but was commanded to carry out the order. When Montholon asked him for an explanation, he replied that he had been forbidden, on pain of court-martial for himself and Dr. Arnott, to discuss the matter. Then, however, unable to restrain himself, he burst out: "What a cowardly business! The wretch! To rebuff a dying man in that fashion!" [2]

Napoleon was told nothing about the incident. When he asked Dr. Arnott if the officers of the 20th were pleased with the book, the doctor managed to turn the conversation. Captain William Crokat was appointed orderly officer and took office on April 26. Napoleon had Montholon write a letter to Captain Lutyens, thanking him for the manner in which he had conducted himself during his residence at Longwood and expressing the hope that he might see him again when his health had improved.

This, however, was not the end of the matter. The indignation of the officers of the 20th regiment, when they learned the facts, was profound. After Napoleon's death they demanded that the book be restored to them. Lord Holland, speaking in the House of Lords, supported their demand. "Dr. Arnott," he said, "was ordered to return the book, first because it had not been transmitted through the Government House, and, secondly, because it was in the name of the Emperor Napoleon and not of *General Bonaparte*. Pitiful, narrow-minded malignity, disgraceful alike to the government and its agents." The Duke of York hastened to authorize Sir William Houston, colonel of the 20th regiment, to accept the book from the hands of Count Montholon.

SIX

On April 10, Napoleon had mentioned to Montholon that he believed the time had come for him to make his will. He had made a will in August, 1819, and had entrusted it to Bertrand, but was no longer satisfied with it. Bertrand had lost much of his good will; Montholon and Marchand had gained. He sent Marchand to the grand marshal's house to fetch the document, glanced through it, then tore it in two and told the valet to throw it into the fire.

[2] Bertrand, *op. cit.*

On April 13, and again the following day, he locked himself up with Montholon and dictated to him for several hours. On the 15th, sitting up in bed and using a sheet of cardboard for a desk, he had the count read to him slowly what he had written and wrote the will with his own hand, taking care to make his handwriting more legible than usual. The five main clauses of the first part of the will read as follows:

"1. I die in the Catholic Apostolic Roman religion, in which I was born more than fifty years ago."

As he was then yet entirely lucid this must have been a political move. We know that he was doubtful about the historical existence of Christ and, only a little more than two weeks before, had told Bertrand that he had no religion, hence no imaginary terror of the future.

"2. I desire that my ashes should repose on the banks of the Seine, in the midst of the French people whom I have loved so well."

Although as a very young man he had been a Corsican patriot and had said that he would do France all the harm he could, that time was long since past. France had been good to him, and he had genuinely loved his soldiers. It was the secret of his success, for love begets love. They had fought and died for him even more than for France.

"3. I have always had reason to be pleased with my dear wife Marie Louise, and retain for her to my last moments the most tender sentiments. I beseech her to watch in order to preserve my son from the snares which yet environ his infancy."

While still at Elba he had learned that she had become the mistress of Count Neipperg, whom she was to marry a few months after his death. Throughout his captivity at Elba and at St. Helena she had never communicated with him although opportunities had not been lacking. But she was the mother of his son, and appearances had to be preserved.

"4. I recommend to my son never to forget that he was born a French prince, and never to allow himself to become an instrument in the hands of the triumvirs who oppress the nations of Europe. He should never fight against France, nor injure her in

379

any way. He should adopt my motto: 'Everything for the French people.'"

The Duke of Reichstadt, who was then ten and was to die at twenty-one, might have been born a French prince, but remained one only in Rostand's *L'Aiglon*. So thoroughgoing an Austrian prince did he become that when visiting the battlefield of Wagram, he was to say to a companion: "Here we were; there the enemy"—the "enemy" being his father.

"5. I die prematurely, murdered by the English oligarchy and its hired assassin. The people of England will not fail to avenge me."

There were three other clauses in the first part of the will. In the sixth clause he charged Marmont, Augereau, Talleyrand, and Lafayette with responsibility for the success of the allies during the invasions of 1814 and 1815. In the seventh he thanked the members of his family for the interest they had shown in him during his captivity, and forgave his brother Louis for the "libel" he had published about him. In the final clause he disavowed the authorship of certain books, supposedly written by him, published during his captivity.

On April 26, when Bertrand translated for him an article in an English newspaper charging Caulaincourt and Savary with responsibility for the death of the Duc d'Enghien, he added the following to the eighth clause: "I caused the Duc d'Enghien to be arrested and tried because that step was essential to the safety and honor of the French people, when the Comte d'Artois was maintaining, as he himself admitted, sixty assassins in Paris. Under similar circumstances I would act in the same way."

SEVEN

Napoleon left no money to his wife, to his son, or to any member of his family, as he knew that they had no need of it. He bequeathed to his son his personal belongings, with the exception of a few that were to go to Letizia, to Cardinal Fesch, and to his brothers and sisters. Among the articles his son was to inherit were his silverware and Sèvres china, of which Marchand had made an inventory; the sword he had worn at Aboukir and the one he wore at Austerlitz; the sword of Sobieski; one of each of his uniforms; the alarm watch of Frederick the Great; four hundred books from his library; and three mahogany caskets —which he himself tied with green ribbon and sealed—containing his collection of snuff-boxes, orders, miniatures, bonbonnières, and other objects of value. A gold snuff-box decorated with a cameo—a present from Pope Pius VI—he left to Lady Holland, together with a note, written in his own hand, reading: *"Napoléon à Lady Holland: témoignage d'estime et d'affection."* The articles intended for his son he apportioned among Bertrand, Montholon, and Marchand, who were to turn them over to him when he had reached the age of sixteen.

He believed himself to be far richer than he was, being under the impression that the deposit at Laffite's, together with the interest, amounted to six million francs. As a matter of fact there remained only 3,140,000 francs, but it was six million he proceeded to apportion among the legatees. Montholon was to receive 2,000,000 francs; Bertrand 500,000; Marchand—about whom he said that he regarded him as a friend rather than as a domestic—400,000. Vignali, Ali, Noverraz, and Pierron 100,000 each; Archambault 50,000; Coursot and Chandelier, 25,000 each. Antommarchi and Gourgaud were not mentioned, but to Las Cases he willed 100,000 francs. There were twenty legacies of 100,000 francs each to various generals and to the offspring of such as had died in battle or who, like Labédoyère, had died before a firing squad. The remainder was to be divided among those who had been wounded at Ligny or at Waterloo or had been with him at Elba. He told Marchand that his hair was to be shaved after his death and fashioned into a watch chain for his son and bracelets for members of his family.

During the succeeding days he was to write a number of codicils. The first formally invested his three executors—Montholon (chief testamentary executor), Bertrand, and Marchand with all his belongings at St. Helena, and again expressed the desire to be buried on the bank of the Seine. This codicil, intended to keep his belongings from falling into the hands of the British, was to be shown to the governor. Thereafter Napoleon gave his

imagination full scope, making numerous bequests from property of which it was no longer in his power to dispose—his private domain in France, which he valued at two hundred million
francs; his private domain in Italy, valued at two million; and
two million francs in specie Marie Louise had taken with her to
Austria. Some of the bequests were made to individuals, others
to towns or parts of France that had suffered from the two allied invasions. He bequeathed ten thousand francs to Cantillon,
a subaltern officer who had been tried for an attempt to assassinate Wellington but had been acquitted. "Cantillon," he wrote,
"had as much right to assassinate that oligarch as the latter had
to send me to perish upon the rock of St. Helena." Dr. Arnott
was to be paid 12,000 francs in gold out of the 300,000 francs
that had been hidden from the British when the baggage was
searched on the *Bellerophon*. In addition to this he was to be
given a gold snuff-box. There being no monogram engraved
upon the shield in the center of the snuff-box, he laboriously
scratched an N upon it with a penknife. "I don't know how good
a doctor he is, but he has a manner," he remarked. The remainder of the gold he divided among his followers. When all these
arrangements were completed, he said to Montholon: "Well,
my son, wouldn't it be a pity not to die when one has put one's
affairs in such good order?" [3]

[3] The commission appointed to distribute the bequests paid the servants
nearly in full; the others received about half. When Louis Napoleon became
Emperor of France an appropriation of ten million francs made it possible
to pay the individual heirs or their descendants in full, and to distribute four
million francs among the collective legatees.

XXVII. Death

On April 16, Napoleon allowed himself to be persuaded to move to the drawing room, larger and more airy than either his study or his bedroom. The following morning he got out of bed and sat down in his favorite armchair, while one of the camp-beds was taken to the drawing room and placed against the wall between the two windows. The grand marshal and Marchand then took hold of the arms of the chair to carry him to the room he was expected to occupy, but he waved them aside. "No! No!" he said. "You will carry me when I am dead; now you need only support me."

That same day Montholon told Captain Lutyens that he did not believe Napoleon had more than two or three weeks to live. He was making preparations to leave the island and sent his servant to Jamestown to inquire where a large trunk could be obtained. On April 20, he wrote to his wife that he expected to join her soon, but that, unfortunately, their longed-for reunion would be the result of the death of a man who, of late, had demonstrated his boundless friendship for him—an allusion to the two million francs he was to inherit. Others, too, were preparing their departure. Madame Bertrand was looking about for a maid to take with her to Europe.

Napoleon had no illusions about his chances for recovery any more than about the disinterestedness of those who were taking care of him, with the possible exception of Marchand. On April 17, he told Dr. Arnott that it was evident medical science could do nothing for him as day by day he felt himself growing weaker. Arnott replied that he had seen many patients in a far weaker state who had recovered. "You must therefore not lose hope," he added.

"Stuff and nonsense!" Napoleon replied with a touch of impatience. "Tell such things to women and children, but to a soldier like me you should tell the truth." [1]

A few days later, when Bertrand complained to him about the favoritism he was showing to Montholon while refusing to receive Madame Bertrand, he said: "I am fully aware that Montholon pays court to me for the sake of what he may inherit, but I have neither wife nor child and must have someone to be fond of me." The pathetic statement recalls the middle-aged woman Balzac tells about in one of his letters who said to the young man who was courting her for her money: "I only ask that you deceive me so completely that I may be able to believe myself beloved."

TWO

Ever since he had been at Longwood Napoleon had demanded that the Venetian blinds be kept lowered and closed. Now he wanted them raised and the windows wide open. In the morning he would have his armchair placed by the window, and when he had been helped into the chair and his legs had been covered with a woolen blanket, he would look up at the sun and say: "Good morning, sun; good morning, my friend." [2] He had said once to Gourgaud: "If I were to choose a religion I think I should become a worshiper of the sun. The sun gives to all things life and fertility. It is the true god of the earth."

On April 21 he sent for the Abbé Vignali and asked him: "Do you know what a *chapelle ardente* is?"

"Yes, Sire."

"Did you ever officiate in one?"

[1] Bertrand, *op. cit.*
[2] *Ibid.*

"No, Sire."

"Well, you will officiate in mine. Every day you will say Mass in the adjoining room. You will expose the Blessed Sacrament, and you will say the prayers of the forty hours. After my death you will place the altar against the wall behind the bed and will continue to celebrate Mass, with all the customary rites. You will continue to do so until I am buried."

Antommarchi, standing at the foot of the bed, smiled sarcastically. The Emperor noticed it and said: "I'm getting tired of your foolish conduct, sir. I can forgive your frivolity and your lack of tact, but not your lack of heart. Leave the room."

The following day he told Bertrand that if the governor would not permit his body to be taken to France, he wished to be buried in Geranium Valley, near the spring from which his drinking water came. He spoke about Antommarchi and said that he would gladly have left him 200,000 francs, but had not done so because of the young doctor's lack of heart and not because of his lack of ability. Then he added: "However, this can still be changed. There is still time to make another codicil."

On April 23, when alone with Marchand, he was examining the contents of one of the mahogany caskets before tying it with a green ribbon and sealing it. He picked up the girdle with the diamond necklace Hortense had given him and handed it to the young man with the words: "Take this; I don't know the state of my affairs in Europe. Good Hortense has given it to me, thinking it might be useful to me. I believe it to be worth 200,000 francs. When you arrive in France it will enable you to live in comfort until you receive the legacy I have left you."

That same day Arnott made a report to Lowe about the Emperor's condition. He said he felt confirmed in his opinion that Napoleon was suffering from "hypochondriasis, having many dyspeptic symptoms." The cure, he said, would be a tedious one, as he could not give him "that which would set him right." Asked what it was he could not give him, he dramatically replied: "Liberty!" He assured the governor, however, that he "saw no symptom of danger about him."

THREE

On April 26, Napoleon complained of pain in the pylorus and kept saying in English: "Drink! Drink! Drink!" Marchand was kept busy bringing him orange-flower water. Madame Bertrand came, but he declined to receive her, telling Montholon that he could not forgive her for having refused to be his mistress but would see her before he died.

That same day Montholon received a note from Sir Hudson, offering the services of Dr. Thomas Shortt, chief medical officer on the island, as consultant. Dr. Shortt had arrived at St. Helena in December of the previous year to take the place of Dr. Baxter. Lady Lowe was to say to Madame Bertrand that he was "the most capable man to have reached the island since she herself had arrived in it, not excepting Dr. Baxter." He was, indeed, a man of parts in his profession, and in 1819 had been appointed "physician extraordinary" to the King of Scotland. But knowing that Shortt looked after the health of the governor and his family, Napoleon rejected the offer of his services.

On the 27th he dictated the following letter to Montholon, which the count was to sign and send to the governor after his death:

MONSIEUR LE GOUVERNEUR,

I have the honor to inform you that the Emperor Napoleon died the . . . after a long and painful illness.

I have been authorized by him to communicate his last wishes to you, if you desire to know them. I beg you to inform me of the arrangements, prescribed by your government for the transportation of his remains to France, as well as those concerning the persons of his suite.

On the 28th Lady Lowe called on Madame Bertrand and told her she wanted her to know that she had had no responsibility whatever for any of the measures the governor had taken regarding Napoleon and his suite, in fact had had no knowledge of them until long after they were put into effect. Whenever Reade called to confer with Sir Hudson she had always been asked to leave the room, unless the two men retired to the governor's study. Then, with tears of compassion in her eyes, she remarked: "It is painful to see such a great man die under such miserable circumstances." [3]

That evening Napoleon summoned Antommarchi and said: "After my death, which cannot be far off, I desire that you open my body. I prefer that no English medical man should touch it, but if assistance is indispensable you will ask Dr. Arnott to aid you. You will remove my heart, place it in a silver vessel, in spirits of wine, and deliver it to the Empress at Parma. I particularly wish that you carefully examine the stomach and make a precise and detailed report of your findings. This you will likewise give to the Empress for my son. I am inclined to believe that I am dying of the disease that killed my father—schirrosis of the pylorus—and the report might enable the doctors to take measures that will save my son from a similar fate."

FOUR

In the morning of the 29th Dr. Arnott told Napoleon he considered it his duty to inform him that his condition was serious, and that if there were any arrangements he wished to make he should do so now. The Emperor's hearing had become so impaired that Bertrand had to shout when he translated the words. Even then the patient did not grasp their meaning, for he was losing his hold on reality. He asked if he had not gone out for a walk in the garden that morning and, when told that he had not, said with a puzzled expression: "That's strange." Then he asked for coffee and, when told that the doctors would not permit it, begged for it again and again. Bertrand wrote in his journal: "At other periods during his illness he had sent his doctors to the devil and had done as he pleased. But now he was as docile as a child. That was what the Great Napoleon had become, a humble and unhappy man." [4]

On May 1, he finally consented to receive Madame Bertrand. She had been coming to the house every day in the hope of be-

[3] *Ibid.*
[4] *Ibid.*

ing admitted to his presence, but he had always declined to see her. Bertrand had told him that she begged for the privilege of nursing him, but he had replied that it was unnecessary, that he was used to Marchand and Montholon. That day, however, when she came in the morning, a little after ten, he said he would receive her. He had not shaved for several days and his face was covered with stubble, so that she hardly knew him. He said: "Good morning, *Madame la Maréchale*," and she noticed how his voice had changed. He motioned her to an armchair at the foot of the bed and said: "You are well now, aren't you? The doctors knew what was the matter with you, so they cured you; but they don't know what is the matter with me." He asked about the children, then spoke about inconsequential things: which did she think was better, the water from Diana's Peak or from the spring? Then he fell silent and after a while said: "Go, *Madame la Maréchale*." She said, "Yes, Sire," rose, curtsied, and left the room. When the door had closed behind her she burst into tears.

FIVE

On April 30, 1817, Napoleon had said to Gourgaud: "Only a fool would say that when he is on his deathbed he will not want a confessor. There are so many things we don't understand, we can't explain." For various reasons, some political, some sentimental, he had told the Abbé Vignali that he wanted him to administer extreme unction to him. Soon after Madame Bertrand had left, the altar was set up against the wall, back of the bed, and Napoleon remained alone with the priest. When Bertrand heard about this he felt annoyed. He told Montholon that it would be better to say the Emperor had expressed the wish to receive communion, but had lost consciousness sooner than had been expected. On May 3, he was to say to Vignali that he could come and see the Emperor whenever he wished, but should not remain constantly with him and should even make it a point "of showing himself to the English, so that ill-wishers, slanderers, and enemies of the Emperor should not be able to say—as he knew it had already been said on the island—that the Emperor, that strong man, was dying like a monk with the priest always in attendance." [5]

On May 2, at half past two in the morning, he awoke suddenly, sat up in bed, eyes wild, and said he wanted to go for a walk. He managed to get out of bed, stood up, and would have fallen had not Montholon and Vignali seized him by the arms. Bertrand ran to wake the doctor. Napoleon struggled for a moment, then seized by an agonizing cramp, fell back on the bed, crying: "My God! My God! My God!" Vignali knelt down and prayed. Marchand, Ali, Bertrand, and Antommarchi came rushing into the room. He was put to bed, and after a while he calmed down, and his breathing became less labored. At five o'clock Dr. Arnott came, noted that the patient's pulse was 108, and expressed the opinion that the end was near.

On May 3, Napoleon's weakness was such that when given something to drink, the glass had to be held to his lips. He would take a few sips of sweetened orange-flower water or sweetened wine and say: "*Bon, bon,*" then, in English: "Good, very good," with a look that wrung the heart.

That day a disagreement arose between the two doctors. The patient had had no bowel movement for three days, and Arnott proposed that he should be given an enema. Antommarchi opposed this, saying the Emperor was too weak. Arnott replied that he must insist, for the sake of the patient as well as "for the sake of my own reputation." Antommarchi remained firm. The orderly officer semaphored news of the disagreement to Plantation House, and toward half past two in the afternoon the governor and Major Gorrequer came on horseback to confer with Montholon. The governor said that he had felt right along that Dr. Shortt and Dr. Mitchell, surgeon on the admiral's flagship, should be given an opportunity to examine the patient, but had not wished to insist. Now that the attending physicians disagreed, he felt they should be consulted. Montholon replied that it had been extremely difficult to get Napoleon to consent to receive Dr. Arnott. To force two more English doctors upon him might bring on a crisis. Dr. Arnott, he said, agreed with him. In the

[5] *Ibid.*

end it was decided that Drs. Shortt and Mitchell should hold
themselves in readiness at Alarm House and should be summoned when, as had happened on several occasions, Napoleon
was only semi-conscious and did not know what went on
around him.

SIX

For several days the sky had been overcast. On the morning of
the 4th of May masses of dark clouds rolled in from the sea and
the rain fell in torrents. A violent squall swept over the plateau,
uprooting trees and flattening the rain against the windows.

Napoleon did not seem to notice. He lay motionless, his hands
on his breast, fingers intertwined. Every little while Marchand
or Montholon held a cup of beef-tea or a glass of orange-flower
water to his lips, and he would take a few sips. Sometimes he
closed his eyes and seemed to be slumbering. Once, when he
opened them, seeing Madame Bertrand sitting in an armchair at
the foot of the bed, he said: "Madame Bertrand. Oh!" The grand
marshal has written that his expression was full of pity. No doubt,
with death so near, he felt sorry for her, sorry for himself, sorry
for all mankind. "Who was ever born, not excepting Job, who did
not die in despair," Columbus has written.

At nine o'clock that evening Dr. Arnott reported to the governor: "I have just left our patient fast asleep. He appears better
than he was two hours ago. He has no hiccup, his respiration is
easy."

One of the charges against Dr. Stokoe had been that in some
of his reports he had referred to Napoleon as "the patient" instead of as "General Bonaparte"; but now Lowe was too preoc-
cupied with what his own fate would be after Napoleon's demise
to pay attention to Arnott's peccadillo. He made arrangements
for Drs. Shortt and Mitchell to remain at the new house overnight—the house which Napoleon had said it would take six
years to build and which, he had predicted, he would never occupy.

That night Bertrand, Montholon, Vignali, Marchand, and Ali
slept as best they could—some in the sick room, some in the ad-

joining chamber. Hiccups and fits of vomiting kept the Emperor awake most of the night. At about five in the morning, while lying with eyes closed, he suddenly opened them and said: 'Who retreats?" and then: "At the head of the army." [6] After that he spoke no more.

Antommarchi came at daybreak and felt his pulse, which was barely perceptible. The storm had subsided during the night. The window draperies were drawn aside and sunlight streamed into the room. In the billiard-room the windows were opened and one could hear the cooing of pigeons and the chirping of other birds. Dr. Arnott came toward seven o'clock. He, too, felt the Emperor's pulse, listened to his breathing, accompanied now and then by a low moaning, and sent a penciled note to the governor reading: "He is dying. Montholon prays I will not leave the bedside. He wishes I should see him breathe his last."

The bed was now turned away from the wall to face the fireplace, so as to enable more of the suite to gather around it. One after another the servants drifted into the room. Noverraz, who had been ill for weeks with dysentery, looked pale and haggard as he leaned against the wall beside his wife Josephine. Madame Bertrand had come at seven in the morning and an armchair had been placed at the foot of the bed for her to sit in. In the afternoon all four of her children came and clustered around her.

Napoleon lay motionless, his eyes half closed, only the whites showing. The two doctors, standing on either side of the bed, from time to time felt his pulse—either by taking hold of his wrist or by placing their fingers against the side of his neck. At one time a tear coursed slowly from the corner of his left eye to his ear and was wiped away by Bertrand.

The governor had started early for Longwood and had been met on the way by a dragoon who had handed him Dr. Arnott's note. He established himself in the new house, where he found Drs. Shortt and Mitchell. At three o'clock he received a

---

[6] This is Bertrand's version. According to Montholon his last words were: "France—l'armée, tête d'armée—Joséphine." According to Marchand: "France—mon fils—armée."

second note from Arnott, reading: "The pulse cannot be felt at the wrist now, and the heat is departing from the surface. But he may hold out some hours yet."

In the sick room nobody spoke. It was so still that one could hear the ticking of the clock on the mantel. At 5:15 Dr. Arnott sent a third note to Lowe, reading: "He is worse. The respiration has become more hurried and difficult."

The sun was setting. A few wisps of rose-hued cloud hung motionless above High Knoll. At 5:40, when the sun sank below the horizon, came the sudden darkness of the tropics and the cannon at Alarm House boomed. The faces of those gathered around the bed were barely distinguishable. Antommarchi bent over and put his ear to the Emperor's breast. When he straightened up again he closed Napoleon's eyes without saying a word. It was forty-nine minutes after five. Dr. Arnott sent a note to the governor, reading: "He has this moment expired."

XXVIII. Autopsy
and Funeral

A servant had brought a candelabrum with lighted candles into the room just before Antommarchi closed the Emperor's eyes. All saw and understood. The women sobbed; few of the men could withhold their tears; even Dr. Arnott wiped his eyes. Bertrand knelt down by the bed on one knee, took the Emperor's small white hand in his, and pressed his lips against it. Montholon, Marchand, and each of the servants followed his example, then the women and the children.

Lowe received Dr. Arnott's note at six o'clock and hurried to Longwood House with Drs. Shortt and Mitchell. He asked to see the deceased, but Montholon persuaded him to wait until the following morning when the body had been washed and laid out. He consented, but insisted that the two doctors be admitted to confirm Napoleon's passing, and instructed Dr. Arnott to remain with the body until midnight, when a colleague would relieve him.

Six hours later the Emperor had been shaved and his body washed with a mixture of water and *eau de Cologne*. He was laid out on the camp-bed and covered with a white sheet, only the face and the throat showing. On his breast Vignali had placed a silver cross, a present from Letizia. On either side of the bed stood a small table on which a silver candelabrum with lighted candles had been placed. Looking at the dead man one

✓ might have been awed by the thought that a miracle had occurred, for on the bed lay not the aging prisoner of fifty-two but
a young man of thirty—the Napoleon of the Consulate—hand-
somer in death than he had ever been in life. Not a touch of
gray in the silken brown hair, not a suggestion of a wrinkle in
the classical features! The lips, slightly contracted, seemed to
smile, as if the dead man were amused at the joke he was playing
on his captors by his metamorphosis. Dr. Shortt was to write to a
friend: "His face was in death the most beautiful I ever beheld,
exhibiting softness and every good expression in the highest
degree, and really seemed formed to conquer."

At seven in the morning of the 6th of May the governor came
with his staff and a numerous retinue—Admiral Lambert, General Coffin, and their staffs; the Marquis de Montchenu and his
secretary de Gors; Messrs. Brooke and Greentree of the St.
Helena council; Commissary Ibbetson; Captains Browne, Hen-
dry, and Marryat of the royal navy; and six doctors. Bertrand
and Montholon, in their resplendent dress uniforms, received
them and led them into the death-chamber, where Marchand,
Pierron, Saint-Denis, and Noverraz stood at the four corners of
the bed in their green silver and gold embroidered livery. Montchenu had expressed the fear that Napoleon's followers might
make use of some drug after his death to make him unrecog-
nizable, so Lowe now turned to the commissioner and asked:
"Do you recognize him?" The marquis nodded and said: "I do."
All were struck by the beauty and youthfulness of the face.
Major Gorrequer has written: "All the superfluous flesh and the
sallowness had disappeared and left a well-proportioned countenance, such as he might have had some twelve or fourteen
years ago. A dozen of those who saw him concurred in saying
that he did not look at the utmost more than forty, and he certainly did not—even less, I think. His hair had retained its natural dark brown, and not a wrinkle or the slightest contortion was
on the face." Dr. Henry wrote: "Every one exclaimed: 'How
beautiful!' for all present acknowledged they had never seen a
finer or more regular and placid countenance."

Before Lowe departed, Montholon told him about Napoleon's desire that an autopsy be performed, believing it might be of great value to his son. The governor raised no objection, and it was agreed that the autopsy was to take place that afternoon at two o'clock.

TWO

What had been known as the billiard-room had some time before been transformed into a "topographical cabinet"—the billiard-table having been moved to the servants' quarters and a trestle-table put in its place, on which Napoleon was wont to spread his maps. At two o'clock on the afternoon of May 6, the Emperor's body was carried to that room, laid on the trestle-table, and covered with a bedsheet. Seventeen persons gathered in the room. The Emperor's following was represented by Bertrand, Montholon, Marchand, Antommarchi, Vignali, Pierron, and Saint-Denis; the governor, by Reade, Major Harrison, and Captain Crokat. Seven English doctors were present: Dr. Shortt, principal medical officer at St. Helena; Dr. Mitchell, surgeon on the *Vigo*, the admiral's flagship; Drs. Arnott and Burton, surgeons of the 20th and 66th regiments, and their assistants Drs. Rutledge and Henry; Dr. Livingstone, superintendent of the East India Company's medical establishment.

Whatever Antommarchi's shortcomings as a physician, as a dissector and anatomist he had few equals in his day, having received his training from an acknowledged master of the profession. It was agreed that he should do the dissecting and that Dr. Rutledge should serve as his assistant. He was in his element and wielded the scalpel skillfully.

According to the official report the lungs were "quite sound," but Antommarchi, in his own report, claims to have noticed "numerous tubercles and small cavities in the upper lobe of the left lung." The fact that during various periods of his career Napoleon had been troubled with a persistent cough, and that his son died of pulmonary tuberculosis at the age of twenty-one, lends color to Antommarchi's statement.

The heart was "of natural size, but thickly covered with fat."

When the stomach was opened there was agreement among

the doctors that it was the cause of Napoleon's death. "The internal surface of the stomach to nearly its whole extent was a mass of cancerous disease and schirrous portions advancing to cancer: this was particularly noticed near the pylorus." One of the ulcers, whether cancerous or not, had penetrated the stomach wall, so that one could put one's little finger through the opening. On May 8, Dr. Shortt was to write to the governor that "had the edges of the ulcer which penetrated the coats of the stomach near the pylorus not firmly adhered to the liver, death would have taken place much sooner, as part of the contents of the stomach would have escaped into the abdomen." [1]

When the liver was examined there arose a disagreement among the doctors. Dr. Shortt pronounced the organ to be "enlarged." Drs. Burton and Arnott took issue with him and were supported by their assistants Rutledge and Henry. Dr. Mitchell sided with the majority. Dr. Livingstone had departed. In evaluating the opinion of those who took issue with Dr. Shortt, it is well to keep in mind that doctors at St. Helena stood in terror of the governor. We have seen that Dr. Verling and Dr. Livingstone, who for several months had treated Madame Montholon for a liver complaint, were unwilling to make a signed statement to that effect for fear of Sir Hudson. They knew that O'Meara and Stokoe had been dismissed because in their medical reports they had stated that Napoleon was suffering from "chronic hepatitis," a diagnosis that conflicted with the opinion of Lord Bathurst's medical authority—General Gourgaud! [2]

[1] Saint-Denis has written that before sewing up the body Antommarchi managed to extract and conceal some of the Emperor's viscera, which on his arrival in England he gave to O'Meara, who presented them to the museum of the Royal College of Surgeons. That he could have done so without its having been noticed by the hawk-eyed Reade, or any of the other Englishmen present—who had been especially warned by the governor not to permit such a thing to happen—is unbelievable. Considering the character of Antommarchi there is reason to believe that the viscera at the museum which Sir James Paget, Lord Moynihan, and other eminent pathologists examined, and about which they made conflicting statements, are not Napoleon's.

[2] Professor Keith, conservator of the museum of the Royal College of Surgeons, said in his Huntarian lecture, delivered in 1913: "No one who has tabulated from the records left by O'Meara, Stokoe, and Antommarchi

Dr. Shortt finally agreed to compromise by stating in the autopsy report that "the liver was perhaps a little larger than natural." Shortt, Mitchell, Arnott, and Burton signed the document. The two assistant-surgeons were not asked to sign. Antommarchi was asked but declined. He said that, since he had been Napoleon's physician and had performed the autopsy, it was for him to write the report. He prepared a report of his own in which he agreed with the British surgeons that the ulcer which had perforated the stomach near the pylorus was cancerous and was the cause of death. About the liver he said that it was "congested and unnaturally large." [3]

When Dr. Shortt presented his report to the governor, the latter was displeased. He wanted the statement "the liver was a little larger than natural" stricken out. Shortt allowed himself to be overawed and rewrote the report, leaving out the offending statement. At the demand of Lowe, Dr. Livingstone, who had not been present when the liver was examined, signed the revised report together with the four other doctors. Dr. Shortt, however, kept the original version. It is still in existence, with a line drawn through the offending statement and a footnote reading: *The words obliterated were suppressed by the orders of Sir Hudson Lowe.* Thomas Shortt, P.M.O [Principal Medical Officer]" [4]

Shortt never forgave Lowe for having put pressure upon him to be unfaithful to the ethics of his profession. Some of the unflattering information concerning Lowe's character Walter Scott used in his *The Life of Napoleon* he obtained from Dr. Shortt.

the symptoms manifested month after month by Napoleon during the first three years of his illness can doubt the recurrent febrile nature of his original disease. It is plain then, that Napoleon suffered, originally from an endemic fever in which the liver was severely affected."

[3] The report he published in his book in 1825 differs considerably from the one he made in 1821. In the 1825 version he says that the liver was "hardened, very large, distended with blood . . . and affected by chronic hepatitis." The report of 1821 can be found in Marchand's memoirs, Vol. II, pp. 343-44.

[4] In 1919 Dr. Arnold Chaplin wrote in his *A St. Helena Who's Who*, p. 156: "The original draft is now in the possession of the Reverend Brook Johnson, and a footnote in Dr. Shortt's handwriting states that the sentence regarding the liver was suppressed by order of Sir Hudson Lowe."

While the autopsy was still in progress, Montholon took Reade aside and told him about the Emperor's wish that his heart be delivered to Marie Louise. Reade permitted it to be removed, but said Sir Hudson would have to decide what should be done with it. Lowe decided that it should be placed in the coffin. It was entrusted to Dr. Rutledge, who was commanded to keep watch over it as well as over the body, so as to prevent "the cavities being opened a second time for the purpose of removing any part of the body." Rutledge has written that he placed the heart in a silver vessel, which he filled with spirit of wine, and the stomach in a silver pepper-box "without any means of preventing the putrefective process."

THREE

In the meantime Napoleon's study had been transformed into a mortuary chapel. The walls had been hung with black cloth and an altar set up against the east wall, before which Vignali was praying. The Emperor's camp-bed had been covered with the blue gold-embroidered cloak he had worn at the battle of Marengo. On this Napoleon was laid out dressed in the uniform of the *chasseurs à cheval de la garde*—green coat with red facings, white cassimere vest and breeches, high riding boots with silver spurs. On his breast were the cordon and the plaque of the Legion of Honor and the cross of the Iron Crown. His sword was at his side and on his head the famed hat with tricolor cockade. Candles were burning in candelabra on the altar and in various other parts of the room. Marchand, Saint-Denis, Noverraz, and Pierron stood motionless at the four corners of the bed. Bertrand and Montholon, in dress uniform, were standing between the bed and the altar. Antommarchi, Arnott, and the remaining servants were lined up in two rows on either side of the door leading to the adjoining chamber, while Captain Crokat was busily engaged marshaling the people who filed past the bed—officers of the 20th and 66th regiments and of the squadron, notables of the island, non-commissioned officers, soldiers and sailors. An atmosphere of solemnity pervaded the

room, and on many of the faces there was an expression
awe. For was not this the man whom emperors and kin
courted—whose word of command could set armies ma
throughout Europe? "Look well, my son. This was the g
man in the world," a soldier was overheard to remark to hi
boy.

FOUR

In the morning of the 7th of May the populace filed throug
room. Many brought flowers which they deposited at the
of the bed. Some of the officers came a second time. One, I
tenant George Horsley Wood of the 20th regiment, son of (
eral Wood, wrote a sonnet commemorating the occasion, w
may well have voiced the feelings of many of his colleagues. "
first two stanzas read:

> Sorrow and pity marked the mournful day
>   Sad sighs were heard and heartfelt tears were shed
> When pale in death upon his lowly bed
>   As in deep sleep the mighty chieftain lay.
>
> Long, long I gazed and bent me o'er the dead,
>   For ne'er before did I in rapture trace
> Such purity and loveliness and peace
>   As o'er the features of that face were spread.

In the evening three coffins arrived from Jamestown—one o
tin, one of mahogany, one of lead. The tin coffin was lined with
white silk padded with cotton, and had a resting place and a
pillow for the head. In this the body was laid after the head had
been shaved, as by Napoleon's orders his hair was to be woven
into a watchchain for his son and bracelets for members of his
family. The sword, too, was removed. The hat was laid upon his
thighs. The silver vessel containing the heart and the silver pepper-box containing the stomach were placed between the legs,
below the knees. A silver plate, knife, fork and spoon, twelve
gold and three silver coins of the Empire and the Kingdom of
Italy were likewise placed in the coffin. Dr. Rutledge, who

superintended these proceedings, had the juvenile vanity of adding another silver plate on which he had scratched his name and address. The lid of the coffin was then soldered down, that of the mahogany screwed down, and of the lead soldered down. Later still another mahogany coffin arrived in which the whole was placed.

Admiral Cockburn had been instructed that in case of death Napoleon's remains were to be transported to England. The government, made uneasy by the fact that Napoleon had many admirers in England—even among members of the royal family—changed its mind, however, and in 1820 Lowe received an order that if Napoleon died he was to be buried at St. Helena. When made acquainted with the Emperor's choice of a resting place on the island, Lowe consented, but was guilty of a final demonstration of officious pettiness. Montholon showed him the inscription they wished to put on the grave. It read:

NAPOLÉON

NÉ À AJACCIO LE 15 AOUT, 1769.

MORT À STE-HÉLÈNE LE 5 MAI, 1821.

Lowe objected. He said the name must read Napoleon Bonaparte. Montholon, after consulting Bertrand, informed him that in that case they preferred no inscription whatever.

Richard Torbett, owner of Geranium Valley, readily agreed to the grave being located on his property. He ultimately was paid £1,200 for the land after having received rental for some years.

Soldiers from the engineering corps dug a large pit between two weeping willows. When it had been lined with solid masonry two feet thick, it was twelve feet deep, eight feet long, and five feet wide. Eight stones, a foot high and five inches thick, were then cemented in the corners and to the sides to serve as a support for a large slab of stone, on which the coffin was to rest. Four other slabs of stones were then cemented to the sides, while still another—set on its edge and held up by ropes fastened to the trees—was ready to be lowered over the coffin.

FIVE

Sir Hudson Lowe had officially notified the Marquis de Montchenu that Napoleon's funeral would take place toward noon of May 9, "with all the honors due to a general officer of the highest rank." At ten o'clock Vignali celebrated Mass in the mortuary chapel. The household and a few English Catholics attended. The governor, the admiral, General Coffin, their staffs, the French commissioner and his secretary, members of the St. Helena council, and notables of the island waited in the garden. In the avenue stood the funeral car to which four of the Emperor's horses were harnessed, soldiers acting as postilions. It had been constructed from Napoleon's old carriage—the seats having been removed, a wooden platform with a canopy put in their place, and the whole festooned with black cloth. From the garden gate, all the way to Hutt's Gate, the garrison, some three thousand strong, stood lined up on the left side of the road, regimental colors bearing in gold lettering the names of victories won by the British over Napoleon's generals in Spain—Minden, Talavera, Albuera, Pyrenees, Orthes.

At eleven o'clock twelve grenadiers of the 20th regiment filed into the mortuary chapel, lifted the heavy coffin upon their shoulders, and carried it to the funeral car. It was then covered with a purple pall on which the Marengo cloak and Napoleon's sword were placed. The Abbé Vignali, in sacerdotal vestments, headed the funeral procession with Henri Bertrand, who carried the silver vessel with holy water and the aspergillum. They were followed by Drs. Antommarchi and Arnott, walking side by side. Then came the funeral car, flanked on each side by six grenadiers without arms. Marchand, Napoleon Bertrand, the grand marshal, and Montholon served as pallbearers. Napoleon's horse "Sheikh," led by the bridle by Archambault, followed. Next came the Longwood servants and a curricle with Madame Bertrand, Hortense, and Arthur. Then came a cavalcade of officers, preceded by midshipmen, headed by the governor and the admiral and followed by the Marquis de Montchenu and his secretary, by St. Helena councilmen and notables of the island—

some on horseback, others on foot. As the procession passed each corps of the garrison, the soldiers stood at attention arms reversed, then fell in behind. At the very end came a phaëton with Lady Lowe and her daughter Miss Johnson. All the while the regimental bands played a mournful dirge, composed for the occasion by Lieutenant Charles McCarthy of the 66th. Along the entire route the populace was massed—white men with their wives and children, Chinese, Lascars, Negro slaves.

From where the alarm gun stood a straight road had been constructed leading downward to Geranium Valley. When the funeral car reached that point, it halted. Bertrand took the sword from the coffin and Montholon the cloak; others removed the velvet pall.[5] Twenty-four men from all the services, in relays of twelve, carried the coffin to the burial place. Officers and dignitaries dismounted and followed. The coffin was placed on wooden supports laid across the grave. Then, at a prearranged signal, the soldiers on the road above fired three volleys of musketry, answered by three salvos of fifteen cannon massed at Hutt's Gate. The minute guns of the squadron boomed, as did the cannon of the forts. The mountains echoed the sound. There was something terrifying and inexpressibly moving in this noisy salute given the dead Emperor by his most inveterate enemies.

When the noise had died out Vignali performed the funeral rites, after which Lowe turned first to Bertrand, then to Montholon asking if they wished to speak. Both declined. Considering the circumstances they could have done nothing more befitting.

The coffin was lowered into the grave with the aid of winches, to be followed by the great slab of stone which was to be cemented to the masonry walls. Two layers of stone masonry were built over this, joined, and clamped to the sidewalls. The remaining depth of eight feet was filled with earth and the whole sealed with three slabs of stone taken from the kitchen of the new house. Later an iron fence, about four and a half feet high, was placed around the grave. Nearby a sentry-box was set up,

[5] Marchand has claimed that fearing Lowe might try to appropriate Napoleon's sword, Bertrand had placed his own sword on the coffin.

and night and day a soldier kept watch. Lowe was as anxious to make sure that the remains of Napoleon should not leave the island without official sanction as he had been about the prisoner. He was still living when, in 1840, the body was transported to France and placed at the Invalides with great pomp and ceremony—one hundred and fifty thousand soldiers and nearly a million people doing honor to the chieftain to whom the Russian representatives at the Congress of Aix-la-Chapelle had referred as "the Revolution concentrated in the person of one man."

XXIX. Fate of
Sir Hudson Lowe

Shortly after the funeral a reconciliation took place between
Napoleon's generals and the governor. Lowe realized that the
generals were in a position to make embarrassing revelations;
as for Bertrand and Montholon, they were aware that being on
good terms with the governor would facilitate their departure
for England and might pave the way for a friendly reception by
the British authorities. To Bertrand, under sentence of death in
France, the latter was particularly important. Madame Bertrand
put out a feeler by telling Admiral Lambert that shortly before
his death Napoleon had expressed the wish that a reconciliation
should take place between her husband and the governor. Since
Bertrand makes no mention of this in his journal and Napoleon
in his will refers to Lowe as a "hired assassin," there is reason to
believe that the story was invented for the occasion. It had, however, the desired effect. Reade called on Madame Bertrand and
told her that the governor had been pleased to learn the grand
marshal was willing to let bygones be bygones and that he would
gladly do the same.

Bertrand and Montholon called at Plantation House and received a friendly reception. There followed a succession of dinners and parties in their honor. When later, in England, Lord
Brougham asked Bertrand how he had found it possible to become reconciled with Sir Hudson, the grand marshal replied

with a shrug: "What will you have? Napoleon was dead, Sir Hudson was very much alive, and I had sat at his table." This was not the only obligation he had incurred. Madame Bertrand had contracted debts with shopkeepers at Jamestown who had insisted that the grand marshal should not be allowed to depart until they were paid. Lowe had offered him a loan of £1,000, which had been gratefully accepted and effectively sealed his lips.

In the meantime Montholon had resumed his friendly intercourse with Montchenu, to whom he confided that a few days before his death Napoleon had burned important notations concerning affairs in France. He quoted the Emperor as having said: "We don't want foreigners to poke their noses into our affairs. Since these memoranda were dictated to you, you know their contents and must not divulge them to anyone except to the King or to my son." It was pure invention, but the commissioner was sufficiently impressed to report to his government that Montholon was a man of parts, able to furnish information that might prove useful to the Crown, and claiming to be the possessor of an immense fortune. "It might therefore be advisable to court him." Of Bertrand he wrote that he had been humiliated, did not hide his resentment, and was not likely to be of any further danger to the regime.

The French left St. Helena on May 27, 1821, on the storeship *Camel*. The governor and Lady Lowe were on hand to see them off, as were Montchenu and his secretary. The old Lothario asked and received permission to give Madame Bertrand a farewell kiss.

TWO

Sir Hudson Lowe, his family, and his staff—with the exception of Major Gorrequer—left St. Helena on July 25, 1821, on the *Lady Melville*. As the island disappeared from view, what were Lowe's thoughts? For over five years he had exercised the power of a viceroy, had lived in a mansion fit for a duke, had had an annual salary of £12,000 and so many perquisites as to enable him to lay by a considerable sum. Would he be rewarded for his services by having his "local" rank of lieutenant general made an "army" rank? He undoubtedly felt that he deserved it. He had been strict—stricter perhaps than his instructions had obliged him to be—but the doctors had agreed that Bonaparte had died of cancer, which meant that he would have died even had he, Lowe, been far more lenient. The important thing was that he had not escaped, and with all his cleverness had been unable to stir up a mutiny. If Europe had been spared another upheaval, it was, Lowe felt, due to his watchfulness and devotion to duty.

When, however, he arrived in England the reception he received from Lord Bathurst was rather cool. The English are a generous-hearted people. Napoleon's early death had convinced them that the government had been lacking in generosity in its treatment of a gallant foe. Public sentiment was running strongly in the dead man's favor. When at a general assembly of the East India Company a member expressed satisfaction at the passing of Napoleon, he was castigated by the press of both parties. Lord Bathurst thought it expedient not to become too involved with Sir Hudson.

Lowe was presented to the King, who shook his hand and thanked him for his services. He was promised an appointment to the first colonelcy that happened to be vacant, and soon after was appointed colonel of the 63rd foot regiment. This, however, was far from what he believed his due. He sensed a feeling of hostility all about him. When he tried to obtain an interview with Lady Holland, she wrote that she would find it as painful to talk to him about the treatment Napoleon had received as he would find it to hear what she thought of it. Reade, too, met with disappointment. He who had been "local" deputy adjutant-general at St. Helena wrote to Lowe on December 3, 1821: "I dread returning to my regiment at Gibraltar as a captain."

THREE

In July, 1822, O'Meara published his two-volume work *Napoleon in Exile* or *A Voice from St. Helena.* Professor Philippe Gonnard, in his *Les Origines de la Légende Napoléonienne*[1] has said of the book: "The work certainly deserved its success, for it is very interesting. The author sinks his own personality, and there is no attempt at declamation or mere literature. O'Meara's only object was to tell the readers about his patient at St. Helena." But he reached the conclusion that "in spite of his apparent impartiality and of his tranquil style there is great violence underneath, and this violence made him sometimes careless of the truth." Lord Rosebery, in his excellent *Napoleon: The Last Phase*, agrees with that conclusion. Yet neither Gonnard, nor Rosebery, nor even Lowe's champions—Forsyth, Seaton, and Young—seem to have been able to point out any serious misstatement in O'Meara's account. True that he put a malicious construction on Lowe's remark that Europe would benefit by Napoleon's death, but this appears in a letter, written in anger to John Wilson Croker, secretary of the admiralty, not in the book. One has but to reread the remarks concerning Lowe made by the Duke of Wellington, Admiral Cockburn, Admiral Malcolm, Dr. Baxter, Dr. Shortt, Count Balmain, Baron Stürmer, and Captain Lutyens to become convinced that O'Meara did not exaggerate. Are we to believe that they conspired to slander Lowe? And should we overlook Lowe's attempts to discredit Admiral Malcolm, Captain Poppleton, and Dr. Verling—for which Lord Bathurst soundly rebuked him—or the letter of the court of directors of the East India Company in which they take him to task for his vindictive persecution of Major Pritchard and Breame, the Company farmer? And why did Lady Lowe feel impelled, on three occasions, to disassociate herself from her husband's treatment of the exiles?

When Lord Rosebery contends that O'Meara was not an honorable man, we agree with him; but honorable or not, it was not necessary for him to resort to mendacity to place Lowe in an unfavorable light. The simple truth sufficed. Count Balmain—to whose veracity, ability, tact, and good sense so staunch a defender of Sir Hudson Lowe as Norwood Young has testified, and

[1] English translation entitled *The Exile of St. Helena*, London, 1909.

of whom Lord Rosebery has written that "obliging, amiable, and unpretentious he is beloved by all who know him"—in his reports to his government presents Lowe in no more favorable a light than O'Meara has done. Indeed, we have seen that he accuses him of resorting to downright falsehood to justify his behavior, and writes that he stands ready "to prove this to all Europe." Haunted by fear and suspicion to such an extent as to read a sinister meaning into the color of beans sent by Montholon to Montchenu, and into a picture painted by Marchand in which O'Meara is shown standing with other persons in front of Longwood House, Lowe is revealed as a paranoid personality more to be pitied than blamed.

FOUR

O'Meara's book had an enormous success. Edition followed edition. Crowds gathered before bookshops to buy copies. It was translated into French and into several other languages. The *Edinburgh Review* commented: "Every branch of the periodical press at home, whether Reviews, Magazines, or Daily and Weekly Journals, Metropolitan and Provincial, has bestowed upon it the most unqualified commendation." Lord Byron wrote:

> And the stiff surgeon who maintained his cause
> Has lost his place and gained the world's applause.

Lowe became a pariah. Friends and acquaintances shunned him. At a *table d'hôte* dinner at a hotel no one wanted to sit beside him. Men he had known for years turned their backs on him at the club. In the *Memoirs of a Highland Lady*, an autobiography of Elizabeth Grant of Rothiemurchus, we read: "He was so truly sent to Coventry that once he [effusively] thanked Colonel Pennington in a coffeehouse for the common civility of handing him a newspaper, saying that any civility was now so new to him he must be excused for gratefully acknowledging it." Young Las Cases, who happened to be in London, waited for him in front of his house, armed with a whip, and when Lowe appeared struck him twice across the face and challenged him to a duel. Lowe did not accept the challenge, although they could have fought in France.

The unfortunate man turned to Lord Bathurst for help. His lordship asked Sir John Copley, the solicitor-general, about the possibility of obtaining redress in the courts. Copley consulted Mr. N. C. Tindal, future chief justice of the Court of Common Pleas, one of the ablest lawyers in England. On November 22, 1822, the two men of the law gave a written opinion to the effect that Sir Hudson would have to prove that certain passages in the book were not only "abusive" but "false." Moreover, since those passages had been put "in the mouth of Bonaparte . . . it will be strongly pressed upon the jury that the publication of all that relates to the history of Bonaparte's latter days is matter of public right; and if the right to publish a free and full account of what he did and what he said is denied, there is an end of the freedom and impartiality of history. And we are of the opinion that the jury will in all probability yield to that suggestion, and will refuse to find the defendant guilty of libel, unless the prosecutor can show that the speeches attributed to Bonaparte were not really his, but that they were falsely put into his mouth, as a cover for the defendent's malignity." They therefore gave the opinion "that it is inexpedient in the present case to commence any prosecution, unless such evidence can be given."

Notwithstanding this advice Lowe insisted on going ahead. He managed to obtain twenty-three affidavits from officers who had been with him at St. Helena and were willing to testify that the charges made against him in the book were unfounded. Even if this were so it would not have proved that Napoleon had not made them. We have seen that in his will he refers to Lowe as a "hired assassin." Needless to say Lowe obtained no affidavit from Admiral Cockburn—who told Lord Dudley that "he was disposed to take O'Meara's part"—from Admiral Malcolm, or from any of the captains who had been orderly officers at Longwood. Nor even from Dr. Arnott. Dr. Baxter, Dr. Verling, Colonel Lascelles, and Balcombe, who signed affidavits in his support, could have done so only from expediency.

Of the fifteen affidavits O'Meara obtained seven were from

British officers. Among them was Captain Poppleton, who had been two years at Longwood and had more precise information than any of his colleagues. Marshal Bertrand, who had placed himself under obligation to Lowe, did not sign. Gourgaud dared not do so, lest the statements come to light he had given to Goulburn and to the French ambassador in London when trying to ingratiate himself with the Bourbons. Montholon, Las Cases and his son, Marchand, Antommarchi, Pierron, Coursot, and Chandelier signed affidavits in support of O'Meara.

The case never came to trial because the solicitor-general and Mr. Tindal delayed taking it into court until it was too late. That two of the foremost lawyers in England should have been ignorant of the law in such a matter is unbelievable. Only one explanation suggests itself. Since Lowe was determined on going ahead, and they were convinced that he would lose, they intentionally delayed proceedings to save him and the government needless embarrassment. "The only satisfaction which Sir Hudson derived from the result of the proceedings was that he was not compelled to pay the cost of his adversary as well as his own!" Forsyth has written.

FIVE

Lowe, discouraged, decided to retire from the army and applied for a pension. Colonel Wilks, his predecessor at St. Helena, had received a retiring allowance of £1,500; but although Lord Bathurst recommended that a pension be granted to Sir Hudson, it was refused.

In December, 1823, Lowe was offered the governorship of a small West Indian island, but declined the appointment. In 1825 he was appointed commander of the garrison at Ceylon, and accepted in the hope of being appointed governor of the colony as soon as a vacancy occurred. His hopes were shattered in 1827 by the appearance of Walter Scott's *The Life of Napoleon*. The archives of the colonial office had been thrown open to the distinguished author in the hope that he would disprove the charges made in O'Meara's book and in Las Cases' *Le Mémorial de St. Hélène*, published in 1823. The opposite happened. Scott's unflattering appraisal of Lowe's character, as revealed by the correspondence, has already been quoted. Concerning his policy he wrote: "His over-anxiety led to frequent changes of his regulations, and to the adoption of measures which were afterwards abandoned and perhaps again resumed. All this uncertainty occasioned just subject of complaint to his prisoner; for though a captive may become gradually accustomed to the fetters which he wears daily in the same manner, he must be driven to impatience if the mode of them is altered from day to day."

It was precisely this "doing, undoing, and redoing" which had been Napoleon's principal complaint against Lowe—a complaint which Count Balmain felt was fully justified.

Lowe obtained a leave of absence and hastened to England to see if any hope remained of his becoming governor of Ceylon. There had been a change in the ministry. Lord Liverpool had resigned; the Duke of Wellington was prime minister. He called on the duke and tried to obtain a promise that if a vacancy occurred he would be appointed governor of Ceylon. Wellington curtly refused to make the promise. Lowe then expressed the wish to retire from the army and asked that a pension be granted him. The duke replied that it would be useless to introduce such a proposal in the House of Commons as it would be rejected. Lowe returned to his military command at Ceylon, broken in spirit.

The long-expected vacancy in the governorship occurred in 1830. The government was now in the hands of the Whigs; Earl Grey was prime minister; but had Wellington remained in power Lowe would not have received the appointment. He resigned his command and returned to England in 1831. The following year he was saddened by the death of his wife, whom Napoleon had never seen, but whom his followers had found sympathetic.

To what extent Lowe's name had become a byword may be judged from a debate that took place in the House of Lords in 1833. A measure was before the House to give the lieutenant general of Ireland, the Marquis of Normanby, extraordinary powers. Lord Teynham objected. "Now suppose the noble Marquis were to be succeeded by a Sir Hudson Lowe," he argued. He was called to order. The Duke of Wellington rose and said: "I have the honor to know Sir Hudson, and I will say, in this House or elsewhere, wherever it may be, that there is not in the army a more respectable officer than Sir Hudson Lowe, nor has His Majesty a more faithful subject." Lord Teynham replied: "I had no intention of aspersing the private character of Sir Hudson Lowe. No doubt the testimony the noble duke bears to it is perfectly correct. But as regards his public conduct while Governor of St. Helena, I say, and will maintain it as a Peer of Parliament, that he is cried out upon by all the people of Europe as a person not fit to be trusted with power."

One need but read Wellington's statement concerning Lowe to Lord Stanhope, quoted in this volume, to be convinced that he agreed with Lord Teynham. An officer whom he himself was to characterize as "a very bad choice," "a man wanting in education and judgment," "a stupid man" who had "a bad and irritable temper," and who was "suspicious and jealous" was assuredly not a man to be trusted with power.

After his return to England Sir Hudson received no other public appointment and no pension. His investments had turned out badly. He died in 1844 at the age of seventy-five, poor, ill, and forsaken. Napoleon had said in his will: "The people of England will not fail to avenge me." They had avenged him on Sir Hudson Lowe, but those whom he had first served as a tool, then as a lightning rod, were not seriously affected.

Bibliography and Index

BIBLIOGRAPHY

Abbott, John, *Napoleon at St. Helena*, 1855

Abell, Mrs., *Recollections of the Emperor Napoleon*, 1845

Advielle, Victor, *La Bibliothèque de Napoléon à Sainte-Hélène*, 1894

Aldanov, M. A., *Saint-Helena, Little Island*, 1924

Allardyce, *Memoirs of Lord Keith*, 1882

Antommarchi, Dr. Francesco, *Les derniers moments de Napoléon.* 1825, 2 vols.

Arnott, Dr. Archibald, *An Account of the Last Illness, Decease, and Post-mortem Appearance of Napoleon Bonaparte*, 1822

Aubry, Octave, *Sainte-Hélène*, 1935, 2 vols.

Bainville, Jacques, *Napoléon*, 1933, 2 vols.

Balmain, Comte de, "*Les prisonniers de Sainte-Hélène*." *Revue Bleue du 8 mai au 12 juin*, 1897. Abridged English translation, *Napoleon in Captivity*, 1927

Barnes, John, *A Tour through the Island of St. Helena*, 1817

Barthe, Félix, *Réfutation de la relation du Capitaine Maitland touchant l'embarquement de Napoléon à son bord*, 1827

Beatson, A., *Tracts Relative to the Island of Saint-Helena*, 1816

Beker, Général, *Relation de la mission du lieutenant-général Beker auprès de l'Empereur Napoléon*, 1841

Bertrand, Général, *Cahiers de Sainte-Hélène, Journal, 1816-1817. Janvier-Mai, 1821. Manuscrit déchiffré et annoté par Paul Fleuriot de Langle*, 1951, 2 vols. English translation of Vol. I, *Napoleon at St. Helena*, 1952

Blackwood's Magazine, "Reminiscences of Napoleon Bonaparte at St. Helena," 1834

Bowerbank, John, *An Extract from a Journal Kept on Board H.M.S. Bellerophon*, 1815

Brooke, T. H., *A History of the Island of St. Helena*, 1808

Cabanès, Docteur, *Les indiscretions de l'histoire*, 1907

Cahuet, Albéric, *Après la mort de l'Empereur*, 1913

Carnet d'un voyageur: un receuil de notes curieuses sur la vie, les occupations, les habitués de Bonaparte à Longwood, 1819

Century Magazine, "New Records of Napoleon by British Officers at Saint-Helena," Jan. 1912

Chaplin, Dr. Arnold, *The Illness and Death of Napoleon Bonaparte*, 1918

———, *A St. Helena Who's Who*, 1919

Cockburn, Sir George, *Buonaparte's Voyage to St. Helena*, 1833

Collection nouvelle de documents historiques sur Napoléon, 1822

Contamine de Latour, "Napoléon et Sainte Hélène." *Revue des études Napoléoniennes*, 15 août, 1920

Corbett, Julian, "Colonel Wilks and Napoleon," *Monthly Review*, Jan. 1901

Cornhill Magazine, "More Light on Saint Helena from the Papers of Sir George Bingham, Major Harrison and Colonel Gorrequer," Jan.-Feb. 1901

Correspondance de Napoléon Ier, Vol. XXXII, 1869

Dacre, Captain, *Letters from the Island of Saint-Helena, Exposing the Unnecessary Severity towards Napoleon*, 1818

Deschamps, Jules, "Napoléon à Plymouth et l'ordonnance d'Habeas Corpus," *Bulletin de l'Académie Royale de Belgique*, 1955

Documents pour servir à l'histoire de la captivité de Napoléon Bonaparte à Sainte-Hélène, 1821

Ellis, Henry, *Journal of the Proceedings of the Late Embassy to China*, 1817

Firmin-Didot, Georges, *La captivité de Ste. Hélène d'après les rapports du Marquis de Montchenu*, 1894

Forsyth, William, *History of the Captivity of Napoleon at Saint Helena; from the Letters and Journals of the Late Lieut.-Gen. Sir Hudson Lowe*, 1853, 3 vols.

Frémeaux, Paul, *Napoléon prisonnier. Mémoires d'un médecin de l'Empereur à Sainte-Hélène*, 1900

———, *Les Derniers Jours de l'Empereur*, 1908. English translation, *The Drama of St. Helena*, 1910

Ganière, Dr. Paul, *Napoléon à Sainte-Hélène*, 1956

Glover, John R., *Napoleon's Last Voyages. Being the Diaries of Admiral Sir Thomas Ussher* (*on board the* Undaunted), *and John R. Glover, Secretary to Rear Admiral Cockburn* (*on board the* Northumberland), 1895

Gonnard, Philippe, *Les origines de la légende Napoléonienne*, 1906. English translation, *The Exile of St. Helena*, 1909

——, *Lettres du Comte et de la Comtesse de Montholon*, 1906

Gourgaud, Gaspard, *Sainte-Hélène: journal inédit de 1815 à 1818*, 1899, 2 vols. Revised edition with preface by Octave Aubry, 1947

Guérard, Albert, *Reflections on the Napoleonic Legend*, 1924

Hall, Captain Basil, *A Voyage to Loo-Choo . . . and Notes of an Interview with Napoleon at St. Helena in August, 1817*, 1826

Hauterive, Ernest d', *Sainte-Hélène au temps de Napoléon et aujourd'hui*, 1933

Henry, Walter, *Events of a Military Life*, 1843, 2 vols.

Holland, Lord, *Foreign Reminiscences*, 1850

Holzhausen, *Napoleon's Tod*, 1902

Hone, William, *Interesting Particulars of Napoleon's Deportation for Life, to St. Helena*, 1816

Hook, Theodore E., *Facts Illustrative of the Treatment of Napoleon Bonaparte in Saint Helena*, 1819

Houssaye, *1815*, 1905

Jackson, Basil, *Notes and Reminiscences of a Staff Officer*, 1877

Jackson, E. L., *St. Helena: The Historic Island: From Its Discovery to the Present Date*, 1903

Janish, Hudson R., *Extracts from the St. Helena Records and Chronicles of Cape Commanders*, 1908

Keith, Arthur, M.D., "An Address on the History and Nature of Certain Specimens Alleged to Have Been Obtained at the Post-mortem Examination of Napoleon the Great," *British Medical Journal*, Jan. 1913

Las Cases, Comte de, *Mémorial de Sainte-Hélène. Edition intégrale et critique établie et annotée par Marcel Dunan*, 1955. Original edition of the *Mémorial*, 1823.

Latimer, E. W., *Talks with Napoleon at St. Helena*, 1904

Lubin, Georges, *Un compagnon de Sainte-Hélène: le grand maréchal Bertrand. Miroir de l'histoire, août*, 1955

Lyttelton, W. H., *Some Account of Napoleon Bonaparte's Coming on Board H.M.S.* Northumberland. *Aug. 1815*, 1836

Maitland, Frederic L., *Narrative of the Surrender of Bonaparte and of His Residence on Board H.M.S.* Bellerophon, 1826

Malcolm, Lady, *Diary of St. Helena (1816-1817)*; *Journal of Lady Malcolm Containing the Conversations of Napoleon with Sir Pulteney Malcolm*, ed. by Sir Arthur Wilson, 1899

Marchand, Louis, *Mémoires de Marchand . . . publié d'après le manuscrit original par Jean Bourguignon et le Commandant Henry Lechouque*, 1955

Masseline, *Mémoire sur l'île de Sainte-Hélène*, 1861

Masson, Frédéric, *Napoléon à Sainte-Hélène*, 1912

———, *Autour de Sainte-Hélène*, 3 vols., 1909, 1911, 1912

Mellis, J. C., *St. Helena, a Physical, Historical, and Topographical Description of the Island*, 1872

Mémoires pour servir à l'histoire de France sous Napoléon, par les généraux qui ont partagé sa captivité, 1822-1825

Merkwürdige Aktenstücke zur Geschichte der Gefangenschaft, Schicksal und letzten Lebensaugenblicke Napoleon Bonapartes auf St. Helena, 1822

Meynell, H., *Conversations with Napoleon at St. Helena*, 1909

Montholon, Charles Tristan, Comte de, *Récit de la Captivité de Napoléon à Sainte-Hélène*, 1847, 2 vols.

Montholon, Comtesse de, *Souvenirs de Sainte-Hélène, publié par le Comte Fleury*, 1901

Napoleon At St. Helena, as Portrayed in the St. James Magazine. (Includes extract from *Scharpe's Magazine:* "Facts connected with the last hours of Napoleon, by Mrs. Major Ward," 1876)

O'Meara, Barry Edward, *Napoleon in Exile: or A Voice from St. Helena*, 1822, 2 vols.

Planat de la Faye, *Rome et Sainte-Hélène de 1815 à 1821*, 1862

Pillans, T. Dundas, *The Real Martyr of St. Helena*, 1913

Robertson, Charles Grant, "Great Britain and the Detention of Napoleon, 1814-1815," *Agenda*, May, 1944

Rosebery, The Earl of, *Napoleon: The Last Phase*, 1900

Runciman, Sir Walter, *The Tragedy of Saint-Helena*, 1911

Saint-Denis, Louis Etienne, *Napoleon from the Tuileries to St. Helena; Personal Recollections of the Emperor's Second Mameluke and Valet*, 1922

Santini, Giovanni Natale, *De Sainte-Hélène aux Invalides*, 1853

Schlitter, Dr. Hanns, *Berichte aus Sainte Helena zur Zeit der dortigen Internierung Napoleon Bonapartes*, 1886

Scott, Sir Walter, *The Life of Napoleon*, Vol. IX, 1827

Seaton, R. C., *Napoleon's Captivity in Relation to Sir Hudson Lowe*, 1903

Shorter, Clement K., *Napoleon and His Fellow Travelers*, 1908
Silvestre, P. J., *De Waterloo à Sainte-Hélène*, 1904
Simmonin, A. J. B., *Histoire des trois derniers mois de la vie de Napoléon Buonaparte*, 1821
Toulouzan de Saint Martin, *De l'île Sainte Hélène et de Buonaparte*, 1815
Tyder, James, *Buonaparte at St. Helena*, 1816
Warden, Dr. William, *Letters Written on Board the* Northumberland *and at St. Helena*, 1816
Watson, G. L. de St. M., *A Polish Exile with Napoleon*, 1912
Young, Norwood, *Napoleon in Exile: Saint Helena*, 1915, 2 vols.

INDEX